12-25-2000

Merry Christmas!
Love
Carole Jim
Colleen + Jenny

CHRISTMAS

IN PROSE AND VERSE

ITS ORIGIN, CELEBRATION AND SIGNIFICANCE
TWO VOLUMES IN ONE

CHRISTMAS
IN PROSE AND VERSE

ITS ORIGIN, CELEBRATION AND SIGNIFICANCE
TWO VOLUMES IN ONE

EDITED BY ALLISON C. PUTALA

PLATINUM PRESS
NEW YORK
2000

Platinum Press Inc.
311 Crossways Park Drive,
Woodbury, NY, 11797

ISBN 1-879582-54-6

PRINTED IN USA

1 2 3 4 5 6 7 8 9

TABLE OF CONTENTS

BOOK I

CONTENTS

II
CELEBRATION

CONTENTS

CONTENTS

III

SIGNIFICANCE AND SPIRIT

CONTENTS

IV
STORIES

V
OLD CAROLS AND EXERCISES

ADDITIONAL PIECES

TABLE OF CONTENTS

BOOK II

In Verse

IN PROSE

PREFACE

Christmas is our most important holiday, and its literature is correspondingly rich. Yet until now no adequate bundle of Christmas treasures in poetry and prose has found its way into the library of Santa Claus.

While this book brings to children of all ages, in school and at home, the best lyrics, carols, essays, plays and stories of Christmas, its scope is yet wider. For the Introduction gives a rapid view of the holiday's origin and development, its relation to cognate pagan festivals, the customs and symbols of its observance in different lands, and the significance and spirit of the day. This Introduction endeavors to be as suggestive as possible to parents and teachers who are personally conducted and introduced to the host of writers learned and quaint, human and pedantic, humorous and brilliant and profound, who have dealt technically with this fascinating subject.

INTRODUCTION

It was the habit of him whose birthday we celebrate to take what was good in men and remould it to higher uses. And so it is peculiarly fitting that the anniversary of Christmas, when it was first celebrated in the second century of our era should have taken from heathen mythology and customs the more beautiful parts for its own use. "Christmas," says Dean Stanley, "brings before us the relations of the Christian religion to the religions which went before; for the birth at Bethlehem was itself a link with the past."

The pagan nations of antiquity * always had a tendency to worship the sun, under different names, as the giver of light and life. And their festivals in its honor took place near the winter solstice, the shortest day in the year, when the sun in December begins its upward course, thrilling men with the first distant promise of spring. This holiday was called *Saturnalia* among the Romans and was marked by great merriment and licence which extended even to the slaves. There were feasting and

* An account of the early history of Christmas may be found in Chamber's Book of Days.

iii

gifts and the houses were hung with evergreens.   A more barbarous form of these rejoicings took place among the rude peoples of
the north where great blocks of wood blazed
in honor of Odin and Thor, and sacrifices of
men and cattle were made to them.   Mistletoe
was cut then from the sacred oaks with a
golden sickle by the Prince of the Druids, between whom and the Fire-Worshippers of Persia there was an affinity both in character and
customs.

The ancient Goths and Saxons called this
festival Yule, which is preserved to us in the
Scottish word for Christmas and also in the
name of the Yule Log.   The ancient Teutons
celebrated the season by decking a fir tree, for
they thought of the sun, riding higher and
higher in the heavens, as the spreading and
blossoming of a great tree.   Thus our own
Christmas fir was decked as a symbol of the
celestial sun tree.   The lights, according to
Professor Schwartz, represent the flashes of
lightning overhead, the golden apples, nuts and
balls symbolize the sun, the moon and the stars,
while the little animals hung in the branches
betoken sacrifices made in gratitude to the sun
god.*

As Christianity replaced paganism, the Chris-

* A delightful account of the origin of the Christmas tree may be found in Elise Traut's Christmas in
Heart and Home.

tians, in the tolerant spirit of their Master, adopted these beautiful old usages, merely changing their spirit. So that the Lord of Misrule who long presided over the Christmas games of Christian England was the direct descendant of the ruler who was appointed, with considerable prerogatives, to preside over the sports of the Saturnalia. In this connection the narrow Puritan author of the "Histrio-Mastix" laments: "If we compare our Bacchanalian Christmasses with these Saturnalia, we shall find such a near affinitye between them, both in regard to time and in manner of solemnizing, that we must needs conclude the one to be but the very issue of the other."

"Merrie old England," writes Walsh,* "was the soil in which Merrie Christmas took its firmest root. Even in Anglo-Saxon days we hear of Alfred holding high revelry in December, 878, so that he allowed the Danes to surprise him, cut his army to pieces and send him a fugitive. The court revelries increased in splendor after the conquest. Christmas, it must be remembered was not then a single day of sport. It had the preliminary novena which began December 16, and it ended on January 6, or Twelfth Night. All this period was devoted to holiday making.

It was a democratic festival. All classes

* Curiosities of Popular Customs.

mixed in its merry-makings. Hospitality was universal. An English country gentleman of the fifteenth and sixteenth centuries held open house. With daybreak on Christmas morning the tenants and neighbors thronged into the hall. The ale was broached. Blackjacks and Cheshire cheese, with toast and sugar and nutmeg, went plentifully round. The Hackin, or great sausage, must be boiled at daybreak, and if it failed to be ready two young men took the cook by the arm and ran her around the market-place till she was ashamed of her laziness.

With the rise of Puritanism the very existence of Christmas was threatened. Even the harmless good cheer of that season was looked upon as pagan, or, what was worse, Popish. 'Into what a stupendous *height* of more than pagan impiety,' cried Prynne (. . .) 'have we not now *degenerated!*' Prynne's rhetoric, it will be seen, is not without an unconscious charm of humor. He complained that the England of his day could not celebrate Christmas or any other festival 'without drinking, roaring, healthing, dicing, carding, dancing, masques and stage-plays. . . . which Turkes and Infidels would abhor to practise.'

Puritanism brought over with it in the Mayflower the anti-Christmas feeling to New England. So early as 1621 Governor Bradford was called upon to administer a rebuke to certain lusty yonge men' who had just come

over in the little ship Fortune. 'On ye day called Christmas day,' says William Bradford, 'ye Govr caled them out to worke (as was used), but ye most of this new company excused themselves and said it went against their consciences to worke on ye day. So ye Govr tould them that if they made it matter of conscience, he would spare them till they were better informed. So he led away ye rest, and left them; but when they came home at noone from their worke, he found them in ye streete at play, openly: some pitching ye barr, and some at stoole-ball and such like sports. So he went to them and tooke away their implements, and tould them that it was against his conscience that they should play and others worke. If they made ye keeping of it matter of devotion, let them kepe their houses, but ther should be no gameing or revelling in ye streets. Since which time nothing hath been attempted that way, at least openly.'

In England the feeling culminated in 1643, when the Roundhead Parliament abolished the observance of saints' days and "the three grand festivals" of Christmas, Easter, and Whitsuntide, "any law, statute, custom, constitution, or canon to the contrary in any wise notwithstanding." The king protested. But he was answered. In London, nevertheless, there was an alarming disposition to observe Christmas. The mob attacked those who by opening their

shops flouted the holiday. In several counties the disorder was threatening. But Parliament adopted strong measures, and during the twelve years in which the great festivals were discountenanced there was no further tumult, and the observance of Christmas as a general holiday ceased.

The General Court of Massachusetts followed the example of the English Parliament in 1659 when it enacted that ' anybody who is found observing, by abstinence from labor, feasting, or any other way, any such day as Christmas day, shall pay for every such offense five shillings.'

The restoration of English royalty brought about the restoration of the English Christmas. It was not till 1681, however, that Massachusetts repealed the ordinance of 1659. But the repeal was bitter to old Puritanism, which kept up an ever attenuating protest even down to the early part of the present century.

There are many superstitions connected with the coming of Christmas itself. The bees are said to sing, the cattle to kneel, in honor of the manger, and the sheep to go in procession in commemoration of the visit of the angel to the shepherds.

Howison in his " Sketches of Upper Canada " relates that on one moonlit Christmas Eve he saw an Indian creeping cautiously through the woods. In response to an inquiry,

he said. ' Me watch to see deer kneel. Christmas night all deer kneel and look up to Great Spirit.'

In the German Alps it is believed that the cattle have the gift of language on Christmas Eve. But it is a sin to attempt to play the eavesdropper upon them. An Alpine story is told of a farmer's servant who did not believe that the cattle could speak, and, to make sure, he hid in his master's stable on Christmas Eve and listened. When the clock struck twelve he was surprised at what he heard. ' We shall have hard work to do this day week,' said one horse. ' Yes; the farmer's servant is heavy,' answered the other horse. ' And the way to the churchyard is long and steep,' said the first. The servant was buried that day week."

There is a beautiful superstition about the cock that Shakespeare put into the mouth of Marcellus, in *Hamlet* —

" Some say, that ever 'gainst that season comes
   Wherein our Saviour's birth is celebrated,
   The bird of dawning singeth all night long:
   And then, they say, no spirit can walk
      abroad;
   The nights are wholesome; then no planets
      strike,
   No fairy takes, nor witch hath power to
      charm;
   So hallow'd and so gracious is the time."

No other holiday has so rich an heritage of old customs and observances as Christmas. The Yule Log has from time immemorial been haled to the open fire-place on Christmas Eve, and lighted with the embers of its predecessor to sanctify the roof-tree and protect it against those evil spirits over whom the season is in everyway a triumph. Then the wassail bowl full of swimming roasted apples, goes its merry round. Then the gift-shadowing Christmas tree sheds its divine brilliance down the path of the coming year; or stockings are hung for Santa Claus (St. Nicholas) to fill during the night. Then the mistletoe becomes a precarious shelter for maids, and the Waits — descendants of the minstrels of old — go through the snow from door to door, singing their mellow old carols, while masquerades and the merry Christmas game of Snapdragon are not forgotten.*

Even the Christmas dinner has its special observances. In many an English hall the stately custom still survives of bearing in a boar's head to inaugurate the meal, as a reminder of the student of Queens College, Oxford, who, attacked by a boar on Christmas day, choked him with a copy of Aristotle and took

---

* An exhaustive study of the history and customs of Christmas has been made by W. F. Dawson in "Christmas and its Associations."

his head back for dinner. The mince pie, sacred to the occasion, is supposed to commemorate in its mixture of oriental ingredients the offerings made by the wise men of the East. As for turkey and plum pudding, they have a deep significance, but it is clearer to the palate than to the brain.

Elise Traut relates the legend that on every Christmas eve the little Christ-child wanders all over the world bearing on its shoulders a bundle of evergreens. Through city streets and country lanes, up and down hill, to proudest castle and lowliest hovel, through cold and storm and sleet and ice, this holy child travels, to be welcomed or rejected at the doors at which he pleads for succor. Those who would invite him and long for his coming set a lighted candle in the window to guide him on his way hither. They also believe that he comes to them in the guise of any alms-craving, wandering person who knocks humbly at their doors for sustenance, thus testing their benevolence. In many places the aid rendered the beggar is looked upon as hospitality shown to Christ.

This legend embodies the true Christmas spirit which realizes, with a rush of love to the heart, the divinity in every one of " the least of these " our brethren. Selfishness is rebuked, the feeling of universal brotherhood is fostered, while the length of this holiday season by en-

couraging the reunion of families and of friends, provides a wonderful rallying place for early affections. A wholesome and joyous current of religious feeling flows through the entire season to temper its extravagance and regulate its mirth.

"Under the sanctions of religion," writes Hervey,* the covenants of the heart are renewed. . . . The lovers of Earth seem to have met together."

Christmas is the birthday of one whose chief contribution to the human heart and mind was his message of boundless, universal love, He brought to the world the greatest thing in the world and that is why the season of his birth has won such an intimate place in our hearts and why its jubilant bells find this echo there:

"Ring out the old, ring in the new,
    Ring, happy bells, across the snow;
    The year is going, let him go;
Ring out the false, ring in the true.

"Ring out the grief that saps the mind,
    For those that here we see no more;
    Ring out the feud of rich and poor,
Ring in redress to all mankind.

*For a beautiful and extended discussion of the significance of the day, see Hervey's "The Book of Christmas."

" Ring out a slowly dying cause,
　　And ancient forms of party strife;
　　Ring in the nobler modes of life,
With sweeter manners, purer laws.

" Ring out the want, the care, the sin,
　　The faithless coldness of the times;
　　Ring out, ring out my mournful rhymes,
But ring the fuller minstrel in.

" Ring out false pride in place and blood,
　　The civic slander and the spite;
　　Ring in the love of truth and right,
Ring in the common love of good.

" Ring out old shapes of foul disease;
　　Ring out the narrowing lust of gold;
　　Ring out the thousand wars of old,
Ring in the thousand years of peace.

" Ring in the valiant man and free,
　　The larger heart, the kindlier hand;
　　Ring out the darkness of the land,
Ring in the Christ that is to be."

CHRISTMAS
IN PROSE AND VERSE

ITS ORIGIN, CELEBRATION AND SIGNIFICANCE
TWO VOLUMES IN ONE

BOOK ONE

CHRISTMAS
ORIGIN

CHRISTMAS

IS THERE A SANTA CLAUS?

The following, reprinted from the editorial page of the New York Sun, was written by the late Mr. Frank P. Church:

We take pleasure in answering at once and thus prominently the communication below, expressing at the same time our great gratification that its faithful author is numbered among the friends of *The Sun:*

DEAR EDITOR: I am 8 years old.
Some of my little friends say there is no Santa Claus.
Papa says "If you see it in *The Sun* it's so."
Please tell me the truth; is there a Santa Claus?
VIRGINIA O'HANLON.

Virginia, your little friends are wrong. They have been affected by the scepticism of a sceptical age. They do not believe except they see. They think that nothing can be which is not comprehensible by their little minds. All minds, Virginia, whether they be men's or children's, are little. In this great universe of ours man is a mere insect, an ant, in his intellect, as compared with the boundless

3

world about him, as measured by the intelligence capable of grasping the whole of truth and knowledge.

Yes, Virginia, there is a Santa Claus. He exists as certainly as love and generosity and devotion exist, and you know that they abound and give to your life its highest beauty and joy. Alas! how dreary would be the world if there were no Santa Claus! It would be as dreary as if there were no Virginias. There would be no childlike faith then, no poetry, no romance to make tolerable this existence. We should have no enjoyment, except in sense and sight. The eternal light with which childhood fills the world would be extinguished.

Not believe in Santa Claus! You might as well not believe in fairies! You might get your papa to hire men to watch in all the chimneys on Christmas Eve to catch Santa Claus, but even if they did not see Santa Claus coming down, what would that prove? Nobody sees Santa Claus, but that is no sign that there is no Santa Claus. The most real things in the world are those that neither children nor men can see. Did you ever see fairies dancing on the lawn? Of course not, but that's no proof that they are not there. Nobody can conceive or imagine all the wonders there are unseen and unseeable in the world.

You may tear apart the baby's rattle and see what makes the noise inside, but there is

a veil covering the unseen world which not
the strongest man, nor even the united strength
of all the strongest men that ever lived, could
tear apart. Only faith, fancy, poetry, love, romance, can push aside that curtain and view
and picture the supernal beauty and glory beyond. Is it all real? Ah, Virginia, in all this
world there is nothing else real and abiding.

No Santa Claus! Thank God! he lives, and
he lives forever. A thousand years from now,
Virginia, nay, ten times ten thousand years
from now, he will continue to make glad the
heart of childhood.

O LITTLE TOWN OF BETHLEHEM

PHILLIPS BROOKS

O little town of Bethlehem,
  How still we see thee lie!
Above thy deep and dreamless sleep
  The silent stars go by;
Yet in thy dark streets shineth
  The everlasting Light;
The hopes and fears of all the years
  Are met in thee to-night.

For Christ is born of Mary,
  And, gathered all above,
While mortals sleep, the angels keep
  Their watch of wondering love.

O morning stars, together
  Proclaim the holy birth!
And praises sing to God the King,
  And peace to men on earth.
How silently, how silently,
  The wondrous gift is given!
So God imparts to human hearts
  The blessings of His heaven.
No ear may hear His coming,
  But in this world of sin,
Where meek souls will receive Him still,
  The dear Christ enters in.

O holy Child of Bethlehem!
  Descend to us, we pray;
Cast out our sin, and enter in,
  Be born in us to-day.
We hear the Christmas angels
  The great glad tidings tell;
Oh, come to us, abide with us,
  Our Lord Emmanuel!

———

THE GLAD EVANGEL

KATE DOUGLAS WIGGIN

When the Child of Nazareth was born, the sun, according to the Bosnian legend, " leaped in the heavens, and the stars around it danced. A peace came over mountain and forest. Even the rotten stump stood straight and healthy on the green hill-side. The grass was beflowered with open blossoms, incense sweet as myrrh pervaded upland and forest, birds sang on the mountain top, and all gave thanks to the great God."

It is naught but an old folk-tale, but it has truth hidden at its heart, for a strange, subtle force, a spirit of genial good-will, a new-born kindness, seem to animate child and man alike when the world pays its tribute to the " heaven-sent youngling," as the poet Drummond calls the infant Christ.

When the Three Wise Men rode from the East into the West on that " first, best Christmas night," they bore on their saddle-bows three caskets filled with gold and frankincense and myrrh, to be laid at the feet of the manger-cradled babe of Bethlehem. Beginning with

7

this old, old journey, the spirit of giving crept into the world's heart. As the Magi came bearing gifts, so do we also; gifts that relieve want, gifts that are sweet and fragrant with friendship, gifts that breathe love, gifts that mean service, gifts inspired still by the star that shone over the City of David nearly two thousand years ago.

Then hang the green coronet of the Christmas-tree with glittering baubles and jewels of flame; heap offerings on 'its emerald branches; bring the Yule log to the firing; deck the house with holly and mistletoe,

> "And all the bells on earth shall ring
> On Christmas day in the morning."

THE SHEPHERDS

WILLIAM DRUMMOND, OF HAWTHORNDEN

O than the fairest day, thrice fairer night!
　Night to blest days in which a sun doth rise
　Of which that golden eye which clears the
　　　skies
Is but a sparkling ray, a shadow-light!
And blessed ye, in silly pastor's sight,
　Mild creatures, in whose warm crib now lies
That heaven-sent youngling, holy-maid-born
　　　wight,
　Midst, end, beginning of our prophecies!

Blest cottage that hath flowers in winter spread,
    Though withered — blessed grass that hath
        the grace
To deck and be a carpet to that place!
Thus sang, unto the sounds of oaten reed,
    Before the Babe, the shepherds bowed on
        knees;
    And springs ran nectar, honey dropped from
        trees.

A CHRISTMAS CAROL

JAMES RUSSELL LOWELL

"What means this glory round our feet,"
    The Magi mused, "more bright than
        morn?"
And voices chanted clear and sweet,
    "To-day the Prince of Peace is born!"

"What means that star," the Shepherds said,
    "That brightens through the rocky glen?"
And angels, answering overhead,
    Sang, "Peace on earth, good-will to men!"

'Tis eighteen hundred years and more
    Since those sweet oracles were dumb;
We wait for Him, like them of yore;
    Alas, He seems so slow to come!

But it was said, in words of gold,
    No time or sorrow e'er shall dim,

That little children might be bold
  In perfect trust to come to Him.

All round about our feet shall shine
  A light like that the wise men saw,
If we our loving wills incline
  To that sweet Life which is the Law.

So shall we learn to understand
  The simple faith of shepherds then,
And, clasping kindly hand in hand,
  Sing, " Peace on earth, good-will to men! "

But they who do their souls no wrong,
  But keep at eve the faith of morn,
Shall daily hear the angel-song,
  " To-day the Prince of Peace is born! "

A CHRISTMAS HYMN

ALFRED DOMETT

It was the calm and silent night!
  Seven hundred years and fifty-three
Had Rome been growing up to might,
  And now was Queen of land and sea.
No sound was heard of clashing wars;
  Peace brooded o'er the hush'd domain;
Apollo, Pallas, Jove and Mars,
  Held undisturb'd their ancient reign,
    In the solemn midnight
      Centuries ago.

'T was in the calm and silent night!
  The senator of haughty Rome
Impatient urged his chariot's flight,
  From lordly revel rolling home.
Triumphal arches gleaming swell
  His breast with thoughts of boundless sway;
What reck'd the Roman what befell
  A paltry province far away,
      In the solemn midnight
        Centuries ago!

Within that province far away
  Went plodding home a weary boor:
A streak of light before him lay,
  Fall'n through a half-shut stable door
Across his path. He pass'd — for nought
  Told what was going on within;
How keen the stars! his only thought;
  The air how calm and cold and thin,
      In the solemn midnight
        Centuries ago!

O strange indifference! — low and high
  Drows'd over common joys and cares:
The earth was still — but knew not why;
  The world was listening — unawares.
How calm a moment may precede
  One that shall thrill the world for ever!
To that still moment none would heed,
  Man's doom was link'd, no more to sever,
      In the solemn midnight
        Centuries ago.

It *is* the calm and solemn night!
　A thousand bells ring out, and throw
Their joyous peals abroad, and smite
　The darkness, charm'd and holy now.
The night that erst no name had worn,
　To it a happy name is given;
For in that stable lay new-born
　　The peaceful Prince of Earth and Heaven,
　　　In the solemn midnight
　　　　Centuries ago.

———

BRIGHTEST AND BEST OF THE SONS OF THE MORNING

REGINALD HEBER

Brightest and best of the Sons of the morning!
　Dawn on our darkness and lend us thine aid!
Star of the East, the horizon adorning,
　Guide where our Infant Redeemer is laid!

Cold on His cradle the dewdrops are shining,
　Low lies His head with the beasts of the
　　　stall;
Angels adore Him in slumber reclining,
　Maker and Monarch and Saviour of all!

Say, shall we yield Him, in costly devotion,
　Odors of Edom and offerings divine?
Gems of the mountain and pearls of the ocean,
　Myrrh from the forest, or gold from the
　　　mine?

Vainly we offer each ample oblation;
  Vainly with gifts would His favor secure:
Richer by far is the heart's adoration;
  Dearer to God are the prayers of the poor.

Brightest and best of the Sons of the morning!
  Dawn on our darkness and lend us thine aid!
Star of the East, the horizon adorning,
  Guide where our Infant Redeemer is laid!

GOD REST YE, MERRY GENTLEMEN

DINAH MARIA MULOCK

God rest ye, merry gentlemen; let nothing you
    dismay,
For Jesus Christ, our Saviour, was born on
    Christmas-day.
The dawn rose red o'er Bethlehem, the stars
    shone through the gray,
When Jesus Christ, our Saviour, was born on
    Christmas-day.

God rest ye, little children; let nothing you af-
    fright,
For Jesus Christ, your Saviour, was born this
    happy night;
Along the hills of Galilee the white flocks sleep-
    ing lay,
When Christ, the child of Nazareth, was born
    on Christmas-day.

God rest ye, all good Christians; upon this
    blessed morn
The Lord of all good Christians was of a
    woman born:
Now all your sorrows He doth heal, your sins
    He takes away;
For Jesus Christ, our Saviour, was born on
    Christmas-day.

THE CHRISTMAS SILENCE

MARGARET DELAND

Hushed are the pigeons cooing low
    On dusty rafters of the loft;
    And mild-eyed oxen, breathing soft,
Sleep on the fragrant hay below.

Dim shadows in the corner hide;
    The glimmering lantern's rays are shed
    Where one young lamb just lifts his head,
Then huddles 'gainst his mother's side.

Strange silence tingles in the air;
    Through the half-open door a bar
    Of light from one low-hanging star
Touches a baby's radiant hair.

No sound: the mother, kneeling, lays
    Her cheek against the little face.
    Oh human love! Oh heavenly grace!
'Tis yet in silence that she prays!

Ages of silence end to-night;
  Then to the long-expectant earth
  Glad angels come to greet His birth
In burst of music, love, and light!

A CHRISTMAS LULLABY

JOHN ADDINGTON SYMONDS

Sleep, baby, sleep! The Mother sings:
Heaven's angels kneel and fold their wings.
        Sleep, baby, sleep!

With swathes of scented hay Thy bed
By Mary's hand at eve was spread.
        Sleep, baby, sleep!

At midnight came the shepherds, they
Whom seraphs wakened by the way.
        Sleep, baby, sleep!

And three kings from the East afar,
Ere dawn came, guided by the star.
        Sleep, baby, sleep!

They brought Thee gifts of gold and gems,
Pure orient pearls, rich diadems.
        Sleep, baby, sleep!

But Thou who liest slumbering there,
Art King of Kings, earth, ocean, air.
        Sleep, baby, sleep!

Sleep, baby, sleep! The shepherds sing:
Through heaven, through earth, hosannas ring.
Sleep, baby, sleep!

———

HYMN FOR THE NATIVITY

EDWARD THRING

Happy night and happy silence downward
    softly stealing,
  Softly stealing over land and sea,
Stars from golden censors swing a silent eager
    feeling
  Down on Judah, down on Galilee;
And all the wistful air, and earth, and sky,
Listened, listened for the gladness of a cry.

Holy night, a sudden flash of light its way is
    winging:
  Angels, angels, all above, around;
Hark, the angel voices, hark, the angel voices
    singing;
  And the sheep are lying on the ground.
Lo, all the wistful air, and earth, and sky,
Listen, listen to the gladness of the cry.

Happy night at Bethlehem; soft little hands are
    feeling,
  Feeling in the manger with the kine:
Little hands, and eyelids closed in sleep, while
    angels kneeling,
  Mary mother, hymn the Babe Divine.

Lo, all the wistful air, and earth, and sky,
Listen, listen to the gladness of the cry.

Wide, as if the light were music, flashes adora-
      tion:
  " Glory be to God, nor ever cease,"
All the silence thrills, and speeds the message of
      salvation:
  " Peace on earth, good-will to men of peace."
Lo, all the wistful air, and earth, and sky,
Listen, listen to the gladness of the cry.

Holy night, thy solemn silence evermore en-
      foldeth
  Angels songs and peace from God on high:
Holy night, thy watcher still with faithful eye
      beholdeth
  Wings that wave, and angel glory nigh,
Lo, hushed is strife in air, and earth, and sky,
Still thy watchers hear the gladness of the cry.

Praise Him, ye who watch the night, the silent
      night of ages:
  Praise Him, shepherds, praise the Holy
      Child;
Praise Him, ye who hear the light, O praise
  . Him, all ye sages;
  Praise Him, children, praise Him meek and
      mild.
Lo, peace on Earth, glory to God on high,
Listen, listen to the gladness of the cry.

MASTERS IN THIS HALL

ANONYMOUS

" To Bethlem did they go, the shepherds three;
To Bethlem did they go to see whe'r it were so
    or no,
Whether Christ were born or no
    To set men free."

Masters, in this hall,
    Hear ye news to-day
Brought over sea,
    And ever I you pray.
        Nowell! Nowell! Nowell! Nowell!
        Sing we clear!
        Holpen are all folk on earth,
        Born is God's Son so dear.

Going over the hills,
    Through the milk-white snow,
Heard I ewes bleat
    While the wind did blow.
        Nowell, &c.

Shepherds many an one
    Sat among the sheep;
No man spake more word
    Than they had been asleep.
        Nowell, &c.

Quoth I 'Fellows mine,
  Why this guise sit ye?
Making but dull cheer,
  Shepherds though ye be?
          Nowell, &c.

'Shepherds should of right
  Leap and dance and sing;
Thus to see ye sit
  Is a right strange thing.'
          Nowell, &c.

Quoth these fellows then
  'To Bethlem town we go,
To see a Mighty Lord
  Lie in manger low.'
          Nowell, &c.

'How name ye this Lord,
  Shepherds?' then said I.
'Very God' they said,
  'Come from Heaven high.'
          Nowell, &c.

Then to Bethlem town
  We went two and two,
And in a sorry place
  Heard the oxen low.
          Nowell, &c.

Therein did we see
  A sweet and goodly May,

And a fair old man;
  Upon the straw she lay.
            Nowell, &c.

And a little CHILD
  On her arm had she;
'Wot ye who this is?'
  Said the hinds to me.
            Nowell, &c.

Ox and ass him know,
  Kneeling on their knee:
Wondrous joy had I
  This little BABE to see.
            Nowell, &c.

This is CHRIST the Lord,
  Masters, be ye glad!
Christmas is come in,
  And no folk should be sad.
            Nowell, &c.

———

THE ADORATION OF THE WISE MEN

CECIL FRANCES ALEXANDER

Saw you never in the twilight,
  When the sun had left the skies,
Up in heaven the clear stars shining,
  Through the gloom like silver eyes?

So of old the wise men watching,
  Saw a little stranger star,
And they knew the King was given,
  And they follow'd it from far.

Heard you never of the story,
  How they cross'd the desert wild,
Journey'd on by plain and mountain,
  Till they found the Holy Child?
How they open'd all their treasure,
  Kneeling to that Infant King,
Gave the gold and fragrant incense,
  Gave the myrrh in offering?

Know ye not that lowly Baby
  Was the bright and morning star,
He who came to light the Gentiles,
  And the darken'd isles afar?
And we too may seek his cradle,
  There our heart's best treasures bring,
Love, and Faith, and true devotion,
  For our Saviour, God, and King.

THE SHEPHERDS IN JUDEA

MARY AUSTIN

Oh, the Shepherds in Judea,
  They are pacing to and fro,
For the air grows chill at twilight
  And the weanling lambs are slow!

Leave, O lambs, the dripping sedges, quit the
    bramble and the brier,
Leave the fields of barley stubble, for we light
    the watching fire;
Twinkling fires across the twilight, and a bit-
    ter watch to keep,
Lest the prowlers come a-thieving where the
    flocks unguarded sleep.

    Oh, the Shepherds in Judea,
       They are singing soft and low —
    Song the blessed angels taught them
       All the centuries ago!

There was never roof to hide them, there were
    never walls to bind;
Stark they lie beneath the star-beams, whom
    the blessed angels find,
With the huddled flocks upstarting, wondering
    if they hear aright,
While the Kings come riding, riding, solemn
    shadows in the night.

    Oh, the Shepherds in Judea,
       They are thinking, as they go,
    Of the light that broke their watching
       On the hillside in the snow! —

Scattered snow along the hillside, white as
    springtime fleeces are,
With the whiter wings above them and the
    glory-streaming star —

Guiding-star across the housetops; never fear
   the Shepherds felt
Till they found the Babe in manger where the
   kindly cattle knelt.

   Oh, the Shepherds in Judea! —
     Do you think the Shepherds know
   How the whole round earth is brightened
     In the ruddy Christmas glow?

How the sighs are lost in laughter, and the
   laughter brings the tears,
As the thoughts of men go seeking back across
   the darkling years
Till they find the wayside stable that the star-
   led Wise Men found,
With the Shepherds, mute, adoring, and the
   glory shining round!

CHRISTMAS CAROL

JAMES S. PARK

So crowded was the little town
   On the first Christmas day,
Tired Mary Mother laid her down
   To rest upon the hay.
(Ah, would my door might have been thrown
   Wide open on her way!)

But when the Holy Babe was born
  In the deep hush of night,
It seemed as if a Sabbath morn
  Had come with sacred light.
Child Jesus made the place forlorn
  With his own beauty bright.

The manger rough was all his rest;
  The cattle, having fed,
Stood silent by, or closer pressed,
  And gravely wonderèd.
(Ah, Lord, if only that my breast
  Had cradled Thee instead!)

NEIGHBORS OF THE CHRIST NIGHT

NORA ARCHIBALD SMITH

Deep in the shelter of the cave,
  The ass with drooping head
Stood weary in the shadow, where
  His master's hand had led.
About the manger oxen lay,
  Bending a wide-eyed gaze
Upon the little new-born Babe,
  Half worship, half amaze.
High in the roof the doves were set,
  And cooed there, soft and mild,
Yet not so sweet as, in the hay,
  The Mother to her Child.

The gentle cows breathed fragrant breath
  To keep Babe Jesus warm,
While loud and clear, o'er hill and dale,
  The cocks crowed, " Christ is born! "
Out in the fields, beneath the stars,
  The young lambs sleeping lay,
And dreamed that in the manger slept
  Another white as they.

These were Thy neighbors, Christmas Child;
  To Thee their love was given,
For in Thy baby face there shone
  The wonder-light of Heaven.

CRADLE HYMN

ISAAC WATTS

Hush, my dear, lie still and slumber;
  Holy angels guard thy bed;
Heavenly blessings without number
  Gently falling on thy head.

Sleep, my babe, thy food and raiment,
  House and home, thy friends provide;
All without thy care, or payment,
  All thy wants are well supplied.

How much better thou'rt attended
  Than the Son of God could be,
When from heaven He descended,
  And became a child like thee!

Soft and easy is thy cradle;
   Coarse and hard thy Saviour lay,
When His birthplace was a stable,
   And His softest bed was hay.

See the kindly shepherds round him,
   Telling wonders from the sky!
When they sought Him, there they found
     Him,
   With his Virgin-Mother by.

See the lovely babe a-dressing;
   Lovely infant, how He smiled!
When He wept, the mother's blessing
   Soothed and hushed the holy child.

Lo, He slumbers in His manger,
   Where the honest oxen fed;
— Peace, my darling! here's no danger!
   Here's no ox a-near thy bed!

Mayst thou live to know and fear Him,
   Trust and love Him all thy days;
Then go dwell forever near Him,
   See His face, and sing His praise!

I could give thee thousand kisses,
   Hoping what I most desire;
Not a mother's fondest wishes
   Can to greater joys aspire.

AN ODE ON THE BIRTH OF OUR SAVIOUR

ROBERT HERRICK

In numbers, and but these few,
I sing thy birth, O Jesu!
Thou pretty baby, born here
With sup'rabundant scorn here:
Who for thy princely port here,
        Hadst for thy place
        Of birth, a base
Out-stable for thy court here.

Instead of neat enclosures
Of interwoven osiers,
Instead of fragrant posies
Of daffodils and roses,
Thy cradle, kingly stranger,
        As gospel tells,
        Was nothing else
But here a homely manger.

But we with silks, not crewels,
With sundry precious jewels,
And lily work will dress thee;
And, as we dispossess thee
Of clouts, we'll make a chamber,
        Sweet babe, for thee
        Of ivory,
And plaster'd round with amber.

CHRISTMAS SONG

EDMUND HAMILTON SEARS

Calm on the listening ear of night
　Come heaven's melodious strains,
Where wild Judea stretches far
　Her silver-mantled plains;
Celestial choirs from courts above
　Shed sacred glories there;
And angels with their sparkling lyres
　Make music on the air.

The answering hills of Palestine
　Send back the glad reply,
And greet from all their holy heights
　The day-spring from on high:
O'er the blue depths of Galilee
　There comes a holier calm,
And Sharon waves, in solemn praise,
　Her silent groves of palm.

" Glory to God! "　The lofty strain
　The realm of ether fills:
How sweeps the song of solemn joy
　O'er Judah's sacred hills!
" Glory to God! "　The sounding skies
　Loud with their anthems ring;
" Peace on the earth; good-will to men,
　From heaven's eternal King! "

Light on thy hills, Jerusalem!
　　The Saviour now is born:
More bright on Bethlehem's joyous plains
　　Breaks the first Christmas morn;
And brighter on Moriah's brow,
　　Crowned with her temple-spires,
Which first proclaim the new-born light,
　　Clothed with its Orient fires.

This day shall Christian lips be mute,
　　And Christian hearts be cold?
Oh, catch the anthem that from heaven
　　O'er Judah's mountains rolled!
When nightly burst from seraph-harps
　　The high and solemn lay,—
" Glory to God! on earth be peace;
　　Salvation comes to-day! "

A HYMN ON THE NATIVITY OF MY SAVIOUR

BEN JONSON

I sing the birth was born to-night,
The author both of life and light;
　　The angels so did sound it.
And like the ravished shepherds said,
Who saw the light, and were afraid,
　　Yet searched, and true they found it.

The Son of God, th' eternal king,
That did us all salvation bring,
  And freed the soul from danger;
He whom the whole world could not take,
The Word, which heaven and earth did make,
  Was now laid in a manger.

The Father's wisdom willed it so,
The Son's obedience knew no No,
  Both wills were in one stature;
And as that wisdom had decreed,
The Word was now made flesh indeed,
  And took on him our nature.

What comfort by him do we win,
Who made himself the price of sin,
  To make us heirs of glory!
To see this babe all innocence;
A martyr born in our defence:
  Can man forget the story?

———

THE SHEPHERD'S SONG

EDMUND BOLTON

Sweet music, sweeter far
  Than any song is sweet:
Sweet music, heavenly rare,
  Mine ears, O peers, doth greet.
You gentle flocks, whose fleeces pearled with
  dew,

Resemble heaven, whom golden drops **make** bright,
Listen, O listen, now, O not to you
  Our pipes make sport to shorten **weary** night:
    But voices most divine
      Make blissful harmony:
    Voices that seem to shine,
      For what else clears the sky?
Tunes can we hear, but not the singers see,
The tunes divine, and so the singers be.

    Lo, how the firmament
      Within an azure fold
    The flock of stars hath pent,
      That we might them behold,
Yet from their beams proceedeth not this light,
  Nor can their crystals such reflection give.
What then doth make the element so bright?
  The heavens are come down upon earth to live
    But hearken to the song,
      Glory to glory's King,
    And peace all men among,
      These quiristers do sing.
Angels they are, as also (shepherds) He
Whom in our fear we do admire to see.

    Let not amazement blind
      Your souls, said he, annoy:
    To you and all mankind
      My message bringeth joy.

For lo! the world's great Shepherd now is
    born,
  A blessed Babe, an Infant full of power:
After long night uprisen is the morn,
    Renowning Bethlem in the Saviour.
        Sprung is the perfect day,
            By prophets seen afar:
        Sprung is the mirthful May,
            Which winter cannot mar.
In David's city doth this Sun appear
Clouded in flesh, yet, shepherds, sit we here?

A CHRISTMAS CAROL

AUBREY DE VERE

They leave the land of gems and gold,
  The shining portals of the East;
For Him, the woman's Seed foretold,
  They leave the revel and the feast.

To earth their sceptres they have cast,
  And crowns by kings ancestral worn;
They track the lonely Syrian waste;
  They kneel before the Babe new born.

O happy eyes that saw Him first;
  O happy lips that kissed His feet:
Earth slakes at last her ancient thirst;
  With Eden's joy her pulses beat.

True kings are those who thus forsake
  Their kingdoms for the Eternal King;
Serpent, her foot is on thy neck;
  Herod, thou writhest, but canst not sting.

He, He is King, and He alone
  Who lifts that infant hand to bless;
Who makes His mother's knee His throne,
  Yet rules the starry wilderness.

A CHRISTMAS HYMN

ANON

Written in the Chapel of the Manger, in the Convent Church of Bethlehem, Palestine:

In the fields where, long ago,
  Dropping tears, amid the leaves,
Ruth's young feet went to and fro,
  Binding up the scattered sheaves,
In the field that heard the voice
  Of Judea's shepherd King,
Still the gleaners may rejoice,
  Still the reapers shout and sing.

For each mount and vale and plain
  Felt the touch of holier feet.
Then the gleaners of the grain
  Heard, in voices full and sweet,
" Peace on earth, good will to men,"
  Ring from angel lips afar,

While, o'er every glade and glen,
   Broke the light of Bethlehem's star.

Star of hope to souls in night,
   Star of peace above our strife,
Guiding, where the gates of death
   Ope to fields of endless life.
Wanderer from the nightly throng
   Which the eastern heavens gem;
Guided, by an angel's song,
   To the Babe of Bethlehem.

Not Judea's hills alone
   Have earth's weary gleaners trod,
Not to heirs of David's throne
   Is it given to " reign with God."
But where'er on His green earth
   Heavenly faith and longing are,
Heavenly hope and life have birth,
   'Neath the smile of Bethlehem's star.

In each lowly heart or home,
   By each love-watched cradle-bed,
Where we rest, or where we roam,
   Still its changeless light is shed.
In its beams each quickened heart,
   Howe'er saddened or denied,
Keeps one little place apart
   For the Hebrew mother's Child.

And that inner temple fair
   May be holier ground than this,

Hallowed by the pilgrim's prayer,
　Warmed by many a pilgrim's kiss.
In its shadow still and dim,
　Where our holiest longings are,
Rings forever Bethlehem's hymn,
　Shines forever Bethlehem's star.

CHRISTMAS DAY

CHARLES WESLEY

Hark! the herald angels sing
Glory to the new-born King!
Peace on earth and mercy mild,
God and sinners reconciled.

Joyful all ye nations rise,
Join the triumph of the skies,
With the angelic host proclaim
Christ is born in Bethlehem!

Hail the heaven-born Prince of Peace!
Hail the Sun of Righteousness!
Light and life to all he brings,
Risen with healing in his wings.

Mild, he lays his glory by;
Born, that man no more may die,
Born to raise the sons of earth,
Born to give them second birth.

CHRISTMAS

ANON

Once in Royal David's city
  Stood a lowly cattle shed,
Where a mother laid her baby
  In a manger for His bed.
Mary was that mother mild,
Jesus Christ that little child.

He came down to earth from Heaven,
  Who is God and Lord of all.
And his shelter was a stable,
  And his cradle was a stall.
With the poor and mean and lowly,
Lived on earth our Saviour Holy.

And our eyes at last shall see Him
  Through His own redeeming love,
For that child so dear and gentle
  Is our Lord in Heaven above;
And He leads His children on
To the place where He is gone.

Not in that poor, lowly stable,
  With the oxen standing by,
We shall see Him; but in Heaven,
  Set at God's right hand on high,
When, like stars, His children crowned
All in white, shall wait around.

CHRISTMAS

NAHUM TATE

While shepherds watch'd their flocks by night,
 All seated on the ground,
The angel of the Lord came down,
 And glory shone around.

" Fear not," said he (for mighty dread
 Had seized their troubled mind);
" Glad tidings of great joy I bring
 To you and all mankind.

" To you, in David's town, this day
 Is born of David's line
The Saviour who is Christ the Lord;
 And this shall be the sign:

" The heavenly Babe you there shall find
 To human view display'd,
All meanly wrapt in swathing bands,
 And in a manger laid."

Thus spake the Seraph; and forthwith
 Appear'd a shining throng
Of angels, praising God, and thus
 Address'd their joyful song:

" All glory be to God on high,
 And to the earth be peace;
Good-will henceforth from heaven to men
 Begin, and never cease! "

"WHILE SHEPHERDS WATCHED
THEIR FLOCKS BY NIGHT"

MARGARET DELAND

Like small curled feathers, white and soft,
   The little clouds went by,
Across the moon, and past the stars,
   And down the western sky:
In upland pastures, where the grass
   With frosted dew was white,
Like snowy clouds the young sheep lay,
   That first, best Christmas night.

The shepherds slept; and, glimmering faint,
   With twist of thin, blue smoke,
Only their fire's crackling flames
   The tender silence broke —
Save when a young lamb raised his head,
   Or, when the night wind blew,
A nesting bird would softly stir,
   Where dusky olives grew —

With finger on her solemn lip,
   Night hushed the shadowy earth,
And only stars and angels saw
   The little Saviour's birth;
Then came such flash of silver light
   Across the bending skies,
The wondering shepherds woke, and hid
   Their frightened, dazzled eyes!

And all their gentle sleepy flock
  Looked up, then slept again,
Nor knew the light that dimmed the stars
  Brought endless Peace to men —
Nor even heard the gracious words
  That down the ages ring —
The Christ is born! the Lord has come,
  Good-will on earth to bring!"

Then o'er the moonlit, misty fields,
  Dumb with the world's great joy,
The shepherds sought the white-walled town,
  Where lay the baby boy —
And oh, the gladness of the world,
  The glory of the skies,
Because the longed-for Christ looked up
  In Mary's happy eyes!

COLONIAL CHRISTMASES *

ALICE MORSE EARLE

The first century of colonial life saw few set times and days for pleasure. The holy days of the English Church were as a stench to the Puritan nostrils, and their public celebration was at once rigidly forbidden by the laws of New England. New holidays were not quickly evolved, and the sober gatherings for matters of Church and State for a time took their place. The hatred of " wanton Bacchanallian Christmasses " spent throughout England, as Cotton said, in " revelling, dicing, carding, masking, mumming, consumed in compotations, in interludes, in excess of wine, in mad mirth," was the natural reaction of intelligent and thoughtful minds against the excesses of a festival which had ceased to be a Christian holiday, but was dominated by a lord of misrule who did not hesitate to invade the churches in time of service, in his noisy revels and sports. English Churchmen long ago revolted also against such Christmas observance.

* From " Customs and Fashions in Old New England." Copyright 1903, by Charles Scribner's Sons.

Of the first Pilgrim Christmas we know but little, save that it was spent, as was many a later one, in work. . . .

By 1659 the Puritans had grown to hate Christmas more and more; it was, to use Shakespeare's words, "the bug that feared them all." The very name smacked to them of incense, stole, and monkish jargon; any person who observed it as a holiday by forbearing of labor, feasting, or any other way was to pay five shillings fine, so desirous were they to "beate down every sprout of Episcopacie." Judge Sewall watched jealously the feeling of the people with regard to Christmas, and noted with pleasure on each succeeding year the continuance of common traffic throughout the day. Such entries as this show his attitude: "Dec. 25, 1685. Carts come to town and shops open as usual. Some somehow observe the day, but are vexed I believe that the Body of people profane it, and blessed be God no authority yet to compel them to keep it." When the Church of England established Christmas services in Boston a few years later, we find the Judge waging hopeless war against Governor Belcher over it, and hear him praising his son for not going with other boy friends to hear the novel and attractive services. He says: "I dehort mine from Christmas keeping and charge them to forbear."

Christmas could not be regarded till this

century as a New England holiday, though in certain localities, such as old Narragansett — an opulent community which was settled by Episcopalians — two weeks of Christmas visiting and feasting were entered into with zest by both planters and slaves for many years previous to the revolution.

THE ANGELS

WILLIAM DRUMMOND

Run, shepherds, run where Bethlehem blest
    appears.
We bring the best of news; be not dismayed:
A Saviour there is born more old than years,
Amidst heaven's rolling height this earth who
    stayed.
In a poor cottage inned, a virgin maid,
A weakling did him bear, who all upbears;
There is he poorly swaddled, in manger laid,
To whom too narrow swaddlings are our
    spheres:
Run, shepherds, run, and solemnize his birth.
This is that night — no, day, grown great with
    bliss,
In which the power of Satan broken is:
In heaven be glory, peace unto the earth!
Thus singing, through the air the angels
    swarm,
And cope of stars re-echoèd the same.

Or say, if this new Birth of ours
Sleeps, laid within some ark of flowers,
Spangled with dew-light; thou canst clear
All doubts, and manifest the where.

Declare to us, bright star, if we shall seek
Him in the morning's blushing cheek,
Or search the beds of spices through,
To find him out?

Star.— No, this ye need not do;
But only come and see Him rest,
A princely babe, in's mother's breast.

HYMN FOR CHRISTMAS

FELICIA HEMANS

Oh! lovely voices of the sky
   Which hymned the Saviour's birth,
Are ye not singing still on high,
   Ye that sang, " Peace on earth "?
      To us yet speak the strains
         Wherewith, in time gone by,
      Ye blessed the Syrian swains,
         Oh! voices of the sky!

Oh! clear and shining light, whose beams
   That hour Heaven's glory shed,

Around the palms, and o'er the streams,
  And on the shepherd's head.
    Be near, through life and death,
      As in that holiest night
    Of hope, and joy, and faith —
      Oh! clear and shining light!

NEW PRINCE, NEW POMP

ROBERT SOUTHWELL

Behold a simple, tender Babe,
  In freezing winter night,.
In homely manger trembling lies;
  Alas! a piteous sight.

The inns are full; no man will yield
  This little Pilgrim bed;
But forced he is with silly beasts
  In crib to shroud his head.

Despise him not for lying there;
  First what he is inquire:
An Orient pearl is often found
  In depth of dirty mire.

Weigh not his crib, his wooden dish,
  Nor beasts that by him feed;
Weigh not his mother's poor attire,
  Nor Joseph's simple weed.

This stable is a Prince's court,
   The crib his chair of state;
The beasts are parcel of his pomp,
   The wooden dish his plate.

The persons in that poor attire
   His royal liveries wear;
The Prince himself is come from heaven:
   This pomp is praisèd there.

With joy approach, O Christian wight!
   Do homage to thy King;
And highly praise this humble pomp,
   Which he from heaven doth bring.

THE THREE KINGS

HENRY WADSWORTH LONGFELLOW

Three Kings came riding from far away,
   Melchior and Gaspar and Baltasar;
Three Wise Men out of the East were they,
And they traveled by night and they slept by
      day,
   For their guide was a beautiful, wonderful
      star.

The star was so beautiful, large and clear,
   That all the other stars of the sky
Became a white mist in the atmosphere;

And by this they knew that the coming was
    near
Of the Prince foretold in the prophecy.

Of bells and pomegranates and furbelows,
Their robes were of crimson silk, with rows
Three caskets they bore on their saddle-bows,
    Three caskets of gold with golden keys;
    Their turbans like blossoming almond-trees.

And so the Three Kings rode into the West,
    Through the dusk of night over hills and
        dells,
And sometimes they nodded with beard on
        breast,
And sometimes talked, as they paused to rest,
    With the people they met at the wayside
        wells.

" Of the child that is born," said Baltasar,
    " Good people, I pray you, tell us the news;
For we in the East have seen his star,
And have ridden fast, and have ridden far,
    To find and worship the King of the Jews."

And the people answered, " You ask in vain;
    We know of no king but Herod the Great!"
They thought the Wise Men were men insane,
As they spurred their horses across the plain
    Like riders in haste who cannot wait.

And when they came to Jerusalem,
  Herod the Great, who had heard this thing,
Sent for the Wise Men and questioned them;
And said, " Go down unto Bethlehem,
  And bring me tidings of this new king."

So they rode away, and the star stood still,
  The only one in the gray of morn;
Yes, it stopped, it stood still of its own free
      will,
Right over Bethlehem on the hill,
  The city of David where Christ was born.

And the Three Kings rode through the gate
      and the guard,
  Through the silent street, till their horses
      turned
And neighed as they entered the great inn-
      yard;
But the windows were closed, and the doors
      were barred,
  And only a light in the stable burned.

And cradled there in the scented hay,
  In the air made sweet by the breath of kine,
The little child in the manger lay,
The Child that would be King one day
  Of a kingdom not human, but divine.

His mother, Mary of Nazareth,
  Sat watching beside his place of rest,

Watching the even flow of his breath,
For the joy of life and the terror of death
   Were mingled together in her breast.

They laid their offerings at his feet:
   The gold was their tribute to a King;
The frankincense, with its odor sweet,
Was for the Priest, the Paraclete;
   The myrrh for the body's burying.

And the mother wondered and bowed her head,
   And sat as still as a statue of stone;
Her heart was troubled yet comforted,
Remembering what the angel had said
   Of an endless reign and of David's throne.

Then the Kings rode out of the city gate,
   With a clatter of hoofs in proud array;
But they went not back to Herod the Great,
For they knew his malice and feared his hate,
   And returned to their homes by another way.

HYMN ON THE NATIVITY

JOHN MILTON

It was the winter wild,
While the heaven-born child
   All meanly wrapt in the rude manger lies;
Nature, in awe of him,

Had doffed her gaudy trim,
  With her great Master so to sympathize:
It was no season then for her
To wanton with the sun, her lusty paramour.

Only with speeches fair
She wooes the gentle air,
  To hide her guilty front with innocent snow;
And on her naked shame,
Pollute with sinful blame,
  The saintly veil of maiden-white to throw;
Confounded, that her Maker's eyes
Should look so near upon her foul deformities.

But he, her fears to cease,
Sent down the meek-eyed Peace:
  She, crowned with olive green, came softly
      sliding
Down through the turning sphere,
His ready harbinger,
  With turtle wing the amorous clouds divid-
      ing;
And, waving wide her myrtle wand,
She strikes a universal peace through sea and
    land.

No war or battle's sound
Was heard the world around:
  The idle spear and shield were high uphung;
The hookèd chariot stood

Unstained with hostile blood;
　The trumpet spake not to the armèd throng;
And kings sat still with awful eye,
As if they surely knew their sovereign lord
　　was by.

But peaceful was the night,
Wherein the Prince of Light
　His reign of peace upon the earth began:
The winds, with wonder whist,
Smoothly the waters kissed,
　Whispering new joys to the mild ocean,
Who now hath quite forgot to rave,
While birds of calm sit brooding on the
　　charmèd wave.

The stars, with deep amaze,
Stand fixed in steadfast gaze,
　Bending one way their precious influence;
And will not take their flight,
For all the morning light,
　Or Lucifer had often warned them thence:
But in their glimmering orbs did glow,
Until their Lord himself bespake, and bid
　　them go.

And, though the shady gloom
Had given day her room,
　The sun himself withheld his wonted speed,
And hid his head for shame,

As his inferior flame
  The new-enlightened world no more should
        need;
He saw a greater sun appear
Than his bright throne, or burning axletree,
        could bear.

The shepherds on the lawn,
Or ere the point of dawn,
  Sat simply chatting in a rustic row;
Full little thought they then
That the mighty Pan
  Was kindly come to live with them below;
Perhaps their loves, or else their sheep,
Was all that did their silly thoughts so busy
        keep.

When such music sweet
Their hearts and ears did greet,
  As never was by mortal fingers strook,
Divinely warbled voice
Answering the stringèd noise,
  As all their souls in blissful rapture took:
The air, such pleasure loath to lose,
With thousand echoes still prolongs each heav-
        enly close.

Nature, that heard such sound,
Beneath the hollow round
  Of Cynthia's seat, the airy region thrilling,
Now was almost won,

To think her part was done,
    And that her reign had here its last fulfill-
      ing;
She knew such harmony alone
Could hold all heaven and earth in happier
    union.

At last surrounds their sight
A globe of circular light,
    That with long beams the shame-faced night
      arrayed;
The helmèd cherubim,
And sworded seraphim,
    Are seen in glittering ranks with wings dis-
      played,
Harping in loud and solemn quire,
With unexpressive notes, to Heaven's new-
    born heir.

Such music as 'tis said
Before was never made,
    But when of old the sons of morning sung,
While the Creator great
His constellations set,
    And the well-balanced world on hinges hung,
And cast the dark foundations deep,
And bid the weltering waves their oozy channel
    keep.

Ring out, ye crystal spheres,
Once bless our human ears,
    If ye have power to touch our senses so;

And let your silver chime
Move in melodious time;
 And let the bass of Heaven's deep organ
  blow;
And, with your ninefold harmony,
Make up full concert to the angelic symphony.

For, if such holy song
Enwrap our fancy long,
 Time will run back, and fetch the age of
  gold;
And speckled Vanity
Will sicken soon and die,
 And leprous Sin will melt from earthly
  mould;
And Hell itself will pass away,
And leave her dolorous mansions to the peer-
 ing day.

Yea, Truth and Justice then
Will down return to men,
 Orbed in a rainbow; and, like glories wear-
  ing,
Mercy will sit between,
Throned in celestial sheen,
 With radiant feet the tissued clouds down
  steering;
And Heaven, as at some festival,
Will open wide the gates of her high palace
 hall.

But wisest Fate says no,
This must not yet be so;
   The babe yet lies in smiling infancy,
That on the bitter cross
Must redeem our loss,
   So both himself and us to glorify:
Yet first, to those chained in sleep,
The wakeful trump of doom must thunder
      through the deep,

With such a horrid clang
As on Mount Sinai rang,
   While the red fire and smouldering clouds
      outbrake;
The aged earth aghast,
With terror of that blast,
   Shall from the surface to the centre shake;
When, at the world's last session,
The dreadful Judge in middle air shall spread
      his throne.

And then at last our bliss,
Full and perfect is,
   But now begins; for, from this happy day,
The old dragon, underground,
In straiter limits bound,
   Not half so far casts his usurpèd sway;
And, wroth to see his kingdom fail,
Swinges the scaly horror of his folded tail.

The oracles are dumb;
No voice or hideous hum
   Runs through the archèd roof in words de-
      ceiving.
Apollo from his shrine
Can no more divine,
   With hollow shriek the steep of Delphos
      leaving.
No nightly trance, or breathèd spell,
Inspires the pale-eyed priest from the prophetic
      cell.

The lonely mountains o'er,
And the resounding shore,
   A voice of weeping heard and loud lament;
From haunted spring and dale,
Edged with poplar pale,
   The parting Genius is with sighing sent;
With flower-inwoven tresses torn,
The nymphs in twilight shade of tangled thick-
      ets mourn.

In consecrated earth,
And on the holy hearth,
   The Lars and Lemures mourn with midnight
      plaint.
In urns and altars round,
A drear and dying sound
   Affrights the Flamens at their service
      quaint;

And the chill marble seems to sweat,
While each peculiar power foregoes his wonted
    seat.

Peor and Baälim
Forsake their temples dim
  With that twice-battered God of Palestine;
And moonèd Ashtaroth
Heaven's queen and mother both,
  Now sits not girt with tapers' holy shine;
The Libyac Hammon shrinks his horn;
In vain the Tyrian maids their wounded Tham-
    muz mourn.

And sullen Moloch, fled,
Hath left in shadows dread
  His burning idol all of blackest hue:
In vain with cymbals' ring
They call the grisly king,
  In dismal dance about the furnace blue:
The brutish gods of Nile as fast,
Isis, and Orus, and the dog Anubis, haste.

Nor is Osiris seen
In Memphian grove or green,
  Trampling the unshowered grass with low-
    ings loud;
Nor can he be at rest
Within his sacred chest,
  Naught but profoundest hell can be his
    shroud;

In vain with timbrelled anthems dark
The sable-stolèd sorcerers bear his worshipped
      ark.

He feels from Judah's land
The dreaded infant's hand,
  The rays of Bethlehem blind his dusky eyne;
Nor all the gods beside
Longer dare abide,
  Not Typhon huge ending in snaky twine;
Our babe, to show his Godhead true,
Can in his swaddling bands control the damnèd
      crew.

So, when the sun in bed,
Curtained with cloudy red,
  Pillows his chin upon an orient wave,
The flocking shadows pale
Troop to the infernal jail,
  Each fettered ghost slips to his several
      grave;
And the yellow-skirted fays
Fly after the night-steeds, leaving their moon-
      loved maze.

But see, the Virgin blest
Hath laid her babe to rest;
  Time is our tedious song should here have
      ending:
Heaven's youngest-teemèd star

Hath fixed her polished car,
   Her sleeping Lord with handmaid lamp at-
      tending;
And all about the courtly stable
Bright-harnessed angels sit in order service-
      able.

CHRISTMAS
CELEBRATION

CHRISTMAS EVE AT MR. WARDLE'S

From " Pickwick Papers "

CHARLES DICKENS

From the center of the ceiling of this kitchen, old Wardle had just suspended with his own hands a huge branch of mistletoe, and this same branch of mistletoe instantaneously gave rise to a scene of general and most delightful struggling and confusion; in the midst of which Mr. Pickwick with a gallantry which would have done honour to a descendant of Lady Trollimglower herself, took the old lady by the hand, led her beneath the mystic branch, and saluted her in all courtesy and decorum. The old lady submitted to this pie e of practical politeness with all the dignity which befitted so important and serious a solemnity, but the younger ladies not being so thoroughly imbued with a superstitious veneration of the custom, or imagining that the value of a salute is very much enhanced if it cost a little trouble to obtain it, screamed and struggled, and ran into corners, and threatened and remonstrated, and did everything but leave the room, until some of the less adventurous gentlemen were on the point of desisting, when they all at once found it useless to resist any longer, and submitted to be kissed with a good grace. Mr. Winkle kissed the young lady with the black eyes, and Mr. Snodgrass kissed Emily; and Mr. Weller, not being particular about the form of being under the mistletoe, kissed Emma and the other female servants, just as he caught them. As to the poor relations, they kissed everybody, not even excepting the plainer portion of the young-lady visitors, who, in their excessive confusion, ran right under the mistletoe, directly it was hung up, without knowing it! Wardle stood with his back to the fire, surveying the whole scene, with the utmost satisfaction; and the fat boy took the opportunity of appropriating to his own use, and summarily devouring, a particularly fine mince-pie, that had been carefully put by for somebody else.

Now the screaming had subsided, and faces were in a glow and curls in a tangle, and Mr. Pickwick, after kissing the old lady as before mentioned, was standing under the mistletoe, looking with a very pleased countenance on all that was passing around him, when the young lady with the black eyes, after a little whispering with the other young ladies, made a sudden dart forward, and, putting her arm around Mr. Pickwick's neck, saluted him affectionately on the left cheek; and before Mr. Pickwick distinctly knew what was the matter, he was sur-

rounded by the whole body, and kissed by every one of them.

It was a pleasant thing to see Mr. Pickwick in the centre of the group, now pulled this way, and then that, and first kissed on the chin and then on the nose, and then on the spectacles, and to hear the peals of laughter which were raised on every side; but it was a still more pleasant thing to see Mr. Pickwick, blinded shortly afterwards with a silk-handkerchief, falling up against the wall, and scrambling into corners, and going through all the mysteries of blind-man's buff, with the utmost relish of the game, until at last he caught one of the poor relations; and then had to evade the blind-man himself, which he did with a nimbleness and agility that elicited the admiration and applause of all beholders. The poor relations caught just the people whom they thought would like it; and when the game flagged, got caught themselves. When they were all tired of blind-man's buff, there was a great game at snapdragon, and when fingers enough were burned with that, and all the raisons gone, they sat down by the huge fire of blazing logs to a substantial supper, and a mighty bowl of wassail, something smaller than an ordinary washhouse copper, in which the hot apples were hissing and bubbling with a rich look, and a jolly sound, that were perfectly irresistible.

" This," said Mr. Pickwick, looking round him, " this is, indeed, comfort."

" Our invariable custom," replied Mr. Wardle. " Everybody sits down with us on Christmas eve, as you see them now — servants and all; and here we wait till the clock strikes twelve, to usher Christmas in, and wile away the time with forfeits and old stories. Trundle, my boy, rake up the fire."

Up flew the bright sparks in myriads as the logs were stirred, and the deep red blaze sent forth a rich glow, that penetrated into the furthest corner of the room, and cast its cheerful tint on every face.

" Come," said Wardell, " a song — a Christmas song. I'll give you one, in default of a better."

" Bravo," said Mr. Pickwick.

" Fill up," cried Wardle. " It will be two hours good, before you see the bottom of the bowl through the deep rich colour of the wassail; fill up all round, and now for the song."

Thus saying, the merry old gentleman, in a good, round, sturdy voice, commenced without more ado —

A CHRISTMAS CAROL

I care not for Spring; on his fickle wing
Let the blossoms and buds be borne:
He woos them amain with his treacherous rain,
And he scatters them ere the morn.

An inconstant elf, he knows not himself,
Or his own changing mind an hour,
He'll smile in your face, and, with wry grimace,
He'll wither your youngest flower.

Let the summer sun to his bright home run,
He shall never be sought by me;
When he's dimmed by a cloud I can laugh aloud,
And care not how sulky he be;
For his darling child is the madness wild
That sports in fierce fever's train;
And when love is too strong, it don't last long,
As many have found to their pain.

A mild harvest night, by the tranquil light
Of the modest and gentle moon,
Has a far sweeter sheen for me, I ween,
Than the broad and unblushing noon,
But every leaf awakens my grief,
As it lieth beneath the tree;
So let Autumn air be never so fair,
It by no means agrees with me.

But my song I troll out, for Christmas stout,
The hearty, the true, and the bold;
A bumper I drain, and with might and main
Give three cheers for this Christmas old.
We'll usher him in with a merry din
That shall gladden his joyous heart,
And we'll keep him up while there's bite or sup,
And in fellowship good, we'll part.

In his fine honest pride, he scorns to hide
One jot of his hard-weather scars;
They're no disgrace, for there's much the same
    trace
On the cheeks of our bravest tars.

Then again I sing 'till the roof doth ring,
And it echoes from wall to wall —
To the stout old wight, fair welcome to-night,
As the King of the Seasons all!

A VISIT FROM ST. NICHOLAS

CLEMENT C. MOORE

'Twas the night before Christmas, when all
    through the house
Not a creature was stirring, not even a mouse;
The stockings were hung by the chimney with
    care,
In hopes that St. Nicholas soon would be
    there;
The children were nestled all snug in their
    beds,
While visions of sugar-plums danced through
    their heads;
And mamma in her kerchief, and I in my cap,
Had just settled our brains for a long winter's
    nap,—
When out on the lawn there arose such a
    clatter,
I sprang from my bed to see what was the
    matter.
Away to the window I flew like a flash,
Tore open the shutters and threw up the sash.
The moon, on the breast of the new-fallen
    snow,

Gave a lustre of midday to objects below;
When what to my wondering eyes should appear,
But a miniature sleigh and eight tiny reindeer,
With a little old driver, so lively and quick
I knew in a moment it must be St. Nick.
More rapid than eagles his coursers they came,
And he whistled and shouted and called them by name:
"Now, Dasher! now, Dancer! now, Prancer and Vixen!
On, Comet! on, Cupid! on, Donder and Blitzen!
To the top of the porch, to the top of the wall!
Now, dash away, dash away, dash away all!"
As dry leaves that before the wild hurricane fly,
When they meet with an obstacle, mount to the sky,
So, up to the house-top the coursers they flew,
With a sleigh full of toys,— and St. Nicholas too.
And then in a twinkling I heard on the roof
The prancing and pawing of each little hoof,
As I drew in my head and was turning around,
Down the chimney St. Nicholas came with a bound.
He was dressed all in fur from his head to his foot,
And his clothes were all tarnished with ashes and soot;

A bundle of toys he had flung on his back,
And he looked like a pedler just opening his
    pack.
His eyes how they twinkled! his dimples how
    merry!
His cheeks were like roses, his nose like a
    cherry;
His droll little mouth was drawn up like a
    bow,
And the beard on his chin was as white as the
    snow.
The stump of a pipe he held tight in his teeth,
And the smoke it encircled his head like a
    wreath.
He had a broad face, and a little round belly
That shook, when he laughed, like a bowl full
    of jelly.
He was chubby and plump,— a right jolly old
    elf —
And I laughed when I saw him, in spite of
    myself.
A wink of his eye and a twist of his head
Soon gave me to know I had nothing to dread.
He spoke not a word, but went straight to his
    work,
And filled all the stockings; then turned with
    a jerk,
And laying his finger aside of his nose,
And giving a nod, up the chimney he rose.
He sprang to his sleigh, to his team gave a
    whistle,

And away they all flew like the down of a
thistle;
But I heard him exclaim, ere he drove out of
sight:
" Happy Christmas to all, and to all a good-
night ! "

A CHRISTMAS PIECE

Of garnered rhyme, from hidden stores of olden time that since the language did begin, have welcomed merry Christmas in, and made the winter nights so long, fleet by on wings of wine and song; for when the snow is on the roof, the house within is sorrow proof, if yule clog blazes on the hearth, and cups and hearts o'er-brim with mirth. Then bring the wassail to the board, with nuts and fruit — the winter's hoard; and bid the children take off shoe, to hang their stockings by the flue; and let the clear and frosty sky, set out its brightest jewelry, to show old Santa Claus the road, so he may ease his gimcrack load. And with the coming of these times, we'll add some old and lusty rhymes, that suit the festive season well, and sound as sweet as Christmas bell.

Now just bethink of castle gate, where humble midnight mummers wait, to try if voices, one and all, can rouse the tipsy seneschal, to give them bread and beer and brawn, for tidings of the Christmas morn; or bid each yelper clear his throat, with water of the castle moat,

for thus they used, by snow and torch, to rear
their voices at the porch:

Fred S. Cozzens.

WASSAILER'S SONG

ROBERT SOUTHWELL

Wassail! wassail! all over the town,
Our toast it is white, and our ale it is brown;
Our bowl is made of a maplin tree;
We be good fellows all;— I drink to thee.

Here's to our horse, and to his right ear,
God send master a happy new year;
A happy new year as e'er he did see,—
With my wassailing bowl I drink to thee.

Here's to our mare, and to her right eye,
God send our mistress a good Christmas pie;
A good Christmas pie as e'er I did see,—
With my wassailing bowl I drink to thee.

Here's to our cow, and to her long tail,
God send our measter us never may fail
Of a cup of good beer: I pray you draw near,
And our jolly wassail it's then you shall hear.

Be here any maids? I suppose here be some;
Sure they will not let young men stand on the
       cold stone!

Sing hey O, maids! come trole back the pin,
And the fairest maid in the house let us all in.

Come, butler, come, bring us a bowl of the best;
I hope your soul in heaven will rest;
But if you do bring us a bowl of the small,
Then down fall butler, and bowl and all.

And here's a Christmas carol meant for children, and most excellent, and though the monk
that wrote it was hung, yet still his verses may
be sung.

A CAROL

As I in a hoarie, winter's night
  Stood shivering in the snow,
Surpriz'd I was with sudden heat,
  Which made my heart to glow;
And lifting up a fearefull eye
  To view what fire was neere,
A prettie babe, all burning bright,
  Did in the aire appeare;
Who, scorchèd with excessive heat,
  Such flouds of teares did shed,
As though his flouds should quench his
      flames,
  Which with his teares were bred:

Alas! (quoth he) but newly borne,
  In fierie heats I frie,
Yet none approach to warm their hearts,
  Or feele my fire, but I;

My faultless brest the furnace is,
  The fuell, wounding thornes:
Love is the fire, and sighs the smoke,
  The ashes, shames and scornes;
The fuell justice layeth on,
  And mercy blows the coales,
The metalls in this furnace wrought,
  Are Men's defiled soules:
For which, as now on fire I am,
  To work them to their good,
So will I melt into a bath,
  To wash them in my blood.
With this he vanisht out of sight,
  And swiftly shrunke away,
And straight I called unto minde
  That it was Christmasse Day.

* * * * * * *

———

CHRISTMAS EVE *

HAMILTON WRIGHT MABIE

The world has been full of mysteries to-day; everybody has gone about weighted with secrets. The children's faces have fairly shone with expectancy, and I enter easily into the universal dream which at this moment holds all the children of Christendom under its spell. Was there ever a wider or more loving conspiracy than that which keeps the venerable figure of Santa Claus from slipping away, with all the other oldtime myths, into the forsaken wonderland of the past? Of all the personages whose marvelous doings once filled the minds of men, he alone survives. He has outlived all the great gods, and all the impressive and poetic conceptions which once flitted between heaven and earth; these have gone, but Santa Claus remains by virtue of a common understanding that childhood shall not be despoiled of one of its most cherished beliefs, either by the mythologist, with his sun myth theory, or the scientist, with his heartless

* From "My Study Fire." Copyright 1890, 1893, 1897, by Dodd, Mead & Company.

diatribe against superstition. There is a good
deal more to be said on this subject, if this
were the place to say it; even superstition has
its uses, and sometimes, its sound heart of
truth. He who does not see in the legend of
Santa Claus a beautiful faith on one side, and
the naive embodiment of a divine fact on the
other, is not fit to have a place at the Christmas board. For him there should be neither
carol, nor holly, nor mistletoe; they only shall
keep the feast to whom all these things are
but the outward and visible signs of an inward
and spiritual grace.

Rosalind and myself are thoroughly orthodox when it comes to the keeping of holidays;
here at least the ways of our fathers are our
ways also. Orthodoxy generally consists in
retaining and emphasizing the disagreeable
ways of the fathers, and as we are both inclined to heterodoxy on these points, we make
the more prominent our observance of the best
of the old-time habits. I might preach a
pleasant little sermon just here, taking as my
text the "survival of the fittest," and illustrat-
ing the truth from our own domestic ritual;
but the season preaches its own sermon, and I
should only follow the example of some ministers and get between the text and my congregation if I made the attempt. For weeks we
have all been looking forward to this eventful
evening, and the still more eventful morrow.

There have been hurried and whispered conferences hastily suspended at the sound of a
familiar step on the stair; packages of every
imaginable size and shape have been surrep-
titiously introduced into the house, and have
immediately disappeared in all manner of out-
of-the-way places; and for several weeks past
one room has been constantly under lock and
key, visited only when certain sharp-sighted
eyes were occupied in other directions.
Through all this scene of mystery Rosalind has
moved sedately and with sealed lips, the common confidant of all the conspirators, and herself the greatest conspirator of all. Blessed is
the season which engages the whole world in
a conspiracy of love!

After dinner, eaten, let it be confessed, with
more haste and less accompaniment of talk
than usual, the parlor doors were opened, and
there stood the Christmas tree in a glow of
light, its wonderful branches laden with all
manner of strange fruits not to be found in
the botanies. The wild shouts, the merry
laughter, the cries of delight as one coveted
fruit after another dropped into long-expectant arms still linger in my ears now that the
little tapers are burnt out, the boughs left bare,
and the actors in the perennial drama are fast
asleep, with new and strange bedfellows selected from the spoils of the night. Cradled

between a delightful memory and a blissful anticipation, who does not envy them?

After this charming prelude is over, Rosalind comes into the study, and studies for the fortieth time the effect of the new design of decoration which she had this year worked out, and which gives these rather somber rows of books a homelike and festive aspect. It pleases me to note the spray of holly that obscures the title of Bacon's solemn and weighty "Essays," and I get half a page of suggestions for my notebook from the fact that a sprig of mistletoe has fallen on old Burton's "Anatomy of Melancholy." Rosalind has reason to be satisfied, and if I read her face aright she has succeeded even in her own eyes in bringing Christmas, with its fragrant memories and its heavenly visions, into the study. I cannot help thinking, as I watch her piling up the fire for a blaze of unusual splendor, that if more studies had their Rosalinds to bring in the genial currents of life there would be more cheer and hope and large-hearted wisdom in the books which the world is reading to-day.

When the fire has reached a degree of intensity and magnitude which Rosalind thinks adequate to the occasion, I take down a well-worn volume which opens of itself at a well-worn page. It is a book which I have read and re-read many times, and always with a kindling sympathy and affection for the man

who wrote it; in whatever mood I take it up there is something in it which touches me with a sense of kinship. It is not a great book, but it is a book of the heart, and books of the heart have passed beyond the outer court of criticism before we bestow upon them that phrase of supreme regard. There are other books of the heart around me, but on Christmas Eve it is Alexander Smith's "Dreamthorp" which always seems to lie at my hand, and when I take it up the well-worn volume falls open at the essay on "Christmas." It is a good many years since Rosalind and I began to read together on Christmas Eve this beautiful meditation on the season, and now it has gathered about itself such a host of memories that it has become part of our common past. It is, indeed, a veritable palimpsest, overlaid with tender and gracious recollections out of which the original thought gains a new and subtle sweetness. As I read it aloud I know that she sees once more the familiar landscape about Dreamthorp, with the low, dark hill in the background, and over it "the tender radiance that precedes the moon"; the village windows are all lighted, and the "whole place shines like a congregation of glowworms." There are the skaters still "leaning against the frosty wind"; there is the "gray church tower amid the leafless elms," around which the echoes of the morn-

ing peal of Christmas bells still hover; the village folk have gathered, "in their best dresses and their best faces"; the beautiful service of the church has been read and answered with heartfelt responses, the familiar story has been told again simply and urgently, with applications for every thankful soul, and then the congregation has gone to its homes and its festivities.

All these things, I am sure, lie within Rosalind's vision, although she seems to see nothing but the ruddy blaze of the fire; all these things I see, as I have seen them these many Christmas Eves agone; but with this familiar landscape there are mingled all the sweet and sorrowful memories of our common life, recalled at this hour that the light of the highest truth may interpret them anew in the divine language of hope. I read on until I come to the quotation from the "Hymn to the Nativity," and then I close the book, and take up a copy of Milton close at hand. We have had our commemoration service of love, and now there comes into our thought, with the organ roll of this sublime hymn, the universal truth which lies at the heart of the season. I am hardly conscious that it is my voice which makes these words audible: I am conscious only of this mighty-voiced anthem, fit for the choral song of the morning stars:

"Ring out, ye crystal spheres,
And bless our human ears,
If ye have power to touch our senses so;
And let your silver chime
Move in melodious time;
And let the bass of heaven's deep organ blow;
And, with your ninefold harmony,
Make up full concert to the angelic symphony.

"For, if such holy song
Enwrap our fancy long,
Time will run back and fetch the age of gold;
And speckled vanity
Will sicken soon and die,
And leprous sin will melt from earthly mold;
And hell itself will pass away,
And leave her dolorous mansions to the peering day.

. . . .

"The oracles are dumb,
No voice or hideous hum
Runs through the archéd roof in words deceiving;
Apollo from his shrine
Can no more divine
With hollow shriek the steep of Delphos leaving,
No nightly trance or breathéd spell
Inspires the pale-eyed priest from the prophetic cell.

"The lonely mountains o'er,
And the resounding shore,
A voice of weeping heard and loud lament;
From haunted spring, and dale
Edgéd with poplars pale,
The parting genius is with sighing sent;
With flower-enwoven tresses torn,
The nymphs in twilight shades of tangled thickets
mourn."

. . . .

Like a psalm the great Hymn fills the air,
and like a psalm it remains in the memory.
The fire has burned low, and a soft and solemn
light fills the room. Neither of us speaks
while the clock strikes twelve. I look out of
the window. The heavens are ablaze with
light, and somewhere amid those circling constellations I know that a new star has found
its place, and is shining with such a ray as
never before fell from heaven to earth.

CHRISTMAS IN THE OLDEN TIME

WALTER SCOTT

On Christmas-eve the bells were rung;
The damsel donned her kirtle sheen;
The hall was dressed with holly green;
Forth to the wood did merry men go,
To gather in the mistletoe.
Thus opened wide the baron's hall
To vassal, tenant, serf and all;
Power laid his rod of rule aside
And ceremony doffed his pride.
The heir, with roses in his shoes,
That night might village partner choose;
The lord, underogating, share
The vulgar game of " Post and Pair."
All hailed, with uncontrolled delight,
And general voice, the happy night

That to the cottage, as the crown,
Brought tidings of salvation down.

The fire, with well-dried logs supplied,
Went roaring up the chimney wide;
The huge hall-table's oaken face,
Scrubbed till it shone, the day to grace,
Bore then upon its massive board
No mark to part the squire and lord.
Then was brought in the lusty brawn
By old blue-coated serving man;
Then the grim boar's head frowned on high,
Crested with bays and rosemary.
Well can the green-garbed ranger tell
How, when and where the monster fell;
What dogs before his death he tore,
And all the baitings of the boar.
The wassal round, in good brown bowls,
Garnished with ribbons, blithely trowls.
There the huge sirloin reeked: hard by
Plum-porridge stood, and Christmas pye;
Nor failed old Scotland to produce,
At such high-tide, her savory goose.

Then came the merry maskers in,
And carols roared with blithesome din.
If unmelodious was the song,
It was a hearty note, and strong;
Who lists may in their murmuring see
Traces of ancient mystery;

White shirts supplied the masquerade,
And smutted cheeks the visors made;
But O, what maskers richly dight,
Can boast of bosoms half so light!
England was " merry England " when
Old Christmas brought his sports again;
'Twas Christmas broached the mightiest ale,
'Twas Christmas told the merriest tale;
A Christmas gambol oft would cheer
The poor man's heart through half the year.

SLY SANTA CLAUS

MRS. C. S. STONE

All the house was asleep,
  And the fire burning low,
When, from far up the chimney,
  Came down a " Ho! ho!"
And a little, round man,
  With a terrible scratching,
Dropped into the room
  With a wink that was catching.
Yes, down he came, bumping,
And thumping, and jumping,
  And picking himself up without sign
    of a bruise!

" Ho! ho!" he kept on,
  As if bursting with cheer.

"Good children, gay children,
  Glad children, see here!
I have brought you fine dolls,
  And gay trumpets, and rings,
Noah's arks, and bright skates,
  And a host of good things!
I have brought a whole sackful,
A packful, a hackful!
  Come hither, come hither, come hither
    and choose!

"Ho! ho! What is this?
  Why, they all are asleep!
But their stockings are up,
  And my presents will keep!
So, in with the candies,
  The books, and the toys;
All the goodies I have
  For the good girls and boys.
I'll ram them, and jam them,
And slam them, and cram them;
  All the stockings will hold while the
    tired youngsters snooze."

All the while his round shoulders
  Kept ducking and ducking;
And his little, fat fingers
  Kept tucking and tucking;
Until every stocking
  Bulged out, on the wall,
As if it were bursting,
  And ready to fall.

And then, all at once,
  With a whisk and a whistle,
And twisting himself
  Like a tough bit of gristle,
He bounced up again,
  Like the down of a thistle,
    And nothing was left but the prints
    of his shoes.

THE WAITS

MARGARET DELAND

At the break of Christmas Day,
  Through the frosty starlight ringing,
Faint and sweet and far away,
  Comes the sound of children, singing,
    Chanting, singing,
     " Cease to mourn,
     For Christ is born,
  Peace and joy to all men bringing!"

Careless that the chill winds blow,
  Growing stronger, sweeter, clearer,
Noiseless footfalls in the snow
  Bring the happy voices nearer;
    Hear them singing,
     " Winter's drear,
     But Christ is here,
  Mirth and gladness with Him bringing!"

" Merry Christmas ! " hear them say,
  As the East is growing lighter;
" May the joy of Christmas Day
  Make your whole year gladder, brighter ! "
    Join their singing,
      " To each home
      Our Christ has come,
    All Love's treasures with Him bringing ! "

THE KNIGHTING OF THE SIRLOIN OF BEEF BY CHARLES THE SECOND

ANON

The Second Charles of England
  Rode forth one Christmas tide,
To hunt a gallant stag of ten,
  Of Chingford woods the pride.

The winds blew keen, the snow fell fast,
  And made for earth a pall,
As tired steeds and wearied men
  Returned to Friday Hall.

The blazing logs, piled on the dogs,
  Were pleasant to behold !
And grateful was the steaming feast
  To hungry men and cold.

With right good-will all took their fill,
  And soon each found relief;

Whilst Charles his royal trencher piled
  From one huge loin of beef.

Quoth Charles, " Odd's fish! a noble dish!
  Ay, noble made by me!
By kingly right, I dub thee knight —
  Sir Loin henceforward be!"

And never was a royal jest
  Received with such acclaim:
And never knight than good Sir Loin
  More worthy of the name.

———

THE CHRISTMAS GOOSE AT THE CRATCHITS'

CHARLES DICKENS

You might have thought a goose the rarest of all birds; a feathered phenomenon, to which a black swan was a matter of course; and in truth, it was something like it in that house. Mrs. Cratchit made the gravy (ready beforehand in a little saucepan) hissing hot; Master Peter mashed the potatoes with incredible vigor; Miss Belinda sweetened up the apple-sauce; Martha dusted the hot plates; Bob took Tiny Tim beside him in a tiny corner, at the table; the two young Cratchits set chairs for everybody, not forgetting themselves, and mounting guard upon their posts, crammed spoons into their mouths, lest they should shriek for goose before their turn came to be helped. At last the dishes were set on, and grace was said. It was succeeded by a breathless pause, as Mrs. Cratchit, looking slowly all along the carving knife, prepared to plunge it in the breast; but when she did, and when the long-expected gush of stuffing issued forth, one murmur of delight arose all around the board, and even Tiny Tim, excited by the two young Cratchits, beat on the table with the handle of his knife, and feebly cried hurrah!

There never was such a goose. Bob said he didn't believe there ever was such a goose cooked. Its tenderness and flavor, size and cheapness, were the themes of universal admiration. Eked out by the apple-sauce and mashed potaoes, it was a sufficient dinner for the whole family; indeed, as Mrs. Cratchit said with great delight (surveying one small atom of a bone on the dish), they hadn't ate it all at last! Yet every one had had enough, and the youngest Cratchits in particular were steeped in sage and onion to the eye-brows! But now, the plates being changed by Miss Belinda, Mrs. Cratchit left the room alone — too nervous to bear witnesses — to take the pudding up, and bring it in.

Suppose it should not be done enough! Suppose it should break in turning out! Suppose somebody should have got over the wall of the backyard, and stolen it, while they were merry with the goose; a supposition at which the two young Cratchits became livid! All sorts of horrors were supposed.

Hallo! A great deal of steam! The pudding was out of the copper. A smell like a washing-day! That was the cloth. A smell like an eating-house and a pastry cook's next door to each other, with a laundress next door

to that! That was the pudding. In half a minute Mrs. Cratchit entered, flushed, but smiling proudly, with the pudding like a speckled cannon-ball, so hard and firm, blazing in half of half-a-quartern of ignited brandy, and bedight with Christmas holly stuck into the top.

Oh, a wonderful pudding! Bob Cratchit said, and calmly too, that he regarded it as the greatest success achieved by Mrs. Cratchit since their marriage. Mrs. Cratchit said that now the weight was off her mind, she would confess she had had her doubts about the quantity of flour. Everybody had something to say about it, but nobody said or thought it was at all a small pudding for so large a family. It would have been flat heresy to do so. Any Cratchit would have blushed to hint at such a thing.

At last the dinner was all done, the cloth was cleared, the hearth swept, and the fire made up. The compound in the jug being tasted and considered perfect, apples and oranges were put upon the table, and a shovelful of chestnuts on the fire. Then all the Cratchit family drew round the hearth, in what Bob Cratchit called a circle, meaning half a one; and at Bob Cratchit's elbow stood the family display of glass — two tumblers, and a custard-cup without a handle.

These held the hot stuff from the jug, however, as well as golden goblets would have

done; and Bob served it out with beaming looks, while the chestnuts on the fire sputtered and cracked noisily.   Then Bob proposed:

"A merry Christmas to us all, my dears. God bless us!"

Which all the family re-echoed.

"God bless us every one!" said Tiny Tim, the last of all.

———

GOD BLESS US EVERY ONE *

JAMES WHITCOMB RILEY

"God bless us every one!" prayed Tiny Tim,
    Crippled, and dwarfed of body, yet so tall
Of soul, we tiptoe earth to look on him,
        High towering over all.

He loved the loveless world, nor dreamed, in-
        deed,
    That it, at best, could give to him, the while,
But pitying glances, when his only need
        Was but a cheery smile.

And thus he prayed, "God bless us every
        one!"
    Enfolding all the creeds within the span
Of his child-heart; and so, despising none,
        Was nearer saint than man.

* From "Sketches in Prose." Copyright 1900, by Bobbs-Merrill Company. Reproduced by special permission.

I like to fancy God, in Paradise,
  Lifting a finger o'er the rhythmic swing
Of chiming harp and song, with eager eyes
    Turned earthward, listening —

The Anthem stilled — the angels leaning there
  Above the golden walls — the morning sun
Of Christmas bursting flower-like with the
      prayer,
    " God bless us Every One! "

———

BELLS ACROSS THE SNOWS

FRANCES RIDLEY HAVERGAL

O Christmas, merry Christmas!
  Is it really come again,
With its memories and greetings,
  With its joy and with its pain?
There's a minor in the carol,
  And a shadow in the light,
And a spray of cypress twining
  With the holly wreath to-night.
And the hush is never broken
  By laughter light and low,
As we listen in the starlight
  To the " bells across the snow."

O Christmas, merry Christmas!
  'Tis not so very long

Since other voices blended
  With the carol and the song!
If we could but hear them singing
  As they are singing now,
If we could but see the radiance
  Of the crown on each dear brow;
There would be no sigh to smother,
  No hidden tear to flow,
As we listen in the starlight
  To the " bells across the snow."

O Christmas, merry Christmas!
  This never more can be;
We cannot bring again the days
  Of our unshadowed glee.
But Christmas, happy Christmas,
  Sweet herald of good-will,
With holy songs of glory
  Brings holy gladness still.
For peace and hope may brighten,
  And patient love may glow,
As we listen in the starlight
  To the " bells across the snow."

———

CHRISTMAS BELLS

HENRY WADSWORTH LONGFELLOW

I heard the bells on Christmas Day
Their old, familiar carols play,

And wild and sweet
The words repeat
Of peace on earth, good-will to men!

And thought how, as the day had come,
The belfries of all Christendom
Had rolled along
The unbroken song
Of peace on earth, good-will to men!

Till, ringing, swinging on its way,
The world revolved from night to day
A voice, a chime,
A chant sublime
Of peace on earth, good-will to men!

Then from each black, accursèd mouth
The cannon thundered in the South
And with the sound
The carols drowned
Of peace on earth, good-will to men!

It was as if an earthquake rent
The hearth-stones of a continent,
And made forlorn
The households born
Of peace on earth, good-will to men!

And in despair I bowed my head;
"There is no peace on earth," I said;
"For hate is strong
And mocks the song
Of peace on earth, good-will to men!"

Then pealed the bells more loud and deep:
"God is not dead; nor doth He sleep!
    The Wrong shall fail,
    The Right prevail,
    With peace on earth, good-will to men!"

MINSTRELS AND MAIDS

WILLIAM MORRIS

Outlanders, whence come ye last?
    *The snow in the street and the wind on the
        door.*
Through what green seas and great have ye
        past?
    Minstrels and maids, stand forth on the floor.

From far away, O masters mine,
    *The snow in the street and the wind on the
        door.*
We come to bear you goodly wine.
    Minstrels and maids, stand forth on the floor.

From far away we come to you,
    *The snow in the street and the wind on the
        door.*
To tell of great tidings strange and true,
    Minstrels and maids, stand forth on the floor.

News, news of the Trinity,
*The snow in the street and the wind on the
door.*
And Mary and Joseph from over the sea!
Minstrels and maids, stand forth on the floor.

For as we wandered far and wide,
*The snow in the street and the wind on the
door.*
What hap do you deem there should us betide!
Minstrels and maids, stand forth on the floor.

Under a bent when the night was deep,
*The snow in the street and the wind on the
door.*
There lay three shepherds tending their sheep.
Minstrels and maids, stand forth on the floor.

" O ye shepherds, what have ye seen,
*The snow in the street and the wind on the
door.*
To slay your sorrow, and heal your teen? "
Minstrels and maids, stand forth on the floor.

" In an ox-stall this night we saw,
*The snow in the street and the wind on the
door.*
A babe and a maid without a flaw.
Minstrels and maids, stand forth on the floor.

"There was an old man there beside,
*The snow in the street and the wind on the
door.*
His hair was white and his hood was wide.
Minstrels and maids, stand forth on the floor.

"And as we gazed this thing upon,
*The snow in the street and the wind on the
door.*
Those twain knelt down to the Little One,
Minstrels and maids, stand forth on the floor.

"And a marvellous song we straight did hear,
*The snow in the street and the wind on the
door.*
That slew our sorrow and healed our care."
Minstrels and maids, stand forth on the floor.

News of a fair and marvellous thing,
*The snow in the street and the wind on the
door.*
Nowell, nowell, nowell, we sing!
Minstrels and maids, stand forth on the floor.

———

INEXHAUSTIBILITY OF THE SUBJECT
OF CHRISTMAS

LEIGH HUNT

So many things have been said of late years about Christmas, that it is supposed by some there is no saying more. O they of little faith! What! do they suppose that every thing has been said that *can* be said about any one Christmas thing?

About beef, for instance?

About plum-pudding?

About mince-pie?

About holly?

About ivy?

About rosemary?

About mistletoe? (Good Heavens! what an immense number of things remain to be said about mistletoe!)

About Christmas Eve?

About hunt-the-slipper?

About hot cockles?

About blind-man's-buff?

About shoeing the wild-mare?

About thread-the-needle?

About he-can-do-little-that-can't-do-this?

About puss-in-the-corner?
About snap-dragon?
About forfeits?
About Miss Smith?
About the bell-man?
About the waits?
About chilblains?
About carols?
About the fire?
About the block on it?
About school-boys?
About their mothers?
About Christmas-boxes?
About turkeys?
About Hogmany?
About goose-pie?
About mumming?
About saluting the apple-trees?
About brawn?
About plum-porridge?
About hobby-horse?
About hoppings?
About wakes?
About " feed-the-dove "?
About hackins?
About yule-doughs?
About going-a-gooding?
About loaf-stealing?
About *Julklaps?* (Who has exhausted that
subject, we should like to know?)
About wad-shooting?

About elder-wine?

About pantomimes?

About cards?

About New-Year's Day?

About gifts?

About wassail?

About Twelfth-cake?

About king and queen?

About characters?

About eating too much?

About aldermen?

About the doctor?

About all being in the wrong?

About charity?

About all being in the right?

About faith, hope, and endeavor?

About the greatest plum-pudding for the greatest number?

Esto perpetua,— that is, faith, hope and charity, and endeavor; and plum-pudding enough by and by, all the year round, for everybody that likes it. Why that should not be the case, we cannot see,— seeing that the earth is big, and human kind teachable, and God very good, and inciting us to do it. Meantime, gravity apart, we ask anybody whether any of the above subjects are exhausted; and we inform everybody, that all the above customs still exist in some parts of our beloved country, however unintelligible they may have become in others. But to give a specimen of

the non-exhaustion of any one of their topics.

Beef, for example. Now, we should like to know who has exhausted the subject of the fine old roast Christmas piece of beef, from its original appearance in the meadows as part of the noble sultan of the herd, glorious old Taurus,— the lord of the sturdy brow and ponderous agility, a sort of thunderbolt of a beast, well chosen by Jove to disguise in, one of Nature's most striking compounds of apparent heaviness and unencumbered activity,— up to its contribution to the noble Christmas-dinner, smoking from the spit, and flanked by the outposts of Bacchus. John Bull (cannibalism apart) hails it like a sort of relation. He makes it part of his flesh and blood; glories in it; was named after it; has it served up, on solemn occasions, with music and a hymn, as it was the other day at the royal city dinner:—

> "Oh the roast beef of old England!
> And oh the old English roast beef!"

"*And* oh!" observe, not merely "oh!" again; but "and" with it; as if, though the same piece of beef, it were also another,— another and the same,— cut, and come again; making two of one, in order to express intensity and reduplication of satisfaction:—

> "Oh the roast beef of old England!
> *And* oh the old English roast beef!"

We beg to assure the reader, that a whole *Seer* might be written on this single point of the Christmas-dinner; and " shall we be told " (as orators exclaim), " and this, too, in a British land," that the subject is *" exhausted "!*

Then plum-pudding! What a word is that! how plump and plump again! How round and repeated and plenipotential! " There are two p's, observe, in plenipotential; and so there are in plum-pudding. We love an exquisite fitness, — a might and wealth of adaptation). Why, the whole round cheek of universal childhood is in the idea of plum-pudding; ay, and the weight of manhood, and the plenitude of the majesty of city dames. Wealth itself is symbolized by the least of its fruity particles. " A plum " is a city fortune,— a million of money. He (the old boy, who has earned it)—

" Puts in his thumb,

videlicet, into his pocket,

And pulls out a plum,
And says, What a *good man* am I ! "

Observe a little boy at a Christmas-dinner, and his grandfather opposite him. What a world of secret similarity there is between them! How hope in one, and retrospection in the other, and appetite in both, meet over the same ground of pudding, and understand it to

a nicety! How the senior banters the little
boy on his third slice! and how the little boy
thinks within himself that he dines that day
as well as the senior! How both look hot and
red and smiling, and juvenile. How the little
boy is conscious of the Christmas-box in his
pocket! (of which, indeed, the grandfather jo-
cosely puts him in mind) ; and how the grandfather is quite as conscious of the plum, or
part of a plum, or whatever fraction it may be,
in his own! How he incites the little boy to
love money and good dinners all his life! and
how determined the little boy is to abide by his
advice,— with a secret addition in favor of
holidays and marbles,— to which there is an
analogy, in the senior's mind, on the side of
trips to Hastings, and a game at whist! Finally, the old gentleman sees his own face in
the pretty smooth one of the child; and if the
child is not best pleased at his proclamation of
the likeness (in truth, is horrified at it, and
thinks it a sort of madness), yet nice observ-
ers, who have lived long enough to see the
wonderful changes in people's faces from
youth to age, probably discern the thing well
enough, and feel a movement of pathos at their
hearts in considering the world of trouble and
emotion that is the causer of the changes.
That old man's face was once like that little
boy's! *That* little boy's will be one day like
that old man's! What a thought to make us

all love and respect one another, if not for our fine qualities, let at least for the trouble and sorrow which we all go through!

Ay, and joy too; for all people have their joys as well as troubles, at one time or another, — most likely both together, or in constant alternation: and the greater part of troubles are not the worst things in the world, but only graver forms of the requisite motion of the universe, or workings towards a better condition of things, the greater or less violent according as we give them violence, or respect them like awful but not ill-meaning gods, and entertain them with a rewarded patience. Grave thoughts, you will say, for Christmas. But no season has a greater right to grave thoughts, in passing; and, for that very reason, no season has a greater right to let them pass, and recur to more light ones.

So a noble and merry season to you, my masters; and may we meet, thick and three-fold, many a time and oft, in blithe yet most thoughtful pages! Fail not to call to mind, in the course of the 25th of this month, that the divinest Heart that ever walked the earth was born on that day: and then smile and enjoy yourselves for the rest of it; for mirth is also of Heaven's making, and wondrous was the wine-drinking at Galilee.

SONG OF THE HOLLY

WILLIAM SHAKESPEARE

BLOW, blow thou winter wind —
Thou art not so unkind
    As man's ingratitude!
Thy tooth is not so keen,
Because thou art not seen,
    Although thy breath be rude.
Heigh ho! sing heigh ho! unto the green holly:
Most friendship is feigning, most loving mere
    folly.
    Then heigh ho! the holly!
    This life is most jolly!

Freeze, freeze, thou bitter sky —
Thou dost not bite so nigh
    As benefits forgot!
Though thou the waters warp,
Thy sting is not so sharp
    As friend remembered not.
Heigh ho! sing heigh ho! unto the green holly,
Most friendship is feigning, most loving mere
    folly.
    Then heigh ho, the holly!
    This life is most jolly!

UNDER THE HOLLY-BOUGH

CHARLES MACKAY

Ye who have scorned each other,
Or injured friend or brother,
  In this fast-fading year;
Ye who, by word or deed,
Have made a kind heart bleed,
  Come gather here!
Let sinned against and sinning
Forget their strife's beginning,
  And join in friendship now.
Be links no longer broken,
Be sweet forgiveness spoken
  Under the Holly-Bough.

Ye who have loved each other,
Sister and friend and brother,
  In this fast-fading year:
Mother and sire and child,
Young man and maiden mild,
  Come gather here;
And let your heart grow fonder,
As memory shall ponder
  Each past unbroken vow;
Old loves and younger wooing
Are sweet in the renewing
  Under the Holly-Bough.

Ye who have nourished sadness,
Estranged from hope and gladness
In this fast-fading year;
Ye with o'erburdened mind,
Made aliens from your kind,
Come gather here.
Let not the useless sorrow
Pursue you night and morrow,
If e'er you hoped, hope now.
Take heart,— uncloud your faces,
And join in our embraces
Under the Holly-Bough.

———

CEREMONIES FOR CHRISTMAS

ROBERT HERRICK

Come, bring with a noise,
My merry, merry boys,
The Christmas log to the firing,
While my good dame, she
Bids ye all be free,
And drink to your heart's desiring.

With the last year's brand
Light the new block, and
For good success in his spending,
On your psalteries play,
That sweet luck may
Come while the log is a-teending.

Drink now the strong beer,
Cut the white loaf here,
The while the meat is a-shredding;
For the rare mince-pie,
And the plums stand by,
To fill the paste that's a kneading.

SANTA CLAUS

ANON

He comes in the night! He comes in the
    night!
  He softly, silently comes;
While the little brown heads on the pillows so
    white
  Are dreaming of bugles and drums.
He cuts through the snow like a ship through
    the foam,
  While the white flakes around him whirl;
Who tells him I know not, but he findeth the
    home
  Of each good little boy and girl.

His sleigh it is long, and deep, and wide;
  It will carry a host of things,
While dozens of drums hang over the side,
  With the sticks sticking under the strings:
And yet not the sound of a drum is heard,
  Not a bugle blast is blown,

As he mounts to the chimney-top like a bird,
　　And drops to the hearth like a stone.

The little red stockings he silently fills,
　　Till the stockings will hold no more;
The bright little sleds for the great snow hills
　　Are quickly set down on the floor.
Then Santa Claus mounts to the roof like a
　　　bird,
　　And glides to his seat in the sleigh;
Not the sound of a bugle or drum is heard
　　As he noiselessly gallops away.

He rides to the East, and he rides to the West,
　　Of his goodies he touches not one;
He eateth the crumbs of the Christmas feast
　　When the dear little folks are done.
Old Santa Claus doeth all that he can;
　　This beautiful mission is his;
Then, children, be good to the little old man,
　　When you find who the little man is.

THE CEREMONIES FOR CHRISTMAS
DAY

ROBERT HERRICK

Kindle the Christmas brand, and then
　　Till sunset let it burn;
Which quench'd, then lay it up again
　　Till Christmas next return.

Part must be kept wherewith to teend
  The Christmas log next year,
And where 'tis safely kept, the fiend
  Can do no mischief there.

———

DECEMBER

HARRIET F. BLODGETT

I

Oh! holly branch and mistletoe.
  And Christmas chimes where'er we go.
And stockings pinned up in a row!
  These are thy gifts, December!

II

And if the year has made thee old,
  And silvered all thy locks of gold,
Thy heart has never been a-cold
  Or known a fading ember.

III

The whole world is a Christmas tree,
  And stars its many candles be.
Oh! sing a carol joyfully
  The year's great feast in keeping!

IV

For once, on a December night
An angel held a candle bright.
And led three wise men by its light
To where a child was sleeping.

———

THE FESTIVAL OF ST. NICHOLAS

MARY MAPES DODGE

We all know how, before the Christmas-tree
began to flourish in the home-life of our country, a certain "right jolly old elf," with
"eight tiny reindeer," used to drive his sleighload of toys up to our housetops, and then
bound down the chimney to fill the stockings
so hopefully hung by the fireplace. His friends
called him Santa Claus; and those who were
most intimate ventured to say, "Old Nick."
It was said that he originally came from Holland. Doubtless he did; but, if so, he certainly, like many other foreigners, changed his
ways very much after landing upon our shores.
In Holland, St. Nicholas is a veritable saint,
and often appears in full costume, with his embroidered robes glittering with gems and gold,
his mitre, his crosier, and his jewelled gloves.
Here Santa Claus comes rollicking along on
the 25th of December, our Holy Christmas
morn; but in Holland, St. Nicholas visits earth
on the 5th, a time especially appropriated to

him. Early on the morning of the 6th, which is St. Nicholas Day, he distributes his candies, toys and treasures, and then vanishes for a year.

Christmas Day is devoted by the Hollanders to church-rites and pleasant family visiting. It is on St. Nicholas Eve that their young people become half wild with joy and expectation. To some of them it is a sorry time; for the saint is very candid, and, if any of them have been bad during the past year, he is quite sure to tell them so. Sometimes he carries a birch-rod under his arm, and advises the parents to give them scoldings in place of confections, and floggings instead of joys.

It was well that the boys hastened to their abodes on that bright winter evening; for, in less than an hour afterwards, the saint made his appearance in half the homes of Holland. He visited the king's palace, and in the self-same moment appeared in Annie Bouman's comfortable home. Probably one of our silver half-dollars would have purchased all that his saintship left at the peasant Bouman's. But a half-dollar's worth will sometimes do for the poor what hundreds of dollars may fail to do for the rich: it makes them happy and grateful, fills them with new peace and love.

Hilda van Gleck's little brothers and sisters were in a high state of excitement that night. They had been admitted into the grand par-

lor: they were dressed in their best, and had
been given two cakes apiece at supper. Hilda
was as joyous as any. Why not? St. Nicholas would never cross a girl of fourteen from
his list, just because she was tall and looked
almost like a woman. On the contrary, he
would probably exert himself to do honor to
such an august-looking damsel. Who could
tell? So she sported and laughed and danced
as gayly as the youngest, and was the soul of
all their merry games. Father, mother and
grandmother looked on approvingly; so did
grandfather, before he spread his large red
handkerchief over his face, leaving only the
top of his skull-cap visible. This kerchief was
his ensign of sleep.

Earlier in the evening, all had joined in the
fun. In the general hilarity, there had seemed
to be a difference only in bulk between grandfather and the baby. Indeed, a shade of solemn expectation, now and then flitting across
the faces of the younger members, had made
them seem rather more thoughtful than their
elders.

Now the spirit of fun reigned supreme. The
very flames danced and capered in the polished grate. A pair of prim candles, that had
been staring at the astral lamp, began to wink
at other candles far away in the mirrors. There
was a long bell-rope suspended from the ceiling
in the corner, made of glass beads, netted over

a cord nearly as thick as your wrist. It generally hung in the shadow, and made no sign; but to-night it twinkled from end to end. Its handle of crimson glass sent reckless dashes of red at the papered wall, turning its dainty blue stripes into purple. Passers-by halted to catch the merry laughter floating through curtain and sash into the street, then skipped on their way with the startled consciousness that the village was wide awake. At last matters grew so uproarious that the grandsire's red kerchief came down from his face with a jerk. What decent old gentleman could sleep in such a racket! Mynheer van Gleck regarded his children with astonishment. The baby even showed symptoms of hysterics. It was high time to attend to business. Mevrouw suggested that, if they wished to see the good St. Nicholas, they should sing the same loving invitation that had brought him the year before.

The baby stared, and thrust his fist into his mouth, as mynheer put him down upon the floor. Soon he sat erect, and looked with a sweet scowl at the company. With his lace and embroideries, and his crown of blue ribbon and whalebone (for he was not quite past the tumbling age), he looked like the king of babies.

The other children, each holding a pretty willow basket, formed at once in a ring, and moved slowly around the little fellow, lifting

their eyes meanwhile; for the saint to whom they were about to address themselves was yet in mysterious quarters.

Mevrouw commenced playing softly upon the piano; soon the voices rose,— gentle, youthful voices, rendered all the sweeter for their tremor,—

"Welcome, friend! St. Nicholas, welcome!
   Bring no rod for us to-night!
While our voices bid thee welcome,
   Every heart with joy is light.

     "Tell us every fault and failing;
      We will bear thy keenest railing
      So we sing, so we sing:
      Thou shalt tell us everything!

"Welcome, friend! St. Nicholas, welcome!
   Welcome to this merry band!
Happy children greet thee, welcome!
   Thou art gladdening all the land.

     "Fill each empty hand and basket;
      'T is thy little ones who ask it.
      So we sing, so we sing:
      Thou wilt bring us everything!"

During the chorus, sundry glances, half in eagerness, half in dread, had been cast towards the polished folding-doors. Now a loud knocking was heard. The circle was broken in an instant. Some of the little ones, with a strange mixture of fear and delight, pressed

against their mother's knee. Grandfather bent forward, with his chin resting upon his hand; grandmother lifted her spectacles; Mynheer van Gleck, seated by the fireplace, slowly drew his meerschaum from his mouth; while Hilda and the other children settled themselves beside him in an expectant group.

The knocking was heard again.

"Come in," said the mevrouw, softly.

The door slowly opened; and St. Nicholas, in full array, stood before them. You could have heard a pin drop. Soon he spoke. What a mysterious majesty in his voice! what kindliness in his tone!

"Karel van Gleck, I am pleased to greet thee, and thy honored *vrouw*, Kathrine, and thy son, and his good *vrouw*, Annie.

"Children, I greet ye all,— Hendrick, Hilda, Broom, Katy, Huygens and Lucretia. And thy cousins,— Wolfert, Diedrich, Mayken, Voost and Katrina. Good children ye have been, in the main, since I last accosted ye. Diedrich was rude at the Haarlem fair last fall; but he has tried to atone for it since. Mayken has failed, of late, in her lessons; and too many sweets and trifles have gone to her lips, and too few stivers to her charity-box. Diedrich, I trust, will be a polite, manly boy for the future; and Mayken will endeavor to shine as a student. Let her remember, too, that economy and thrift are needed in the foun-

dation of a worthy and generous life. Little Katy has been cruel to the cat more than once. St. Nicholas can hear the cat cry when its tail is pulled. I will forgive her, if she will remember from this hour that the smallest dumb creatures have feeling, and must not be abused."

As Katy burst into a frightened cry, the saint graciously remained silent until she was soothed.

" Master Broom," he resumed, " I warn thee that boys who are in the habit of putting snuff upon the foot-stove of the school-mistress may one day be discovered, and receive a flogging —"

(Master Broom colored, and stared in great astonishment.)

" But, thou art such an excellent scholar, I shall make thee no further reproof.

" Thou, Hendrick, didst distinguish thyself in the archery match last spring, and hit the *doel*,* though the bird was swung before it to unsteady thine eye. I give thee credit for excelling in manly sport and exercise; though I must not unduly countenance thy boat-racing, since it leaves thee too little time for thy proper studies.

" Lucretia and Hilda shall have a blessed sleep to-night. The consciousness of kindness to the poor, devotion in their souls, and cheer-

* Bull's-eye.

ful, hearty obedience to household rule, will render them happy.

"With one and all I avow myself well content. Goodness, industry, benevolence and thrift have prevailed in your midst. Therefore, my blessing upon you; and may the New Year find all treading the paths of obedience, wisdom and love! To-morrow you shall find more substantial proofs that I have been in your home. Farewell!"

With these words came a great shower of sugar-plums upon a linen sheet spread out in front of the doors. A general scramble followed. The children fairly tumbled over each other in their eagerness to fill their baskets. Mevrouw cautiously held the baby down upon the sheet till the chubby little fists were filled. Then the bravest of the youngsters sprang up and threw open the closed doors. In vain they searched the mysterious apartment. St. Nicholas was nowhere to be seen.

Soon they all sped to another room, where stood a table, covered with the whitest of linen damask. Each child, in a flutter of pleasure, laid a shoe upon it, and each shoe held a little hay for the good saint's horse. The door was then carefully locked, and its key hidden in the mother's bedroom. Next followed good-night kisses, a grand family procession to the upper floor, merry farewells at bedroom doors,

and silence, at last, reigned in the Van Gleck mansion.

Early the next morning, the door was solemnly unlocked and opened in the presence of the assembled household; when, lo! a sight appeared, proving good St. Nicholas to be a saint of his word.

Every shoe was filled to overflowing; and beside each stood a many-colored pile. The table was heavy with its load of presents,— candies, toys, trinkets, books and other articles. Every one had gifts, from grandfather down to the baby.

THE CHRISTMAS HOLLY

ELIZA COOK

The holly! the holly! oh, twine it with bay —
  Come give the holly a song;
For it helps to drive stern winter away,
  With his garment so sombre and long;

It peeps through the trees with its berries of
     red,
  And its leaves of burnished green,
When the flowers and fruits have long been
     dead,
  And not even the daisy is seen.
Then sing to the holly, the Christmas holly,
  That hangs over peasant and king;

While we laugh and carouse 'neath its glitter-
    ing boughs,
  To the Christmas holly we'll sing.

The gale may whistle, the frost may come
  To fetter the gurgling rill;
The woods may be bare, and warblers dumb,
  But holly is beautiful still.
In the revel and light of princely halls
  The bright holly branch is found;
And its shadow falls on the lowliest walls,
  While the brimming horn goes round.

The ivy lives long, but its home must be
  Where graves and ruins are spread;
There's beauty about the cypress tree,
  But it flourishes near the dead;
The laurel the warrior's brow may wreathe,
  But it tells of tears and blood;
I sing the holly, and who can breathe
  Aught of that that is not good?
Then sing to the holly, the Christmas holly,
  That hangs over peasant and king;
While we laugh and carouse 'neath its glitter-
    ing boughs,
  To the Christmas holly we'll sing.

———

TO THE FIR-TREE

FROM THE GERMAN

O Fir-tree green! O Fir-tree green!
    Your leaves are constant ever,
Not only in the summer time,
But through the winter's snow and rime
    You're fresh and green forever.

O Fir-tre green! O Fir-tree green!
    I still shall love you dearly!
How oft to me on Christmas night
Your laden boughs have brought delight.
O Fir-tree green! O Fir-tree green!
    I still shall love you dearly.

THE MAHOGANY-TREE

WILLIAM MAKEPEACE THACKERAY

Christmas is here;
Winds whistle shrill,
Icy and chill,
Little care we;
Little we fear
Weather without,
Sheltered about
The Mahogany-Tree.

Once on the boughs
Birds of rare plume
Sang in its bloom;
Night-birds are we;
Here we carouse,
Singing, like them,
Perched round the stem
Of the jolly old tree.

Here let us sport,
Boys, as we sit —
Laughter and wit
Flashing so free.
Life is but short —
When we are gone,
Let them sing on,
Round the old tree.

Evenings we knew,
Happy as this;
Faces we miss,
Pleasant to see.
Kind hearts and true,
Gentle and just,
Peace to your dust!
We sing round the tree.

Care like a dun,
Lurks at the gate;
Let the dog wait;
Happy we'll be!

Drink, every one;
Pile up the coals;
Fill the red bowls,
Round the old tree!

Drain we the cup.—
Friend, art afraid?
Spirits are laid
In the Red Sea.
Mantle it up;
Empty it yet;
Let us forget,
Round the old tree!

Sorrows begone!
Life and its ills,
Duns and their bills,
Bid we to flee.
Come with the dawn,
Blue-devil sprite;
Leave us to-night,
Round the old tree!

———

CHRISTMAS

WASHINGTON IRVING

But is old, old, good old Christmas gone? Nothing but the hair on his good, gray, old head and beard left? Well, I will have that, seeing I cannot have more of him.

HUE AND CRY AFTER CHRISTMAS.

A man might then behold
    At Christmas, in each hall,
Good fires to curb the cold,
    And meat for great and small.
The neighbors were friendly bidden,
    And all had welcome true,
The poor from the gates were not chidden,
    When this old cap was new.

OLD SONG.

There is nothing in England that exercises a more delightful spell over my imagination than the lingerings of the holiday customs and rural games of former times. They recall the pictures my fancy used to draw in the May morning of life, when as yet I only knew the world through books, and believed it to be all that poets had painted it; and they bring with them the flavor of those honest days of yore,

129

in which, perhaps with equal fallacy, I am apt to think the world was more homebred, social, and joyous than at present. I regret to say that they are daily growing more and more faint, being gradually worn away by time, but still more obliterated by modern fashion. They resemble those picturesque morsels of Gothic architecture, which we see crumbling in various parts of the country, partly dilapidated by the waste of ages, and partly lost in the additions and alterations of latter days. Poetry, however, clings with cherishing fondness about the rural game and holiday revel, from which it has derived so many of its themes — as the ivy winds its rich foliage about the Gothic arch and mouldering tower, gratefully repaying their support, by clasping together their tottering remains, and, as it were, embalming them in verdure.

Of all the old festivals, however, that of Christmas awakens the strongest and most heartfelt associations. There is a tone of solemn and sacred feeling that blends with our conviviality, and lifts the spirit to a state of hallowed and elevated enjoyment. The services of the church about this season are extremely tender and inspiring: they dwell on the beautiful story of the origin of our faith, and the pastoral scenes that accompanied its announcement; they gradually increase in fervor and pathos during the season of Advent,

until they break forth in full jubilee on the morning that brought peace and good-will to men. I do not know a grander effect of music on the moral feelings than to hear the full choir and the pealing organ performing a Christmas anthem in a cathedral, and filling every part of the vast pile with triumphant harmony.

It is a beautiful arrangement, also, derived from the days of yore, that this festival, which commemorates the announcement of the religion of peace and love, has been made the season for gathering together of family connections, and drawing closer again those bands of kindred hearts, which the cares and pleasures and sorrows of the world are continually operating to cast loose; of calling back the children of a family, who have launched forth in life, and wandered widely asunder, once more to assemble about the paternal hearth, that rallying-place of the affections, there to grow young and loving again among the endearing mementos of childhood.

There is something in the very season of the year, that gives a charm to the festivity of Christmas. At other times, we derive a great portion of our pleasures from the mere beauties of Nature. Our feelings sally forth and dissipate themselves over the sunny landscape, and we " live abroad and everywhere." The song of the bird, the murmur of the stream, the

breathing fragrance of spring, the soft voluptuousness of summer, the golden pomp of autumn; earth with its mantle of refreshing green,
and heaven with its deep, delicious blue and its
cloudy magnificence,— all fill us with mute but
exquisite delight, and we revel in the luxury of
mere sensation. But in the depth of winter,
when Nature lies despoiled of every charm,
and wrapped in her shroud of sheeted snow,
we turn for our gratifications to moral sources.
The dreariness and desolation of our landscape,
the short gloomy days and darksome nights,
while they circumscribe our wanderings, shut
in our feelings also from rambling abroad, and
make us more keenly disposed for the pleasures
of the social circle. Our thoughts are more
concentrated; our friendly sympathies more
aroused. We feel more sensibly the charm of
each other's society, and are brought more
closely together by dependence on each other
for enjoyment. Heart calleth unto heart, and
we draw our pleasures from the deep wells of
living kindness which lie in the quiet recesses
of our bosoms; and which, when resorted to,
furnish forth the pure element of domestic
felicity.

The pitchy gloom without makes the heart
dilate on entering the room filled with the glow
and warmth of the evening fire. The ruddy
blaze diffuses an artificial summer and sunshine
through the room, and lights up each counte-

nance with a kindlier welcome. Where does the honest face of hospitality expand into a broader and more cordial smile — where is the shy glance of love more sweetly eloquent — than by the winter fireside? and as the hollow blast of wintry wind rushes through the hall, claps the distant door, whistles about the casement, and rumbles down the chimney, what can be more grateful than that feeling of sober and sheltered security, with which we look around upon the comfortable chamber, and the scene of domestic hilarity?

The English, from the great prevalence of rural habits throughout every class of society, have always been fond of those festivals and holidays which agreeably interrupt the stillness of country life; and they were in former days particularly observant of the religious and social rights of Christmas. It is inspiring to read even the dry details which some antiquaries have given of the quaint humors, the burlesque pageants, the complete abandonment to mirth and good fellowship, with which this festival was celebrated. It seemed to throw open every door, unlock every heart. It brought the peasant and the peer together, and blended all ranks in one warm generous flow of joy and kindness. The old halls of castles and manor-houses resounded with the harp and the Christmas carol, and their ample boards groaned under the weight of hospitality. Even the

poorest cottage welcomed the festive season with green decorations of bay and holly — the cheerful fire glanced its rays through the lattice, inviting the passenger to raise the latch, and join the gossip knot huddled round the hearth beguiling the long evening with legendary jokes, and oft-told Christmas tales.

One of the least pleasing effects of modern refinement is the havoc it has made among the hearty old holiday customs. It has completely taken off the sharp touchings and spirited reliefs of these embellishments of life, and has worn down society into a more smooth and polished, but certainly a less characteristic surface. Many of the games and ceremonials of Christmas have entirely disappeared, and, like the sherris sack of old Falstaff, are become matters of speculation and dispute among commentators. They flourished in times full of spirit and lustihood, when men enjoyed life roughly, but heartily and vigorously: times wild and picturesque, which have furnished poetry with its richest materials, and the drama with its most attractive variety of characters and manners. The world has become more worldly. There is more of dissipation and less enjoyment. Pleasure has expanded into a broader, but a shallower stream, and has forsaken many of those deep and quiet channels, where it flowed sweetly through the calm bosom of domestic life. Society has acquired

a more enlightened and elegant tone; but it has lost many of its strong local peculiarities, its homebred feelings, its honest fireside delights. The traditionary customs of golden-hearted antiquity, its feudal hospitalities, and lordly wassailings, have passed away with the baronial castles and stately manor-houses in which they were celebrated. They comported with the shadowy hall, the great oaken gallery, and the tapestried parlor, but are unfitted for the light showy saloons and gay drawing-rooms of the modern villa.

Shorn, however, as it is, of its ancient and festive honors, Christmas is still a period of delightful excitement in England. It is gratifying to see that home feeling completely aroused which holds so powerful a place in every English bosom. The preparations making on every side for the social board that is again to unite friends and kindred — the presents of good cheer passing and repassing, those tokens of regard and quickeners of kind feelings — the evergreens distributed about houses and churches, emblems of peace and gladness — all these have the most pleasing effect in producing fond associations, and kindling benevolent sympathies. Even the sound of the waits, rude as may be their minstrelsy, breaks upon the midwatches of a winter night with the effect of perfect harmony. As I have been awakened by them in that still and solemn hour

"when deep sleep falleth upon man," I have listened with a hushed delight, and connecting them with the sacred and joyous occasion, have almost fancied them into another celestial choir, announcing peace and good-will to mankind. How delightfully the imagination, when wrought upon by these moral influences, turns everything to melody and beauty! The very crowing of the cock, heard sometimes in the profound repose of the country, "telling the night-watches to his feathery dames," was thought by the common people to announce the approach of the sacred festival:

"Some say that ever 'gainst that season comes
 Wherein our Saviour's birth was celebrated,
 This bird of dawning singeth all night long:
 And then, they say, no spirit dares stir abroad;
 The nights are wholesome — then no planets strike,
 No fairy takes. no witch hath power to charm,
 So hallowed and so gracious is the time."

Amidst the general call to happiness, the bustle of the spirits, and stir of the affections, which prevail at this period, what bosom can remain insensible? It is, indeed, the season of regenerated feeling — the season for kindling not merely the fire of hospitality in the hall, but the genial flame of charity in the heart. The scene of early love again rises green to memory beyond the sterile waste of years, and the idea of home, fraught with the

fragrance of home-dwelling joys, reanimates the drooping spirit — as the Arabian breeze will sometimes waft the freshness of the distant fields to the weary pilgrim of the desert.

Stranger and sojourner as I am in the land — though for me no social hearth may blaze, no hospitable roof throw open its doors, nor the warm grasp of friendship welcome me at the threshold — yet I feel the influence of the season beaming into my soul from the happy looks of those around me. Surely happiness is reflective, like the light of heaven; and every countenance bright with smiles, and glowing with innocent enjoyment, is a mirror transmitting to others the rays of a supreme and ever-shining benevolence. He who can turn churlishly away from contemplating the felicity of his fellow-beings, and can sit down darkling and repining in his loneliness when all around is joyful, may have his moments of strong excitement and selfish gratification, but he wants the genial and social sympathies which constitute the charm of a merry Christmas.

CHURCH DECKING AT CHRISTMAS

WILLIAM WORDSWORTH

Would tnat our scrupulous sires had dared to
    leave
Less scanty measure of those graceful rites

And usages, whose due return invites
A stir of mind too natural to deceive;
Giving the memory help when she could weave
  A crown for Hope! — I dread the boasted
     lights
  That all too often are but fiery blights,
Killing the bud o'er which in vain we grieve.
Go, seek, when Christmas snows discomfort
     bring,
  The counter Spirit found in some gay
     church
  Green with fresh holly, every pew a perch
In which the linnet or the thrush might sing,
  Merry and loud, and safe from prying
     search,
Strains offered only to the genial spring.

SO, NOW IS COME OUR JOYFULST FEAST

GEORGE WITHER

So, now is come our joyfulst feast,
  Let every man be jolly;
Each room with ivy leaves is drest,
  And every post with holly.
Though some churls at our mirth repine,
Round your foreheads garlands twine;
Drown sorrow in a cup of wine,
  And let us all be merry.

Now all our neighbours' chimnies smoke,
  And Christmas logs are burning;
Their ovens they with baked meats choke,
  And all their spits are turning.
Without the door let sorrow lie;
And if for cold it hap to die,
We'll bury't in a Christmas pie,
  And evermore be merry.

Now every lad is wondrous trim,
  And no man minds his labour;
Our lasses have provided them
  A bag-pipe and a tabor;
Young men and maids, and girls and boys,
Give life to one another's joys;
And you anon shall by their noise
  Perceive that they are merry.

Rank misers now do sparing shun;
  Their hall of music soundeth;
And dogs thence with whole shoulders run,
  So all things there aboundeth.
The country folks themselves advance
For crowdy-mutton's * come out of France;
And Jack shall pipe, and Jill shall dance,
  And all the town be merry.

  * Fiddlers.

FAIRY FACES

ANON

Out of the mists of childhood,
   Steeped in a golden glory,
Come dreamy forms and faces,
   Snatches of song and story;
Whispers of sweet, still faces;
   Rays of ethereal glimmer,
That gleam like sunny heavens,
   Ne'er to grow colder or dimmer:
Now far in the distance, now shining near,
Lighting the snows of the shivering year.

Faces there are that tremble,
   Bleared with a silent weeping,
Weird in a shadowy sorrow,
   As if endless vigil keeping.
Faces of dazzling brightness,
   With childlike radiance lighted,
Flashing with many a beauty,
   Nor care nor time had blighted.
But o'er them all there 's a glamour thrown,
Bright with the dreamy distance alone.

Aglow in the Christmas halo,
   Shining with heavenly lustre,
These are the fairy faces
   That round the hearthstone cluster.

These the deep, tender records,
   Sacred in all their meetness,
That, wakening purest fancies,
   Soften us with their sweetness;
As, gathered where flickering fagots burn,
We welcome the holy season's return.

MERRY CHRISTMAS

ANON

In the rush of the merry morning,
   When the red burns through the gray,
And the wintry world lies waiting
   For the glory of the day;
Then we hear a 'fitful rushing
   Just without upon the stair,
See two white phantoms coming,
   Catch the gleam of sunny hair.

Are they Christmas fairies stealing
   Rows of little socks to fill?
Are they angels floating hither
   With their message of good-will?
What sweet spell are these elves weaving,
   As like larks they chirp and sing?
Are these palms of peace from heaven
   That these lovely spirits bring?

Rosy feet upon the threshold,
   Eager faces peeping through,

With the first red ray of sunshine,
 Chanting cherubs come in view;
Mistletoe and gleaming holly,
 Symbols of a blessed day,
In their chubby hands they carry,
 Streaming all along the way.

Well we know them, never weary
 Of this innocent surprise;
Waiting, watching, listening always
 With full hearts and tender eyes,
While our little household angels,
White and golden in the sun,
Greet us with the sweet old welcome,—
 " Merry Christmas, every one ! "

A MERRY CHRISTMAS TO YOU

THEODORE LEDYARD CUYLER

My own boyhood was spent in a delightful home on one of the most beautiful farms in Western New York — an experience that any city-bred boy might envy. We had no religious festivals except Thanksgiving Day and Christmas, and the latter was especially welcome, not only on account of the good fare but its good gifts. Christmas was sacred to Santa Claus, the patron saint of good boys and girls. We counted the days until its arrival. If the night before the longed-for festival was one of eager expectation in all our houses, it was a sad time in all barn-yards and turkey-coops and chicken-roosts; for the slaughter was terrible, and the cry of the feathered tribes was like " the mourning of Hadadrimmon." As to our experiences within doors, they are portrayed in Dr. Clement C. Moore's immortal lines, " The Night Before Christmas," which is probably the most popular poem for children ever penned in America.

143

As the visits of Santa Claus in the night could only be through the chimney, we hung our stockings where they would be in full sight. Three score and ten years ago such modern contrivances as steam pipes, and those unpoetical holes in the floor called "hot-air registers," were as entirely unknown in our rural regions as gas-burners or telephones. We had a genuine fire-place in our kitchen, big enough to contain an enormous back-log, and broad enough for eight or ten people to form "a circle wide" before it and enjoy the genial warmth.

The last process before going to bed was to suspend our stockings in the chimney jambs; and then we dreamed of Santa Claus, or if we awoke in the night, we listened for the jingling of his sleigh-bells. At the peep of day we were aroused by the voice of my good grandfather, who planted himself in the stairway and shouted in a stentorian tone, "I wish you all a Merry Christmas!" The contest was as to who should give the salutation first, and the old gentleman determined to get the start of us by sounding his greeting to the family before we were out of our rooms. Then came a race for the chimney corner; all the stockings came down quicker than they had gone up. What could not be contained in them was disposed upon the mantelpiece, or elsewhere. I remember that I once received an autograph

letter from Santa Claus, full of good counsels; and our colored cook told me that she awoke in the night and, peeping into the kitchen, actually saw the veritable old visitor light a candle and sit down at the table and write it! I believed it all as implicitly as I believed the Ten Commandments, or the story of David and Goliath. Happy days of childish credulity, when fact and fiction were swallowed alike without a misgiving! During my long life I have seen many a day-dream and many an air-castle go the way of Santa Claus and the wonderful "Lamp of Aladdin."

In after years, when I became a parent, my beloved wife and I, determined to make the Christmastide one of the golden days of the twelve months. In mid-winter, when all outside vegetation was bleak and bare, the Christmas-tree in our parlor bloomed in many-colored beauty and bounty. When the tiny candles were all lighted the children and our domestics gathered round it and one of the youngsters rehearsed some pretty juvenile effusion; as "they that had found great spoil." After the happy harvesting of the magic tree in my own home, it was my custom to spend the afternoon or evening in some mission-school and to watch the sparkling eyes of several hundreds of children while a huge Christmas-tree shed down its bounties. Fifty years ago, when the degradation and miseries of the

"Five-Points" were first invaded by pioneer philanthropy, it was a thrilling sight to behold the denizens of the slums and their children as they flocked into Mr. Pease's new "House of Industry" and the "Brewery Mission" building. The angelic host over the hills of Bethlehem did not make a more welcome revelation to them "who had sat in darkness and the shadow of death." In these days the squalid regions of our great cities are being explored and improved by various methods of systematic beneficence. "Christian Settlements" are established; Bureaus of Charity are formed and Associations for the relief of the poor are organized. A noble work; but, after all, the most effective "bureau" is one that, in a water-proof and a stout pair of shoes, sallies off on a wintry night to some abode of poverty with not only supplies for suffering bodies, but kind words of sympathy for lonesome hearts. A dollar from a warm hand with a warm word is worth two dollars sent by mail or by a messenger-boy. The secret of power in doing good is *personal contact*. Our incarnate "Elder Brother" went in person to the sick chamber. He anointed with His own hand the eyes of the blind man and He touched the loathsome leper into health. The portentous chasm between wealth and poverty must be bridged by a span of personal kindness over which the footsteps must turn in only one di-

rection. The personal contact of self sacrificing benevolence with darkness, filth and misery — that is the only remedy. Heart must touch heart. Benevolence also cannot be confined to calendars. Those good people will exhibit the most of the spirit of our Blessed Master who practice Christmas-giving and cheerful, unselfish and zealous Christmas-living through all the circling year.

CHRISTMAS BELLS

ANON

There are sounds in the sky when the year
    grows old,
  And the winds of the winter blow —
When night and the moon are clear and cold,
  And the stars shine on the snow,
Or wild is the blast and the bitter sleet
  That beats on the window-pane;
But blest on the frosty hills are the feet
  Of the Christmas time again!
    Chiming sweet when the night wind swells,
    Blest is the sound of the Christmas Bells!

Dear are the sounds of the Christmas chimes
  In the land of the ivied towers,
And they welcome the dearest of festival times
  In this Western world of ours!

Bright on the holly and mistletoe bough
   The English firelight falls,
And bright are the wreathed evergreens now
  That gladden our own home walls!
    And hark! the first sweet note that tells,
    The welcome of the Christmas Bells!

The owl that sits in the ivy's shade,
  Remote from the ruined tower,
Shall start from his drowsy watch afraid
  When the clock shall strike the hour;
And over the fields in their frosty rhyme
  The cheery sounds shall go,
And chime shall answer unto chime
  Across the moonlit snow!
    How sweet the lingering music dwells,—
    The music of the Christmas Bells.

It fell not thus in the East afar
  Where the Babe in the manger lay;
The wise men followed their guiding star
  To the dawn of a milder day;
And the fig and the sycamore gathered green,
  And the palm-tree of Deborah rose;
'T was the strange first Christmas the world
    had seen —
    And it came not in storm and snows.
    Not yet on Nazareth's hills and dells
    Had floated the sound of Christmas Bells.

The cedars of Lebanon shook in the blast
  Of their own cold mountain air;

But nought o'er the wintry plain had passed
  To tell that the Lord was there!
The oak and the olive and almond were still,
  In the night now worn and thin;
No wind of the winter-time roared from the hill
  To waken the guests at the inn;
    No dream to them the music tells
    That is to come from the Christmas Bells!

The years that have fled like the leaves on the
      gale
  Since the morn of the Miracle-Birth,
Have widened the fame of the marvellous tale
  Till the tidings have filled the earth!
And so in the climes of the icy North,
  And the lands of the cane and the palm,
By the Alpine cotter's blazing hearth,
  And in tropic belts of calm,
    Men list to-night the welcome swells,
    Sweet and clear, of Christmas Bells!

They are ringing to-night through the Norway
      firs,
  And across the Swedish fells,
And the Cuban palm-tree dreamily stirs
  To the sound of those Christmas Bells!
They ring where the Indian Ganges rolls
  Its flood through the rice-fields wide;
They swell the far hymns of the Lapps and
      Poles

To the praise of the Crucified.
    Sweeter than tones of the ocean's shells
    Mingle the chimes of the Christmas Bells!

The years come not back that have circled
    away
  With the past of the Eastern land,
When He plucked the corn on the Sabbath day
  And healed the withered hand;
But the bells shall join in a joyous chime
  For the One who walked the sea,
And ring again for the better time
  Of the Christ that is to be!
    Then ring! — for earth's best promise
    dwells
    In ye, O joyous Prophet Bells!

Ring out at the meeting of night and morn
  For the dawn of a happier day!
Lo, the stone from our faith's great sepulchre
    torn
  The angels have rolled away!
And they come to us here in our low abode,
  With words like the sunrise gleam,—
Come down and ascend by that heavenly road
  That Jacob saw in his dream.
    Spirit of love, that in music dwells,
    Open our hearts with the Christmas Bells!

Help us to see that the glad heart prays
  As well as the bended knees;

That there are in our own as in ancient days
  The Scribes and the Pharisees;
That the Mount of Transfiguration still
  Looks down on these Christian lands,
And the glorified ones from that holy hill
  Are reaching their helping hands.
    These be the words our music tells
    Of solemn joy, O Christmas Bells!

THE BIRTH OF CHRIST

ALFRED TENNYSON

The time draws near the birth of Christ;
  The moon is hid — the night is still;
  The Christmas bells from hill to hill
Answer each other in the mist.

Four voices of four hamlets round,
  From far and near, on mead and moor,
  Swell out and fail, as if a door
Were shut between me and the sound.

Each voice four changes on the wind,
  That now dilate and now decrease,
  Peace and good-will, good-will and peace,
Peace and good-will to all mankind.

Rise, happy morn! rise, holy morn!
  Draw forth the cheerful day from night;
  O Father! touch the east, and light
The light that shone when hope was born!

THE CHRISTMAS CAROL

WILLIAM WORDSWORTH

The minstrels played their Christmas tune
　To-night beneath my cottage eaves;
While, smitten by a lofty moon,
　The encircling laurels, thick with leaves,
Gave back a rich and dazzling sheen
That overpowered their natural green.

Through hill and valley every breeze
　Had sunk to rest, with folded wings:
Keen was the air, but could not freeze
　Nor check the music of the strings;
So stout and hardy were the band
That scraped the chords with strenuous hand!

And who but listened — till was paid
　Respect to every inmate's claim:
The greeting given, the music played,
　In honor of each household name,
Duly pronounced with lusty call,
And " Merry Christmas " wished to all!

How touching, when, at midnight, sweep
　Snow-muffled winds, and all is dark,
To hear, and sink again to sleep!
　Or, at an earlier call, to mark
By blazing fire, the still suspense
Of self-complacent innocence;

The mutual nod,— the grave disguise
  Of hearts with gladness brimming o'er;
And some unbidden tears that rise
  For names once heard, and heard no more;
Tears brightened by the serenade
For infant in the cradle laid.

Hail ancient Manners! sure defence,
  Where they survive, of wholesome laws;
Remnants of love whose modest sense
  Thus into narrow room withdraws;
Hail, Usages of pristine mould,
And ye that guard them, Mountains old!

———

CHRISTMAS AT FEZZIWIG'S WARE-HOUSE

CHARLES DICKENS

" Yo ho! my boys," said Fezziwig. " No more work to-night; Christmas Eve, Dick! Christmas, Ebenezer! Let's have the shutters up," cried old Fezziwig with a sharp clap of his hands, " before a man can say Jack Robinson. . . ."

" Hilli-ho!" cried old Fezziwig, skipping down from the high desk with wonderful agility. " Clear away, my lads, and let's have lots of room here! Hilli-ho, Dick! Cheer up, Ebenezer!"

Clear away! There was nothing they wouldn't have cleared away, or couldn't have cleared away, with old Fezziwig looking on. It was done in a minute. Every movable was packed off, as if it were dismissed from public life forevermore; the floor was swept and watered, the lamps were trimmed, fuel was heaped upon the fire; and the warehouse was as snug, and warm, and dry, and bright a ball-room as you would desire to see upon a winter's night.

In came a fiddler with a music-book, and

went up to the lofty desk and made an orchestra of it and tuned like fifty stomach-aches. In came Mrs. Fezziwig, one vast, substantial smile. In came the three Misses Fezziwig, beaming and lovable. In came the six followers whose hearts they broke. In came all the young men and women employed in the business. In came the housemaid with her cousin the baker. In came the cook with her brother's particular friend the milkman. In came the boy from over the way, who was suspected of not having board enough from his master, trying to hide himself behind the girl from next door but one who was proved to have had her ears pulled by her mistress; in they all came, anyhow and everyhow. Away they all went, twenty couple at once; hands half round and back again the other way; down the middle and up again; round and round in various stages of affectionate grouping, old top couple always turning up in the wrong place; new top couple starting off again, as soon as they got there; all top couples at last, and not a bottom one to help them.

When this result was brought about the fiddler struck up "Sir Roger de Coverley." Then old Fezziwig stood out to dance with Mrs. Fezziwig. Top couple, too, with a good stiff piece of work cut out for them; three or four and twenty pairs of partners; people who

were not to be trifled with; people who would dance and had no notion of walking.

But if they had been thrice as many — Oh, four times as many — old Fezziwig would have been a match for them, and so would Mrs. Fezziwig. As to her, she was worthy to be his partner in every sense of the term. If that's not high praise, tell me higher and I'll use it. A positive light appeared to issue from Fezziwig's calves. They shone in every part of the dance like moons. You couldn't have predicted at any given time what would become of them next. And when old Fezziwig and Mrs. Fezziwig had gone all through the dance; advance and retire; both hands to your partner, bow and courtesy, corkscrew, thread the needle, and back again to your place; Fezziwig "cut"— cut so deftly that he appeared to wink with his legs, and came upon his feet again without a stagger.

When the clock struck eleven the domestic ball broke up. Mr. and Mrs. Fezziwig took their stations, one on either side of the door, and shaking hands with every person individually, as he or she went out, wished him or her a MERRY CHRISTMAS!

CHRISTMAS BELLS

JOHN KEBLE

Wake me to-night, my mother dear,
That I may hear
The Christmas Bells, so soft and clear,
To high and low glad tidings tell,
How God the Father loved us well;
How God the Eternal Son
Came to undo what we had done.

CHRISTMAS
SIGNIFICANCE AND SPIRIT

A CHRISTMAS CARMEN

JOHN G. WHITTIER

I

Sound over all waters, reach out from all lands,
The chorus of voices, the clasping of hands;
Sing hymns that were sung by the stars of the
    morn,
Sing songs of the angels when Jesus was born!
    With glad jubilations
    Bring hope to the nations!
The dark night is ending and dawn has begun:
Rise, hope of the ages, arise like the sun,
    All speech flow to music, all hearts beat as
    one!

II

Sing the bridal of nations! with chorals of love
Sing out the war-vulture and sing in the dove,
Till the hearts of the peoples keep time in ac-
    cord,
And the voice of the world is the voice of the
    Lord!
    Clasp hands of the nations
    In strong gratulations:

The dark night is ending and dawn has begun;
Rise, hope of the ages, arise like the sun,
    All speech flow to music, all hearts beat as
      one!

III

Blow, bugles of battle, the marches of peace;
East, west, north, and south let the long quar-
    rel cease:
Sing the song of great joy that the angels
    began,
Sing of glory to God and of good-will to man!
    Hark! joining in chorus
    The heavens bend o'er us!
The dark night is ending and dawn has begun;
Rise, hope of the ages, arise like the sun,
    All speech flow to music, all hearts beat as
      one!

THE SPIRIT OF CHRISTMAS

From " Pickwick Papers."

CHARLES DICKENS

And numerous indeed are the hearts to
which Christmas brings a brief season of happiness and enjoyment. How many families
whose members have been dispersed and scattered far and wide, in the restless struggles of
life, are then re-united, and meet once again in
that happy state of companionship and mutual

good-will, which is a source of such pure and unalloyed delight, and one so incompatible with the cares and sorrows of the world, that the religious belief of the most civilized nations, and the rude traditions of the roughest savages, alike number it among the first joys of a future state of existence, provided for the blest and happy! How many old recollections, and how many dormant sympathies, does Christmas time awaken!

We write these words now, many miles distant from the spot at which, year after year, we met on that day, a merry and joyous circle. Many of the hearts that throb so gaily then, have ceased to beat; many of the looks that shone so brightly then, have ceased to glow; the hands we grasped, have grown cold; the eyes we sought, have hid their lustre in the grave; and yet the old house, the room, the merry voices and smiling faces, the jest, the laugh, the most minute and trivial circumstance connected with those happy meetings, crowd upon our mind at each recurrence of the season, as if the last assemblage had been but yesterday. Happy, happy Christmas, that can win us back to the delusions of our childish days, that can recall to the old man the pleasures of his youth, and transport the sailor and the traveller, thousands of miles away, back to his own fireside and his quiet home!

*   *   *   *   *   *

ON GOOD WISHES AT CHRISTMAS

FRISWELL

At Christmas, which is a good holiday for most of us, but especially for that larger and better half of us, the young, there is, as everybody knows, a profusion of good things. The final cause of a great many existences is Christmas Day. How many of that vast flock of geese, which are now peacefully feeding over the long, cold wolds of Norfolk, or are driven gabbling and hissing by the gozzard to their pasture — how many of those very geese were called into being simply for Christmas Day! In the towns, with close streets and fetid courts, where the flaring gas at the corner of an alley marks the only bright spot, a gin-palace, there a goose-club is held; and there, for a short time, is the resting-place, side by side with a bottle of gin, of one of those wise-looking and self-concentrated gobblers, whose name men have generally, and, as we think, unjustly, applied to the silly one amongst themselves.

But it is only the profusion of good things, of cakes, puddings, spices, oranges, and fruits, from sunny Italy and Spain, from India and from Asia, from America, North and South, and even from distant Australia; it is not that amongst us, as long ago with the *Franklin* in Chaucer, that at this time —

> " It snowës in our house
> Of meate and drinke;"

it is not that we have huge loads of beef chines, ribs, sirloins, legs, necks, breasts, and shoulders of mutton, fillets of veal, whole hogs, and pigs in various stages, from the tender suckling to the stiff-jointed father of a family, whose " back hair " makes good clothes-brushes, and whose head is brought in at college feasts; it is not that the air gives up its choicest fowl, and the waters yield their best fish: plentiful as these are with us, they are nothing in profusion to the kindly greeting and good wishes that fly about in the cold weather, and that circulate from land's end to land's end. The whole coast of England is surrounded by a general " shake hands." The coast-guard on their wintry walks do not greet each other more surely than old friends all over England do: one clasps another, and another a third, till from Dover to London and so on to York, from Yarmouth on the east to Bristol on the west, from John O'Groat's house at the extreme north to the Land's End, the very toe-nail of England on the south — a kindly greeting, we may be sure, will pass.

And a cheerful thing it is, on this day of universal equality, on this day which —

> "To the cottage and the crown,
>   Brought tidings of salvation down,"

to think that we can touch and hold each other with friendly hands all over our land. We all of us shake hands on Christmas Day. Leigh Hunt had a quaint fancy that he had, as it were, by lineal descent, shaken hands with Milton. He would argue thus: he knew a man who had shaken hands with Dr. Johnson, who had clasped the hand of him who had shaken Dryden's right hand, who himself had thus greeted Andrew Marvell, who knew Master Elwood, the Quaker friend of Milton, who knew Milton himself; and thus, though our Sovereign has her hand kissed, not shaken, by her subjects, yet doubtless she will clasp the hands of her children, who, shaking those of others, will let the greeting and the good wishes descend to the lowest on that ladder of society which we are all trying to climb.

As for hearty good wishes, spoken in all kinds of voices, from the deepest bass to the shrillest treble, we are sure that they circulate throughout the little island, and are borne on the wings of the post all over the seas. Erasmus, coming to England in Henry VIII's time, was struck with the deep heartiness of our wishes — good, ay, and bad too; but he most

admired the good ones. Other nations ask in their greetings how a man carries himself, or how doth he stand with the world, or how doth he find himself; but the English greet with a pious wish that God may give one a good morning or a good evening, good day, or "god'd'en," as the old writers have it; and when we part we wish that "God may be with you," though we now clip it into "Good b'ye."

A CHRISTMAS SONG

WILLIAM COX BENNETT

Blow, wind, blow,
Sing through yard and shroud;
Pipe it shrilly and loud,
    Aloft as well as below;
Sing in my sailor's ear
The song I sing to you,
"Come home, my sailor true,
For Christmas that comes so near."

Go, wind, go,
Hurry his home-bound sail,
Through gusts that are edged with hail,
    Through winter, and sleet, and snow;
Song, in my sailor's ear,
Your shrilling and moans shall be,
For he knows they sing him to me
And Christmas that comes so near.

SERY

RICHARD WATSON GILDER

With wild surprise
Four great eyes
In two small heads,
From neighboring beds
Looked out — and winked —
And glittered and blinked
At a very queer sight
In the dim starlight.
As plain as can be

A fairy tree
Flashes and glimmers
And shakes and shimmers.
Red, green and blue
Meet their view;
Silver and gold
Their sharp eyes behold;
Small moon, big stars;
And jams in jars,
And cakes, and honey
And thimbles, and money,
Pink dogs, blue cats,
Little squeaking rats,
And candles, and dolls,
And crackers, and polls,
A real bird that sings,
And tokens and favors,
And all sorts of things
For the little shavers.

Four black eyes
Grow big with surprise;
And then grow bigger
When a tiny figure,
Jaunty and airy,
(Is it a fairy?)
From the tree-top cries,
" Open wide! Black Eyes!
Come, children, wake now!
Your joys you may take now!"

Quick as you can think
　Twenty small toes
　In four pretty rows,
Like little piggies pink,
　All kick in the air —
And before you can wink
　The tree stands bare!

A CHRISTMAS SONG

TUDOR JENKS

When mother-love makes all things bright,
When joy comes with the morning light,
When children gather round their tree,
　Thou Christmas Babe,
　We sing of Thee!

When manhood's brows are bent in thought,
To learn what men of old have taught,

When eager hands seek wisdom's key,
    Wise Temple Child,
    We learn of Thee!

When doubts assail, and perils fright,
When, groping blindly in the night,
We strive to read life's mystery,
    Man of the Mount,
    We turn to Thee!

When shadows of the valley fall,
When sin and death the soul appall,
One light we through the darkness see —
    Christ on the Cross,
    We cry to Thee!

And when the world shall pass away,
And dawns at length the perfect day,
In glory shall our souls made free,
    Thou God enthroned,
    Then worship Thee.

CHRISTMAS

(A Selection from " Dreamthorp ")

ALEXANDER SMITH

Sitting here, I incontinently find myself holding a levee of departed Christmas nights. Silently, and without special call, into my study

of imagination come these apparitions, clad in
snowy mantles, brooched and gemmed with
frosts. Their numbers I do not care to count,
for I know they are the numbers of many
years. The visages of two or three are sad
enough, but on the whole 'tis a congregation
of jolly ghosts. The nostrils of my memory
are assailed by a faint odor of plum-pudding
and burnt brandy. I hear a sound as of light
music, a whisk of women's dresses whirled
round in dance, a click as of glasses pledged
by friends. Before one of these apparitions is
a mound, as of a new-made grave, on which
the snow is lying. I know, I know! Drape
thyself not in white like the others, but in
mourning stole of crape; and instead of dance
music, let there haunt around thee the service
for the dead! I know that sprig of mistletoe,
O Spirit in the midst! Under it I swung the
girl I loved — girl no more now than I am a
boy — and kissed her spite of blush and pretty
shriek. And thee, too, with fragrant trencher
in hand, over which blue tongues of flame are
playing, I do know — most ancient apparition
of them all. I remember thy reigning night.
Back to very days of childhood am I taken by
the ghostly raisins simmering in a ghostly
brandy flame. Where now the merry boys and
girls that thrust their fingers in thy blaze?
And now, when I think of it, thee also would I

drape in black raiment, around thee also would I make the burial service murmur.

*   *   *   *   *   *

This, then, is Christmas, 1862. Everything is silent in Dreamthorp. The smith's hammer reposes beside the anvil. The weaver's flying shuttle is at rest. Through the clear wintry sunshine the bells this morning rang from the gray church tower amid the leafless elms, and up the walk the villagers trooped in their best dresses and their best faces — the latter a little reddened by the sharp wind: mere redness in the middle aged; in the maids, wonderful bloom to the eyes of their lovers — and took their places decently in the ancient pews. The clerk read the beautiful prayers of our Church, which seem more beautiful at Christmas than at any other period. For that very feeling which breaks down at this time the barriers which custom, birth, or wealth have erected between man and man, strikes down the barrier of time which intervenes between the worshipper of to-day and the great body of worshippers who are at rest in their graves. On such a day as this, hearing these prayers, we feel a kinship with the devout generations who heard them long ago. The devout lips of the Christian dead murmured the responses which we now murmur; along this road of prayer did their thoughts of our innumerable dead, our brothers and sisters in faith and hope, approach the

Maker, even as ours at present approach Him.
Prayers over, the clergyman — who is no
Boanerges, of Chrysostom, golden-mouthed, but
a loving, genial-hearted, pious man, the whole
extent of his life from boyhood until now, full
of charity and kindly deeds, as autumn fields
with heavy wheaten ears; the clergyman, I say
— for the sentence is becoming unwieldy on my
hands, and one must double back to secure con-
nexion — read out in that silvery voice of his,
which is sweeter than any music to my ear,
those chapters of the New Testament that deal
with the birth of the Saviour. And the red-
faced rustic congregation hung on the good
man's voice as he spoke of the Infant brought
forth in a manger, of the shining angels that
appeared in the mid-air to the shepherds, of
the miraculous star that took its station in the
sky, and of the wise men who came from afar
and laid their gifts of frankincense and myrrh
at the feet of the child. With the story every
one was familiar, but on that day, and backed
by the persuasive melody of the reader's voice,
it seemed to all quite new — at least, they listened attentively as if it were. The discourse
that   followed   possessed   no   remarkable
thoughts; it dealt simply with the goodness of
the Maker of heaven and earth, and the short-
ness of time, with the duties of thankfulness
and charity to the poor; and I am persuaded
that every one who heard returned to his house

in a better frame of mind. And so the service remitted us all to our own homes, to what roast-beef and plum-pudding slender means permitted, to gatherings around cheerful fires, to half-pleasant, half-sad remembrances of the dead and the absent.

From sermon I have returned like the others, and it is my purpose to hold Christmas alone. I have no one with me at table, and my own thoughts must be my Christmas guests. Sitting here, it is pleasant to think how much kindly feeling exists this present night in England. By imagination I can taste of every table, pledge every toast, silently join in every roar of merriment. I become a sort of universal guest. With what propriety is this jovial season, placed amid dismal December rains and snows! How one pities the unhappy Australians, with whom everything is turned topsy-turvy, and who holds Christmas at midsummer! The face of Christmas glows all the brighter for the cold. The heart warms as the frost increases. Estrangements which have embittered the whole year, melt in to-night's hospitable smile. There are warmer handshakings on this night than during the by-past twelve months. Friend lives in the mind of friend. There is more charity at this time than at any other. You get up at midnight and toss your spare coppers to the half-benumbed musicians whiffling beneath your windows, although at

any other time you would consider their performance a nuisance, and call angrily for the
police. Poverty, and scanty clothing, and fire-
less grates, come home at this season to the
bosoms of the rich, and they give of their abun-
dance. The very red-breast of the woods enjoys his Christmas feast. Good feeling incar-
nates itself into plum-pudding. The Master's
words, "The poor ye have always with you,"
wear at this time a deep significance. For at
least one night on each year over all Christendom there is brotherhood. And good men, sitting amongst their families, or by a solitary
fire like me, when they remember the light that
shone over the poor clowns huddling on the
Bethlehem plains eighteen hundred years ago,
the apparition of shining angels overhead, the
song "Peace on earth and good-will toward
men," which for the first hallowed the midnight
air,— pray for that strain's fulfilment, that battle and strife may vex the nations no more, that
not only on Christmas eve, but the whole year
round, men shall be brethren owning one
Father in heaven.

*   *   *   *   *   *   *

Once again, for the purpose of taking away
all solitariness of feeling, and of connecting
myself, albeit only in fancy, with the proper
gladness of the time, let me think of the comfortable family dinners now being drawn to a
close, of the good wishes uttered, and the pres-

ents made, quite valueless in themselves, yet felt to be invaluable from the feelings from which they spring; of the little children, by sweetmeats lapped in Elysium; and of the pantomime, pleasantest Christmas sight of all, with the pit a sea of grinning delight, the boxes a tier of beaming juvenility, the galleries, piled up to the far-receding roof, a mass of happy laughter which a clown's joke brings down in mighty avalanches. In the pit, sober people relax themselves, and suck oranges, and quaff ginger-pop; in the boxes, Miss, gazing through her curls, thinks the Fairy Prince the prettiest creature she ever beheld, and Master, that to be a clown must be the pinnacle of human happiness: while up in the galleries the hard literal world is for an hour sponged out and obliterated; the chimney-sweep forgets, in his delight when the policeman comes to grief, the harsh call of his master, and Cinderella, when the demons are foiled, and the long parted lovers meet and embrace in a paradise of light and pink gauze, the grates that must be scrubbed to-morrow. All bands and trappings of toil are for one hour loosened by the hands of imaginative sympathy. What happiness a single theatre can contain! And those of maturer years, or of more meditative temperament, sitting at the pantomime, can extract out of the shifting scenes meanings suitable to themselves; for the pantomime is a symbol or adumbration of human life.

Have we not all known Harlequin, who rules the roast, and has the pretty Columbine to himself? Do we not all know that rogue of a clown with his peculating fingers, who brazens out of every scrape, and who conquers the world by good humour and ready wit? And have we not seen Pantaloons not a few, whose fate it is to get all the kicks and lose all the halfpence, to fall through all the trap doors, break their shins over all the barrows, and be forever captured by the policeman, while the true pilferer, the clown, makes his escape with the booty in his possession? Methinks I know the realities of which these things are but the shadows; have met with them in business, have sat with them at dinner. But to-night no such notions as these intrude; and when the torrent of fun, and transformation, and practical joking which rushed out of the beautiful fairy world gathered up again, the high-heaped happiness of the theatre will disperse itself, and the Christmas pantomime will be a pleasant memory the whole year through. Thousands on thousands of people are having their midriffs tickled at this moment; in fancy I see their lighted faces, in memory I see their mirth.

By this time I should think every Christmas dinner at Dreamthorp or elsewhere has come to an end. Even now in the great cities the theatres will be dispersing. The clown has wiped the paint off his face. Harlequin has laid aside his

wand, and divested himself of his glittering raiment; Pantaloon, after refreshing himself with a pint of porter, is rubbing his aching joints; and Columbine, wrapped up in a shawl, and with sleepy eyelids, has gone home in a cab. Soon, in the great theatre, the lights will be put out, and the empty stage will be left to ghosts. Hark! midnight from the church tower vibrates through the frosty air. I look out on the brilliant heaven, and see a milky way of powdery splendour wandering through it, and clusters and knots of stars and planets shining serenely in the blue frosty spaces; and the armed apparition of Orion, his spear pointing away into immeasurable space, gleaming overhead; and the familiar constellation of the Plough dipping down into the west; and I think when I go in again that there is one Christmas the less between me and my grave.

* * * * * * *

CHRISTMAS CAROL

PHILLIPS BROOKS

The earth has grown old with its burden of
    care,
  But at Christmas it always is young,
The heart of the jewel burns lustrous and fair,

And its soul full of music bursts forth on the
        air,
    When the song of the angels is sung

It is coming, Old Earth, it is coming to-night!
    On the snowflakes which cover thy sod
The feet of the Christ-child fall gentle and
        white,
And the voice of the Christ-child tells out with
        delight
    That mankind are the children of God.

On the sad and the lonely, the wretched and
        poor,
    The voice of the Christ-child shall fall;
And to every blind wanderer open the door
Of hope that he dared not to dream of before,
    With a sunshine of welcome for all.

The feet of the humblest may walk in the field
    Where the feet of the Holiest trod,
This, then, is the marvel to mortals revealed
When the silvery trumpets of Christmas have
        pealed,
    That mankind are the children of God.

THE END OF THE PLAY

WILLIAM MAKEPEACE THACKERAY

The play is done — the curtain drops,
    Slow-falling to the prompter's bell:

A moment yet the actor stops,
  And looks around, to say farewell.
It is an irksome word and task;
  And, when he's laughed and said his say,
He shows, as he removes his mask,
  A face that's anything but gay.

One word, ere yet the evening ends,
  Let's close it with a parting rhyme;
And pledge a hand to all young friends,
  As fits the merry Christmas time.
On life's wide scene you, too, have parts
  That fate erelong shall bid you play;
Good-night! — with honest, gentle hearts
  A kindly greeting go alway!

Good-night! — I'd say the griefs, the joys,
Just hinted in this mimic page,
The triumphs and defeats of boys,
  Are but repeated in our age.
I'd say your woes were not less keen,
  Your hopes more vain than those of men,
Your pangs or pleasures of fifteen
  At forty-five played o'er again.

I'd say we suffer and we strive,
  Not less nor more as men than boys,
With grizzled beards at forty-five
  As erst at twelve in corduroys;
And if, in time of sacred youth,
  We learned at home to love and pray,

Pray Heaven that early love and truth
  May never wholly pass away.

And in the world as in the school
  I'd say how fate may change and shift,
The prize be sometimes to the fool,
  The race not always to the swift:
The strong may yield, the good may fall,
  The great man be a vulgar clown,
The knave be lifted over all,
  The kind cast pitilessly down.

Who knows the inscrutable design?
  Blessèd be He who took and gave!
Why should your mother, Charles, not mine,
  Be weeping at her darling's grave?
We bow to Heaven that willed it so,
  That darkly rules the fate of all,
That sends the respite or the blow,
  That's free to give or to recall.

This crowns his feast with wine and wit,—
  Who brought him to that mirth and state?
His betters, see, below him sit,
  Or hunger hopeless at the gate!
Who bade the mud from Dives's wheel
  To spurn the rags of Lazarus?
Come, brother, in that dust we'll kneel,
  Confessing Heaven that ruled it thus.

So each shall mourn, in life's advance,
   Dear hopes, dear friends, untimely killed;
Shall grieve for many a forfeit chance,
   And longing passion unfulfilled.
Amen! — whatever fate be sent,
   Pray God the heart may kindly glow,
Although the head with cares be bent,
   And whitened with the winter snow!

Come wealth or want, come good or ill,
   Let young and old accept their part,
And bow before the awful will,
   And bear it with an honest heart.
Who misses or who wins the prize,
   Go, lose or conquer, as you can;
But if you fail, or if you rise,
   Be each, pray God, a gentleman!

A gentleman, or old or young!
   (Bear kindly with my humble lays;)
The sacred chorus first was sung
   Upon the first of Christmas days;
The shepherds heard it overhead,—
   The joyful angels raised it then:
"Glory to Heaven on high," it said,
   "And peace on earth to gentle men!"

My song, save this, is little worth;
   I lay the weary pen aside,
And wish you health and love and mirth,
   As fits the solemn Christmas-tide.

As fits the holy Christmas birth,
  Be this, good friends, our carol still:
Be peace on earth, be peace on earth
  To men of gentle will!

CHRIST'S NATIVITY

HENRY VAUGHAN

Awake, glad heart! get up and sing!
It is the Birthday of thy King.
    Awake! awake!
    The sun doth shake
Light from his locks, and, all the way
Breathing perfumes, doth spice the day.

Awake! awake! hark how th' wood rings,
Winds whisper, and the busy springs
    A concert make!
    Awake! awake!
Man is their high-priest, and should rise
To offer up the sacrifice.

I would I were some bird, or star,
Fluttering in woods, or lifted far
    Above this inn,
    And road of sin!
Then either star or bird should be
Shining or singing still to thee.

I would I had in my best part
Fit rooms for thee! or that my heart

Where so clean as
Thy manger was!
But I am all filth, and obscene;
Yet, if thou wilt, thou canst make clean.

Sweet Jesu! will then.   Let no more
This leper haunt and soil thy door!
Cure him, ease him,
O release him!
And let once more, by mystic birth,
The Lord of life be born in earth.

CHRISTMAS DREAMS

CHRISTOPHER NORTH

*   *   *   *   *   *   *

To-morrow is Merry Christmas; and when
its night descends there will be mirth and music,
and the light sounds of the merry-twinkling
feet within these now so melancholy walls —
and sleep now reigning over all the house save
this one room, will be banished far over the
sea — and morning will be reluctant to allow
her light to break up the innocent orgies.

Were every Christmas of which we have been
present at the celebration, painted according to
nature — what a Gallery of Pictures! True
that a sameness would pervade them all — but
only that kind of sameness that pervades the
nocturnal heavens. One clear night always is,
to common eyes, just like another; for what
hath any night to show but one moon and
some stars — a blue vault, with here a few
braided, and there a few castellated, clouds?
yet no two nights ever bore more than a family
resemblance to each other before the studious
and instructed eye of him who has long com-
muned with Nature, and is familiar with every

186

smile and frown on her changeful, but not capricious, countenance. Even so with the Annual Festivals of the heart. Then our thoughts are the stars that illumine those skies — and on ourselves it depends whether they shall be black as Erebus, or brighter than Aurora.

"Thoughts! that like spirits trackless come and go"— is a fine line of Charles Lloyd's. But no bird skims, no arrow pierces the air, without producing some change in the Universe, which will last to the day of doom. No coming and going is absolutely trackless; nor irrecoverable by Nature's law is any consciousness, however ghostlike; though many a one, even the most blissful, never does return, but seems to be buried among the dead. But they are not dead — but only sleep; though to us who recall them not, they are as they had never been, and we, wretched ingrates, let them lie for ever in oblivion! How passing sweet when of their own accord they arise to greet us in our solitude! — as a friend who, having sailed away to a foreign land in our youth, has been thought to have died many long years ago, may suddenly stand before us, with face still familiar and name reviving in a moment, and all that he once was to us brought from utter forgetfulness close upon our heart.

My Father's House! How it is ringing like a grove in spring, with the din of creatures

happier, a thousand times happier, than all the birds on earth. It is the Christmas Holidays — Christmas Day itself — Christmas Night — and Joy in every bosom intensifies Love. Never before were we brothers and sisters so dear to one another — never before had our hearts so yearned towards the authors of our being — our blissful being! There they sat — silent in all that outcry — composed in all that disarray — still in all that tumult; yet, as one or other flying imp sweeps round the chair, a father's hand will playfully strive to catch a prisoner — a mother's gentler touch on some sylph's disordered symar be felt almost as a reproof, and for a moment slacken the fairy flight. One old game treads on the heels of another — twenty within the hour — and many a new game never heard of before nor since, struck out by the collision of kindred spirits in their glee, the transitory fancies of genius inventive through very delight. Then, all at once, there is a hush, profound as ever falls on some little plat within a forest when the moon drops behind the mountain, and small green-robed People of Peace at once cease their pastime, and vanish. For she — the Silver-Tongued — is about to sing an old ballad, words and air alike hundreds of years old — and sing she doth, while tears begin to fall, with a voice too mournfully beautiful long to breathe below — and, ere another Christmas

shall have come with the falling snows, doomed to be mute on earth — but to be hymning in Heaven.

Of that House — to our eyes the fairest of earthly dwellings — with its old ivyed turrets, and orchard-garden bright alike with fruit and with flowers, not one stone remains. The very brook that washed its foundations has vanished along with them — and a crowd of other buildings, wholly without character, has long stood where here a single tree, and there a grove, did once render so lovely that small demesne; which, how could we, who thought it the very heart of Paradise, even for one moment have believed was one day to be blotted out of being, and we ourselves — then so linked in love that the band which bound us altogether was, in its gentle pressure, felt not nor understood — to be scattered far and abroad, like so many leaves that after one wild parting rustle are separated by roaring wind-eddies, and brought together no more! The old Abbey — it still survives; and there, in that corner of the burial-ground, below that part of the wall which was last in ruins, and which we often climbed to reach the flowers and nests — there, in hopes of a joyful resurrection, lie the Loved and Venerated — for whom, even now that so many grief-deadening years have fled, we feel, in this holy hour, as if it were impiety so utterly to have ceased

to weep — so seldom to have remembered! — And then, with a powerlessness of sympathy to keep pace with youth's frantic grief, the floods we all wept together — at no long interval — on those pale and placid faces as they lay, most beautiful and most dreadful to behold, in their coffins.

We believe that there is genius in all childhood. But the creative joy that makes it great in its simplicity dies a natural death or is killed, and genius dies with it. In favored spirits, neither few nor many, the joy and the might survive; for you must know that unless it be accompanied with imagination, memory is cold and lifeless. The forms it brings before us must be inspired with beauty — that is, with affection or passion. All minds, even the dullest, remember the days of their youth; but all cannot bring back the indescribable brightness of that blessed season. They who would know what they once were, must not merely recollect but they must imagine, the hills and valleys — if any such there were — in which their childhood played, the torrents, the waterfalls, the lakes, the heather, the rocks, the heaven's imperial dome, the raven floating only a little lower than the eagle in the sky. To imagine what he then heard and saw, he must imagine his own nature. He must collect from many vanished hours the power of his untamed heart, and he must, perhaps, transfuse

also something of his maturer mind into these
dreams of his former being, thus linking the
past with the present by a continuous chain,
which, though often invisible, is never broken.
So is it too with the calmer affections that
have grown within the shelter of a roof. We
do not merely remember, we imagine our
father's house, the fireside, all his features then
most living, now dead and buried; the very
manner of his smile, every tone of his voice.
We must combine with all the passionate and
plastic power of imagination the spirit of a
thousand happy hours into one moment; and
we must invest with all that we ever felt
to be venerable such an image as alone can
satisfy our filial hearts. It is thus that imagination, which first aided the growth of all
our holiest and happiest affections, can preserve
them to us unimpaired —

"For she can give us back the dead,
Even in the loveliest looks they wore."

Then came a New Series of Christmases,
celebrated, one year in this family, another
year in that — none present but those whom
Charles Lamb the Delightful calleth the "old
familiar faces;" something in all features, and
all tones of voice, and all manners, betokening
origin from one root — relations all, happy,
and with no reason either to be ashamed or
proud of their neither high nor humble birth,

their lot being cast within that pleasant realm, "the Golden Mean," where the dwellings are connecting links between the hut and the hall — fair edifices resembling manse or mansion-house, according as the atmosphere expands or contracts their dimensions — in which Competence is next-door neighbor to Wealth, and both of them within the daily walk of Contentment.

Merry Christmases they were indeed — one Lady always presiding, with a figure that once had been the stateliest among the stately, but then somewhat bent, without being bowed down, beneath an easy weight of most venerable years. Sweet was her tremulous voice to all her grandchildren's ears. Nor did these solemn eyes, bedimmed into a pathetic beauty, in any degree restrain the glee that sparkled in orbs that had as yet shed not many tears, but tears of joy or pity. Dearly she loved all those mortal creatures whom she was soon about to leave; but she sat in sunshine even within the shadow of death; and the " voice that called her home " had so long been whispering in her ear, that its accents had become dear to her, and consolatory every word that was heard in the silence, as from another world.

Whether we were indeed all so witty as we thought ourselves — uncles, aunts, brothers, sisters, nephews, nieces, cousins, and " the

rest," it might be presumptuous in us, who
were considered by ourselves and a few others
not the least amusing of the whole set, at this
distance of time to decide — especially in the
affirmative; but how the roof did ring with
sally, pun, retort, and repartee! Ay, with pun
— a species of impertinence for which we have
therefore a kindness even to this day. Had
incomparable Thomas Hood had the good fortune to have been born a cousin of ours, how
with that fine fancy of his would he have shone
at those Christmas festivals, eclipsing us all!
Our family, through all its different branches,
has ever been famous for bad voices, but good
ears; and we think we hear ourselves — all
those uncles and aunts, nephews and nieces,
and cousins — singing now! Easy it is to
" warble melody " as to breathe air. But we
hope harmony is the most difficult of all things
to people in general, for to us it was impossible; and what attempts ours used to be
at Seconds! Yet the most woful failures were
rapturously encored; and ere the night was
done we spoke with most extraordinary voices
indeed, every one hoarser than another, till at
last, walking home with a fair cousin, there
was nothing left it but a tender glance of the
eye — a tender pressure of the hand — for
cousins are not altogether sisters, and although
partaking of that dearest character, possess, it
may be, some peculiar and appropriate charms

of their own; as didst thou, Emily the " Wild-
cap!"—That *soubriquet* all forgotten now —
for now thou art a matron, nay a Grandam,
and troubled with an elf fair and frolicsome
as thou thyself wert of yore, when the gravest
and wisest withstood not the witchery of thy
dancings, thy singings, and thy showering
smiles.

On rolled Suns and Seasons — the old died
— the elderly became old — and the young, one
after another, were wafted joyously away on
the wings of hope, like birds almost as soon as
they can fly, ungratefully forsaking their nests
and the groves in whose safe shadow they
first essayed their pinions; or like pinnaces that,
after having for a few days trimmed their
snow-white sails in the land-locked bay, close
to whose shores of silvery sand had grown the
trees that furnished timber both for hull and
mast, slip their tiny cables on some summer
day, and gathering every breeze that blows, go
dancing over the waves in sunshine, and melt
far off into the main. Or, haply, some were
like fair young trees, transplanted during no
favorable season, and never to take root in
another soil, but soon leaf and branch to wither
beneath the tropic sun, and die almost un-
heeded by those who knew not how beautiful
they had been beneath the dews and mists of
their own native climate.

Vain images! and therefore chosen by fancy

not too plainly to touch the heart. For some hearts grew cold and forbidding with selfish cares — some, warm as ever in their own generous glow, were touched by the chill of Fortune's frowns, ever worst to bear when suddenly succeeding her smiles — some, to rid themselves of painful regrets, took refuge in forgetfulness, and closed their eyes to the past — duty banished some abroad, and duty imprisoned others at home — estrangements there were, at first unconscious and unintended, yet erelong, though causeless, complete — changes were wrought insensibly, invisibly, even in the innermost nature of those who being friends knew no guile, yet came thereby at last to be friends no more — unrequited love broke some bonds — requited love relaxed others — the death of one altered the conditions of many — and so — year after year — the Christmas Meeting was interrupted — deferred — till finally it ceased with one accord, unrenewed and unrenewable. For when Some Things cease for a time — that time turns out to be forever.

Survivors of those happy circles! wherever ye be — should these imperfect remembrances of days of old chance, in some thoughtful pause of life's busy turmoil, for a moment to meet your eyes, let there be towards the inditer a few throbs of revived affection in your hearts — for his, though " absent long and distant

far," has never been utterly forgetful of the loves and friendships that charmed his youth. To be parted in body is not to be estranged in spirit — and many a dream and many a vision, sacred to nature's best affections, may pass before the mind of one whose lips are silent. " Out of sight out of mind " is rather the expression of a doubt — of a fear — than a belief or a conviction.   The soul surely has eyes that can see the objects it loves, through all intervening darkness — and of those more especially dear it keeps within itself almost undimmed images, on which, when they know it not, think it not, believe it not, it often loves to gaze, as on relics imperishable as they are hallowed.

All hail! rising beautiful and magnificent through the mists of morning — ye Woods, Groves, Towers, and Temples, overshadowing that famous Stream beloved by all the Muses! Through this midnight hush — methinks we hear faint and far-off sacred music —

"Where through the long-drawn aisle and fretted vault,
The pealing anthem swells the note of praise!"

How steeped now in the stillness of moonlight are all those pale, pillared Churches, Courts and Cloisters, Shrines and Altars, with here and there a Statue standing in the shade, or Monument sacred to the memory of the pious — the immortal dead. Some great clock is

striking from one of many domes — from the majestic Tower of St. Mary Magdalen — and in the deepened hush that follows the solemn sound, the mingling waters of the Cherwell and the Isis soften the severe silence of the holy night.

Remote from kindred, and from all the friendships that were the native growth of the fair fields where our boyhood and our youth had roamed and meditated and dreamed, those were indeed years of high and lofty mood which held us in converse with the shades of great Poets and ages of old in Rhedicyna's hallowed groves, still, serene, and solemn, as that Attic Academe where divine Plato, with all Hybla on his lips, discoursed such excellent music that his life seemed to the imagination spiritualized — a dim reminiscence of some former state of being. How sank then the Christmas Service of that beautiful Liturgy into our hearts! Not faithless we to the simple worship that our forefathers had loved; but Conscience told us there was no apostasy in the feelings that rose within us when that deep organ began to blow, that choir of youthful voices so sweetly to join the diapason,— our eyes fixed all the while on that divine Picture over the Altar, of our Saviour

"Bearing his cross up rueful Calvary."

The City of Palaces disappears — and in the

setting sunlight we behold mountains of soft
crimson snow! The sun hath set, and even
more beautiful are the bright-starred nights
of winter, than summer in all its glories beneath the broad moons of June. Through the
woods of Windermere, from cottage to cottage, by coppice-pathways winding up to dwellings among the hill-rocks where the birch-trees
cease to grow —

> "Nodding their heads, before us go,
>   The merry minstrelsy."

They sing a salutation at every door, familiarly
naming old and young by their Christian
names; and the eyes that look upward from
the vales to the hanging huts among the plats
and cliffs, see the shadows of the dancers ever
and anon crossing the light of the star-like window, and the merry music is heard like an echo
dwelling in the sky. Across those humble
thresholds often did we on Christmas-week
nights of yore — wandering through our solitary silvan haunts, under the branches of trees
within whose hollow trunks the squirrel slept
— venture in, unasked perhaps, but not unwel-
come, and, in the kindly spirit of the season,
did our best to merrify the Festival by tale
or song. And now that we behold them not,
are all those woods, and cliffs, and rivers, and
tarns, and lakes, as beautiful as when they
softened and brightened beneath our living

eyes, half-creating, as they gazed, the very world they worshipped! And are all those hearths as bright as of yore, without the shadow of our figure! And the roofs, do they ring as mirthfully, though our voice be forgotten. We hang over Westmoreland, an unobserved — but observant star. Mountains, hills, rocks, knolls, vales, woods, groves, single trees, dwelling — all asleep! O Lakes! but we are indeed, by far too beautiful! O fortunate Isles! too fair for human habitation, fit abode for the Blest! It will not hide itself — it will not sink into the earth — it will rise; and risen, it will stand steady with its shadow in the overpowering moonlight, that ONE TREE! that ONE HOUSE! — and well might the sight of ye two together — were it harder — break our heart. But hard at all it is not — therefore it is but crushed.

Can it be that there we are utterly forgotten! No star hanging higher than the Andes in heaven — but sole-sitting at midnight in a small chamber — a melancholy man are we — and there seems a smile of consolation, O Wordsworth! on thy sacred Bust.

Alas! how many heavenly days, " seeming immortal in their depth of rest," have died and been forgotten! Treacherous and ungrateful is our memory even of bliss that overflowed our being as light our habitation. Our spirit's deepest intercommunion with nature has no

place in her records — blanks are there that ought to have been painted with imperishable imagery, and steeped in sentiment fresh as the morning on life's golden hills. Yet there is mercy in this dispensation — for who can bear to behold the light of bliss re-arising from the past on the ghastlier gloom of present misery? The phantoms that will not come when we call on them to comfort us, are too often at our side when in our anguish we could almost pray that they might be reburied in oblivion. Such hauntings as these are not as if they were visionary — they come and go like forms and shapes still imbued with life. Shall we vainly stretch out our arms to embrace and hold them fast, or as vainly seek to intrench ourselves by thought of this world against their visitation? The soul in its sickness knows not whether it be the duty of love to resign itself to indifference or to despair. Shall it enjoy life, they being dead? Shall we, the survivors, for yet a little while, walk in other companionship out into the day, and let the sunbeams settle on their heads as they used to do, or cover them with dust and ashes, and show to those in heaven that love for them is now best expressed by remorse and penitence?

Sometimes we have fears about our memory — that it is decaying; for, lately, many ordinary yet interesting occurrences and events, which we regarded at the time with pain or

pleasure, have been slipping away almost into oblivion, and have often alarmed us of a sudden by their return, not to any act of recollection, but of themselves, sometimes wretchedly out of place and season, the mournful obtruding upon the merry, and worse, the merry upon the mournful — confusion, by no fault of ours, of piteous and gladsome faces — tears where smiles were a duty as well as a delight, and smiles where nature demanded, and religion hallowed, a sacrifice of tears.

For a good many years we have been tied to town in winter by fetters as fine as frostwork filigree, which we could not break without destroying a whole world of endearment. That seems an obscure image; but it means what the Germans would call in English — our winter environment. We are imprisoned in a net; yet we can see it when we choose — just as a bird can see, when he chooses, the wires of his cage, that are invisible in his happiness, as he keeps hopping and fluttering about all day long, or haply dreaming on his perch with his poll under his plumes — as free in confinement as if let loose into the boundless sky. That seems an obscure image too; but we mean, in truth, the prison unto which we doom ourselves no prison is; and we have improved on that idea, for we have built our own — and are prisoner, turnkey, and jailer all in one, and 'tis noiseless as the house of

sleep.   Or what if we declare that Christopner
North is a king in his palace, with no subjects
but his own thoughts — his rule peaceful over
those lights and shadows — and undisputed to
reign over them his right divine.

The opening year in a town, now answers in
all things to our heart's desire. How beautiful
the smoky air! The clouds have a homely
look as they hang over the happy families of
houses, and seem as if they loved their birthplace;— all unlike those heartless clouds that
keep *stravaigging* over mountain-tops, and
have no domicile in the sky! Poets speak of
living rocks, but what is their life to that of
houses? Who ever saw a rock with eyes —
that is, with windows? Stone-blind all, and
stone-deaf, and with hearts of stone; whereas
who ever saw a house without eyes — that is,
windows? Our own is an Argus; yet the good
old Conservative grudges not the assessed taxes
— his optics are as cheerful as the day that
lends them light, and they love to salute the
setting sun, as if a hundred beacons, level above
level, were kindled along a mountain side. He
might safely be pronounced a madman who
preferred an avenue of trees to a street. Why,
trees have no chimneys; and, were you to kindle a fire in the hollow of an oak, you would
soon be as dead as a Druid. It won't do to
talk to us of sap, and the circulation of sap.
A grove in winter, bole and branch — leaves

it has none — is as dry as a volume of sermons. But a street, or a square, is full of "vital sparks of heavenly flame" as a volume of poetry, and the heart's blood circulates through the system like rosy wine.

But a truce to comparisons; for we are beginning to feel contrition for our crime against the country, and, with humbled head and heart, we beseech you to pardon us — ye rocks of Pavey-Ark, the pillared palaces of the storms — ye clouds, now wreathing a diadem for the forehead of Helvellyn — ye trees, that hang the shadows of your undying beauty over the "one perfect chrysolite," of blessed Windermere!

Our meaning is transparent now as the hand of an apparition waving peace and good-will to all dwellers in the land of dreams. In plainer but not simpler words (for words are like flowers, often rich in their simplicity — witness the Lily, and Solomon's Song) — Christian people all, we wish you a Merry Christmas and Happy New-Year. in town or in country — or in ships at sea.

KEEPING CHRISTMAS

Romans, xiv, 6: *He that regardeth the day, regardeth it unto the Lord,*

HENRY VAN DYKE

It is a good thing to observe Christmas day. The mere marking of times and seasons, when men agree to stop work and make merry together, is a wise and wholesome custom. It helps one to feel the supremacy of the common life over the individual life. It reminds a man to set his own little watch, now and then, by the great clock of humanity which runs on sun time.

But there is a better thing than the observance of Christmas day, and that is, keeping Christmas.

Are you willing to forget what you have done for other people, and to remember what other people have done for you; to ignore what the world owes you, and to think what you owe the world; to put your rights in the background, and your duties in the middle distance, and your chances to do a little more than your duty in the foreground; to see that your fellow-men are just as real as you are, and try to look behind their faces to their hearts, hungry for joy; to own that probably the only good reason for your existence is not what you are going to get out of life, but what you are going to give to life; to close your book of complaints against the management of the universe, and look around you for a place where you can sow a few seeds of happiness — are you willing to do these things even for a day? Then you can keep Christmas.

Are you willing to stoop down and consider the needs and the desires of little children; to remember the weakness and loneliness of people who are growing old; to stop asking how much your friends love you, and ask yourself whether you love them enough; to bear in mind the things that other people have to bear in their hearts; to try to understand what those who live in the same house with you really want, without waiting for them to tell you; to trim your lamp so that it will give more light and less smoke, and to carry it in front so that your shadow will fall behind you; to make a grave for your ugly thoughts and a garden for your kindly feelings, with the gate open — are you willing to do these things even for a day? Then you can keep Christmas.

Are you willing to believe that love is the strongest thing in the world — stronger than hate, stronger than evil, stronger than death — and that the blessed life which began in Beth-

lehem nineteen hundred years ago is the image
and brightness of the Eternal Love? Then
you can keep Christmas,

And if you keep it for a day, why not always?
But you can never keep it alone.

MARK WELL MY HEAVY DOLEFUL TALE

ANONYMOUS

Mark well my heavy doleful tale,
For Twelfth-day now is come,
And now I must no longer sing,
And say no words but mum;
For I perforce must take my leave
Of all my dainty cheer,
Plum-porridge, roast beef, and minced pies,
My strong ale and my beer.

Kind-hearted Christmas, now adieu,
For I with thee must part,
And for to take my leave of thee
Doth grieve me at the heart;
Thou wert an ancient housekeeper,
And mirth with meat didst keep,
But thou art going out of town,
Which makes me for to weep.

God knoweth whether I again
Thy merry face shall see,

Which to good-fellows and the poor
  That was so frank and free.
Thou lovedst pastime with thy heart,
  And eke good company;
Pray hold me up for fear I swoon,
  For I am like to die.

Come, butler, fill a brimmer up
  To cheer my fainting heart,
That to old Christmas I may drink
  Before he doth depart;
And let each one that's in this room
  With me likewise condole,
And for to cheer their spirits sad
  Let each one drink a bowl.

And when the same it hath gone round
  Then fall unto your cheer,
For you do know that Christmas time
  It comes but once a year.
But this good draught which I have drunk
  Hath comforted my heart,
For I was very fearful that
  My stomach would depart.

Thanks to my master and my dame
  That doth such cheer afford;
God bless them, that each Christmas they
  May furnish thus their board.
My stomach having come to me,
  I mean to have a bout,
Intending to eat most heartily;
  Good friends, I do not flout.

A CHRISTMAS CAROL

CHRISTINA G. ROSSETTI

In the bleak mid-winter
  Frosty wind made moan,
Earth stood hard as iron,
  Water like a stone;
Snow had fallen, snow on snow,
  Snow on snow,
In the bleak mid-winter
  Long ago.

Our God, Heaven cannot hold him
  Nor earth sustain;
Heaven and earth shall flee away,
  When he comes to reign.
In the bleak mid-winter
  A stable-place sufficed
The Lord God Almighty,
  Jesus Christ.

Angels and archangels
  May have gathered there;
Cherubim and seraphim
  Thronged the air.
But only His Mother,
  In her maiden bliss,
Worshipped her Beloved
  With a kiss.

What can I give Him,
　　Poor as I am?
If I were a shepherd
　　I would bring a lamb;
If I were a wise man,
　　I would do my part,—
Yet what I can I give Him,
　　Give my heart.

THE GLORIOUS SONG OF OLD

EDMUND H. SEARS

It came upon the midnight clear,
　　That glorious song of old,
From angels bending near the earth
　　To touch their harps of gold,
" Peace on the earth, good-will to men,
　　From heaven's all-gracious King "—
The world in solemn stillness lay
　　To hear the angels sing.

Still through the cloven skies they come.
　　With peaceful wings unfurled,
And still their heavenly music floats
　　O'er all the weary world;
Above its sad and lowly plains
　　They bend on hovering wing,
And ever o'er its Babel-sounds
　　The blessed angels sing.

But with the woes of sin and strife
  The world has suffered long;
Beneath the angel-strain have rolled
  Two thousand years of wrong.
And man at war with man hears not
  The love-song which they bring;
Oh, hush the noise, ye men of strife,
  And hear the angels sing!

And ye beneath life's crushing load,
  Whose forms are bending low,
Who toil along the climbing way
  With painful steps and slow,
Look now! for glad and golden hours
  Come swiftly on the wing:—
Oh, rest beside the weary road
  And hear the angels sing!

For lo! the days the hastening on
  By prophet-bards foretold,
When with the ever-circling years
  Comes round the age of gold;
When peace shall over all the earth
  Its ancient splendors fling,
And the whole world give back the song
  Which now the angels sing.

———

A CHRISTMAS CAROL FOR CHILDREN

MARTIN LUTHER

Good news from heaven the angels bring,
Glad tidings to the earth they sing:
To us this day a child is given,
To crown us with the joy of heaven.

This is the Christ, our God and Lord,
Who in all need shall aid afford:
He will Himself our Saviour be,
From sin and sorrow set us free.

To us that blessedness He brings,
Which from the Father's bounty springs:
That in the heavenly realm we may
With Him enjoy eternal day.

All hail, Thou noble Guest, this morn,
Whose love did not the sinner scorn!
In my distress Thou cam'st to me:
What thanks shall I return to Thee?

Were earth a thousand times as fair,
Beset with gold and jewels rare,
She yet were far too poor to be
A narrow cradle, Lord, for Thee.

Ah, dearest Jesus, Holy Child!
Make Thee a bed, soft, undefiled,

Within my heart, that it may be
A quiet chamber kept for Thee.

Praise God upon His heavenly throne,
Who gave to us His only Son:
For this His hosts, on joyful wing,
A blest New Year of mercy sing.

ON SANTA CLAUS

GEORGE A. BAKER, JR.

Brave old times those were. In the first half of the seventeenth century, we mean; before there was any such place as New York and Manhattan Island was occupied mostly by woods, and had a funny little Dutch town, known as New Amsterdam, sprouting out of the southern end of it. Those were the days of solid comfort, of mighty pipes, and unctuous doughnuts. Winter had not yet been so much affected by artificiality as he is now-a-days, and was contented to be what he is, not trying to pass himself off for Spring; and Christmas — well, it was Christmas. Do you know why? Because in those times Santa Claus used to live in a great old house in the midst of an evergreen forest, just back of the Hudson, and about half-way between New Amsterdam and Albany. A house built out of funny little Dutch bricks, with gables whose sides looked like stair-cases, and a roof of red tiles with more weathercocks and chimneys sticking out of it than you could count. Phew, how cold it was there! The wind roared and

shouted around the house, and the snow fell steadily half the year, so that the summers never melted it away till winter came again. And Santa Claus thought that was the greatest pleasure in life: for he loved to have enormous fires in the great fire-places, and the colder it was, the bigger fires he would have, and the louder the winds roared around his chimney. There he sat and worked away all the year round, making dolls, and soldiers, and Noah's arks, and witches, and every other sort of toy you can think of. When Christmas Eve came he'd harness up his reindeers, Dasher, and Prancer, and Vixen, and the rest of them, and wrap himself up in furs, and light his big pipe, and cram his sled full of the doll-babies and Noah's arks, and all the other toys he'd been making, and off he'd go with a great shout and tremendous ringing of sleigh-bells. Before morning he'd be up and down every chimney in New Amsterdam, filling the stout grey yarn stockings with toys, and apples, and ginger-bread, laughing and chuckling so all the while, that the laughs and chuckles didn't get out of the air for a week afterwards.

But the old house has gone to ruin, and Santa Claus doesn't live there any longer. You see he married about forty years ago; his wife was a Grundy, daughter of old Mrs. Grundy, of Fifth Avenue, of whom you've all heard.

She married him for his money, and couldn't put up with his plain way of living and his careless jollity. He is such an easy-going, good natured old soul, that she manages him without any trouble. So the first thing she did was to make him change his name to St. Nicholas; then she made him give up his old house, and move into town; then she sent away the reindeers, for she didn't know what Ma *would* say to such an outlandish turn-out; then she threw away his pipe because it was vulgar, and the first Christmas Eve that he went off and stayed out all night she had hysterics, and declared she'd go home to her Ma, and get a divorce if he ever did such a thing again. She'd have put a stop to his giving away toys every year, too, only she thought it looked well, and as it was, she wouldn't let him make them himself any more, but compelled him to spend enormous sums in bringing them from Paris, and Vienna, and Nuremberg.

So now Santa Claus is St. Nicholas, and lives in a brown stone house on Fifth Avenue, a great deal handsomer than he can afford, and keeps a carriage, not because he wants it, but because Mrs. Shoddy, next door, keeps one; and loves, not to be jolly himself and to make everybody else so, but to please his wife's mother. He has to give an awful pull, what with his wife's extravagance, and the high prices of Parisian and Viennese toys, to make

both ends meet, although he does speculate in stocks, and is very lucky. Instead of looking forward to Christmas with pleasure, and thinking what a good time he will have, he pulls out his ledger, and groans, and wonders how on earth he's going to make his presents this year, and thinks he would stop giving them entirely, only he's so mortally afraid of his mother-in-law, and he knows what she'd say if he did. So he borrows money wherever he can, and sends over to Paris for fans, and opera-glasses, and bon-bon boxes, and jewelry, and when they come he sits down in his parlor and lets his wife tell him just what to do with them. So she takes out her list and runs over the names; she has all the rich people down, for she is a religious woman, and the Bible says " unto him that hath, it shall be given." This is the way she talks: " The little Crœsuses must have some very elegant things, of course; their mother's a horrid old cat, but Crœsus could help you very much in business. And there are the Centlivres; we must pick out something magnificent for them; they give a party Christmas night: of course the presents will be on exhibition, and I shall sink with shame if any one else's are handsomer than ours." So she goes on, until all the rich people are disposed of. Then Santa Claus asks: " How about the Brinkers, my dear?" The Brinkers are great favorites of his. " Good

gracious, dearest! How often have I told you, you mustn't manifest such an interest in those Brinkers? What would Ma say if she knew you associated with such common people!" "But, I'm Dutch myself, pet." "Of course you are, darling, but there's no need of letting every one know it!" St. Nicholas hardly dares to do it, but he finally suggests very meekly: "The poor children, my darling." "Bother the poor children, my dear!" They're a most affectionate couple, you know. Then St. Nicholas sighs and sighs, and sends for his messengers, and they all come in with long faces, and take off big packages to the Crœsuses and the Centlivres, and the rest of them. The messengers do their work entirely as a matter of business, so there isn't a sign of a laugh, nor a symptom of a chuckle in the air next day. The little Crœsuses first cry, because they haven't received more, and then fight over what they have; then they eat too much French candy, and get sick and cross, and the whole house is filled with their noise. So mamma has a headache; and papa longs for his office, and misses the tick-tick of the stock telegraph, and thinks what a confounded nuisance holidays are. That is what Christmas is like in good society.

But I must tell you a secret. Away up in the fourth-story of his grand house, where his wife never goes, St. Nicholas has a little workshop, and there he sits whenever he gets a

chance, making the most wonderful dolls, and gorgeous soldiers, and miraculous jumping-jacks, and tin horns — such quantities of tin horns! Some one ought to speak to him about those tin horns. But after all they please the poor children, so we suppose it's all right. Now do you know what he does with these things? On Christmas Eve he gets his old sled down from the stable away up by the North Pole, and as soon as his wife is fast asleep, he puts on his old furs and gets out from under his shirts in his bureau drawer a Dutch pipe, three times as big as the one his wife threw away, and off he goes. He tumbles down all the poor people's chimneys, and fills up the stockings to overflowing, and plants gorgeous Christmas trees in all the Mission schools.

He has a glorious good time, and laughs and chuckles tremendously, except when, once in a while, he thinks of what would happen if his wife found him out.

So there's a little fun going on after all.

Do you know, if it were not for this performance of his, we should wish with all our heart that St. Nicholas were dead and buried. But we must say, we wish his wife would die, and that all the Grundy family would follow her good example, for between them they've spoiled a good many jolly people besides St. Nicholas.

A CHRISTMAS CAROL

JOSIAH GILBERT HOLLAND

There's a song in the air!
There's a star in the sky!
There's a mother's deep prayer
And a baby's low cry!
And the star rains its fire while the Beautiful
   sing,
For the manger of Bethlehem cradles a king.

There's a tumult of joy
O'er the wonderful birth,
For the virgin's sweet boy
Is the Lord of the earth,
Ay! the star rains its fire and the Beautiful
   sing,
For the manger of Bethlehem cradles a king.

In the light of that star
Lie the ages impearled;
And that song from afar
Has swept over the world.
Every hearth is aflame, and the Beautiful sing
In the homes of the nations that Jesus is King.

We rejoice in the light,
And we echo the song
That comes down through the night
From the heavenly throng.

Ay! we shout to the lovely evangel they bring,
And we greet in his cradle our Saviour and
    King!

———

AN OFFERTORY

MARY MAPES DODGE

Oh, the beauty of the Christ Child,
    The gentleness, the grace,
    The smiling, loving tenderness,
    The infantile embrace!
      All babyhood he holdeth,
      All motherhood enfoldeth —
    Yet who hath seen his face?

Oh, the nearness of the Christ Child,
    When, for a sacred space,
    He nestles in our very homes —
    Light of the human race!
      We know him and we love him,
      No man to us need prove him —
    Yet who hath seen his face?

———

CHRISTMAS SONG

LYDIA A. C. WARD

Why do bells for Christmas ring?
Why do little children sing?

Once a lovely, shining star,
Seen by shepherds from afar,
Gently moved until its light
Made a manger-cradle bright.

There a darling baby lay
Pillowed soft upon the hay.
And his mother sang and smiled,
"This is Christ, the holy child."

So the bells for Christmas ring,
So the little children sing.

A CHRISTMAS CAROL

CHRISTIAN BURKE

The trees are hung with crystal lamps, the
    world lies still and white,
And the myriad little twinkling stars are sharp
    with keener light;
The moon sails up the frost-clear sky and sil-
    vers all the snow,
As she did, perchance, that Christmas night,
    two thousand years ago!
    Good people, are you waking?
      Give us food and give us wine,
    For the sake of blessed Mary
      And her Infant Son Divine,
    Who was born the world's Redeemer —
      A Saviour — yours and mine!

Long ago angelic harpers sang the song we
    sing to-day,
And the drowsy folk of Bethlehem may have
    listened as they lay!
But eager shepherds left their flocks, and o'er
    the desert wild
The kingly sages journeyed to adore the Holy
    Child!
    Has any man a quarrel?
      Has another used you ill?
    The friendly word you meant to say,
      Is that unspoken still? —
    Then, remember, 'twas the Angels
      Brought glad tidings of good will!

Of all the gifts of Christmas, are you fain to
    win the best?
Lo! the Christ-child still is waiting Himself to
    be your guest;
No lot so high or lowly but He will take His
    part,
If you do but bid Him welcome to a clean and
    tender heart.
    Are you sleeping, are you waking?
      To the Manger haste away,
    And you shall see a wond'rous sight
      Amid the straw and hay.—
    'Tis Love Himself Incarnate
      As on this Christmas Day!

A SIMPLE BILL OF FARE FOR A CHRISTMAS DINNER

H. H.

All good recipe-books give bills of fare for
different occasions, bills of fare for grand dinners, bills of fare for little dinners; dinners
to cost so much per head; dinners " which can
be easily prepared with one servant," and so
on. They give bills of fare for one week;
bills of fare for each day in a month, to avoid
too great monotony in diet. There are bills
of fare for dyspeptics; bills of fare for con-
sumptives; bills of fare for fat people, and
bills of fare for thin; and bills of fare for
hospitals, asylums, and prisons, as well as for
gentlemen's houses. But among them all, we
never saw the one which we give below. It
has never been printed in any book; but it has
been used in families. We are not drawing on
our imagination for its items. We have sat at
such dinners; we have helped prepare such
dinners; we believe in such dinners; they are
within everybody's means. In fact, the most
marvellous thing about this bill of fare is that
the dinner does not cost a cent. Ho! all ye

that are hungry and thirsty, and would like so cheap a Christmas dinner, listen to this:

BILL OF FARE FOR A CHRISTMAS DINNER

First Course — Gladness.

This must be served hot. No two house-keepers make it alike; no fixed rule can be given for it. It depends, like so many of the best things, chiefly on memory; but, strangely enough, it depends quite as much on proper forgetting as on proper remembering. Worries must be forgotten. Troubles must be forgotten. Yes, even sorrow itself must be denied and shut out. Perhaps this is not quite possible. Ah! we all have seen Christmas days on which sorrow would not leave our hearts nor our houses. But even sorrow can be compelled to look away from its sorrowing for a festival hour which is so solemnly joyous at Christ's Birthday. Memory can be filled full of other things to be remembered. No soul is entirely destitute of blessings, absolutely without comfort. Perhaps we have but one. Very well; we can think steadily of that one, if we try. But the probability is that we have more than we can count. No man has yet numbered the blessings, the mercies, the joys of God. We are all richer than we think; and if we once set ourselves to reckoning up the things of which we are glad, we shall be astonished at their number.

Gladness, then, is the first item, the first course on our bill of fare for a Christmas dinner.

Entrées.— Love garnished with Smiles.

GENTLENESS, with sweet-wine sauce of Laughter.

GRACIOUS SPEECH, cooked with any fine, savory herbs, such as Frollery, which is always in season, or Pleasant Reminiscence, which no one need be without, as it keeps for years, sealed or unsealed.

Second Course — HOSPITALITY.

The precise form of this also depends on individual preferences. We are not undertaking here to give exact recipes, only a bill of fare.

In some houses Hospitality is brought on surrounded with Relatives. This is very well. In others, it is dished up with Dignitaries of all sorts; men and women of position and estate for whom the host has special likings or uses. This gives a fine effect to the eye, but cools quickly, and is not in the long-run satisfying.

In a third class, best of all, it is served in simple shapes, but with a great variety of Unfortunate Persons,— such as lonely people from lodging-houses, poor people of all grades, widows and childless in their affliction. This is the kind most preferred; in fact, never abandoned by those who have tried it.

For Dessert.— MIRTH, in glasses.

GRATITUDE and FAITH beaten together and piled up in snowy shapes. These will look light if run over night in the moulds of Solid Trust and Patience.

A dish of the bonbons Good Cheer and Kindliness with every-day mottoes; Knots and Reasons in shape of Puzzles and Answers; the whole ornamented with Apples of Gold in Pictures of Silver, of the kind mentioned in the Book of Proverbs.

This is a short and simple bill of fare. There is not a costly thing in it; not a thing which cannot be procured without difficulty.

If meat be desired, it can be added. That is another excellence about our bill of fare. It has nothing in it which makes it incongruous with the richest or the plainest tables. It is not overcrowded by the addition of roast goose and plum-pudding; it is not harmed by the addition of herring and potatoes. Nay, it can give flavor and richness to broken bits of stale bread served on a doorstep and eaten by beggars.

We might say much more about this bill of fare. We might, perhaps, confess that it has an element of the supernatural; that its origin is lost in obscurity; that, although, as we said, it has never been printed before, it has been known in all ages; that the martyrs feasted upon it; that generations of the poor, called

blessed by Christ, have laid out banquets by it; that exiles and prisoners have lived on it; and the despised and forsaken and rejected in all countries have tasted it. It is also true that when any great king ate well and throve on his dinner, it was by the same magic food. The young and the free and the glad, and all rich men in costly houses, even they have not been well fed without it.

And though we have called it a Bill of Fare for a Christmas Dinner, that is only that men's eyes may be caught by its name, and that they, thinking it a specialty for festival, may learn and understand its secret, and henceforth, laying all their dinners according to its magic order, may " eat unto the Lord."

A BALLADE OF OLD LOVES

CAROLYN WELLS

Who is it stands on the polished stair,
    A merry, laughing, winsome maid,
From the Christmas rose in her golden hair
    To the high-heeled slippers of spangled suede
A glance, half daring and half afraid,
    Gleams from her roguish eyes downcast;
Already the vision begins to fade —
    ' Tis only a ghost of a Christmas Past.

Who is it sits in that high-backed chair,
  Quaintly in ruff and patch arrayed,
With a mockery gay of a stately air
  As she rustles the folds of her old brocade,—
Merriest heart at the masquerade?
  Ah, but the picture is passing fast
Back to the darkness from which it strayed —
  'Tis only a ghost of a Christmas Past.

Who is it whirls in a ball-room's glare,
  Her soft white hand on my shoulder laid,
Like a radiant lily, tall and fair,
  While the violins in the corner played
The wailing strains of the Serenade?
  Oh, lovely vision, too sweet to last —
E'en now my fancy it will evade —
  'Tis only a ghost of a Christmas Past.

L' ENVOI

Rosamond! look not so dismayed,
  All of my heart, dear love, thou hast
Jealous, beloved? Of a shade?—
  'Tis only a ghost of a Christmas Past.

BALLADE OF CHRISTMAS GHOSTS

ANDREW LANG

Between the moonlight and the fire
In winter twilights long ago,

What ghosts we raised for your desire,
To make your merry blood run slow!
How old, how grave, how wise we grow!
No Christmas ghost can make us chill,
Save those that troop in mournful row,
The ghosts we all can raise at will!

The beasts can talk in barn and byre
On Christmas Eve, old legends know.
As year by year the years retire,
We men fall silent then I trow,
Such sights hath memory to show,
Such voices from the silence thrill,
Such shapes return with Christmas snow,—
The ghosts we all can raise at will.

Oh, children of the village choir,
Your carols on the midnight throw,
Oh, bright across the mist and mire,
Ye ruddy hearths of Christmas glow!
Beat back the dread, beat down the woe,
Let's cheerily descend the hill;
Be welcome all, to come or go,
The ghosts we all can raise at will.

ENVOY

Friend, sursum corda, soon or slow
We part, like guests who've joyed their fill;
Forget them not, nor mourn them so,
The ghosts we all can raise at will.

HANG UP THE BABY'S STOCKING

Hang up the baby's stocking:
  Be sure you don't forget;
The dear little dimpled darling!
  She ne'er saw Christmas yet;

But I've told her all about it,
  And she opened her big blue eyes,
And I'm sure she understood it —
  She looked so funny and wise.

Dear! what a tiny stocking!
  It doesn't take much to hold
Such little pink toes as baby's
  Away from the frost and cold.
But then for the baby's Christmas
  It will never do at all;
Why, Santa wouldn't be looking
  For anything half so small.

I know what will do for the baby.
  I've thought of the very best plan:
I'll borrow a stocking of grandma,
  The longest that ever I can;
And you'll hang it by mine, dear mother,
  Right here in the corner, so!
And write a letter to Santa,
  And fasten it on to the toe.

Write, " This is the baby's stocking
   That hangs in the corner here;
You never have seen her, Santa,
   For she only came this year;
But she's just the blessedest baby!
   And now, before you go,
Just cram her stocking with goodies,
   From the top clean down to the toe."

THE NEWEST THING IN CHRISTMAS CAROLS

ANONYMOUS

God rest you, merry gentlemen!
   May nothing you dismay;
Not even the dyspeptic plats
   Through which you'll eat your way;
Nor yet the heavy Christmas bills
   The season bids you pay;
No, nor the ever tiresome need
   Of being to order gay;

Nor yet the shocking cold you'll catch
   If fog and slush hold sway;
Nor yet the tumbles you must bear
   If frost should win the day;
Nor   sleepless   nights — they're   sure   to
      come —
   When " waits " attune their lay;

Nor pantomimes, whose dreariness
  Might turn macassar gray;

Nor boisterous children, home in heaps,
  And ravenous of play;
Nor yet — in fact, the host of ills
  Which Christmases array.
God rest you, merry gentlemen,
  May none of these dismay!

———

A CHRISTMAS LETTER FROM AUSTRALIA

DOUGLAS SLADEN

'Tis Christmas, and the North wind blows;
      'twas two years yesterday
Since from the Lusitania's bows I looked o'er
      Table Bay,
A tripper round the narrow world, a pilgrim of
      the main,
Expecting when her sails unfurled to start for
      home again.

'Tis Christmas, and the North wind blows; to-
      day our hearts are one,
Though you are 'mid the English snows and I
      in Austral sun;
You, when you hear the Northern blast, pile
      high a mightier fire,

Our ladies cower until it's past in lawn and lace
    attire.

I fancy I can picture you upon this Christmas
    night,
Just sitting as you used to do, the laughter at its
    height;
And then a sudden, silent pause intruding on
    your glee,
And kind eyes glistening because you chanced
    to think of me.

This morning when I woke and knew 'twas
    Christmas come again,
I almost fancied I could view white rime upon
    the pane,
And hear the ringing of the wheels upon the
    frosty ground,
And see the drip that downward steals in icy
    casket bound.

I daresay you'll be on the lake, or sliding on the
    snow,
And breathing on your hands to make the cir-
    culation flow,
Nestling your nose among the furs of which
    your boa's made,—
The Fahrenheit here registers a hundred in the
    shade.

It is not quite a Christmas here with this un-
    clouded sky,

This pure transparent atmosphere, this sun mid-
    heaven-high;
To see the rose upon the bush, young leaves
    upon the trees,
And hear the forest's summer hush or the low
    hum of bees.

But cold winds bring not Christmastide, nor
    budding roses June,
And when it's night upon your side we're bask-
    ing in the noon.
Kind hearts make Christmas — June can bring
    blue sky or clouds above;
The only universal spring is that which comes
    of love.

And so it's Christmas in the South as on the
    North-sea coasts,
Though we are staved with summer-drouth and
    you with winter frosts.
And we shall have our roast beef here, and
    think of you the while,
Though all the watery hemisphere cuts off the
    mother isle.

Feel sure that we shall think of you, we who
    have wandered forth,
And many a million thoughts will go to-day
    from south to north;
Old heads will muse on churches old, where
    bells will ring to-day —

The very bells, perchance, which tolled their
    fathers to the clay.

And now, good-night! and I shall dream that
    I am with you all,
Watching the ruddy embers gleam athwart the
    panelled hall;
Nor care I if I dream or not, though severed
    by the foam,
My heart is always in the spot which was my
    childhood's home.

CHRISTMAS

ROSE TERRY COOKE

Here comes old Father Christmas,
    With sound of fife and drums;
With mistletoe about his brows,
    So merrily he comes!
His arms are full of all good cheer,
    His face with laughter glows,
He shines like any household fire
    Amid the cruel snows.
He is the old folks' Christmas;
    He warms their hearts like wine;
He thaws their winter into spring,
    And makes their faces shine.
Hurrah for Father Christmas!
    Ring all the merry bells!

And bring the grandsires all around
  To hear the tale he tells.

Here comes the Christmas angel,
  So gentle and so calm;
As softly as the falling flakes
  He comes with flute and psalm.
All in a cloud of glory,
  As once upon the plain
To shepherd-boys in Jewry,
  He brings good news again.
He is the young folks' Christmas;
  He makes their eyes grow bright
With words of hope and tender thought,
  And visions of delight.
Hail to the Christmas angel!
  All peace on earth he brings;
He gathers all the youths and maids
  Beneath his shining wings.

Here comes the little Christ-child,
  All innocence and joy,
And bearing gifts in either hand
  For every girl and boy.
He tells the tender story
  About the Holy Maid,
And Jesus in the manger
  Before the oxen laid.
Like any little winter bird
  He sings his sweetest song,
Till all the cherubs in the sky
  To hear his carol throng.

He is the children's Christmas;
   They come without a call,
To gather round the gracious Child,
   Who bringeth joy to all.

But who shall bring *their* Christmas
   Who wrestle still with life?
Not grandsires, youths, or little folks,
   But they who wage the strife —
The fathers and the mothers
   Who fight for homes and bread,
Who watch and ward the living,
   And bury all the dead?
Ah! by their side at Christmas-tide
   The Lord of Christmas stands:
He smooths the furrows from their brow
   With strong and tender hands.
" I take my Christmas gift," He saith,
   " From thee, tired soul, and he
Who giveth to My little ones
   Gives also unto Me."

CHRISTMAS
STORIES

THE FIR TREE

HANS CHRISTIAN ANDERSEN

Out in the forest stood a pretty little Fir
Tree. It had a good place; it could have sunlight, air there was in plenty, and all around
grew many larger comrades — pines as well
as firs. But the little Fir Tree wished ardently
to become greater. It did not care for the
warm sun and the fresh air; it took no notice
of the peasant children, who went about talking together, when they had come out to look
for strawberries and raspberries. Often they
came with a whole pot-full, or had strung berries on a straw; then they would sit down by
the little Fir Tree and say, "How pretty and
small that one is!" and the Tree did not like
to hear that at all.

Next year he had grown a great joint, and
the following year he was longer still, for in
fir trees one can always tell by the number of
rings they have how many years they have
been growing.

"Oh, if I were only as great a tree as the
others!" sighed the little Fir, "then I would
spread my branches far around, and look out

from my crown into the wide world. The birds would then build nests in my boughs, and when the wind blew I could nod just as grandly as the others yonder."

He took no pleasure in the sunshine, in the birds, and in the red clouds that went sailing over him morning and evening.

When it was winter, and the snow lay all around, white and sparkling, a hare would often come jumping along, and spring right over the little Fir Tree. Oh! this made him so angry. But two winters went by, and when the third came the little Tree had grown so tall that the hare was obliged to run around it.

"Oh! to grow, to grow, and become old; that's the only fine thing in the world," thought the Tree.

In the autumn woodcutters always came and felled a few of the largest trees; that was done this year too, and the little Fir Tree, that was now quite well grown, shuddered with fear, for the great stately trees fell to the ground with a crash, and their branches were cut off, so that the trees looked quite naked, long, and slender — they could hardly be recognized. But then they were laid upon waggons, and horses dragged them away out of the wood. Where were they going? What destiny awaited them?

In the spring, when the swallows and the

Stork came, the Tree asked them, " Do you know where they were taken? Did you not meet them?"

The swallows knew nothing about it, but the Stork looked thoughtful, nodded his head, and said,

" Yes, I think so. I met many new ships when I flew out of Egypt; on the ships were stately masts; I fancy that these were the trees. They smelt like fir. I can assure you they're stately — very stately."

" Oh that I were only big enough to go over the sea! What kind of thing is this sea, and how does it look?"

" It would take too long to explain all that," said the Stork, and he went away.

" Rejoice in thy youth," said the Sunbeams; " rejoice in thy fresh growth, and in the young life that is within thee."

And the wind kissed the Tree, and the dew wept tears upon it; but the Fir Tree did not understand that.

When Christmas-time approached, quite young trees were felled, sometimes trees which were neither so old nor so large as this Fir Tree, that never rested but always wanted to go away. These young trees, which were almost the most beautiful, kept all their branches; they were put upon wagons, and horses dragged them away out of the wood.

" Where are they all going?" asked the Fir

Tree. "They are not greater than I — indeed, one of them was much smaller. Why do they keep all their branches? Whither are they taken?"

"We know that! We know that!" chirped the Sparrows. "Yonder in the town we looked in at the windows. We know where they go. Oh! they are dressed up in the greatest pomp and splendor that can be imagined. We have looked in at the windows, and have perceived that they are planted in the middle of the warm room, and adorned with the most beautiful things — gilt apples, honey-cakes, playthings, and many hundreds of candles."

"And then?" asked the Fir Tree, and trembled through all its branches. "And then? What happens then?"

"Why, we have not seen anything more. But it was incomparable."

"Perhaps I may be destined to tread this glorious path one day!" cried the Fir Tree rejoicingly. "That is even better than traveling across the sea. How painfully I long for it! If it were only Christmas now! Now I am great and grown up, like the rest who were led away last year. Oh, if I were only on the carriage! If I were only in the warm room, among all the pomp and splendor! And then? Yes, then something even better will come, something far more charming, or else why should they adorn me so? There must be

something grander, something greater still to come; but what? Oh, I'm suffering, I'm longing! I don't know myself what is the matter with me!"

"Rejoice in us," said Air and Sunshine. "Rejoice in thy fresh youth here in the woodland."

But the Fir Tree did not rejoice at all, but it grew and grew; winter and summer it stood there, green, dark green. The people who saw it said, "That's a handsome tree!" and at Christmas-time it was felled before any one of the others. The axe cut deep into its marrow, and the tree fell to the ground with a sigh: it felt a pain, a sensation of faintness, and could not think at all of happiness, for it was sad at parting from its home, from the place where it had grown up: it knew that it should never again see the dear old companions, the little bushes and flowers all around — perhaps not even the birds. The parting was not at all agreeable.

The Tree only came to itself when it was unloaded in a yard, with other trees, and heard a man say,

"This one is famous; we only want this one!"

Now two servants came in gay liveries, and carried the Fir Tree into a large beautiful saloon. All around the walls hung pictures, and by the great stove stood large Chinese vases

with lions on the covers; there were rocking-chairs, silken sofas, great tables covered with picture-books, and toys worth a hundred times a hundred dollars, at least the children said so. And the Fir Tree was put into a great tub filled with sand; but no one could see that it was a tub, for it was hung round with green cloth, and stood on a large many-colored carpet. Oh, how the Tree trembled! What was to happen now? The servants, and the young ladies also, decked it out. On one branch they hung little nets, cut out of colored paper; every net was filled with sweetmeats; golden apples and walnuts hung down as if they grew there, and more than a hundred little candles, red, white, and blue, were fastened to the different boughs. Dolls that looked exactly like real people — the Tree had never seen such before — swung among the foliage, and high on the summit of the Tree was fixed a tinsel star. It was splendid, particularly splendid.

"This evening," said all, "this evening it will shine."

"Oh," thought the Tree, "that it were evening already! Oh that the lights may be soon lit up! When may that be done? I wonder if trees will come out of the forest to look at me? Will the sparrows fly against the panes? Shall I grow fast here, and stand adorned in summer and winter?"

Yes, he did not guess badly. But he had a

complete backache from mere longing, and the backache is just as bad for a Tree as the headache for a person.

At last the candles were lighted. What a brilliance, what splendor! The Tree trembled so in all its branches that one of the candles set fire to a green twig, and it was scorched.

" Heaven preserve us!" cried the young ladies; and they hastily put the fire out.

Now the Tree might not even tremble. Oh, that was terrible! It was so afraid of setting fire to some of its ornaments, and it was quite bewildered with all the brilliance. And now the folding doors were thrown open, and a number of children rushed in as if they would have overturned the whole Tree; the older people followed more deliberately. The little ones stood quite silent, but only for a minute; then they shouted till the room rang: they danced gleefully round the Tree, and one present after another was plucked from it.

" What are they about?" laughed the Tree. " What's going to be done?"

And the candles burned down to the twigs, and as they burned down they were extinguished, and then the children received permission to plunder the Tree. Oh! they rushed in upon it, so that every branch cracked again: if it had not been fastened by the top and by the golden star to the ceiling, it would have fallen down.

The children danced about with their pretty toys. No one looked at the Tree except one old man, who came up and peeped among the branches, but only to see if a fig or an apple had not been forgotten.

"A story! a story!" shouted the children: and they drew a little fat man towards the Tree; and he sat down just beneath it,—"for then we shall be in the green wood," said he, "and the tree may have the advantage of listening to my tale. But I can only tell one. Will you hear the story of Ivede-Avede, or of Klumpey-Dumpey, who fell down stairs, and still was raised up to honor and married the Princess?"

"Ivede-Avede!" cried some, "Klumpey-Dumpey!" cried others, and there was a great crying and shouting. Only the Fir Tree was quite silent, and thought, "Shall I not be in it? shall I have nothing to do in it?" But he had been in the evening's amusement, and had done what was required of him.

And the fat man told about Klumpey-Dumpey, who fell down stairs, and yet was raised to honor and married the Princess. And the children clapped their hands, and cried, "Tell another! tell another!" for they wanted to hear about Ivede-Avede; but they only got the story of Klumpey-Dumpey. The Fir Tree stood quite silent and thoughtful; never had the birds in the wood told such a story as that.

Klumpey-Dumpey fell down stairs, and yet came to honor and married the Princess!

"Yes, so it happens in the world!" thought the Fir Tree, and believed it must be true, because that was such a nice man who told it. "Well, who can know? Perhaps I shall fall down stairs too, and marry a Princess!" And it looked forward with pleasure to being adorned again, the next evening, with candles and toys, gold and fruit. "To-morrow I shall not tremble," it thought. "I will rejoice in all my splendor. To-morrow I shall hear the story of Klumpey-Dumpey again, and, perhaps, that of Ivede-Avede too."

And the Tree stood all night quiet and thoughtful.

In the morning the servants and the chambermaid came in.

"Now my splendor will begin afresh," thought the Tree. But they dragged him out of the room, and up stairs to the garret, and here they put him in a dark corner where no daylight shone.

"What's the meaning of this?" thought the Tree. "What am I to do here? What is to happen?"

And he leaned against the wall, and thought, and thought. And he had time enough, for days and nights went by, and nobody came up; and when at length some one came, it was only to put some great boxes in a corner.

Now the Tree stood quite hidden away, and the supposition was that it was quite forgotten.

"Now it's winter outside," thought the Tree. "The earth is hard and covered with snow, and people cannot plant me; therefore I suppose I'm to be sheltered here until spring comes. How considerate that is! How good people are! If it were only not so dark here, and so terribly solitary! — not even a little hare! That was pretty out there in the wood, when the snow lay thick and the hare sprang past; yes, even when he jumped over me; but then I did not like it. It is terribly lonely up here!"

"Piep! piep!" said a little Mouse, and crept forward, and then came another little one. They smelt at the Fir Tree, and then slipped among the branches.

"It's horribly cold," said the two little Mice, "or else it would be comfortable here. Don't you think so, you old Fir Tree?"

"I'm not old at all," said the Fir Tree. "There are many much older than I."

"Where do you come from?" asked the Mice. "And what do you know?" They were dreadfully inquisitive. "Tell us about the most beautiful spot on earth. Have you been there? Have you been in the store-room, where cheeses lie on the shelves, and hams hang from the ceiling, where one dances on

tallow candles, and goes in thin and comes out fat?"

"I don't know that!" replied the Tree; "but I know the wood, where the sun shines, and where the birds sing."

And then it told all about its youth.

And the little Mice had never heard anything of the kind; and they listened and said,

"What a number of things you have seen! How happy you must have been!"

"I?" said the Fir Tree; and it thought about what it had told. "Yes, those were really quite happy times." But then he told of the Christmas-eve, when he had been hung with sweetmeats and candles.

"Oh!" said the little Mice, "how happy you have been, you old Fir Tree!"

"I'm not old at all," said the Tree. "I only came out of the wood this winter. I'm only rather backward in my growth."

"What splendid stories you can tell!" said the little Mice.

And next night they came with four other little Mice, to hear what the Tree had to relate; and the more it said, the more clearly did it remember everything, and thought, "Those were quite merry days! But they may come again. Klumpey-Dumpey fell down stairs, and yet he married the Princess. Perhaps I may marry a Princess too!" And then the Fir Tree thought of a pretty little birch tree that

grew out in the forest: for the Fir Tree, that birch was a real Princess.

"Who's Klumpey-Dumpey?" asked the little Mice.

And then the Fir Tree told the whole story. It could remember every single word: and the little Mice were ready to leap to the very top of the tree with pleasure. Next night a great many more Mice came, and on Sunday two Rats even appeared; but these thought the story was not pretty, and the little Mice were sorry for that, for now they also did not like it so much as before.

"Do you only know one story?" asked the Rats.

"Only that one," replied the Tree. "I heard that on the happiest evening of my life; I did not think then how happy I was."

"That's a very miserable story. Don't you know any about bacon and tallow candles — a store-room story?"

"No," said the Tree.

"Then we'd rather not hear you," said the Rats.

And they went back to their own people. The little Mice at last stayed away also; and then the Tree sighed and said,

"It was very nice when they sat round me, the merry little Mice, and listened when I spoke to them. Now that's past too. But I shall

remember to be pleased when they take me out."

But when did that happen? Why, it was one morning that people came and rummaged in the garret: the boxes were put away, and the Tree brought out; they certainly threw him rather roughly on the floor, but a servant dragged him away at once to the stairs, where the daylight shone.

"Now life is beginning again," thought the Tree.

It felt the fresh air and the first sunbeams, and now it was out in the courtyard. Everything passed so quickly that the Tree quite forgot to look at itself, there was so much to look at all round. The courtyard was close to a garden, and here everything was blooming; the roses hung fresh and fragrant over the little paling, the linden trees were in blossom, and the swallows cried, "Quinze-wit! quinze-wit! my husband's come!" But it was not the Fir Tree that they meant.

"Now I shall live!" said the Tree, rejoicingly, and spread its branches far out; but, alas! they were all withered and yellow; and it lay in the corner among nettles and weeds. The tinsel star was still upon it, and shone in the bright sunshine.

In the courtyard a couple of the merry children were playing, who had danced round the tree at Christmas-time, and had rejoiced over

it. One of the youngest ran up and tore off the golden star.

"Look what is sticking to the ugly old fir tree," said the child, and he trod upon the branches till they cracked again under his boots.

And t_e Tree looked at all the blooming flowers and the splendor of the garden, and then looked at itself, and wished it had remained in the dark corner of the garret; it thought of its fresh youth in the wood, of the merry Christmas-eve, and of the little Mice which had listened so pleasantly to the story of Klumpey-Dumpey.

"Past! past!" said the old Tree. "Had I but rejoiced when I could have done so! Past! past!"

And the servant came and chopped the Tree into little pieces; a whole bundle lay there, it blazed brightly under the great brewing copper, and it sighed deeply, and each sigh was like a little shot: and the children who were at play there ran up and seated themselves at the fire, looked into it, and cried, "Puff! puff!" But at each explosion, which was a deep sigh, the Tree thought of a summer day in the woods, or of a winter night there, when the stars beamed; he thought of Christmas-eve and of Klumpey-Dumpey, the only story he had ever heard or knew how to tell; and then the Tree was burned.

The boys played in the garden, and the youngest had on his breast a golden star, which the Tree had worn on its happiest evening. Now that was past, and the Tree's life was past, and the story is past too: past! past! — and that's the way with all stories.

LITTLE ROGER'S NIGHT IN THE CHURCH

SUSAN COOLIDGE

The boys and girls had fastened the last sprig of holly upon the walls, and then gone to their homes, leaving the old church silent and deserted. The sun had set in a sky clear and yellow as topaz. Christmas eve had fairly come, and now the moon was rising, a full moon, and all the world looked white in the silver light. Every bough of every tree sparkled with a delicate coating of frost, the pines and cedars were great shapes of dazzling snow, even the ivy on the gothic tower hung a glittering arabesque on the gray wall. Never was there a lovelier night.

That light that you see yonder comes from the window of old Andrew, the sexton, and inside sits his grandson, little Roger, eating his supper of porridge. The kitchen is in apple-pie order, chairs and tables have been scrubbed as white as snow, the tins on the dresser shine like silver, the hearth is swept clean, and Grandfather's chair is drawn into the warmest corner. Grandfather is not sitting in it though; he has gone to the church to put the fire in order for the night, lock up the doors, and make all safe.

Grandmother, in her clean stuff gown and apron, is mounted upon a chair to stick a twig of holly on the tall clock in the corner. And now, as she turns round, what a pleasant face she shows us, does she not? Old and wrinkled, to be sure, but so good-natured and gentle that she is prettier than many a young girl even now. Is it any wonder that little Roger there is so fond of her?

Now another bit-of holly is wanted on the chimney-piece; and it is while putting this up that the dear old dame gives sign that something has gone wrong. "Ts, ts, ts,— deary me!"

"What's the matter, Granny?" said Roger.

"Why, Roger," replied Granny, carefully dismounting from her chair, "look here, Grandfather has gone off and forgot his keys. He took 'em from the door this morning, because last year some of the young folks let 'em drop in the snow, and had a sad time hunting for them. He knew they would be in and out all day, so he just opened the door and brought the keys home. Deary me! it's a cold night for old bones to be out of doors. Would'st be afeard, little 'un, to run up with them?"

"Not a bit," said Roger, stoutly, as he crammed the last spoonful of porridge in his

mouth, and seized hat and mittens from the table. "I'll take 'em down in a minute, Granny, and then run home. Mother'll want me in the morning, likely."

For Roger's parents lived in a cottage near the old people, and the boy often said that he had two homes, and belonged half in one and half in the other, and the small press-bed in Granny's loft seemed as much his own as the cot in the corner of his mother's sleeping-room, and was occupied almost as often. So, after a good-night hug from Granny, off he ran. The church was near, and the moon light as day, so he never thought of being afraid, not even when, as he brushed by the dark tower, something stirred overhead, and a long, melancholy cry came shuddering from the ivy. Roger knew the owls in the belfry well, and now he called out to them cheerily: "To-whit-whit-whoo!"

"Whoo-whoo-whit!" answered the owls, startled by the cry. Roger could hear them fluttering in the nest.

The church-door stood ajar, and he peeped in. The glow from the open door of the stove showed Grandfather's figure, red and warm, stooping to cover the fire with ashes for the night. He was so busy he never knew the boy was there till he got close to him and jingled the keys in his ear; but after one start he laughed, well pleased.

"I but just missed them," he said. "Thou'rt a good boy to fetch them up. Art going home with me to-night?"

"No, I'm to sleep at my mother's," said Roger, "but I'll wait and walk with you, Grandfather." So he slipped into a pew, and sat down till the work should be finished, and they ready to go; and as he looked up he saw all at once how beautiful the old church was looking.

The moon outside was streaming in so brightly, that you hardly missed the sun. Roger could see distinctly way up to the carved beams of the roof, and trace the figures on the great arched windows over the altar, whose colors had so often dazzled him on Sundays. The colors were soft and dim now, but the figures were there. Roger could see them plainly,— the sitting figure of the Lord Christ, with St. Matthew and two other apostles, and the fisher-lad with his basket of fish. He had often asked Granny to read him the story.

That gleam at the further end of the nave came from the organ-loft, where the moon-beams had found out the great brass pipes, and were playing all manner of tricks with them. Almost the red of the holly-berries could be seen, and every pointed ivy-leaf and spike of evergreen in the wreathings of the windows stood out in bold relief against the shining panes. With this beautiful whiteness

the red glow of the fire blended, and flooded the chancel with a lovely pink light, in which shone the gilded letters on the commandment-tables, and the brasses of the tablets on the walls. It was a wonderful thing to see.

To study the roof better, Roger thought he would lie flat on the cushion awhile, and look straight up. So he arranged himself comfortably, and somehow — it *will* happen, even when we are full of enjoyment and pleasure — his eyes shut, and the first thing he knew he was rubbing them open again, only a minute afterward, as it seemed; but Grandfather was gone. There was the stove closed for the night, and the great door at the end of the aisle was shut. He jumped up in a fright, as you can imagine, and ran to see, and shook it hard. No: it was locked, and poor Roger was fastened in for the night.

He understood it all in a moment. The tall pew had hidden him from sight. Grandfather had thought him gone home; his mother would never doubt that he was safe at the other cottage; no one would miss him, and there was no chance of being let out before morning.

He was only six years old, so no wonder that at first he felt choked and frightened, and inclined to cry. But he was a brave lad, and that idea soon left him. He began to think that he was not badly off, after all,— the church was warm, the pew-cushion as soft as

his bed. No one could get in to harm him. In fact, after the first moment, there was something so exciting and adventurous in the idea of spending the night in such a place, that he was almost glad the accident had happened. So he went back to the pew, and tried to go to sleep again.

That was not so easy. Did you ever get thoroughly waked up in the night by a sudden fright? Do you remember how your eyes wouldn't stay shut afterward, even when you closed them tight, but jerked open almost against your will, as if a string was fastened to them and some one was twitching it? Just so poor Roger felt. He lay still and kept himself quiet for a moment, and then some little noise would come, and his heart beat and his eyes be wide open in a minute. It was a coal dropping from the fire, or a slight crack on the frosty panes: once a little mouse crept out from the chancel, glaring shyly about with his bright eyes, nibbled a moment at a leaf on the carpet and then crept back again. No other living thing disturbed the quiet.

He had heard the clock strike eleven a long time since, and was lying with eyes half shut, gazing at the red fire-grate, and feeling at last a little drowsy, when all at once a strange rush and thrill seemed to come to him in the air, like a cool clear wind blowing through the church, and in one minute he was wide awake

and sitting upright, with ears strained to catch some sound afar off. It was too distant and faint for ordinary sense, but a new and sharper power of hearing seemed given him. Little voices were speaking high in the air, outside the church,— very odd ones, like birds' notes, and yet the words were plain. He listened and listened, and made out at last that it was the owls in the tower talking together.

"Hoo, hoo, why don't you lie still there?" said one.

"Whit-whoo-whit," said the other, "I can't. I know what is coming too well for that."

"What is coming,— what, what?" said two voices together.

"Ah! you'll see soon," replied the first. "The elves are coming, the hateful Christmas elves. You'll not get a wink of sleep to-night."

"Why not? What will they do to us?" chirped the young ones.

"You'll see," hooted the old owl. "You'll see! They'll pull your tails, and tickle your feathers, and prick you with thorns. I know them, the tricksy, troublesome things! I've been here many a long year. You were only hatched last summer. To-whoo, to-whoo!"

Just at this moment the church-clock began to strike twelve. At the first clang the owls ceased to hoot, and Roger listened to the deep notes, almost awe-struck, as they sounded one

by one. He knew the voice of the clock well, but it never before sounded so loud or so solemn: five — six — seven — eight — nine — ten — eleven — twelve. It was Christmas Day.

As the last echo died away, a new sound took its place. From afar off came the babble of tiny voices drawing nearer. Anything so gay and charming was never dreamed of before,— half a laugh, half a song, the tones blended into an enchanting peal, like bells on a frolic. Above the old tower the sounds clustered and increased,— then a long, distressed cry came from the owl, and a bubbling laugh floated in on the wind. Roger could not stand it. Wild to see, he flew to the window, and tried to stretch his neck in such a way as to catch what was going on above; but it was a vain attempt, and just then the church-bells began to ring all together, a chime, a Christmas chime, only the sounds were infinitely small, as if baby hands had laid hold on the ropes. But his sharpened senses brought every note and change to Roger's ears, and they were so merry and so lovely that he felt he must get nearer or die; and almost before he knew it he was climbing the dark belfry-stairs as fast as his feet could carry him, never thinking of fear or darkness, only of the elfin bells which were pealing overhead.

Up, up, through the long slits in the tower the moon could be seen sailing in the cold,

clear blue.   Higher, higher,— at last he gained
the belfry.   There hung the four great bells,
but nobody was pulling at their heavy ropes.
On each iron tongue was perched a fay; on
the chains which suspended them clustered
others, all keeping time by the swaying of their
bodies as they swung to and fro, just grazing
either side, and bringing forth a clear, delicate stroke, sweet as laughter,— just loud
enough for fairy ears.

Through the windows the crowd of floating
fays could be seen whirling about in the moonlight like glittering gossamer.   They floated
in and out of the tower, they mounted the great
bells and sat atop in swarms, they chased and
pushed each other, playing all sorts of pranks.
Below, others were attacking the owl's nest.
Roger could hear their hoots and grunts and
the gleeful laughter of the elves.   The moon
made the tower light as noon; all the time the
elves sang or talked,— which, he could not tell;
there were words, but all so blent with laughs
and mirthful trills that it was nothing less than
music.

To and fro, to and fro, keeping time to a
fairy rhythm, they swayed in unison with the
tiny peal they rang.   Little quarrels arose.
Once Roger watched an elf trying to mount the
clapper, and whenever he neared the top a mischievous comrade pushed him off again.   Then
the elf pouted, and, flying away, he returned

with a holly-leaf. Small as it was, it curled over his head like a huge umbrella. With the spiky point he slyly pricked the elf above; and he, taken by surprise, lost his hold, and came tumbling down, while the other danced for glee and clapped his hands mockingly. Pretty soon, however, all was made up again,— they kissed and were friends,— and Roger saw them perched opposite each other, and moving to and fro like children in a swing.

How long the pretty sight lasted he could not tell. So fearful was he of marring the sport that he never stirred a finger; but all at once there came a strain of music in the air, solemn, and sweeter than ever mortal heard before. In a moment the elves left their sports; they clustered like bees together in the window, and then flew from the tower in one sparkling drift, and were gone, leaving Roger alone, and the owls hooting below in the ivy.

And then he felt afraid,— which he had not been as long as the fays were there,— and down he ran in a fright over the stone steps of the stairs, and entered the church again. The red glow of the fire was grateful to him, for he was shivering with cold and excitement; but hardly had he regained his old seat, when, lo! a great marvel came to pass.

The wide window over the altar swung open, and a train of angels slowly floated through. How he knew them to be angels, Roger could

not have told; but that they were, he was sure,
— Christmas angels, with faces of calm, glorious beauty, and robes as white as snow.   Over
the altar they hovered, and a wonderful song
rose and filled the church — no bird's strain
was ever half so sweet.   The words were few,
but again and again and again they came:
" Glory to God in the highest, on earth peace,
good-will to men! "

Roger knew the oft-repeated words,— they
were those of the great evergreen motto which
overarched the chancel; but I think he never
forgot the beautiful meaning they seemed to
bear as the angels sang them over and over.
It was so wondrous sweet that he could not
feel afraid,— he could only gaze and gaze, and
hold his breath lest he should lose a note.

And the song rang on, clear and triumphant,
even as the white-robed choir parted and
floated like soft summer clouds to and fro in
the church, pausing ever and anon as in blessing.   They touched the leaves of the Christmas
green as they passed; they hung over the organ and brushed the keys with their wings; a
long time they clustered above the benches of
the poor, as if to leave a fragrance in the air;
and then they rested before a tablet which had
been put up but a few months before, and
which bore the name of the rector's eldest son,
and the dates of his birth and death.   Roger
had been told of this brave lad, and how he had

lost his life in plunging from his ship to save the drowning child of an emigrant; and now the angel-song seemed sweeter than ever, as over and again they chanted, "Good-will to men,— good-will to men."

At last one of the white-winged ones left the others, and hovered awhile above the Squire's pew, near which our little boy was hidden. A prayer-book lay open on the rail, and over this the fair angel bent as in benediction. A girl had sat there once,— the Squire's only daughter. Roger remembered her well, and the mourning of the whole parish when, only a twelvemonth ago, the lovely child had been buried from their sight; and now, as he timidly glanced into the glorious face above him, it seemed to him to have the same look, only so ineffably beautiful that he closed his dazzled eyes to shut out the vision and the light that shone from the white wings,— only for a moment, then he opened them again, as a gentle rustling filled the air, and he saw the bending figure stoop, leave a kiss or a blessing on the pages of the open book, and then glide away with the others. Again the group hovered above the altar,— louder and clearer rose the triumphant strain, and, noiseless as a cloud, the snowy train floated to the window. For one moment their figures could be seen against the sky, then the song died away,— they were gone, and Roger saw them no more.

And now the light of dawn began to creep into the windows, twittering sounds showed the birds awakening outside, and a pink streak appeared in the sky. Too much rapt by his vision to feel impatience, the boy sat and waited; and by and by a jingling in the lock showed Grandfather at hand,— the door opened, and he came in.

You can guess his surprise when his little grandson flew to meet him with his wonderful story. As for the story, he pooh-poohed *that,* — sleeping in such a strange place might well bring about a queer dream, he said; but he took the boy home to the cottage, and Granny, full of wonderment and sympathy, speedily prepared a breakfast for her darling after his adventure. But, even with his mouth full of scalding bread and milk, Roger would go on telling of angels and fairies, and the owls' talk in their nest, till both grandparents began to think him bewitched.

Perhaps he was, for to this day he persists in the story. And though the villagers that morning exclaimed that at no time had their old church, in its Christmas dress, looked so beautiful before, and though the organ sent forth a rarer, sweeter music than fingers had ever drawn from it, still nobody believed a word of it. And though the poor mother, kneeling in her lonely pew, and missing her darling from beside her, felt a strange peace

and patience enter her heart, and came away
calmed and blessed, still no one listened to the
story.   "Roger had dreamed it all," they said;
and perhaps he had,— only the owls knew.

MR. BLUFF'S EXPERIENCES OF HOLIDAYS

OLIVER BELL BUNCE

"I hate holidays," said Bachelor Bluff to me, with some little irritation, on a Christmas a few years ago. Then he paused an instant, after which he resumed: "I don't mean to say that I hate to see people enjoying themselves. But I hate holidays, nevertheless, because to me they are always the dreariest and saddest days of the year. I shudder at the name of holiday. I dread the approach of one, and thank Heaven when it is over. I pass through, on a holiday, the most horrible sensations, the bitterest feelings, the most oppressive melancholy; in fact, I am not myself at holiday-times."

"Very strange," I ventured to interpose.

"A plague on it!" said he, almost with violence. "I'm not inhuman. I don't wish anybody harm. I'm glad people can enjoy themselves. But I hate holidays all the same. You see, this is the reason: I am a bachelor; I am without kin; I am in a place that did not know me at birth. And so, when holidays come around, there is no place anywhere for me. I have friends, of course; I don't think I've been a very sulky, shut-in, reticent fellow; and there is many a board that has a place for me — but not at Christmas-time. At Christmas, the dinner is a family gathering; and I've no family. There is such a gathering of kindred on this occasion, such a reunion of family folk, that there is no place for a friend, even if the friend be liked. Christmas, with all its kindliness and charity and good-will, is, after all, deuced selfish. Each little set gathers within its own circle; and people like me, with no particular circle, are left in the lurch. So you see, on the day of all the days in the year that my heart pines for good cheer, I'm without an invitation.

"Oh, it's because I pine for good cheer," said the bachelor, sharply, interrupting my attempt to speak, "that I hate holidays. If I were an infernally selfish fellow, I wouldn't hate holidays. I'd go off and have some fun all to myself, somewhere or somehow. But, you see, I hate to be in the dark when all the rest of the world is in light. I hate holidays, because I ought to be merry and happy on holidays, and can't.

"Don't tell me," he cried, stopping the word that was on my lips; "I tell you, I hate holidays. The shops look merry, do they, with their bright toys and their green branches? The pantomime is crowded with merry hearts, is it?

The circus and the show are brimful of fun and laughter, are they? Well, they all make me miserable. I haven't any pretty-faced girls or bright-eyed boys to take to the circus or the show, and all the nice girls and fine boys of my acquaintance have their uncles or their grand-dads or their cousins to take them to those places; so, if I go, I must go alone. But I don't go. I can't bear the chill of seeing everybody happy, and knowing myself so lonely and desolate. Confound it, sir, I've too much heart to be happy under such circumstances! I'm too humane, sir! And the result is, I hate holidays. It's miserable to be out, and yet I can't stay at home, for I get thinking of Christmases past. I can't read — the shadow of my heart makes it impossible. I can't walk — for I see nothing but pictures through the bright windows, and happy groups of pleasure-seekers. The fact is, I've nothing to do but to hate holidays.— But will you not dine with me?"

Of course, I had to plead engagement with my own family circle, and I couldn't quite invite Mr. Bluff home *that* day, when Cousin Charles and his wife, and Sister Susan and her daughter and three of my wife's kin, had come in from the country, all to make a merry Christmas with us. I felt sorry, but it was quite impossible, so I wished Mr. Bluff a "merry Christmas," and hurried homeward through the cold and nipping air.

I did not meet Bachelor Bluff again until a week after Christmas of the next year, when I learned some strange particulars of what occurred to him after our parting on the occasion just described.   I will let Bachelor Bluff tell his adventure for himself:

" I went to church," said he, " and was as sad there as everywhere else.   Of course, the evergreens were pretty, and the music fine; but all around me were happy groups of people, who could scarcely keep down *merry* Christmas long enough to do reverence to *sacred* Christmas. And nobody was alone but me.   Every happy paterfamilias in his pew tantalized me, and the whole atmosphere of the place seemed so much better suited to every one else than me that I came away hating holidays worse than ever. Then I went to the play, and sat down in a box all alone by myself.   Everybody seemed on the best of terms with everybody else, and jokes and banter passed from one to another with the most good-natured freedom.   Everybody but me was in a little group of friends.   I was the only person in the whole theater that was alone.   And then there was such clapping of hands, and roars of laughter, and shouts of delight at all the fun going on upon the stage, all of which was rendered doubly enjoyable by everybody having somebody with whom to share and interchange the pleasure, that my loneliness got simply un-

bearable, and I hated holidays infinitely worse
than ever.

"By five o'clock the holiday became so intolerable that I said I'd go and get a dinner.
The best dinner the town could provide. A
sumptuous dinner. A sumptuous dinner for
one. A dinner with many courses, with wines
of the finest brands, with bright lights, with a
cheerful fire, with every condition of comfort—
and I'd see if I couldn't for once extract a little pleasure out of a holiday!

"The handsome dining-room at the club
looked bright, but it was empty. Who dines at
this club on Christmas but lonely bachelors?
There was a flutter of surprise when I ordered
a dinner, and the few attendants were, no
doubt, glad of something to break the monotony of the hours.

"My dinner was well served. The spacious
room looked lonely; but the white, snowy cloths,
the rich window-hangings, the warm tints of
the walls, the sparkle of the fire in the steel
grate, gave the room an air of elegance and
cheerfulness; and then the table at which I
dined was close to the window, and through the
partly-drawn curtains were visible centers of
lonely, cold streets, with bright lights from
many a window, it is true, but there was a
storm, and snow began whirling through the
street. I let my imagination paint the streets
as cold and dreary as it would, just to extract

a little pleasure by way of contrast from the brilliant room of which I was apparently sole master.

"I dined well, and recalled in fancy old, youthful Christmases, and pledged mentally many an old friend, and my melancholy was mellowing into a low, sad undertone, when, just as I was raising a glass of wine to my lips, I was startled by a picture at the window-pane. It was a pale, wild, haggard face, in a great cloud of black hair, pressed against the glass. As I looked, it vanished. With a strange thrill at my heart, which my lips mocked with a derisive sneer, I finished the wine and set down the glass. It was, of course, only a beggar-girl that had crept up to the window and stole a glance at the bright scene within; but still the pale face troubled me a little, and threw a fresh shadow on my heart. I filled my glass once more with wine, and was again about to drink, when the face reappeared at the window. It was so white, so thin, with eyes so large, wild, and hungry-looking, and the black, unkempt hair, into which the snow had drifted, formed so strange and weird a frame to the picture, that I was fairly startled. Replacing, untasted, the liquor on the table, I rose and went close to the pane. The face had vanished, and I could see no object within many feet of the window. The storm had increased, and the snow was driving in wild gusts through the streets, which were

empty, save here and there a hurrying way-
farer. The whole scene was cold, wild, and
desolate, and I could not repress a keen thrill of
sympathy for the child, whoever it was, whose
only Christmas was to watch, in cold and storm,
the rich banquet ungratefully enjoyed by the
lonely bachelor. I resumed my place at the
table; but the dinner was finished, and the wine
had no further relish. I was haunted by the
vision at the window, and began, with an un-
reasonable irritation at the interruption, to repeat with fresh warmth my detestation of holidays. One couldn't even dine alone on a holiday with any sort of comfort, I declared. On
holidays one was tormented by too much pleasure on one side, and too much misery on the
other. And then, I said, hunting for justifica-
tion of my dislike of the day, ' How many other
people are, like me, made miserable by seeing
the fullness of enjoyment others possessed!

"Oh, yes, I know," sarcastically replied the
bachelor to a comment of mine; "of course, all
magnanimous, generous, and noble-souled people delight in seeing other people made happy,
and are quite content to accept this vicarious
felicity. But I, you see, and this dear little
girl —"

"Dear little girl!"

"Oh, I forgot," said Bachelor Bluff, blushing
a little, in spite of a desperate effort not to do
so. "I didn't tell you. Well, it was so absurd!

I kept thinking, thinking of the pale, haggard, lonely little girl on the cold and desolate side of the window-pane, and the over-fed, discontented, lonely old bachelor on the splendid side of the window-pane ; and I didn't get much happier thinking about it, I can assure you. I drank glass after glass of the wine — not that I enjoyed its flavor any more, but mechanically, as it were, and with a sort of hope thereby to drown unpleasant reminders. I tried to attribute my annoyance in the matter to holidays, and so denounced them more vehemently than ever. I rose once in a while and went to the window, but could see no one to whom the pale face could have belonged.

" At last, in no very amiable mood, I got up, put on my wrappers, and went out; and the first thing I did was to run against a small figure crouching in the doorway. A face looked up quickly at the rough encounter, and I saw the pale features of the window-pane. I was very irritated and angry, and spoke harshly; and then, all at once, I am sure I don't know how it happened, but it flashed upon me that I, of all men, had no right to utter a harsh word to one oppressed with so wretched a Christmas as this poor creature was. I couldn't say another word, but began feeling in my pocket for some money, and then I asked a question or two, and then I don't quite know how it came about — isn't it very warm here?" exclaimed Bachelor

Bluff, rising and walking about, and wiping the perspiration from his brow.

"Well, you see," he resumed nervously, "it was very absurd, but I did believe the girl's story — the old story, you know, of privation and suffering, and all that — and just thought I'd go home with the brat and see if what she said was all true. And then I remembered that all the shops were closed, and not a purchase could be made. I went back and persuaded the steward to put up for me a hamper of provisions, which the half-wild little youngster helped me carry through the snow, dancing with delight all the way.— And isn't this enough?"

"Not a bit, Mr. Bluff. I must have the whole story.

"I declare," said Bachelor Bluff, "there's no whole story to tell. A widow with children in great need, that was what I found; and they had a feast that night, and a little money to buy them a load of wood and a garment or two the next day; and they were all so bright, and so merry, and so thankful, and so good, that, when I got home that night, I was mightily amazed that, instead of going to bed sour at holidays, I was in a state of great contentment in regard to holidays. In fact, I was really merry. I whistled. I sang. I do believe I cut a caper. The poor wretches I had left had been so merry over their unlooked-for Christmas banquet that their spirits infected mine.

"And then I got thinking again. Of course, holidays had been miserable to me, I said. What right had a well-to-do, lonely old bachelor hovering wistfully in the vicinity of happy circles, when all about there were so many people as lonely as he, and yet oppressed with want? 'Good gracious!' I exclaimed, 'to think of a man complaining of loneliness with thousands of wretches yearning for his help and comfort, with endless opportunities for work and company, with hundreds of pleasant and delightful things to do! Just to think of it! It put me in a great fury at myself to think of it. I tried pretty hard to escape from myself and began inventing excuses and all that sort of thing, but I rigidly forced myself to look squarely at my own conduct. And then I reconciled my conscience by declaring that, if ever after that day I hated a holiday again, might my holidays end at once and forever!

"Did I go and see my *protégés* again? What a question! Why — well, no matter. If the widow is comfortable now, it is because she has found a way to earn without difficulty enough for her few wants. That's no fault of mine. I would have done more for her, but she wouldn't let me. But just let me tell you about New Year's — the New-Year's-day that followed the Christmas I've been describing. It was lucky for me there was another holiday only a week off. Bless you! 1 had so much to do that day

that I was completely bewildered, and the hours weren't half long enough. I did make a few social calls, but then I hurried them over; and then hastened to my little girl, whose face had already caught a touch of color; and she, looking quite handsome in her new frock and her ribbons, took me to other poor folk, and — well, that's about the whole story.

"Oh, as to the next Christmas. Well, I didn't dine alone, as you may guess. It was up three stairs, that's true, and there was none of that elegance that marked the dinner of the year before; but it was merry, and happy, and bright; it was a generous, honest, hearty, Christmas dinner, that it was, although I do wish the widow hadn't talked so much about the mysterious way a turkey had been left at her door the night before. And Molly — that's the little girl — and I had a rousing appetite. We went to church early; then we had been down to the Five Points to carry the poor outcasts there something for their Christmas dinner; in fact, we had done wonders of work, and Molly was in high spirits, and so the Christmas dinner was a great success.

"Dear me, sir, no! Just as you say. Holidays are not in the least wearisome any more. Plague on it! When a man tells me now that he hates holidays, I find myself getting very wroth. I pin him by the button-hole at once, and tell him my experience. The fact is, if I

were at dinner on a holiday, and anybody should ask me for a sentiment, I should say, God bless all holidays!' "

SANTA CLAUS AT SIMPSON'S BAR

It was nearly midnight when the festivities were interrupted. "Hush!" said Dick Bullen, holding up his hand. It was the querulous voice of Johnny from his adjacent closet: "Oh, dad!"

The Old Man arose hurriedly and disappeared in the closet. Presently he reappeared. "His rheumatiz is coming on agin bad," he explained, "and he wants rubbin'." He lifted the demijohn of whiskey from the table and shook it. It was empty. Dick Bullen put down his tin cup with an embarrassed laugh. So did the others. The Old Man examined their contents, and said hopefully, "I reckon that's enough; he don't need much. You hold on, all o' you, for a spell, and I'll be back;" and vanished in the closet with an old flannel shirt and the whiskey. The door closed but imperfectly, and the following dialogue was distinctly audible:—

"Now, sonny, whar does she ache worst?"

" Sometimes over yar and sometimes under yer; but it's most powerful from yer to yer. Rub yer, dad."

A silence seemed to indicate a brisk rubbing. Then Johnny: —

" Hevin' a good time out yar, dad? "

" Yes, sonny."

" Tomorrer's Chrismiss,— ain't it? "

" Yes, sonny. How does she feel now? "

" Better. Rub a little furder down. Wot's Chrismiss, anyway? Wot's it all about? "

" Oh, it's a day."

This exhaustive definition was apparently satisfactory, for there was a silent interval of rubbing. Presently Johnny again: —

" Mar sez that everywhere else but yer everybody gives things to everybody Chrismiss, and then she jist waded inter you. She sez thar's a man they call Sandy Claws, not a white man, you know, but a kind o' Chinemin, comes down the chimbley night afore Chrismiss and gives things to chillern,— boys like me. Puts 'em in their butes! Thet's what she tried to play upon me. Easy, now, pop, whar are you rubbin' to, — thet's a mile from the place. She jest made that up, didn't she, jest to aggrewate me and you? Don't rub thar — Why, dad! "

In the great quiet that seemed to have fallen upon the house the sigh of the near pines and the drip of leaves without was very distinct. Johnny's voice, too, was lowered as he went on:

"Don't you take on now, for I'm gettin' all right fast. Wot's the boys doin' out thar?"

The Old Man partly opened the door and peered through. His guests were sitting there sociably enough, and there were a few silver coins and a lean buckskin purse on the table. "Bettin' on suthin',— some little game or 'nother. They're all right," he replied to Johnny, and recommenced his rubbing.

"I'd like to take a hand and win some money," said Johnny reflectively, after a pause.

The Old Man glibly repeated what was evidently a familiar formula, that if Johnny would wait until he struck it rich in the tunnel, he'd have lots of money, etc., etc.

"Yes," said Johnny, "but you don't. And whether you strike it or I win it, it's about the same. It's all luck. But it's mighty cur'o's about Chrismiss,— ain't it? Why do they call it Chrismiss?"

Perhaps from some instinctive deference to the overhearing of his guests, or from some vague sense of incongruity, the Old Man's reply was so low as to be inaudible beyond the room.

"Yes," said Johnny, with some slight abatement of interest, "I've heerd o' him before. Thar, that'll do dad. I don't ache near so bad as I did. Now wrap me tight in this yer blanket. So. Now," he added in a muffled whisper, "sit down yer by me till I go asleep."

To assure himself of obedience he disengaged one hand from the blanket, and, grasping his father's sleeve, again composed himself to rest.

For some moments the Old Man waited patiently. Then the unwonted stillness of the house excited his curiosity, and without moving from the bed he cautiously opened the door with hid disengaged hand, and looked into the main room. To his infinite surprise it was dark and deserted. But even then a smoldering log on the hearth broke, and by the upspringing blaze he saw the figure of Dick Bullen sitting by the dying embers.

" Hello! "

Dick started, rose, and came somewhat unsteadily toward him.

" Whar's the boys? " said the Old Man.

" Gone up the canon on a little pasear. They're coming back for me in a minit. I'm waitin' round for 'em. What are you starin' at, Old Man? " he added, with a forced laugh; " do you think I'm drunk? "

The Old Man might have been pardoned the supposition, for Dick's eyes were humid and his face flushed. He loitered and lounged back to the chimney, yawned, shook himself, buttoned up his coat and laughed. " Liquor ain't so plenty as that, Old Man. Now don't you git up," he continued, as the Old Man made a movement to release his sleeve from Johnny's hand. " Don't you mind manners. Sit jest

whar you be; I'm goin' in a jiffy. Thar, that's them now."

There was a low tap at the door. Dick Bullen opened it quickly, nodded "Good-night" to his host, and disappeared. The Old Man would have followed him but for the hand that still unconsciously grasped his sleeve. He could have easily disengaged it; it was small, weak and emaciated. But perhaps because it was small, weak and emaciated he changed his mind, and, drawing his chair closer to the bed, rested his head upon it. In this defenceless attitude the potency of his earlier potations surprised him. The room flickered and faded before his eyes, reappeared, faded again, went out, and left him —asleep.

Meantime Dick Bullen, closing the door, confronted his companions. "Are you ready?" said Staples. "Ready," said Dick; "what's the time?" "Past twelve," was the reply; "can you make it? — it's nigh on fifty miles, the round trip hither and yon." "I reckon,' returned Dick shortly. "Whar's the mare?" "Bill and Jack's holdin' her at the crossin'." "Let 'em hold on a minit longer," said Dick.

He turned and reentered the house softly. By the light of the guttering candle and dying fire he saw that the door of the little room was open. He stepped toward it on tiptoe and looked in. The Old Man had fallen back in his chair, snoring, his helpless feet thrust out

in a line with his collapsed shoulders, and his
hat pulled over his eyes. Beside him, on a
narrow wooden bedstead, lay Johnny, muffled
tightly in a blanket that hid all save a strip of
forehead and a few curls damp with perspiration. Dick Bullen made a step forward, hesitated, and glanced over his shoulder into the
deserted room. Everything was quiet. With
a sudden resolution he parted his huge mus-
taches with both hands, and stooped over the
sleeping boy. But even as he did so a mischievous blast, lying in wait, swooped down the
chimney, rekindled the hearth, and lit up the
room with a shameless glow, from which Dick
fled in bashful terror.

His companions were already waiting for him
at the crossing. Two of them were struggling
in the darkness with some strange misshapen
bulk, which as Dick came nearer took the semblance of a great yellow horse.

It was the mare. She was not a pretty picture. From her Roman nose to her rising
haunches, from her arched spine hidden by the
stiff *machillas* of a Mexican saddle, to her thick,
straight, bony legs, there was not a line of
equine grace. In her half blind but wholly vicious white eyes, in her protruding under-lip,
in her monstrous color, there was nothing but
ugliness and vice.

"Now, then," said Staples, "stand cl'ar of
her heels, boy, and up with you. Don't miss

your first holt of her mane, and mind ye get your off stirrup quick. Ready!"

There was a leap, a scrambling, a bound, a wild retreat of the crowd, a circle of flying hoofs, two springless leaps that jarred the earth, a rapid play and jingle of spurs, a plunge, and then the voice of Dick somewhere in the darkness. " All right!"

" Don't take the lower road back onless you're pushed hard for time! Don't hold her in down hill. We'll be at the ford at five. G'lang! Hoopa! Mula! GO!"

A splash, a spark struck from the ledge in the road, a clatter in the rocky cut beyond, and Dick was gone.

. . . .

Sing, O Muse, the ride of Richard Bullen! Sing, O Muse, of chivalrous men! the sacred quest, the doughty deeds, the battery of low churls, the fearsome ride and gruesome perils of the Flower of Simpson's Bar! Alack! she is dainty, this Muse! She will have none of this bucking brute and swaggering, ragged rider, and I must fain follow him in prose, afoot!

It was one o'clock, and yet he had only gained Rattlesnake Hill. For in that time Jovita had rehearsed to him all her imperfections and practised all her vices. Thrice had she stumbled. Twice had she thrown up her Roman nose in a straight line with the reins, and, re-

sisting bit and spur, struck out madly across country. Twice had she reared, and, rearing, fallen backward; and twice had the agile Dick, unharmed, regained his seat before she found her vicious legs again. And a mile beyond them, at the foot of a long hill, was Rattlesnake Creek. Dick knew that here was the crucial test of his ability to perform his enterprise, set his teeth grimly, put his knees well into her flanks, and changed his defensive tactics to brisk aggression. Bullied and maddened, Jovita began the descent of the hill. Here the artful Richard pretended to hold her in with ostentatious objurgation and well-feigned cries of alarm. It is unnecessary to add that Jovita instantly ran away. Nor need I state the time made in the descent; it is written in the chronicles of Simpson's Bar. Enough that in another moment, as it seemed to Dick, she was splashing on the overflowed banks of Rattlesnake Creek. As Dick expected, the momentum she had acquired carried her beyond the point of balking, and, holding her well together for a mighty leap, they dashed into the middle of the swiftly flowing current. A few moments of kicking, wading, and swimming, and Dick drew a long breath on the opposite bank.

The road from Rattlesnake Creek to Red Mountain was tolerably level. Either the plunge into Rattlesnake Creek had dampened her baleful fire, or the art which led to it had

shown her the superior wickedness of her rider, for Jovita no longer wasted her surplus energy in wanton conceits. Once she bucked, but it was from force of habit; once she shied, but it was from a new, freshly-painted meeting-house at the crossing of the country road. Hollows, ditches, gravelly deposits, patches of freshly-springing grasses, flew from beneath her rattling hoofs. She began to smell unpleasantly; once or twice she coughed slightly, but there was no abatement of her strength or speed. By two o'clock he had passed Red Mountain and begun the descent to the plain. Ten minutes later the driver of the fast Pioneer coach was overtaken and passed by a " man on a Pinto hoss,"— an event sufficiently notable for remark. At half past two Dick rose in his stirrups with a great shout. Stars were glittering through the rifted clouds, and beyond him, out of the plain, rose two spires, a flagstaff, and a straggling line of black objects. Dick jingled his spurs and swung his *riata*, Jovita bounded forward, and in another moment they swept into Tuttleville, and drew up before the wooden piazza of " The Hotel of All Nations."

What transpired that night at Tuttleville is not strictly a part of this record. Briefly I may state, however, that after Jovita had been handed over to a sleepy ostler, whom she at once kicked into unpleasant consciousness, Dick sallied out with the barkeeper for a tour of the

sleeping town. Lights still gleamed from a few saloons and gambling houses; but, avoiding these, they stopped before several closed shops, and by persistent tapping and judicious outcry roused the proprietors from their beds, and made them unbar the doors of their magazines and expose their wares. Sometimes they were met by curses, but oftener by interest and some concern in their needs. It was three o'clock before this pleasantry was given over, and with a small waterproof bag of India rubber strapped on his shoulders Dick returned to the hotel. And then he sprang to the saddle, and dashed down the lonely street and out into the lonelier plain, where presently the lights, the black line of houses, the spires, and the flagstaff sank into the earth behind him again and were lost in the distance.

The storm had cleared away, the air was brisk and cold, the outlines of adjacent landmarks were distinct, but it was half-past four before Dick reached the meeting-house and the crossing of the country road. To avoid the rising grade he had taken a longer and more circuitous road, in whose viscid mud Jovita sank fetlock deep at every bound. It was a poor preparation for a steady ascent of five miles more; but Jovita, gathering her legs under her, took it with her usual blind, unreasoning fury, and a half hour later reached the long level that led to Rattlesnake Creek. Another half hour

would bring him to the Creek. He threw the reins lightly upon the neck of the mare, chirruped to her, and began to sing.

Suddenly Jovita shied with a bound that would have unseated a less practised rider. Hanging to her rein was a figure that had leaped from the bank, and at the same time from the road before her arose a shadowy horse and rider. " Throw up your hands," commanded the second apparition, with an oath.

Dick felt the mare tremble, quiver, and apparently sink under him. He knew what it meant, and was prepared.

" Stand aside, Jack Simpson. I know you, you d—d thief! Let me pass, or —"

He did not finish the sentence. Jovita rose straight in the air with a terrific bound, throwing the figure from her bit with a single shake of her vicious head, and charged with deadly malevolence down on the impediment before her. An oath, a pistol-shot, horse and highwayman rolled over in the road, and the next moment Jovita was a hundred yards away. But the good right arm of her rider, shattered by a bullet, dropped helplessly at his side.

Without slacking his speed he lifted the reins to his left hand. But a few moments later he was obliged to halt and tighten the saddle-girths that had slipped in the onset. This in his crippled condition took some time. He had no fear of pursuit, but, looking up, he saw that

the eastern stars were already paling, and that the distant peaks had lost their ghostly whiteness, and now stood out blackly against a lighter sky. Day was upon him. Then completely absorbed in a single idea, he forgot the pain of his wound, and, mounting again, dashed on towards Rattlesnake Creek. But now Jovita's breath came broken by gasps, Dick reeled in his saddle, and brighter and brighter grew the sky.

Ride, Richard; run, Jovita; linger, O day!

For the last few rods there was a roaring in his ears. Was it exhaustion from a loss of blood, or what? He was dazed and giddy as he swept down the hill, and did not recognize his surroundings. Had he taken the wrong road, or was this Rattlesnake Creek?

It was. But the brawling creek he had swam a few hours before had risen, more than doubled its volume, and now rolled a swift and resistless river between him and Rattlesnake Hill. For the first time that night Richard's heart sank within him. The river, the mountain, the quickening east, swam before his eyes. He shut them to recover his self-control. In that brief interval, by some fantastic mental process, the little room at Simpson's Bar and the figures of the sleeping father and son rose upon him. He opened his eyes wildly, cast off his coat, pistol, boots, and saddle, bound his precious pack tightly to his shoulders, grasped the bare flanks

of Jovita with his bared knees, and with a shout dashed into the yellow water. A cry arose from the opposite bank as the head of a man and horse struggled for a few moments against the battling current, and then were swept away amidst uprooted trees and whirling driftwood.

.　.　.　.　.　.　.　.　.　.

The Old man started and woke. The fire on the hearth was dead, the candle in the outer room flickering in its socket, and somebody was rapping at the door. He opened it, but fell back with a cry before the dripping, half-naked figure that reeled against the doorpost.

" Dick ? "

" Hush ! Is he awake yet ? "

" No ; but Dick — "

"Dry up, you old fool! Get me some whiskey, quick ! " The Old Man flew, and returned with — an empty bottle ! Dick would have sworn, but his strength was not equal to the occasion. He staggered, caught at the handle of the door, and motioned to the Old Man.

" Thar's suthin' in my pack yer for Johnny. Take it off. I can't."

The Old Man unstrapped the pack, and laid it before the exhausted man.

" Open it, quick."

He did so with trembling fingers. ⸱It contained only a few poor toys,— cheap and barbaric enough, goodness knows, but bright with

paint and tinsel. One of them was broken;
another, I fear, was irretrievably ruined by
water; and on the third — ah me! there was a
cruel spot.

"It don't look like much, that's a fact," said
Dick ruefully . . . "But it's the best we
could do. . . . Take 'em Old Man, and put
'em in his stocking, and tell him — tell him, you
know — hold me, Old Man —" The Old Man
caught at his sinking figure. "Tell him," said
Dick, with a weak little laugh,—"tell him
Sandy Claus has come."

And even so, bedraggled, ragged, unshaven
and unshorn, with one arm hanging helplessly
at his side, Santa Claus came to Simpson's Bar,
and fell fainting on the first threshold. The
Christmas dawn came slowly after, touching the
remoter peaks with the rosy warmth of ineffa-
ble love. And it looked so tenderly on Simpson's Bar that the whole mountain, as if caught
in a generous action, blushed to the skies.

THE GOLDEN COBWEBS

A TALE FOR SMALL CHILDREN

[This story was told the author in the mother-tongue of
a German friend, at the kindly instance of a common friend
of both; the narrator had heard it at home from the lips
of a father of story-loving children for whom he often invented such tales. The present adaptation has passed by
hearsay through so many minds that it is perhaps little like
the original, but I venture to hope it has a touch of the original fancy, at least.]

I am going to tell you a story about something wonderful that happened to a Christmas
tree like this, ever and ever so long ago, when
it was once upon a time.

It was before Christmas, and the tree was
all trimmed with pop-corn and silver nuts and
(name the trimmings of the tree before you),
and stood safely out of sight in a room where
the doors were locked, so that the children
should not see it before it was time. But ever
so many other little house-people had seen it.
The big black pussy saw it with her great green
eyes; the little gray Kitty saw it with her little
blue eyes; the kind house-dog saw it with his
steady brown eyes; the yellow Canary saw it
with his wise, bright eyes. Even the wee, wee
mice that were so afraid of the cat had peeped
one peek when no one was by.

But there was some one who hadn't seen the Christmas tree. It was the little gray spider!

You see, the spiders lived in the corners,— the warm corners of the sunny attic and the dark corners of the nice cellar. And they were expecting to see the Christmas Tree as much as anybody. But just before Christmas a great cleaning-up began in the house. The house-mother came sweeping and dusting and wiping and scrubbing, to make everything grand and clean for the Christ-child's birthday. Her broom went into all the corners, poke, poke,— and of course the spiders had to run. Dear, dear, how the spiders had to run! Not one could stay in the house while the Christmas cleanness lasted. So, you see, they couldn't see the Christmas Tree.

Spiders like to know all about everything, and see all there is to see, and they were very sad. So at last they went to the Christ-child and told him all about it.

" All the others see the Christmas Tree, dear Christ-child," they said; " but we, who are so domestic and so fond of beautiful things, we are cleaned up! We cannot see it at all."

The Christ-child was very sorry for the little spiders when he heard this, and he said they should see the Christmas Tree.

The day before Christmas when nobody was noticing, he let them all go in, to look as long as ever they liked.

They came creepy, creepy, down the attic stairs, creepy, creepy, up the cellar stairs, creepy, creepy, along the halls,— and into the beautiful room. The fat mother spiders and the old papa spiders were there, and all the little teenty, tonty, curly spiders, the baby ones. And then they looked! Round and round the Tree they crawled, and looked and looked and looked. Oh, what a good time they had! They thought it was perfectly beautiful. And when they looked at everything they could see from the floor, they started up the tree to see some more. All over the tree they ran, creepy, crawly, looking at every single thing. Up and down, in and out, over every branch and twig the little spiders ran, and saw every one of the pretty things right up close.

They stayed until they had seen all there was to see, you may be sure, and then they went away at last, quite happy.

Then, in the still, dark night before Christmas Day, the dear Christ-child came, to bless the Tree for the Children. But when he looked at it — what do you suppose? — it was covered with cobwebs! Everywhere the little spiders had been they had left a spider-web; and you know they had been just everywhere. So the tree was covered from its trunk to its tip with spider-webs, all hanging from the branches and looped around the twigs; it was a strange sight.

What could the Christ-child do? He knew

that house-mothers do not like cobwebs; it would never, never do to have a Christmas Tree covered with those.   No, indeed.

So the dear Christ-child touched the spiders' webs, and turned them all to gold!   Wasn't that a lovely trimming?   They shone and shone, all over the beautiful tree.   And that is the way the Christmas Tree came to have golden cobwebs on it.

———

CHRISTMAS
OLD CAROLS
AND EXERCISES

GOD REST YOU, MERRY GENTLEMEN

OLD CAROL

God rest you, merry gentlemen,
  Let nothing you dismay,
For Jesus Christ, our Saviour,
  Was born upon this day.
To save us all from Satan's pow'r
  When we were gone astray.
    O tidings of comfort and joy!
    For Jesus Christ, our Saviour,
  Was born on Christmas Day.

In Bethlehem, in Jewry,
  This blessed Babe was born,
And laid within a manger,
  Upon this blessed morn;
The which His mother, Mary,
  Nothing did take in scorn.

From God our Heavenly Father,
  A blessed angel came;
And unto certain shepherds
  Brought tidings of the same:
How that in Bethlehem was born
  The Son of God by name.

" Fear not," then said the angel,
   " Let nothing you affright,
This day is born a Saviour
   Of virtue, power, and might,
So frequently to vanquish all
   The friends of Satan quite."

The shepherds at those tidings
   Rejoicèd much in mind,
And left their flocks a-feeding
   In tempest, storm, and wind,
And went to Bethlehem straightway,
   This blessed Babe to find.

But when to Bethlehem they came,
   Whereat this infant lay,
They found Him in a manger,
   Where oxen feed on hay,
His mother Mary kneeling,
   Unto the Lord did pray.

Now to the Lord sing praises,
   All you within this place,
And with true love and brotherhood
   Each other now embrace;
This holy tide of Christmas
   All others doth deface.
     O tidings of comfort and joy!
For Jesus Christ, our Saviour,
   Was born on Christmas Day.

OLD CHRISTMAS RETURNED

All you that to feasting and mirth are inclined,
Come here is good news for to pleasure your
  mind,
Old Christmas is come for to keep open house,
He scorns to be guilty of starving a mouse:
Then come, boys, and welcome for diet the
  chief,
Plum-pudding, goose, capon, minced pies, and
  roast beef.

The holly and ivy about the walls wind
And show that we ought to our neighbors be
  kind,
Inviting each other for pastime and sport,
And where we best fare, there we most do re-
  sort;
We fail not of victuals, and that of the chief,
Plum-pudding, goose, capon, minced pies, and
  roast beef.

All travellers, as they do pass on their way,
At gentlemen's halls are invited to stay,
Themselves to refresh, and their horses to rest,
Since that he must be Old Christmas's guest;
Nay, the poor shall not want, but have for re-
  lief,
Plum-pudding, goose, capon, minced pies, and
  roast beef.

CHRISTMAS CAROL

As Joseph was a-waukin'
   He heard an angel sing,
" This night shall be the birthnight
   Of Christ our heavenly King.

" His birth-bed shall be neither
   In housen nor in hall,
Nor in the place of paradise,
   But in the oxen stall.

" He neither shall be rocked
   In silver nor in gold,
But in the wooden manger
   That lieth in the mould.

" He neither shall be washen
   With white wine nor with red,
But with the fair spring water
   That on you shall be shed.

" He neither shall be clothèd
   In purple nor in pall,
But in the fair, white linen
   That usen babies all."

As Joseph was a-waukin',
   Thus did the angel sing,
And Mary's son at midnight
   Was born to be our King.

Then be you glad, good people,
    At this time of the year;
And light you up your candles,
    For His star it shineth clear.

"IN EXCELSIS GLORIA"

When Christ was born of Mary free,
In Bethlehem, in that fair citie,
Angels sang there with mirth and glee,
                In Excelsis Gloria!

Herdsmen beheld these angels bright,
To them appearing with great light,
Who said, " God's Son is born this night,"
                In Excelsis Gloria!

This King is come to save mankind,
As in Scripture truths we find,
Therefore this song have we in mind,
                In Excelsis Gloria!

Then, dear Lord, for Thy great grace,
Grant us the bliss to see Thy face,
That we may sing to Thy solace,
                In Excelsis Gloria!

THE BOAR'S HEAD CAROL

(Sung at Queen's College, Oxford.)

The boar's head in hand bear I,
Bedecked with bays and rosemary;
And I pray you, my masters, be merry,
    Quot estis in convivio.
      Caput apri defero
      Reddens laudes domino.

The boar's head, as I understand,
Is the rarest dish in all this land,
Which thus bedeck'd with a gay garland
    Let us servire cantico.
      Caput apri defero
      Reddens laudes domino.

Our steward hath provided this
In honour of the King of bliss;
Which on this day to be served is
    In Reginensi Atrio.
      Caput apri defero
      Reddens laudes domino.

CHRISTMAS CAROL

Listen, lordings, unto me, a tale I will you tell;
Which, as on this night of glee, in David's
    town befell.

Joseph came from Nazareth with Mary, that
　　sweet maid;
Weary were they nigh to death, and for a lodg-
　　ing prayed.

In the inn they found no room; a scanty bed
　　they made;
Soon a babe, an angel pure, was in the manger
　　laid.
Forth He came, as light through glass, He
　　came to save us all.
In the stable, ox and ass before their Maker
　　fall.

Shepherds lay afield that night to keep the silly
　　sheep,
Hosts of angels in their sight came down from
　　Heaven's high steep:—
Tidings! tidings unto you! to you a child is
　　born,
Purer than the drops of dew, and brighter than
　　the morn!

Onward then the angels sped, the shepherds
　　onward went,—
God was in His manger bed; in worship low
　　they bent.
In the morning see ye mind, my masters one
　　and all,
At the altar Him to find, who lay within the
　　stall.

Chorus.

Sing high, sing low,
Sing to and fro,
Go tell it out with speed,
Cry out and shout,
All round about,
That Christ is born indeed!
Pray whither sailed those ships all three
On Christmas day in the morning?

Oh, they sailed into Bethlehem
On Christmas day, on Christmas day;
Oh, they sailed into Bethlehem
On Christmas day in the morning.

And all the bells on earth shall ring
On Christmas day, on Christmas day;
And all the bells on earth shall ring
On Christmas day in the morning.

And all the angels in heaven shall sing
On Christmas day, on Christmas day;
And all the angels in heaven shall sing
On Christmas day in the morning.

And all the souls on earth shall sing
On Christmas day, on Christmas day;
And all the souls on earth shall sing
On Christmas day in the morning.

Then let us all rejoice amain
  On Christmas day, on Christmas day;
Then let us all rejoice amain
  On Christmas day in the morning.

———

THE HOLY NIGHT

FLORENCE CONVERSE

BEING A MASQUE TO BE PERFORMED BY YOUNG
CHILDREN AT CHRISTMAS-TIDE

PERSONS OF THE MASQUE

Mary.— *She shall be a little maiden, fair-haired,
and her gown shall be white, covered
over with a long hooded cloak, sky blue.
The hood she weareth about her face.*

Joseph.— *He is a sturdy lad in a rough gown,
long and brown. In his hand he holdeth
a carpenter's wooden mallet; at his girdle
do hang three iron nails, very large.
Joseph hath a grizzled head, which may
be powdered.*

The Holy Child.— *This may be a little figure of
wax or porcelain, fashioned very delicately.*

The Three Shepherds.— *They be three little
lads, wearing short gowns of a light
tanned color, and mantles of sheeps'
skins; but if these be not convenient,
they may wear cloaks of cotton-flannel,
unbleached. And they must carry shepherds' crooks.*

The Three Wise Men.— *These shall be three boys of divers age. The one which is* Melchior *shall be fourteen years of age, or thereabout. He shall go bent, on a staff, with a beard flowing as far as to his waistband, and yet farther. This beard shall be white cotton, and tied about his chin. In his hand he beareth a crown of bright gold, or that appeareth like gold, which he shall give to* The Holy Child.

The other king, which is Caspar, *shall be of a swarthy countenance, of even a young negro, if such an one be at hand. Ten years of age shall he be; and walking he swingeth a censer.*

Now Balthasar *is the most youngest of these three kings. He is a little lad of eight years. In his hand he lifteth up the box of ointment. And all they three be turbaned as to their heads, and richly clad in long robes, and girded with a sash.*

The Angels.— *All the little girls and young maidens shall be* Angels. *Their robes are white, long, and there are no sleeves; and crosswise on the breast be two bands of braided gold, narrow, and underneath a girdle of a third narrow band, a high girdle. These Angels' wings shall be tall, pointed, and white, or else golden.*

The Cock.—*He weareth a yellow vest, made to be rounded out with a little pillow beneath. A red coat he weareth, and the sleeves of this be cut and sewn after such a fashion that when he flappeth his arms these make a semblance of wings. And a green tail he weareth, which is made with many strips of cambric curved by wires and caught in a clustering knot. He hath a black cap, and on the top of this there standeth upright a cock's comb, bright red. Over his nose he weareth a sharp beak, but his mouth remaineth uncovered, that he may speak the more easily. Yellow are his stockings, and his shoes cut in three points on the toe. But at his heels there is a long spur. And if any little boy have very fat legs he shall not play the part of the cock.*

The Raven.—*This is a black bird. His tail standeth out stiff behind him. His beak is very long. His wings he must spread very wide when he will. Let him have black hair.*

The Lamb.—*He lieth on the ground beside the Shepherds. He weareth a sheep's skin, or a white coat, and a little tail that he may frisk by a string what time he bleateth.*

The Ox and the Ass.— *These two be only heads
of pasteboard, which do lean out of window. It needs but one boy that shall
speak for them twain, and nod the head
of the Ox and wag the Ass his ears.*

And Now Beginneth the Masque to Play

The Stage appeareth so and so: To the one side there may be the gable end of a little shed. This hath a door that shall open down its mid length when the time appointed is come. Above, on the gable, sitteth an Angel; *wherefore this framework needs be stout builded. To the one side and the other of the door* Angels *stand likewise. All these three have a face as of one that waiteth, thinking his own thoughts; neither are they observed of the* Shepherds *nor the* Beasts. *In that side of the shed most near the front of the stage shall be a little window, and the* Ox *and the* Ass *look forth. Over against this shed a little mound riseth up — and mayhap it is made of sand — and on this the* Cock *is perched, who anon doth rake with his toes in the sand, anon he pecketh at the* Raven, *which walketh sedate about the heap of sand, or resteth still with his head covered underneath his wing in the seemly fashion of his kind. But ere long he must walk again. Now midway betwixt this little shed and this mound, and in the front of the stage, the* Shepherds *lie on the ground, and their* Lamb *with them. And the* Shepherds *sing.*

THE SHEPHERD'S SONG

King David was a shepherd lad,
A ruddy countenance he had,
He harped for Saul when Saul was sad.
            Alleluia!

He slew the lion and the bear;
No hungry beast henceforth may dare
Draw nigh the flock in David's care.
            Alleluia!

A shepherd reigned in Israel,
A shepherd reigned, our fathers tell,
A shepherd reigned, and all was well.
            Alleluia!

King David's greater Son shall reign,
Shall reign and triumph yet again,
And lead the nations in His train.
            Alleluia!

O Shepherds, now rejoice, and weep!
This Shepherd-King, His flock to keep,
Shall lay His life down for the sheep.
            Alleluia!

The Cock: (he flappeth his wings and crieth)
Cock-a-doodle-doo! Cock-a-doodle-doo!

The Ox: (he noddeth his head) Ooooee!
Ooooee!

*The Raven: (he spreadeth his two broad
wings)* Cawn! Cawn!

First Shepherd: What a clatter do these
beasts make!

The Ass: (*he waggeth one ear and the other alternate*)   Haw Hay!   Haw Hay!

The Lamb: (*he maketh his little tail to frisk*) Ba-a-a-a!

Second Shepherd: And thou too, silly one! Go to sleep!

Third Shepherd: My Grandam saith that one day the beasts shall speak.

Second Shepherd: When?

Third Shepherd: 'Tis but a tale of my Grandam.

First Shepherd: Tell it!

Second Shepherd: Yea; tell it!   The night is long.

The Ass: Haw Hay!   Haw Hay!

Third Shepherd: My Grandam saith, that night Messias is born all the beasts shall speak. 'Twas a wise woman told her.

Second Shepherd: When think you Messias shall be born?

First Shepherd: Not in our time, I trow. Shall not hap in our time but these heavy taxings.

Second Shepherd: Grumble not —'tis a good year with the sheep.

The Lamb: Ba-a-a!

The Three Angels: (*they put the finger to the lip and say*)   Hush-sh!

Third Shepherd: (*he speaketh soft*)   Heard you not a voice?   What was't?

The Three Angels: Hush-sh!

(And for a full minute shall not be any sound in that place. Only the Star *of* Bethlehem *shall rise, being drawn up on a thread, till it hang above the gable of the little shed. Then shall the* Cock *flap his wings and cry in a mighty voice.)*

The Cock: Christus natus est! Christus natus est!

Second Shepherd: Hark you! the bird spake!

First Shepherd: And in the Roman tongue.

(Then these Shepherds sit as lost in a maze.)

The Cock: Christus natus est! Christus natus est!

The Raven: (he stretcheth his wings) Quando? Quando?

Third Shepherd: But these be learned fowl!

The Raven: (as he were impatient) Quando?

The Ass: (he twirleth one of his ears) Hac nocte! Hac nocte!

Second Shepherd: (he whispereth as it were fearfully to his brethren) Didst hear the Ass said, Messias is born to-night?

First Shepherd: How shall an Ass know?

The Cock: Christus natus est! Christus natus est!

The Raven: Quando?

The Ass: Hac nocte!

The Ox: (he noddeth his head and speaketh slow) Ubi? — Ubi?

Third Shepherd: Yea; where?

The Lamb: Be-e-e-e-th-le-hem! Be-e-e-e-th-le-hem!

Second Shepherd: Nay; I'll not believe that!

The Cock: Christus natus est! Christus natus est!

The Raven: Quando? Quando?

The Ass: Hac nocte! Hac nocte!

The Ox: Ubi? — Ubi?

The Lamb: Be-e-e-e-th-le-hem! Be-e-e-e-th-le-hem!

The Three Angels: Alleluia!

(*And there is a sound as of many voices of Angels which sing unseen*) Alleluia!

The Angel on the Gable: (she speaketh to the Shepherds) "Fear not! for behold, I bring you good tidings of great joy, which shall be to all people. For unto you is born this day, in the city of David, a Saviour, which is Christ the Lord. And this shall be a sign unto you; ye shall find the babe wrapped in swaddling clothes lying in a manger."

The Three Angels: Alleluia!

(*Now immediately are the heavens opened, which by-meaneth that there hath been around the back and sides of this stage, some two feet separate from the wall, a dark curtain, and, this being withdrawn, there are disclosed* Angels, *as many as may be, which stand in a long row a four foot space from the floor, on a narrow scaffold builded close by the wall. The* Angels *be garmented like to the three, but they stand*

*close one after one: their hands be laid cross-
wise on their breasts and their wings do rise
up in points folded above their heads. And
from henceforth while this* Masque *dureth the*
Angels *shall stand here, and it is their part to
sing* "Alleluia!" *But first do they chaunt, immediately the curtain is withdrawn:*)

The Angels: "Glory to God in the highest,
and on earth, peace, good-will to men." "The
people that walked in darkness have seen a
great light: they that dwell in the land of the
shadow of death, upon them hath the light
shined."

"For unto us a child is born, unto us a son
is given: and the government shall be upon his
shoulder: and his name shall be called Wonderful, Counsellor, The Mighty God, the Everlasting Father, The Prince of Peace."

(*Now while the* Heavenly Host *chaunteth
after this fashion, the two* Angels *beside the
door of the little shed do fold back the leaves of
the door. And within is seen* Mary *and* Joseph,
sitting, and betwixt them two the Holy Child
*lieth on a tuft of straw in a little box which
shall be called the* Manger.)

Mary: (*she foldeth one against the other her
two hands and singeth soft to the* Holy Child.)
      Sleep, little Shepherd-King,
      Sleep while I sing.
Angels: (*very soft*)   Alleluia!
      Sweet Son, wilt suffer pain?

King — be not King in vain!
Conquer and reign!

Angels: (*very soft*)   Alleluia!
Shepherd — Thy flock wilt keep?
Fall not in death asleep;
Stay with the sheep!

Angels: (*very soft*)   Alleluia!
My little Lamb, my Son,
My little Human One,
Thy will be done.

Angels: (*very soft*)   Alleluia!
Sleep, little Shepherd-King,
Sleep while I sing.

Angels: (*very soft*)   Alleluia!

(The Shepherds *draw anear. They kneel one after one, in a straight row.*)

First Shepherd: Is this Messias?

Mary: Yea.

Third Shepherd: (*he peereth over his brother's shoulder*) Born in a stable?

Second Shepherd: 'Tis a shepherd, bethink thee. I have slept in a stable full oft; yet many a time had I not even a shed to cover me. I have slept 'neath the open sky.

First Shepherd: And I too.

Third Shepherd: And I.

Second Shepherd: If this be King, must He not be worshipped?

Mary: Yea; come nigh! See, He is a very child.

(*They come yet more close to the door.*)

Angels: Alleluia!

(*Now the* Three Wise Men *do enter.* Melchior *is the first.* After *him cometh* Caspar, *and* Balthasar *is the last.*)

Melchior: What may this place be?

The Lamb: Be-e-e-e-th-le-hem.

Angels: Alleluia!

Balthasar: "Where is He that is born King of the Jews? for we have seen His star in the east, and are come to worship Him."

The Cock: Christus natus ets!

The Shepherds: (*they stand aside out of the door*) This is He — this Babe. Come and worship!

The Three Wise Men: (*they sing that old hymn,* "We Three Kings of Orient are," *After, they do kneel beside the* Holy Child.)

The Shepherds: Why may we not give gifts?

Caspar: Yea, do so!

Second Shepherd: What have we, poor shepherds? Nothing!

First Shepherd: I have a little ball; Babe likes a ball.

Third Shepherd: Here have I a bob o' cherries, red cherries. Would Babe laugh to see the red?

Second Shepherd: This lamb is my little lamb, wilt have him for thy little Lamb, Mother? Two lambs, snow white.

(*Now do the Shepherds give these gifts.*)

Angels: Alleluia!

The Angel on the Gable: Joseph!

Joseph: (*he cometh out of the door and look-eth up*) Here am I.

The Angel on the Gable: "Arise, and take the young child and His mother, and flee into Egypt, and be thou there until I bring thee word; for Herod will seek the young child to destroy Him."

Joseph: Well, I must saddle the ass; we go away.

The Ass: (*he speaketh in surprise and some discontent*) Hac nocte?

Joseph: Yea; it must be. We go away.

The Ox: Ubi?

Joseph: Into Egypt, the Angel said.

Mary: But He shall come again to dwell in Nazareth.

The Raven: Quando?

Mary: That shall be when the Lord willeth.

The Cock: Christus natus est! Christus natus est!

..(*Now doth* Mary *arise.* Joseph *hath his hand on the head of the* Ass. *On the one side of the door there stand an* Angel *and the* Three Shepherds, *on the other side of the door an* Angel *and the* Three Wise Men.

The Cock *standeth still upon his mound, the* Raven *is below. Then do all the* Angels, *the* Shepherds, *the* Wise Men, *the* Cock, *the* Raven, *the* Lamb, *the* Ox, *the* Ass, Mary, Joseph, *and*

all they that do sit in Audience *to hear this* Masque, *sing with a loud voice and right joyfully, the first stanza and the third of the hymn called* Adeste Fidelis.)

"Oh, come, all ye faithful, joyful and triumphant;
Oh, come ye, oh, come ye to Bethlehem;
Come and behold Him, born the King of angels;
  Oh, come, let us adore Him,
  Oh, come, let us adore Him,
  Oh, come, let us adore Him, Christ the Lord.

"Sing choirs of angels, sing in exultation,
Sing, all ye citizens of heaven above;
Glory to God in the highest;
  Oh, come, let us adore Him,
  Oh, come, let us adore Him,
  Oh, come, let us adore Him, Christ the Lord."

And this is the End of the Masque.

Mark these things:

If there be any child that knoweth no Latin, *he is to be told that* Christus natus est, *signifieth* Christ is born, Quando *signifieth* When, Hac nocte *signifieth* This night, Ubi *signifieth* Where.

Now this shall be the music of The Shepherds' Song, *the old tune,* "Oh, Sons and Daughters, Let us sing."

CHRISTMAS
ADDITIONAL PIECES

A CHRISTMAS INSURRECTION

ANNE P. L. FIELD

In the hush of a shivery Christmas-tide dawn
    Sing hey! sing ho! heigho!
Three small frozen figures hung stiff and forlorn
    Sing hey! sing ho! heigho!
Three dim ghostly forms in the glimmering gray
Locked up in dark cold storage quarters were
    they
Awaiting the coming of glad Christmas day
    Sing hey! sing ho! heigho!

Suspended each one from a hickory twig
    Sing hey! sing ho! heigho!
A turkey, a goose, and a little fat pig
    Sing hey! sing ho! heigho!
With chestnuts the turkey was garnished and
    stuffed
With onions and sage was the goose-carcass
    puffed,
While piggy was spiced, and his neck was be
    ruffed
    Sing hey! sing ho! heigho!

Three spirits regretful were hovering near
    Sing hey! sing ho! heigho!

" Look!" gobbled the turkey's, "what tragedy's
      here!"
    Sing hey! sing ho! heigho!
" For this did they tempt me with fattening food,
For this did I bring up my beautiful brood,
I always thought farmers uncommonly rude!"
    Sing hey! sing ho! heigho!

The goose spirit trembled, then hissingly said
    Sing hey! sing ho! heigho!
" Most men care for nothing except to be fed!"
    Sing hey! sing ho! heigho!
" What horror is this, filled with onions and sage
To be served on a platter at my tender age!
'Tis enough any well-disposed fowl to enrage!"
    Sing hey! sing ho! heigho!

The phantom pig grunted, "Do please look at
      that!"
    Sing hey! sing ho! heigho!
" Oh! why did I grow up so rosy and fat!"
    Sing hey! sing ho! heigho!
" They put in my mouth a sweet, juicy corncob
Just when of sensations my palate they rob,
Do you wonder such sights make a spirit-pig
      sob!"
    Sing hey! sing ho! heigho!

Conferring, the spirits resolved on a plan
    Sing hey! sing ho! heigho!

By which to wreak vengeance on merciless man
Sing hey! sing ho! heigho!
" We'll each disagree with the human inside,
We'll cause indigestion and damage his pride,
And the pains of this Christmas we'll spread
far and wide! "
Sing hey! sing ho! heigho!

THE NIGHT AFTER CHRISTMAS

ANNE P. L. FIELD

'Twas the night after Christmas in Santa-Claus
land
And to rest from his labors St. Nicholas planned.
The reindeer were turned out to pasture and all
The ten thousand assistants discharged till the
fall.
The furry great-coat was laid safely away
With the boots and the cap with its tassel so gay,
And toasting his toes by a merry wood fire,
What more could a weary old Santa desire?
So he puffed at his pipe and remarked to his wife,
" This amply makes up for my strenuous life!
From climbing down chimneys my legs fairly
ache,
But it's well worth the while for the dear chil-
dren's sake.
I'd bruise every bone in my body to see
The darlings' delight in a gift-laden tree! "

Just then came a sound like a telephone bell—
Though why they should have such a thing I
    can't tell—
St. Nick gave a snort and exclaimed in a rage,
" Bad luck to inventions of this modern age!"
He grabbed the receiver—his face wore a frown
As he roared in the mouth-piece, "I will not
    come down
To exchange any toys like an up-to-date store,
Ring off, I'll not listen to anything more!"
Then he settled himself by the comforting blaze
And waxed reminiscent of halycon days
When children were happy with simplest of toys:
A doll for the girls and a drum for the boys—
But again came that noisy disturber of peace
The telephone bell—would the sound never cease?
" Run and answer it, wife, all my patience has
    fled,
If they keep this thing up I shall wish I were
    dead!
I have worked night and day the best part of a
    year
To supply all the children, and what do I hear—
A boy who declares he received roller-skates
When he wanted a gun—and a cross girl who
    states
That she asked for a new Victor talking machine
And I brought her a sled, so she thinks I am
    ' mean!'"
Poor St. Nicholas looked just the picture of woe,
He needed some auto-suggestion, you know,

To make him think things were all coming out
    right,
For he didn't get one wink of slumber that night!
The telephone wire was kept sizzling hot
By children disgusted with presents they'd got,
And when the bright sun showed its face in the
    sky
The Santa-Claus family were ready to cry!
Just then something happened—a way of escape,
Though it came in the funniest possible shape—
An aeronaut, sorely in need of a meal,
Descended for breakfast—it seemed quite ideal!
For the end of it was, he invited his host
Out to try the balloon, of whose speed he could
    boast.
St. Nick, who was nothing if not a good sport,
Was delighted to go, and as quick as a thought
Climbed into the car for a flight in the air—
" No telephone bells can disturb me up there!
And, wife, if it suits me I'll count it no crime
To stay up till ready for next Christmas time! "
Thus saying—he sailed in the giant balloon,
And I fear that he will not return very soon.
Now, when you ask " Central " for Santa-Claus
    land
She'll say, " discontinued "—and you'll under-
    stand.

WHEN THE STARS OF MORNING SANG

ANNE P. L. FIELD

When the stars of morning sang
    Long ago,
Sweet the air with music rang
    Through the snow,
There beside the mother mild
Slept the blessed Christmas child,—
Slumber holy, undefiled—
    Here below.

When the wise men traveled far
    Through the night,
Following the guiding star
    Pure and bright,
Lo! it stood above the place
Sanctified by Heaven's grace,
And upon the Christ-Child's face
    Shed its light.

When the world lay hushed and still
    Christmas morn,
Suddenly were skies athrill—
    " Christ is born!"
Angel voices, high and clear,
Chanted tidings of good cheer,
" See, the Infant King is here,
    Christ is born!"

A PRAYER AT BETHLEHEM

ANNE P. L. FIELD

O pulsing earth with heart athrill
With infinite creative will!
O watchful shepherds in whose eyes
Sweet hopes and promises arise!
O angel-host whose chanting choir
Proclaims fulfillment of desire!
O flaming star so purely white
Against the black Judean night!
O blessed Mary bending low
With sense of motherhood aglow!
O holy Babe with haloed head
Soft pillowed in a manger bed!
O Mystery divine and deep
Help us Thy prophecies to keep!

THE CHRISTMAS FIRES

ANNE P. L. FIELD

The Christmas fires brightly gleam
    And dance among the holly boughs,
The Christmas pudding's spicy steam
    With fragrance fills the house,
While merry grows each friendly soul
Over the foaming wassail bowl.

Resplendent stands the glitt'ring tree,
    Weighted with gifts for old and young,
The children's faces shine with glee,
    And joyous is each tongue,
While lads and lassies come and go
Under the festive mistletoe.

When suddenly the frosty air
    Is filled with music, voices sweet,
Lo! see the Christmas waits are there
    Snow-crowned and bare of feet,
Yet high and clear their voices ring,
And glad their Christmas carolling.

CAROL

O Child of Mary's tender care!
O little Child so pure and fair!
Cradled within the manger hay
On that divine first Christmas day!
The hopes of every age and race
Are centered in Thy radiant face!

O Child whose glory fills the earth!
O little Child of lowly birth!
The shepherds, guided from afar,
Stood worshiping beneath the star,
And wise-men fell on bended knee
And homage offered unto Thee!

O Child of whom the angels sing!
O little Child, our Infant King!
What balm for every sorrow lies
Within those clear, illumined eyes!
O precious gift to mortals given
To win us heritage in Heaven!

THE MOTHER

ROBERT HAVEN SCHAUFFLER

All day her watch had lasted on the plateau above the town. And now the sun slanted low over the dull, blue sheen of the western sea, playing changingly with the angular mountain which rose abruptly from its surge.

The young matron did not heed the magic which was transforming the theater of hills to the north and lingering lovingly at last on the eastern summit. Nor had she any eyes for the changing hue of the ivy-clad cubes of stone that formed the village over which her hungry gaze passed, sweeping the length and breadth of the plain below.

She seemed not much above thirty: tall, erect, and lithe. Her throat, bared to the breeze, was of the purest modeling; her skin of a whiteness unusual in that warm climate. Her head, a little small for her rounded figure, was crowned with a coil of chestnut hair, and her eyes glowed with a look strange to the common light of every day. It was her soul that was scanning that southward country.

339

From time to time she would fondle a small object hidden beneath the white folds of her robe. Once she threw her arms out in a passionate gesture toward the plain, and tears overflowed the beautiful eyes. Again she fell on her knees, and the throes of inner prayer found relief at her lips:

"Father, my Father, grant me to see him ere the dusk!"

Once again she sank down, moaning:

"He is in Thine everlasting arms. But Thou, who knowest times and seasons, give him to me on this day of days!"

Under the curve of a shielding hand her vision strained through the clear, pure air,— strained and found at last two specks far out in the plain, and followed them breathlessly as they crept nearer. One traveler was clad in a dark garment, and stopped presently, leaving his light-robed companion to hasten on alone toward the hungry-eyed woman on the plateau.

All at once she gathered her skirt with a joyous cry and ran with lithe, elastic steps down through the village.

They met on a low, rounded hill near the plain.

"My son, my darling!" she cried, catching him passionately to her bosom. "We have searched, and waited, and agonized," she continued after a pause, smiling at him through her happy tears. "But it matters nothing now. I have thee again."

"My mother," said the boy as he caressed her cheek, looking at her dreamily, "I have been with my cousin. Even now he waits below for me. I must bid thee farewell. I must pass from thy face forever."

His lip trembled a little, but he smiled bravely. "For it is the will of God, the Father."

The mother's face went ashen. She tottered and would have fallen but for his slender arm about her.

Her thoughts were whirling in wild confusion, yet she knew that she must decide calmly, wisely, quickly.

Her lips moved, but made no sound.

"Oh, lay Thy wise and gracious hand upon me!" was what she breathed in silence.

Then her voice sounded rich and happy and fresh, as it had always sounded for him.

"His will be done. Thou comest to bid farewell to thy brothers and father?"

"It may not be," he answered. "My lot henceforth is to flee the touch of the world, the unsympathetic eye, the ribald tongue of those like my brothers—the defilement of common life."

The mother pressed him closer.

"Say all that is in thine heart," she murmured. "We will bide here."

They sank down together on the soft, bright turf, facing the brilliance of the west, she holding her child as of old in the hollow of her arm.

He began to speak.

"For long and long a voice within me said, 'Go and seek thy cousin.' So I sought and found, and we abode together in the woods and fields, and were friends with our dear brothers the beasts, and the fishes, and the birds. There, day by day, my cousin would tell me of the dream that filled his soul and of the holy men who had put the dream there."

The mother's eyes grew larger with a swift terror, but she held her peace.

"And at the last, when the beauty, the wind, the sun, the rain, and the voice of God, had purified me in some measure, my cousin brought me to visit these holy men."

The clear, boyish voice rose and began to vibrate with enthusiasm.

"Ah, mother, *they* are the chosen ones of God! Sweet and grave and gentle they are, and theirs is the perfect life. They dwell spotless and apart from the world. They own one common purse, and spend their lives working with their hands and pondering and dreaming on purity, goodness, and the commands of the great law."

He sprang up in his excitement from her encircling arm and stood erect and wide-eyed before her.

"Ah, mother, they are so good that they would do nothing on the Sabbath, even to saving their own lives or the lives of their animals, or their brothers. They bathe very often in sacred water.

They have no wives, and mortify the flesh, and——"

"What is their aim in this?" the mother interrupted gently.

The boy was aflame with his subject.

"Ah, that is it—the great goal toward which they all run," he cried. "They are doing my Father's work, and I must help! Hear, hear what is before me: When a young novice comes to them they give him the symbols of purity: a spade, an apron, and a white robe to wear at the holy meals. In a year he receives a closer fellowship and the baths of purification. After that he enters the state of bodily purity. Then little by little he enters into purity of the spirit, meekness, holiness. He becomes a temple of the Holy Spirit, and prophesies. Ah, think, mother, how sweet it would be to lie entranced there for days and weeks in an earthly paradise, with no rough world to break the spell, while the angels sing softly in one's ears! I, even I, have already tasted of that bliss."

"Say on," she breathed. "What does the holy man do then?"

"Then," the inspired, boyish tones continued—"then he performs miracles, and finally—" he clasped her hand convulsively—"he becomes Elias, the forerunner of the Messiah!"

From far out in the wilderness came a melancholy cry.

"It is John, my cousin," said the boy, radiant,

half turning himself at the sound. " I must go to him."

She drew in her breath sharply, and rose to her feet.

" Bear a message to John," she said. " Not pourings of water, nor white robes; not times and seasons, nor feasts in darkness and silence, shall hasten the kingdom of heaven; neither formulas, nor phylacteries, nor madness on the Sabbath. Above all, no selfish, proud isolation shall usher in the glorious reign of the Messiah. These holy men,—these Essenes,—are but stricter, sterner, nobler Pharisees. Tell thy cousin to take all the noble and fine, to reject all the selfish and unmeaning, in their lives. Doctrine is not in heaven. Not by fasts and scourgings, not by vigils and scruples about the law; not by selfishly shutting out the world, but by taking all poor, suffering, erring, striving humanity into his heart will he become the true Elias."

There·was a breathless, thrilling moment of perfect silence as the glowing eyes of the mother looked deep into the astonished, questioning eyes of the son.

Then she rested both hands on his shoulders and spoke almost in a whisper.

"As for thee, the time is now come. Does my son know what this day means? "

He looked at her wonderingly and was silent.

The mother spoke:

"For many years I have kept these things and pondered them in my heart.   Now, *now* the hour is here when thou must know them."

She bent so close that a strand of loosened hair swept his forehead.

"In the time before thou wert born came as in a dream a wondrous visitor to me straight from the Father. And that pure, ecstatic messenger announced that the power of the Highest would overshadow me, and that my child was to be the son of the Highest, who should save His people from their sins—the Prince of Peace—the Messiah!"

From the wilderness came a long, melancholy cry, but the rapt boy heard not.

The mother continued in the soft, tender voice that began to tremble with her in her ecstasy.

"This day is thy birthday.   Twelve years ago this eventide, when thou camest into the world of men, men came to worship and praise God for thee,—the lowliest and the highest,—as a token that thou wert to be not only Son of God but Son of Man as well.   Poor, ignorant shepherds crowded about us in that little stable where we lay, and left the sweet savor of their prayers, and tears, and rejoicings.   And great, wise kings from another part of the earth came also."

From beneath the folds of her robe she drew forth by a fine-spun chain an intricately chased casket of soft, yellow gold.

The boy took it dreamily into his hands, and

as his fingers opened it, there floated forth upon the air of the hills of Nazareth the sacred odor of incense mingled with a perfume indescribably delicate and precious.

"Read!" whispered the mother.

The boy held his breath suddenly.

There, on the lower surface of the lid, graven in rude characters, as if on the inspiration of the moment, stood the single word

LOVE

She flung wide her arms as if to embrace the universe.

"Love! Love! Love!" she cried in her rich mother's voice. "It is the greatest thing in the world! It is the message of the Messiah!"

The heavens over the sea were of molten gold, and a golden glow seemed to radiate from the boyish face that confronted them. In their trance-like ecstasy the wonderful eyes gazed full into the blinding west—gazed on and on until day had passed into night.

One iterant sound alone, as it drew closer, stirred the silence of that evening: it was the voice of one crying in the wilderness.

THE END

INDEX

CHRISTMAS
IN PROSE AND VERSE

ITS ORIGIN, CELEBRATION AND SIGNIFICANCE
IN TWO VOLUMES

BOOK TWO

CHRISTMAS
IN VERSE

CHRISTMAS CAROL
PAUL LAURENCE DUNBAR

Ring out, ye bells!
All Nature swells
With gladness of the wondrous story,
The world was lorn,
But Christ is born
To change our sadness into glory.

Sing, earthlings, sing!
To-night a King
hath come from heaven's high throne to
  bless us.
The outstretched hand
O'er all the land
Is raised in pity to caress us.

Come at His call;
Be joyful all;
Away with mourning and with sadness!
The heavenly choir
With holy fire
Their voices raise in songs of gladness.

The darkness breaks
And Dawn awakes,
Her cheeks suffused with youthful blushes.
The rocks and stones
In holy tones
Are singing sweeter than the thrushes.

Then why should we
In silence be,
When Nature lends her voice to praises;
When heaven and earth
Proclaim the truth
Of Him for whom that lone star blazes?

No, be not still,
But with a will
Strike all your harps and set them ringing;
On hill and heath
Let every breath
Throw all its power into singing!

ON THE INFANCY OF OUR SAVIOR
FRANCIS QUARLES

Hail! blessed Virgin, full of heavenly grace,
Blest above all that sprang from human race,
Whose heaven-saluted womb brought forth
  in one
A blessed Savior and a blessed Son.
O what a ravishment 't had been to see
Thy little Savior perking on thy knee!
To see Him nuzzle in thy virgin breast,
His milk-white body all unclad, undressed;
To see thy busy fingers clothe and wrap
His spraddling limbs in thy indulgent lap;
To see His desperate eyes with childish grace
Smiling upon His smiling mother's face;
And when His forward strength began to bloom
To see Him diddle up and down the room.
O who would think so sweet a Babe as this
Should ere be slain by a false-hearted kiss?
Had I a rag, if sure Thy body wore it,
Pardon, sweet Babe, I think I should adore it;
Till then, O grant this boon, a boon far dearer:
The weed not being, I may adore the Wearer.

CHRISTMAS (I)
GEORGE HERBERT

After all pleasures as I rid one day,
My horse and I, both tired, body and mind,
With full cry of affections, quite astray;
I took up the next inn I could find.

There when I came, whom found I but my dear,
My dearest Lord, expecting till the grief
Of pleasures brought me to Him, ready there
To be all passengers' most sweet relief?

Oh Thou, whose glorious, yet contracted light,
Wrapt in night's mantle, stole into a manger;
Since my dark soul and brutish is Thy right,
To man of all beasts be not Thou a stranger:

Furnish and deck my soul, that Thou
  mayst have
A better lodging, than a rack, or grave.

CHRISTMAS (II)
GEORGE HERBERT

The shepherds sing; and shall I silent be?
    My God, no hymn for Thee?
My soul's a shepherd too; a flock it feeds
    Of thoughts, and words, and deeds.
The pasture is Thy word: the streams, Thy grace
    Enriching all the place.
Shepherd and flock shall sing, and all my powers
    Outsing the daylight hours.
Then will we chide the sun for letting night
    Take up his place and right:
We sing one common Lord; wherefore he should
    Himself the candle hold.
I will go searching, till I find a sun
    Shall stay, till we have done;
A willing shiner, that shall shine as gladly,
    As frost-nipped suns look sadly.
Then will we sing, and shine all our own day,
    And one another pay:
His beams shall cheer my breast, and both so
    twine,
Till ev'n His beams sing, and my music shine.

A CHRISTMAS CAROL
GEORGE WITHER

So now is come our joyful feast,
  Let every man be jolly;
Each room with ivy leaves is dressed,
  And every post with holly.
    Though some churls at our mirth repine,
    Round your foreheads garlands twine,
    Drown sorrow in a cup of wine,
  And let us all be merry.

Now all our neighbors' chimnies smoke,
  And Christmas blocks are burning;
Their ovens they with baked meats choke,
  And all their spits are turning.
    Without the door let sorrow lie,
    And if for cold it hap to die,
    We'll bury it in a Christmas pie,
  And evermore be merry.

Now every lad is wondrous trim,
  And no man minds his labor;
Our lasses have provided them
  A bagpipe and a tabor.
    Young men and maids, and girls and boys,
    Give life to one another's joys;
    And you anon shall by their noise
  Perceive that they are merry.

Rank misers now do sparing shun,
  Their hall of music soundeth;
And dogs thence with whole shoulders run,

So all things aboundeth.
 The country-folk themselves advance,
 For crowdy-mutton's come out of France;
 And Jack shall pipe and Jill shall dance,
And all the town be merry.

Ned Swatch hath fetched his bands from pawn,
 And all his best apparel;
Brisk Nell hath bought a ruff of lawn
 With droppings of the barrel.
  And those that hardly all the year
  Had bread to eat or rags to wear,
  Will have both clothes and dainty fare,
And all the day be merry.

Now poor men to the justices
 With capons make their errands;
And if they hap to fail of these,
They plague them with their warrants.
  But now they feed them with good cheer,
  And what they want they take in beer,
  For Christmas comes but once a year,
And then they shall be merry.

Good farmers in the country nurse
 The poor, that else were undone;
Some landlords spend their money worse,
 On lust and pride at London.
  There the roisters they do play,
  Drab and dice their land away,
  Which may be ours another day;
And therefore let's be merry.

The client now his suit forbears,
  The prisoner's heart is eased;
The debtor drinks away his cares,
  And for the time is pleased.
    Though others' purses be more fat,
    Why should we pine or grieve at that;
    Hang sorrow, care will kill a cat,
  And therefore let's be merry.

Hark how the wags abroad do call
  Each other forth to rambling;
Anon you'll see them in the hall,
  For nuts and apples scrambling;
    Hark how the roofs with laughters sound,
    Anon they'll think the house goes round;
    For they the cellar's depths have found,
  And there they will be merry.

The wenches with their wassail-bowls
  About the streets are singing;
The boys are come to catch the owls,
  The wild mare in is bringing.
    Our kitchen boy hath broke his box,
    And to the dealing of the ox
    Our honest neighbors come by flocks,
  And here they will be merry.

Now kings and queens poor sheep-cotes have,
  And mate with everybody;
The honest now may play the knave,
  And wise men play at noddy.
    Some youths will now a mumming go,
    Some others play at rowland-hoe,

And twenty other gameboys moe;
Because they will be merry.

Then wherefore in these merry days
  Should we, I pray, be duller?
No, let us sing some roundelays
  To make our mirth the fuller.
    And whilst we thus inspired sing,
    Let all the streets with echoes ring;
    Woods, and hills, and everything
Bear witness we are merry.

HEIGH HO, THE HOLLY!
WILLIAM SHAKESPEARE

Blow, blow, thou winter wind,
Thou art not so unkind
As man's ingratitude;
Thy tooth is not so keen,
Because thou art not seen,
Although thy breath be rude.
Heigh ho, sing heigh ho, unto the green holly;
ost friendship is feigning, most loving mere folly:
Then, heigh ho, the holly!
This life is most jolly.

Freeze, freeze, thou bitter sky,
That dost not bite so nigh
As benefits forgot:
Though thou the waters warp,
Thy sting is not so sharp
As friend remember'd not.
Heigh ho, sing heigh ho, unto the green holly:
ost friendship is feigning, most loving mere folly:
Then, heigh ho, the holly!
This life is most jolly.

CHRIST'S NATIVITY
HENRY VAUGHAN

II
How kind is heaven to man! If here
    One sinner doth amend
Straight there is joy, and every sphere
    In music doth contend;
And shall we then no voices lift?
    Are mercy, and salvation
Not worth our thanks? Is life a gift
    Of no more acceptation?
Shall He that did come down from thence,
    And here for us was slain,
Shall He be now cast off? No sense
    Of all His woes remain?
Can neither Love, nor sufferings bind?
    Are we all stone, and earth?
Neither His bloody passions mind,
    Nor one day bless His birth?
  Alas, my God! Thy birth now here
  Must not be numbered in the year.

THE SHEPHERDS
HENRY VAUGHAN

Sweet, harmless lives! (on whose holy leisure
    Waits innocence and pleasure),
Whose leaders to those pastures, and clear
    springs,
    Were patriarchs, saints, and kings,
How happened it that in the dead of night
    You only saw true light,
While Palestine was fast asleep, and lay
    Without one thought of day?
Was it because those first and blessed swains
    Were pilgrims on those plains
When they received the promise, for which now
    'Twas there first shown to you?
'Tis true, He loves that dust whereon they go
    That serve Him here below,
And therefore might for memory of those
    His love there first disclose;
But wretched Salem, once His love, must now
    No voice, nor vision know,
Her stately piles with all their height and pride
    Now languished and died,
And Bethlem's humble cotes above them stepped
    While all her seers slept;
Her cedar, fir, hewed stones and gold were all
    Polluted through their fall,
And those once sacred mansions were now
    Mere emptiness and show;
This made the angel call at reeds and thatch,
    Yet where the shepherds watch,

And God's own lodging (though He could not lack)
    To be a common rack;
No costly pride, no soft-clothed luxury
    In those thin cells could lie,
Each stirring wind and storm blew through their
    cots
    Which never harbored plots,
Only content, and love, and humble joys
    Lived there without all noise,
Perhaps some harmless cares for the next day
    Did in their bosoms play,
As where to lead their sheep, what silent nook,
    What springs or shades to look,
But that was all; and now with gladsome care
    They for the town prepare,
They leave their flock, and in a busy talk
    All towards Bethlem walk
To see their souls' Great Shepherd, Who was
    come
    To bring all stragglers home,
Where now they find Him out, and taught before
    That Lamb of God adore,
That Lamb whose days great kings and prophets
    wished
    And longed to see, but missed.
The first light they beheld was bright and gay
    And turned their night to day,
But to this later light they saw in Him,
    Their day was dark, and dim.

THE TRUE CHRISTMAS
HENRY VAUGHAN

So stick up ivy and the bays,
And then restore the heathen ways.
Green will remind you of the spring,
Though this great day denies the thing.
And mortifies the earth and all
But your wild revels, and loose hall.
Could you wear flowers, and roses strow
Blushing upon your breasts' warm snow,
That very dress your lightness will
Rebuke, and wither at the ill.
The brightness of this day we owe
Not unto music, masque, nor show:
Nor gallant furniture, nor plate;
But to the manger's mean estate.
His life while here, as well as birth,
Was but a check to pomp and mirth;
And all man's greatness you may see
Condemned by His humility.
     Then leave your open house and noise,
To welcome Him with holy joys,
And the poor shepherd's watchfulness:
Whom light and hymns from heaven did bless.
What you abound with, cast abroad
To those that want, and ease your load.
Who empties thus, will bring more in;
But riot is both loss and sin.
Dress finely what comes not in sight,
And then you keep your Christmas right.

THE NATIVITY
HENRY VAUGHAN

Peace? and to all the world? sure, One
And He the Prince of Peace, hath none.
He travels to be born, and then
Is born to travel more again.
Poor Galilee! thou canst not be
The place for His nativity.
His restless mother's called away,
And not delivered till she pay.
   A tax? 'tis so still! we can see
The church thrive in her misery;
And like her Head at Bethlem, rise
When she, oppressed with troubles, lies.
Rise? should all fall, we cannot be
In more extremities than He.
Great Type of passions! come what will,
Thy grief exceeds all copies still.
Thou cam'st from heaven to earth, that we
Might go from earth to heaven with Thee.
And though Thou foundest no welcome here,
Thou didst provide us mansions there.
A stable was Thy court, and when
Men turned to beasts, beasts would be men.
They were Thy courtiers, others none;
And their poor manger was Thy throne.
No swaddling silks Thy limbs did fold,
Though Thou couldst turn Thy rays to gold.
No rockers waited on Thy birth,
No cradles stirred, nor songs of mirth;
But her chaste lap and sacred breast

Which lodged Thee first did give Thee rest.
　　But stay: what light is that doth stream,
And drop here in a gilded beam?
It is Thy star runs page, and brings
Thy tributary Eastern kings.
Lord! grant some light to us, that we
May with them find the way to Thee.
Behold what mists eclipse the day:
How dark it is! shed down one ray
To guide us out of this sad night,
And say once more, "Let there be light."

ANNUNCIATION
JOHN DONNE

Salvation to all that will is nigh;
That All, which always is all everywhere,
Which cannot sin, and yet all sins must bear,
Which cannot die, yet cannot choose but die,
Lo, faithful virgin, yields Himself to lie
In prison, in thy womb; and though He there
Can take no sin, nor thou give, yet He will wear,
Taken from thence, flesh, which death's force
    may try.
Ere by the spheres time was created, thou
Wast in His mind, who is thy Son and Brother;
Whom thou conceivst, conceived; yea thou art
    now
Thy Maker's maker, and thy Father's mother;
Thou hast light in dark, and shutst in little
    room,
Immensity cloistered in thy dear womb.

NATIVITY
JOHN DONNE

Immensity cloistered in thy dear womb,
Now leaves His well-belov'd imprisonment,
There He hath made Himself to His intent
Weak enough, now into the world to come;
But O, for thee, for Him, hath the inn no room?
Yet lay Him in this stall, and from the Orient,
Stars and wise men will travel to prevent
The effect of Herod's jealous general doom.
Seest thou, my soul, with thy faith's eyes,
    how He
Which fills all place, yet none holds Him, d
    oth lie?
Was not His pity towards thee wondrous high,
That would have need to be pitied by thee?
Kiss Him, and with Him into Egypt go,
With His kind mother, who partakes thy woe.

ON THE MORNING OF CHRIST'S NATIVITY
JOHN MILTON

This is the month, and this the happy morn
Wherein the Son of Heav'n's eternal King,
Of wedded Maid, and Virgin Mother born,
Our great redemption from above did bring;
For so the holy sages once did sing,
    That he our deadly forfeit should release,
And with his Father work us a perpetual peace.

That glorious Form, that Light unsufferable,
And that far-beaming blaze of Majesty,
Wherewith he wont at Heav'n's high
   council-table,
To sit the midst of Trinal Unity,
He laid aside, and here with us to be,
  Forsook the courts of everlasting day,
And chose with us a darksome house of
   mortal clay.

Say Heav'nly Muse, shall not thy sacred vein
Afford a present to the Infant God?
Hast thou no verse, no hymn, or solemn strain,
To welcome him to this his new abode,
Now while the heav'n, by the Sun's team untrod,
  Hath took no print of the approaching light,
And all the spangled host keep watch in
   squadrons bright?

See how from far upon the eastern road
The star-led wizards haste with odours sweet:
O run, prevent them with thy humble ode,
And lay it lowly at his blessed feet;
Have thou the honour first thy Lord to greet,
  And join thy voice unto the angel quire,
From out his secret altar touched with
   hallowed fire.

THE HYMN
JOHN MILTON

I

It was the winter wild,
While the Heav'n-born child,
  All meanly wrapt in the rude manger lies;
Nature in awe to him
Had doffed her gaudy trim,
  With her great Master so to sympathize:
It was no season then for her
To wanton with the Sun, her lusty paramour.

II

Only with speeches fair
She woos the gentle air
  To hide her guilty front with innocent snow,
And on her naked shame,
Pollute with sinful blame,
  The saintly veil of maiden white to throw,
Confounded, that her Maker's eyes
Should look so near upon her foul deformities.

III

But he, her fears to cease,
Sent down the meek-eyed Peace:
  She, crowned with olive green, came softly
  sliding
Down through the turning sphere,
His ready harbinger,
  With turtle wing the amorous clouds dividing;
And waving wide her myrtle wand,
She strikes a universal peace through sea and
  land.

IV

No war or battle's sound
Was heard the world around;
  The idle spear and shield were high uphung;
The hooked chariot stood
Unstained with hostile blood;
  The trumpet spake not to the armed throng;
And kings sate still with awful eye,
  As if they surely knew their sovran Lord
  was by.

V

But peaceful was the night
Wherein the Prince of Light
  His reign of peace upon the earth began:
The winds with wonder whist,
Smoothly the waters kist,
  Whispering new joys to the mild Ocean,
Who now hath quite forgot to rave,
While birds of calm sit brooding on the
  charmed wave.

VI

The Stars with deep amaze
Stand fixed in steadfast gaze,
  Bending one way their precious influence;
And will not take their flight,
For all the morning light,
  Or Lucifer that often warned them thence,
But in their glimmering orbs did glow,
Until their Lord himself bespake, and bid
  them go.

VII

And though the shady gloom
Had given day her room,
  The Sun himself withheld his wonted speed,
And hid his head for shame,
As his inferior flame
  The new-enlightened world no more should
  need:
He saw a greater Sun appear
Than his bright throne or burning axle-tree
  could bear.

VIII

The shepherds on the lawn,
Or ere the point of dawn,
  Sate simply chatting in a rustic row;
Full little thought they than
That the mighty Pan
  Was kindly come to live with them below:
Perhaps their loves, or else their sheep,
Was all that did their silly thoughts so
  busy keep;

IX

When such music sweet
Their hearts and ears did greet,
  As never was by mortal finger strook,
Divinely warbled voice
Answering the stringed noise,
  As all their souls in blissful rapture took:
The air such pleasure loth to lose,
With thousand echoes still prolongs each
  heav'nly close.

X

Nature, that heard such sound
Beneath the hollow round
  Of Cynthia's seat, the Airy region thrilling,
Now was almost won
To think her part was done,
  And that her reign had here its last fulfilling:
She knew such harmony alone
Could hold all heav'n and earth in happier union.

XI

At last surrounds their sight
A globe of circular light,
  That with long beams the shame-faced
  Night arrayed;
The helmed Cherubim
And sworded Seraphim
  Are seen in glittering ranks with wings
  displayed,
Harping in loud and solemn quire,
With unexpressive notes to Heav'n's new-born
  Heir.

XII

Such music (as 'tis said)
Before was never made,
  But when of old the sons of morning sung,
While the Creator great
His constellations set,
  And the well-balanced world on hinges hung,
And cast the dark foundations deep,
And bid the welt'ring waves their oozy
  channel keep.

XIII

Ring out ye crystal spheres!
Once bless our human ears
  (If ye have power to touch our senses so)
And let your silver chime
Move in melodious time,
  And let the bass of Heav'n's deep organ blow;
And with your ninefold harmony
Make up full consort to th'angelic symphony.

XIV

For if such holy song
Enwrap our fancy long,
  Time will run back and fetch the age of gold,
And speckled Vanity
Will sicken soon and die,
  And leprous Sin will melt from earthly mould;
And Hell itself will pass away,
And leave her dolorous mansions to the peering
  Day.

XV

Yea, Truth and Justice then
Will down return to men,
  Orbed in a rainbow; and, like glories wearing,
Mercy will sit between,
Throned in celestial sheen,
  With radiant feet the tissued clouds down
steering;
And Heav'n, as at some festival,
Will open wide the gates of her high palace hall.

XVI

But wisest Fate says no:
This must not yet be so;
  The Babe lies yet in smiling infancy,
That on the bitter cross
Must redeem our loss,
  So both himself and us to glorify:
Yet first to those ychained in sleep,
The wakeful trump of doom must thunder
  through the deep,

XVII

With such a horrid clang
As on Mount Sinai rang
  While the red fire and smould'ring clouds
  outbrake:
The aged Earth, aghast
With terror of that blast,
  Shall from the surface to the centre shake,
When at the world's last session,
The dreadful Judge in middle air shall spread
  his throne.

XVIII

And then at last our bliss
Full and perfect is,
  But now begins; for from this happy day
Th'old Dragon under ground,
In straiter limits bound,
  Not half so far casts his usurped sway,
And, wrath to see his kingdom fail,
Swinges the scaly horror of his folded tail.

XIX

The Oracles are dumb;
No voice or hideous hum
  Runs through the arched roof in words deceiving.
Apollo from his shrine
Can no more divine,
  With hollow shriek the steep of Delphos leaving.
No nightly trance or breathed spell
Inspires the pale-eyed priest from the
    prophetic cell.

XX

The lonely mountains o'er,
And the resounding shore,
  A voice of weeping heard and loud lament;
From haunted spring, and dale
Edged with poplar pale,
  The parting Genius is with sighing sent;
With flow'r-inwoven tresses torn
The Nymphs in twilight shade of tangled
    thickets mourn.

XXI

In consecrated earth,
And on the holy hearth,
  The Lars and Lemures moan with
    midnight plaint;
In urns and altars round,
A drear and dying sound
  Affrights the flamens at their service quaint;
And the chill marble seems to sweat,
While each peculiar power forgoes his
    wonted seat.

XXII

Peor and Baalim
Forsake their temples dim,
  With that twice-battered god of Palestine;
And mooned Ashtaroth,
Heav'n's queen and mother both,
  Now sits not girt with tapers' holy shine;
The Libyc Hammon shrinks his horn;
In vain the Tyrian maids their wounded
  Thammuz mourn.

XXIII

And sullen Moloch, fled,
Hath left in shadows dread
  His burning idol all of blackest hue:
In vain with cymbals' ring
They call the grisly king,
  In dismal dance about the furnace blue.
The brutish gods of Nile as fast,
Isis and Orus, and the dog Anubis, haste.

XXIV

Nor is Osiris seen
In Memphian grove or green,
  Trampling the unshower'd grass with
  lowings loud;
Nor can he be at rest
Within his sacred chest,
  Naught but profoundest Hell can be his shroud:
In vain with timbreled anthems dark
The sable-stoled sorcerers bear his
  worshipped ark.

XXV

He feels from Juda's land
The dreaded Infant's hand,
　The rays of Bethlehem blind his dusky eyn;
Nor all the gods beside
Longer dare abide,
　Not Typhon huge ending in snaky twine:
Our Babe, to show his Godhead true,
Can in his swaddling bands control the
　damned crew.

XXVI

So when the Sun in bed,
Curtained with cloudy red,
　Pillows his chin upon an orient wave,
The flocking shadows pale
Troop to th'infernal jail,
　Each fettered ghost slips to his several grave,
And the yellow-skirted fays
Fly after the night-steeds, leaving their
　moon-loved maze.

XXVII

But see, the Virgin blest
Hath laid her Babe to rest:
　Time is our tedious song should here
　have ending.
Heav'n's youngest-teemed star,
Hath fixed her polished car,
　Her sleeping Lord with handmaid lamp
　attending;
And all about the courtly stable,
Bright-harnessed Angels sit in order serviceable.

JESUS INTER UBERA MARIAE
[JESUS BETWEEN MARY'S BREASTS]
JOSEPH BEAUMONT

In the coolness of the day,
The old world even, God all undressed went
   down
   Without His robe, without His crown,
Into His private garden, there to lay
     On spicy bed
     His sweeter head.

There He found two beds of spice,
A double mount of lilies in whose top
   Two milky fountains bubbled up.
He soon resolved: "And well I like!" He cries,
     "My table spread
     Upon my bed."

Scarcely had He 'gun to feed
When troops of cherubs hovered round about,
   And on their golden wings they brought
All Eden's flowers. But we cried out: "No need
     Of flowers here!
     Sweet spirits, forbear."

"True, He needs no sweets," say they;
"But sweets have need of Him, to keep them so;
   Now paradise springs new with you,
Old Eden's beauty all inclined this way;
     And we are come
     To bring them home.

"Paradise spring new with you,
Where 'twixt those beds of lilies you may see
   Of life the everlasting Tree."
"Sweet is your reason," then said we: "come
   strew
     Your pious showers
     Of eastern flowers."

[CHORUS] Winds awake! and with soft gale
Awake the odors of our garden too;
   By which yourselves perfumed go
Through every quarter of your world, that all
     Your sound may hear
     And breathe your air.

A CAROL [I]
MILDMAY FANE, SECOND EARL OF WESTMORELAND

If nothing else, may not this season move,
Or time become the true chronicle of love?
And so allay the fury, stint the rage
Or madness doth predominize this age?
When for to ransom man, whose least offense
Was charactered in disobedience,
He who knew no sin came, that to fulfill
The mercy statute of His Father's will:
Thus he forgave, and gave, to let us know
What to our very enemies we owe,
By his example; and decrees this fate
To the posterity unfortunate
Of too-believing Adam, that they must
Give themselves over to no other trust
Than what His Word assures; nor to make less
That first of sins, create them numberless
In envy, malice, and ambition,
But join to charity contrition
For by-past faults, and resolutions raise
To spend the future in our Maker's praise:
  Obey Him first, then those His glorious powers
  Shall substitute for our superiors:
  And with our own condition whatsoever
  Content, enjoy a full harmonious sphere;
  Leaving no orb for discord's fond increase,
  Since He that's born for us was Prince of Peace.

A CAROL [II]
MILDMAY FANE, SECOND EARL OF WESTMORELAND

What though 't be cold, and freeze,
Let no good Christian leese
So much of heat and zeal
As not for to remember
That blest day of December,
And what to shepherds angels did reveal,
Which doth of right claim lay
To all that ever man can write or say.

A savior's born for us:
What news more precious?
Were 't but some neighbor's son,
The bells would straightways ring—
In cakes for gossiping,
So soon the tidings o'er the town would run,
And many a light brain tossed
Among the goodwives, where to place their cost.

And shall my frozen heart
Not thaw and bear its part
In jollity for this,
Whereby not I alone
But each believing one
May promise to himself eternal bliss?
For such can ne'er be cold,
Who have this birthday in their hearts enrolled.

But may be said to burn,
Till some thanks they return,
Which though far short they reach,
The comfort is most sure,
'T hath healing wings to cure
Not for reward, but to make up the breach,
Which so repaired 'tis we
Must make it good 'gainst Satan's battery:

Whereto belongs this care
In chief and singular,
That stricter guards we keep,
Because both night and day
Th' artillery doth play,
Nor doth our adversary ever sleep:
Then we shall show hereby
Christ's favor hath not slipped our memory.

A CAROL [III]
MILDMAY FANE, SECOND EARL OF WESTMORELAND

Awake dull soul, and from thy fold of clay
Receive the blessed tidings of the day:
Not of a fox's cub, whose guile might be
A promise of successive tyranny,
Nor o' th' victorious eagle's far-spread wing,
The chiefest of the world's parts covering,
But of a lamb that's yeaned, a child that's born,
No spectacle of glory but of scorn;
For in the house of bread, this Bread of Life,
For us is come to Joseph and his wife,
And though the city David's were, therein

His Son no throne possesses, but an inn.
There thou may'st find Him at Whose mean, low
   birth
The mightiest potentates of all the earth,
Nay, oracles, are silenced and gone,
Nor longer serve the devil's delusion.
  The Delphian fiend confesses he's o'ercome
  And by an Hebrew-born child stricken dumb.
The letters of th' Old Law effaced are;
Down falls the statue of great Jupiter,
With th' twins and their nursing beast—which
  shower
Of prodigies rouse up the emperor,
Who thus far in the dark could see, t' erect
In honor of th' Almighty Architect,
An altar in the Capitol to's Son
First-born, with the sole dedication.
  If light thus through darkness shone, why is't
  That thou who hast the Gospel's beams, the
  mist
  Of errors canst not dissipate, but still
  Becom'st idolater in doing ill?
How doth thy pride and envy hatch deceit,
And fond ambition raise thee in conceit
Of thine own worth, when all such honors can
But dress thee up more stately beast, no man?
The serpent's brood like twins do always pair,
Which by thy beastly humors fostered are:
Thy tongue no more thy heart's cross-row doth
  spell,
Than if thou wert another oracle.
Be silent then, nor longer more profane
That holy Temple for which thou art ta'en,

But let the Lamb's blood wash away the stains
And characters were written in thy veins
By thy first parents, and which since thou hast
By thy endeavors into volumes cast,
  Throw down thyself for Him who meekly came
  Into the world for thee, a Child, a Lamb,
  Born to be slain for thee, yet slain before,
  To make the victory and conquest more.
Humility's a child; a giant, pride:
Goliath from the hand of David died—
So though like foes, thy ill affections grow
Unto immensity, a powerful throw
Out of the sling of faith, of hope, and love
May all that monstrous-uncouth brood remove.
  Then mayst thou reign without suspicion, free,
  As Pharaoh did, till this nativity;
  Then shall thy conscience oraclize thy fate,
  Than was Augutus's more fortunate;
    Nor in the Capitol but in thy heart
    Erect an altar to Him, let each part
    Express thou art awake, and seeing canst tell,
    That now salvation's come to Israel.

A CAROL [IV]
MILDMAY FANE, SECOND EARL OF WESTMORELAND

When we a gem or precious stone have lost,
   Is not the fabric or the frame
Of fancy busied, and each thing tossed
     And turned within the room,
       Till we the same
Can find again? Is't not a martyrdom?

Doth vanity affect us so, yet are
   We slumber-charmed, nor can employ
A thought that backward might reduce, so far,
     Lively to represent
       Our misery,
Who fell and thus incurred a banishment?

Shall we leave any corner reason lends
   To give sense light, unsought, untried?
To find how far our liberty extends,
     And how refound we were
       Re-edified
By th' Shepherd, and by the Son of the carpenter?

May not this skill and love in him requite
   The white and better stone to mark,
And t' raise this time above all others higher,
     Wherein He came (through Light)
       Into the dark,
For to restore unto mankind its sight?

Most sure it will: and where neglect denies
   To be observant of the day,

It proves not only forfeiture of eyes,
　　But all parts seem asleep
　　　Or gone astray—
So's the house again unbuilt, and lost the sheep.

IN THE HOLY NATIVITY OF OUR LORD GOD: A HYMN SUNG AS BY SHEPHERDS
RICHARD CRASHAW

[CHORUS] Come we shepherds, whose blest
　sight
Hath met love's noon in nature's night;
　Come lift up our loftier song
And wake the sun that lies too long.

To all the world of well-stol'n joy
　He slept; and dreamt of no such thing.
While we found out Heaven's fairer eye
　And kissed the cradle of our King.
Tell him he rises now, too late
To show us aught worth looking at.

Tell him we now can show him more
　Than he e'er showed to mortal sight;
Than he himself e'er saw before;
　Which to be seen needs not his light.
Tell him, Tityrus, where thou hast been,
Tell him, Tityrus, what thou hast seen.

[TITYRUS] Gloomy night embraced the place
　Where the noble Infant lay.
The Babe looked up and showed His face;

In spite of darkness, it was day.
It was Thy day, Sweet! and did rise
Not from the East, but from Thine eyes.

[CHORUS] It was Thy day, Sweet! and did rise
Not from the East, but from Thine eyes.

[THYRSIS] Winter chid aloud; and sent
  The angry North to wage his wars.
The North forgot his fierce intent,
  And left perfumes instead of scars.
By those sweet eyes' persuasive powers,
Where he meant frost, he scattered flowers.

[CHORUS] By those sweet eyes' persuasive powers,
Where he meant frost, he scattered flowers.

[BOTH] We saw Thee in Thy balmy nest,
  Young Dawn of our eternal day!
We saw Thine eyes break from Their East
  And chase the trembling shades away.
We saw Thee; and we blessed the sight,
We saw Thee by Thine own sweet light.

[TITYRUS] Poor world (said I), what wilt thou do
  To entertain this starry Stranger?
Is this the best thou canst bestow?
  A cold, and not too cleanly, manger?
Contend, ye powers of heaven and earth
To fit a bed for this huge birth.

[CHORUS] Contend, ye powers of heaven and
   earth
To fit a bed for this huge birth.

[THYRSIS] Proud world, said I; cease your
   contest
   And let the mighty Babe alone.
The phoenix builds the phoenix' nest,
   Love's architecture is his own.
The Babe whose birth embraves this morn,
Made His own bed ere He was born.

[CHORUS] The Babe whose birth embraves this
   morn,
Made His own bed ere He was born.

[TITYRUS] I saw the curled drops, soft and slow,
   Come hovering o'er the place's head;
Offering their whitest sheets of snow
   To furnish the fair Infant's bed:
Forbear, said I; be not too bold:
Your fleece is white, but 'tis too cold.

[CHORUS] Forbear, said we; be not too bold:
Your fleece is white, but 'tis too cold.

[THYRSIS] I saw the obsequious seraphims
   Their rosy fleece of fire bestow.
For well they now can spare their wings,
   Since heaven itself lies here below.
Well done, said I: but are you sure
Your down, so warm, will pass for pure?

[CHORUS] Well done, said we: but are you sure
Your down, so warm, will pass for pure?

[TITYRUS] No, no, your King's not yet to seek
  Where to repose His royal head.
See, see, how soon His bloomed cheek
  Twixt 's mother's breasts is gone to bed.
Sweet choice, said I! no way but so:
Not to lie cold, yet sleep in snow.

[CHORUS] Sweet choice, said we! no way but so:
Not to lie cold, yet sleep in snow.

[BOTH] We saw Thee in Thy balmy nest,
  Young Dawn of our eternal day!
We saw Thine eyes break from Their East
  And chase the trembling shades away.
We saw Thee; and we blessed the sight,
We saw Thee by Thine own sweet light.

[CHORUS] We saw Thee; and we blessed the
sight,
We saw Thee by Thine own sweet light.

[FULL CHORUS] Welcome, all Wonders in one
  sight!
  Eternity shut in a span.
Summer to winter, day in night,
  Heaven in earth, and God in man.
Great little One! Whose all-embracing birth
Lifts earth to heaven, stoops heaven to earth.

Welcome, though nor to gold nor silk,
  To more than Caesar's birthright is;
Twin sister-seas of virgin-milk,
  With many rarely-tempered kiss
That breathes at once both maid and mother,
Warms in the one, cools in the other.

Welcome, though not to those gay flies,
  Gilded in the beams of earthly kings,
Slippery souls in smiling eyes;
  But to poor shepherds, home-spun things,
Whose wealth's their flock, whose wit, to be
Well read in their simplicity.

Yet when April's husband showers
  Shall bless the fruitful Maia's bed,
We'll bring the first-born of her flowers
  To kiss Thy feet and crown Thy head.
To Thee, dread Lamb! whose love must keep
The shepherds, more than they their sheep.

To Thee, meek Majesty! soft King
  Of simple graces and sweet loves.
Each of us his lamb will bring,
  Each his pair of silver doves;
Till burnt at last in fire of Thy fair eyes,
Ourselves become our own best sacrifice.

CEREMONIES FOR CHRISTMAS
ROBERT HERRICK

Come, bring with a noise,
My merry, merry boys,
The Christmas Log to the firing;
While my good Dame, she
Bids ye all be free;
And drink to your heart's desiring.

With the last year's brand
Light the new block, and
For good success in his spending,
On your Psaltries play,
That sweet luck may
Come while the log is a-tinding.

Drink now the strong beer,
Cut the white loaf here,
The while the meat is a-shredding;
For the rare mince-pie
And the plums stand by
To fill the paste that's a-kneading.

CHRISTMAS-EVE, ANOTHER CEREMONY
ROBERT HERRICK

Come guard this night the Christmas-Pie,
That the thief, though ne'er so sly,
With his flesh-hooks, don't come nigh
      To catch it
From him, who all alone sits there,
Having his eyes still in his ear,
And a deal of nightly fear
      To watch it.

ANOTHER
ROBERT HERRICK

Wassail the trees, that they may bear
You many a plum, and many a pear:
For more or less fruits they will bring,
As you do give them wassailing.

THE NEW-YEAR'S GIFT
ROBERT HERRICK

Let others look for pearl and gold,
Tissues, or tabbies manifold:
One only lock of that sweet hay
Whereon the blessed Baby lay,
Or one poor swaddling-clout, shall be
The richest New-year's gift to me.

A CHRISTMAS CAROL, SUNG TO THE KING
IN THE PRESENCE AT WHITE-HALL
ROBERT HERRICK

[CHORUS] What sweeter music can we bring,
Than a carol, for to sing
The birth of this our heavenly King?
Awake the voice! Awake the string!
Heart, ear, and eye, and everything.
Awake! the while the active finger
Runs division with the singer.

[VOICE 1] Dark and dull night, fly hence away,
And give the honor to this day,
That sees December turned to May.

[2] If we may ask the reason, say
The why, and wherefore, all things here
Seem like the springtime of the year?

[3] Why does the chilling Winter's morn
Smile, like a field beset with corn?
Or smell, like to a mead new-shorn,
Thus, on the sudden?

[4] Come and see
The cause, why things thus fragrant be:
'Tis He is born, whose quickening birth
Gives life and luster, public mirth,
To heaven, and the under-earth.

[CHORUS] We see Him come, and know
Him ours,

Who, with His sunshine, and His showers,
Turns all the patient ground to flowers.

[1] The darling of the world is come,
And fit it is, we find a room
To welcome Him. [2] The nobler part
Of all the house here, is the heart,

[CHORUS] Which we will give Him; and
  bequeath
This holly, and this ivy wreath,
To do Him honor; who's our King,
And Lord of all this reveling.

THE STAR-SONG: A CAROL TO THE KING; SUNG AT WHITE-HALL
ROBERT HERRICK

[KING 1] Tell us, thou clear and heavenly tongue,
Where is the Babe but lately sprung?
Lies He the lily-banks among?

[KING 2] Or say, if this new birth of ours
Sleeps, laid within some ark of flowers,
Spangled with dew-light; thou canst clear
All doubts, and manifest the where.

[KING 3] Declare to us, bright star, if we
  shall seek
Him in the morning's blushing cheek,
Or search the beds of spices through,
To find Him out?

[STAR] No, this ye need not do;
But only come, and see Him rest
A princely Babe in's mother's breast.

[CHORUS] He's seen, He's seen, why then
  a round,
Let's kiss the sweet and holy ground;
And all rejoice, that we have found
A King, before conception crowned.

[3 KINGS] Come then, come then, and let
  us bring
Unto our pretty Twelfth-tide King,
Each one his several offering;

[CHORUS] And when night comes, we'll give
  Him wassailing:
And that His treble honors may be seen,
We'll choose Him King, and make His
  mother Queen.

THE BURNING BABE
ROBERT SOUTHWELL

As I in hoary winter's night stood shivering in the
    snow,
Surprised I was with sudden heat which made my
    heart to glow;
And lifting up a fearful eye to view what fire was
    near,
A pretty babe all burning bright did in the air
    appear;
Who, though scorched with excessive heat, such
    floods of tears did shed,
As though his floods should quench his flames,
    which with his tears were fed.
"Alas," quoth he, "but newly born, in fiery heats I
    fry,
Yet none approach to warm their hearts, or feel
    my fire but I!
My faultless breast the furnace is, the fuel
    wounding thorns,
Love is the fire, and sighs the smoke, the ashes
    shame and scorns;
The fuel justice layeth on, and mercy blows the
    coals,
The metal in this furnace wrought are men's
    defiled souls,
For which, as now on fire I am to work them to
    their good,
So will I melt into a bath to wash them in my
    blood."
With this he vanished out of sight and swiftly
    shrunk away,
And straight I called unto mind that it was
    Christmas Day.

UPON CHRIST'S NATIVITY, OR CHRISTMAS
ROWLAND WATKYNS

From three dark places Christ came forth this
    day;
From first His Father's bosom, where He lay,
Concealed till now; then from the typic law,
Where we His manhood but by figures saw;
And lastly from His mother's womb He came
To us, a perfect God and perfect Man.
    Now in a manger lies the eternal Word:
The Word He is, yet can no speech afford;
He is the Bread of Life, yet hungry lies;

The Living Fountain, yet for drink He cries;
He cannot help or clothe Himself at need
Who did the lilies clothe and ravens feed;
He is the Light of Lights, yet now doth shroud
His glory with our nature as a cloud.
He came to us a Little One, that we
Like little children might in malice be;
Little He is, and wrapped in clouts, lest He
Might strike us dead if clothed with majesty.
    Christ had four beds and those not soft nor
    brave:
The Virgin's womb, the manger, cross, and
    grave.
The angels sing this day, and so will I
That have more reason to be glad than they.

THE SHEPHERDS HAD AN ANGEL
CHRISTINA G. ROSSETTI

The shepherds had an angel,
The wise men had a star;
But what have I, a little child,
To guide me home from far,
Where glad stars sing together,
And singing angels are?

Lord Jesus is my Guardian
so I can nothing lack;
The lambs lie in His bosom
Along life's dangerous track:
The wilful lambs that go astray
He, bleeding, brings them back.

Those shepherds thro' the lonely night
Sat watching by their sheep,
Until they saw the heav'nly host
Who neither tire nor sleep,
All singing glory, glory,
In festival they keep.

Christ watches me, His little lamb,
Cares for me day and night,
That I may be His own in heav'n,
So angels clad in white
Shall sing their Glory, glory,
For my sake in the height.

Lord, bring me nearer day by day,
Till I my voice unite,

And sing my Glory, glory,
With angels clad in white,
All Glory, glory, giv'n to Thee,
Thro' all the heav'nly height.

MINSTRELS
WILLIAM WORDSWORTH

The minstrels played their Christmas tune
To-night beneath my cottage-eaves;
While, smitten by a lofty moon,
The encircling laurels, thick with leaves,
Gave back a rich and dazzling sheen,
That overpowered their natural green.

Through hill and valley every breeze
Had sunk to rest with folded wings:
Keen was the air, but could not freeze,
Nor check, the music of the strings;
So stout and hardy were the band
That scraped the chords with strenuous hand.

And who but listened?—till was paid
Respect to every inmate's claim,
The greeting given, the music played
In honour of each household name,
Duly pronounced with lusty call,
And "Merry Christmas" wished to all.

VOICES IN THE MIST
ALFRED, LORD TENNYSON

The time draws near the birth of Christ:
The moon is hid; the night is still;
The Christmas bells from hill to hill
Answer each other in the mist.

Four voices of four hamlets round,
From far and near, on mead and moor,
Swell out and fail, as if a door
Were shut between me and the sound:

Each voice four changes on the wind,
That now dilate, and now decrease,
Peace and goodwill, goodwill and peace,
Peace and goodwill, to all mankind.

BEFORE THE PALING OF THE STARS
CHRISTINA G. ROSSETTI

Before the paling of the stars,
Before the winter morn,
Before the earliest cock-crow
Jesus Christ was born:
Born in a stable,
Cradled in a manger,
In the world His hands had made
Born a stranger.

Priest and King lay fast asleep
In Jerusalem,
Young and old lay fast asleep
In crowded Bethlehem:
Saint and Angel, ox and ass,
Kept a watch together,
Before the Christmas daybreak
In the winter weather.

Jesus on his mother's breast
In the stable cold,
Spotless Lamb of God was He
Shepherd of the fold:
Let us kneel with Mary Maid,
With Joseph bent and hoary,
With Saint and Angel, ox and ass,
To hail the King of Glory.

CHRISTMAS
IN PROSE

THE CHRISTMAS CUCKOO
FRANCES BROWNE (ADAPTED)

Once upon a time there stood in the midst of a
bleak moor, in the North Country, a certain
village. All its inhabitants were poor, for their
fields were barren, and they had little trade; but
the poorest of them all were two brothers called
Scrub and Spare, who followed the cobbler's
craft. Their hut was built of clay and wattles.
The door was low and always open, for there was
no window. The roof did not entirely keep out
the rain and the only thing comfortable was a
wide fireplace, for which the brothers could
never find wood enough to make sufficient fire.
There they worked in most brotherly friendship,
though with little encouragement.

On one unlucky day a new cobbler arrived in the
village. He had lived in the capital city of the
kingdom and, by his own account, cobbled for
the queen and the princesses. His awls were
sharp, his lasts were new; he set up his stall in a
neat cottage with two windows. The villagers
soon found out that one patch of his would
outwear two of the brothers'. In short, all the
mending left Scrub and Spare, and went to the
new cobbler.

The season had been wet and cold, their barley
did not ripen well, and the cabbages never half-
closed in the garden. So the brothers were poor
that winter, and when Christmas came they had

nothing to feast on but a barley loaf and a piece of rusty bacon. Worse than that, the snow was very deep and they could get no firewood.

Their hut stood at the end of the village; beyond it spread the bleak moor, now all white and silent. But that moor had once been a forest; great roots of old trees were still to be found in it, loosened from the soil and laid bare by the winds and rains. One of these, a rough, gnarled log, lay hard by their door, the half of it above the snow, and Spare said to his brother:—

"Shall we sit here cold on Christmas while the great root lies yonder? Let us chop it up for firewood, the work will make us warm."

"No," said Scrub, "it's not right to chop wood on Christmas; besides, that root is too hard to be broken with any hatchet."

"Hard or not, we must have a fire," replied Spare. "Come, brother, help me in with it. Poor as we are there is nobody in the village will have such a yule log as ours."

Scrub liked a little grandeur, and, in hopes of having a fine yule log, both brothers strained and strove with all their might till, between pulling and pushing, the great old root was safe on the hearth, and beginning to crackle and blaze with the red embers.

In high glee the cobblers sat down to their bread
and bacon. The door was shut, for there was
nothing but cold moonlight and snow outside;
but the hut, strewn with fir boughs and ornamented with holly, looked cheerful as the ruddy
blaze flared up and rejoiced their hearts.

Then suddenly from out the blazing root they
heard: "Cuckoo! cuckoo!" as plain as ever the
spring-bird's voice came over the moor on a May
morning.

"What is that?" said Scrub, terribly frightened;
"it is something bad!"

"Maybe not," said Spare.

And out of the deep hole at the side of the root,
which the fire had not reached, flew a large, gray
cuckoo, and lit on the table before them. Much
as the cobblers had been surprised, they were
still more so when it said:—

"Good gentlemen, what season is this?"

"It's Christmas," said Spare.

"Then a merry Christmas to you!" said the
cuckoo. "I went to sleep in the hollow of that old
root one evening last summer, and never woke
till the heat of your fire made me think it was
summer again. But now since you have burned
my lodging, let me stay in your hut till the

spring comes round,—I only want a hole to sleep in, and when I go on my travels next summer be assured I will bring you some present for your trouble."

"Stay and welcome," said Spare, while Scrub sat wondering if it were something bad or not.

"I'll make you a good warm hole in the thatch," said Spare. "But you must be hungry after that long sleep,—here is a slice of barley bread. Come help us to keep Christmas!"

The cuckoo ate up the slice, drank water from a brown jug, and flew into a snug hole which Spare scooped for it in the thatch of the hut.

Scrub said he was afraid it wouldn't be lucky; but as it slept on and the days passed he forgot his fears.

So the snow melted, the heavy rains came, the cold grew less, the days lengthened, and one sunny morning the brothers were awakened by the cuckoo shouting its own cry to let them know the spring had come.

"Now I'm going on my travels," said the bird, "over the world to tell men of the spring. There is no country where trees bud, or flowers bloom, that I will not cry in before the year goes round. Give me another slice of barley bread to help me

on my journey, and tell me what present I shall bring you at the twelvemonth's end."

Scrub would have been angry with his brother for cutting so large a slice, their store of barley being low, but his mind was occupied with what present it would be most prudent to ask for.

"There are two trees hard by the well that lies at the world's end," said the cuckoo; "one of them is called the golden tree, for its leaves are all of beaten gold. Every winter they fall into the well with a sound like scattered coin, and I know not what becomes of them. As for the other, it is always green like a laurel. Some call it the wise, and some the merry, tree. Its leaves never fall, but they that get one of them keep a blithe heart in spite of all misfortunes, and can make themselves as merry in a hut as in a palace."

"Good master cuckoo, bring me a leaf off that tree!" cried Spare.

"Now, brother, don't be a fool!" said Scrub; "think of the leaves of beaten gold! Dear master cuckoo, bring me one of them!"

Before another word could be spoken the cuckoo had flown out of the open door, and was shouting its spring cry over moor and meadow.

The brothers were poorer than ever that year. Nobody would send them a single shoe to mend, and Scrub and Spare would have left the village but for their barley-field and their cabbage-garden. They sowed their barley, planted their cabbage, and, now that their trade was gone, worked in the rich villagers' fields to make out a scanty living.

So the seasons came and passed; spring, summer, harvest, and winter followed each other as they have done from the beginning. At the end of the latter Scrub and Spare had grown so poor and ragged that their old neighbors forgot to invite them to wedding feasts or merrymakings, and the brothers thought the cuckoo had forgotten them, too, when at daybreak on the first of April they heard a hard beak knocking at their door, and a voice crying:—

"Cuckoo! cuckoo! Let me in with my presents!"

Spare ran to open the door, and in came the cuckoo, carrying on one side of its bill a golden leaf larger than that of any tree in the North Country; and in the other side of its bill, one like that of the common laurel, only it had a fresher green.

"Here," it said, giving the gold to Scrub and the green to Spare, "it is a long carriage from the world's end. Give me a slice of barley bread, for I must tell the North Country that the spring has come."

Scrub did not grudge the thickness of that slice, though it was cut from their last loaf. So much gold had never been in the cobbler's hands before, and he could not help exulting over his brother.

"See the wisdom of my choice," he said, holding up the large leaf of gold. "As for yours, as good might be plucked from any hedge, I wonder a sensible bird would carry the like so far."

"Good master cobbler," cried the cuckoo, finishing its slice, "your conclusions are more hasty than courteous. If your brother is disappointed this time, I go on the same journey every year, and for your hospitable entertainment will think it no trouble to bring each of you whichever leaf you desire."

"Darling cuckoo," cried Scrub, "bring me a golden one."

And Spare, looking up from the green leaf on which he gazed as though it were a crown-jewel, said:—

"Be sure to bring me one from the merry tree."

And away flew the cuckoo.

"This is the feast of All Fools, and it ought to be your birthday," said Scrub. "Did ever man fling

away such an opportunity of getting rich? Much good your merry leaves will do in the midst of rags and poverty!"

But Spare laughed at him, and answered with quaint old proverbs concerning the cares that come with gold, till Scrub, at length getting angry, vowed his brother was not fit to live with a respectable man; and taking his lasts, his awls, and his golden leaf, he left the wattle hut, and went to tell the villagers.

They were astonished at the folly of Spare, and charmed with Scrub's good sense, particularly when he showed them the golden leaf, and told that the cuckoo would bring him one every spring.

The new cobbler immediately took him into partnership; the greatest people sent him their shoes to mend. Fairfeather, a beautiful village maiden, smiled graciously upon him; and in the course of that summer they were married, with a grand wedding feast, at which the whole village danced except Spare, who was not invited, be-cause the bride could not bear his low-mindedness, and his brother thought him a disgrace to the family.

As for Scrub he established himself with Fairfeather in a cottage close by that of the new cobbler, and quite as fine. There he mended

shoes to everybody's satisfaction, had a scarlet coat and a fat goose for dinner on holidays. Fairfeather, too, had a crimson gown, and fine blue ribbons; but neither she nor Scrub was content, for to buy this grandeur the golden leaf had to be broken and parted with piece by piece, so the last morsel was gone before the cuckoo came with another.

Spare lived on in the old hut, and worked in the cabbage-garden. (Scrub had got the barley-field because he was the elder.) Every day his coat grew more ragged, and the hut more weather-beaten; but people remarked that he never looked sad or sour. And the wonder was that, from the time any one began to keep his company, he or she grew kinder, happier, and content.

Every first of April the cuckoo came tapping at their doors with the golden leaf for Scrub, and the green for Spare. Fairfeather would have entertained it nobly with wheaten bread and honey, for she had some notion of persuading it to bring two golden leaves instead of one; but the cuckoo flew away to eat barley bread with Spare, saying it was not fit company for fine people, and liked the old hut where it slept so snugly from Christmas till spring.

Scrub spent the golden leaves, and remained always discontented; and Spare kept the merry ones.

I do not know how many years passed in this
manner, when a certain great lord, who owned
that village, came to the neighborhood. His
castle stood on the moor. It was ancient and
strong, with high towers and a deep moat. All
the country as far as one could see from the
highest turret belonged to its lord; but he had
not been there for twenty years, and would not
have come then only he was melancholy. And
there he lived in a very bad temper. The servants
said nothing would please him, and the villagers
put on their worst clothes lest he should raise
their rents.

But one day in the harvest-time His Lordship
chanced to meet Spare gathering water-cresses
at a meadow stream, and fell into talk with the
cobbler. How it was nobody could tell, but from
that hour the great lord cast away his melancholy. He forgot all his woes, and went about
with a noble train, hunting, fishing, and making
merry in his hall, where all travelers were entertained, and all the poor were welcome.

This strange story spread through the North
Country, and great company came to the
cobbler's hut,—rich men who had lost their
money, poor men who had lost their friends,
beauties who had grown old, wits who had gone
out of fashion, —all came to talk with Spare,
and, whatever their troubles had been, all went
home merry.

The rich gave him presents, the poor gave him thanks. Spare's coat ceased to be ragged, he had bacon with his cabbage, and the villagers began to think there was some sense in him.

By this time his fame had reached the capital city, and even the court. There were a great many discontented people there; and the king had lately fallen into ill humor because a neighboring princess, with seven islands for her dowry, would not marry his eldest son.

So a royal messenger was sent to Spare, with a velvet mantle, a diamond ring, and a command that he should repair to court immediately.

"To-morrow is the first of April," said Spare, "and I will go with you two hours after sunrise."

The messenger lodged all night at the castle, and the cuckoo came at sunrise with the merry leaf.

"Court is a fine place," it said, when the cobbler told it he was going, "but I cannot come there; they would lay snares and catch me; so be careful of the leaves I have brought you, and give me a farewell slice of barley bread."

Spare was sorry to part with the cuckoo, little as he had of its company, but he gave it a slice which would have broken Scrub's heart in former times, it was so thick and large. And having sewed up the leaves in the lining of his

leather doublet, he set out with the messenger on his way to court.

His coming caused great surprise there. Everybody wondered what the king could see in such a common-looking man; but scarcely had His Majesty conversed with him half an hour, when the princess and her seven islands were forgotten and orders given that a feast for all comers should be spread in the banquet hall.

The princes of the blood, the great lords and ladies, the ministers of state, after that discoursed with Spare, and the more they talked the lighter grew their hearts, so that such changes had never been seen at court.

The lords forgot their spites and the ladies their envies, the princes and ministers made friends among themselves, and the judges showed no favor.

As for Spare, he had a chamber assigned him in the palace, and a seat at the king's table. One sent him rich robes, and another costly jewels; but in the midst of all his grandeur he still wore the leathern doublet, and continued to live at the king's court, happy and honored, and making all others merry and content.

THE CHRISTMAS FAIRY OF STRASBURG
A GERMAN FOLK-TALE
J. STIRLING COYNE (ADAPTED)

Once, long ago, there lived near the ancient city
of Strasburg, on the river Rhine, a young and
handsome count, whose name was Otto. As the
years flew by he remained unwed, and never so
much as cast a glance at the fair maidens of the
country round; for this reason people began to
call him "Stone-Heart."

It chanced that Count Otto, on one Christmas
Eve, ordered that a great hunt should take place
in the forest surrounding his castle. He and his
guests and his many retainers rode forth, and
the chase became more and more exciting. It led
through thickets, and over pathless tracts of
forest, until at length Count Otto found himself
separated from his companions.

He rode on by himself until he came to a spring
of clear, bubbling water, known to the people
around as the "Fairy Well." Here Count Otto
dismounted. He bent over the spring and began
to lave his hands in the sparkling tide, but to his
wonder he found that though the weather was
cold and frosty, the water was warm and delightfully caressing. He felt a glow of joy pass through
his veins, and, as he plunged his hands deeper,
he fancied that his right hand was grasped by
another, soft and small, which gently slipped
from his finger the gold ring he always wore.

And, lo! when he drew out his hand, the gold ring was gone.

Full of wonder at this mysterious event, the count mounted his horse and returned to his castle, resolving in his mind that the very next day he would have the Fairy Well emptied by his servants.

He retired to his room, and, throwing himself just as he was upon his couch, tried to sleep; but the strangeness of the adventure kept him restless and wakeful.

Suddenly he heard the hoarse baying of the watch-hounds in the courtyard, and then the creaking of the drawbridge, as though it were being lowered. Then came to his ear the patter of many small feet on the stone staircase, and next he heard indistinctly the sound of light footsteps in the chamber adjoining his own.

Count Otto sprang from his couch, and as he did so there sounded a strain of delicious music, and the door of his chamber was flung open. Hurrying into the next room, he found himself in the midst of numberless Fairy beings, clad in gay and sparkling robes. They paid no heed to him, but began to dance, and laugh, and sing, to the sound of mysterious music.

In the center of the apartment stood a splendid Christmas Tree, the first ever seen in that country. Instead of toys and candles there hung on its lighted boughs diamond stars, pearl necklaces, bracelets of gold ornamented with colored jewels, aigrettes of rubies and sapphires, silken belts embroidered with Oriental pearls, and daggers mounted in gold and studded with the rarest gems. The whole tree swayed, sparkled, and glittered in the radiance of its many lights.

Count Otto stood speechless, gazing at all this wonder, when suddenly the Fairies stopped dancing and fell back, to make room for a lady of dazzling beauty who came slowly toward him.

She wore on her raven-black tresses a golden diadem set with jewels. Her hair flowed down upon a robe of rosy satin and creamy velvet. She stretched out two small, white hands to the count and addressed him in sweet, alluring tones:—

"Dear Count Otto," said she, "I come to return your Christmas visit. I am Ernestine, the Queen of the Fairies. I bring you something you lost in the Fairy Well."

And as she spoke she drew from her bosom a golden casket, set with diamonds, and placed it in his hands. He opened it eagerly and found within his lost gold ring.

Carried away by the wonder of it all, and overcome by an irresistible impulse, the count
pressed the Fairy Ernestine to his heart, while
she, holding him by the hand, drew him into the
magic mazes of the dance. The mysterious music
floated through the room, and the rest of that
Fairy company circled and whirled around the
Fairy Queen and Count Otto, and then gradually
dissolved into a mist of many colors, leaving the
count and his beautiful guest alone.

Then the young man, forgetting all his former
coldness toward the maidens of the country
round about, fell on his knees before the Fairy
and besought her to become his bride. At last
she consented on the condition that he should
never speak the word "death" in her presence.

The next day the wedding of Count Otto and
Ernestine, Queen of the Fairies, was celebrated
with great pomp and magnificence, and the two
continued to live happily for many years.

Now it happened on a time, that the count and
his Fairy wife were to hunt in the forest around
the castle. The horses were saddled and bridled,
and standing at the door, the company waited,
and the count paced the hall in great impatience; but still the Fairy Ernestine tarried long
in her chamber. At length she appeared at the
door of the hall, and the count addressed her in
anger.

"You have kept us waiting so long," he cried, "that you would make a good messenger to send for Death!"

Scarcely had he spoken the forbidden and fatal word, when the Fairy, uttering a wild cry, vanished from his sight. In vain Count Otto, overwhelmed with grief and remorse, searched the castle and the Fairy Well, no trace could he find of his beautiful, lost wife but the imprint of her delicate hand set in the stone arch above the castle gate.

Years passed by, and the Fairy Ernestine did not return. The count continued to grieve. Every Christmas Eve he set up a lighted tree in the room where he had first met the Fairy, hoping in vain that she would return to him.

Time passed and the count died. The castle fell into ruins. But to this day may be seen above the massive gate, deeply sunken in the stone arch, the impress of a small and delicate hand.

And such, say the good folk of Strasburg, was the origin of the Christmas Tree.

THE CHRISTMAS THORN OF GLASTONBURY
A LEGEND OF ANCIENT BRITAIN
ADAPTED FROM WILLIAM OF MALMESBURY AND
OTHER SOURCES

There is a golden Christmas legend and it relates how Joseph of Arimathea—that good man and just, who laid our Lord in his own sepulcher, was persecuted by Pontius Pilate, and how he fled from Jerusalem carrying with him the Holy Grail hidden beneath a cloth of samite, mystical and white.

For many moons he wandered, leaning on his staff cut from a white-thorn bush. He passed over raging seas and dreary wastes, he wandered through trackless forests, climbed rugged mountains, and forded many floods. At last he came to Gaul where the Apostle Philip was preaching the glad tidings to the heathen. And there Joseph abode for a little space.

Now, upon a night while Joseph lay asleep in his hut, he was wakened by a radiant light. And as he gazed with wondering eyes he saw an angel standing by his couch, wrapped in a cloud of incense.

"Joseph of Arimathea," said the angel, "cross thou over into Britain and preach the glad tidings to King Arvigarus. And there, where a Christmas miracle shall come to pass, do thou build the first Christian church in that land."

And while Joseph lay perplexed and wondering in his heart what answer he should make, the angel vanished from his sight.

Then Joseph left his hut and calling the Apostle Philip, gave him the angel's message. And, when morning dawned, Philip sent him on his way, accompanied by eleven chosen followers. To the water's side they went, and embarking in a little ship, they came unto the coasts of Britain.

And they were met there by the heathen who carried them before Arvigarus their king. To him and to his people did Joseph of Arimathea preach the glad tidings; but the king's heart, though moved, was not convinced. Nevertheless he gave to Joseph and his followers Avalon, the happy isle, the isle of the blessed, and he bade them depart straightway and build there an altar to their God.

And a wonderful gift was this same Avalon, sometimes called the Island of Apples, and also known to the people of the land as Ynis-witren, the Isle of Glassy Waters. Beautiful and peaceful was it. Deep it lay in the midst of a green valley, and the balmy breezes fanned its apple orchards, and scattered afar the sweet fragrance of rosy blossoms or ripened fruit. Soft grew the green grass beneath the feet. The smooth waves gently lapped the shore, and water-lilies floated on the surface of the tide; while in the blue sky above sailed the fleecy clouds.

And it was on the holy Christmas Eve that Joseph and his companions reached the Isle of
Avalon. With them they carried the Holy Grail
hidden beneath its cloth of snow-white samite.
Heavily they toiled up the steep ascent of the hill
called Weary-All. And when they reached the top
Joseph thrust his thorn-staff into the ground.

And, lo! a miracle! the thorn-staff put forth
roots, sprouted and budded, and burst into a
mass of white and fragrant flowers! And on the
spot where the thorn had bloomed, there Joseph
built the first Christian church in Britain. And
he made it "wattled all round" of osiers gathered
from the water's edge. And in the chapel they
placed the Holy Grail.

And so, it is said, ever since at Glastonbury
Abbey—the name by which that Avalon is known
to-day—on Christmas Eve the white thorn buds
and blooms.

THE CHRISTMAS ROSE
AN OLD LEGEND
LIZZIE DEAS (ADAPTED)

When the Magi laid their rich offerings of myrrh, frankincense, and gold, by the bed of the sleeping Christ Child, legend says that a shepherd maiden stood outside the door quietly weeping.

She, too, had sought the Christ Child. She, too, desired to bring him gifts. But she had nothing to offer, for she was very poor indeed. In vain she had searched the countryside over for one little flower to bring Him, but she could find neither bloom nor leaf, for the winter had been cold.

And as she stood there weeping, an angel passing saw her sorrow, and stooping he brushed aside the snow at her feet. And there sprang up on the spot a cluster of beautiful winter roses,— waxen white with pink tipped petals.

"Nor myrrh, nor frankincense, nor gold," said the angel, "is offering more meet for the Christ Child than these pure Christmas Roses."

Joyfully the shepherd maiden gathered the flowers and made her offering to the Holy Child.

LITTLE PICCOLA
CELIA THAXTER

In the sunny land of France there lived many years ago a sweet little maid named Piccola.

Her father had died when she was a baby, and her mother was very poor and had to work hard all day in the fields for a few sous.

Little Piccola had no dolls and toys, and she was often hungry and cold, but she was never sad nor lonely.

What if there were no children for her to play with! What if she did not have fine clothes and beautiful toys! In summer there were always the birds in the forest, and the flowers in the fields and meadows,—the birds sang so sweetly, and the flowers were so bright and pretty!

In the winter when the ground was covered with snow, Piccola helped her mother, and knit long stockings of blue wool.

The snow-birds had to be fed with crumbs, if she could find any, and then, there was Christmas Day.

But one year her mother was ill and could not earn any money. Piccola worked hard all the day long, and sold the stockings which she knit, even when her own little bare feet were blue with the cold.

As Christmas Day drew near she said to her mother, "I wonder what the good Saint Nicholas will bring me this year. I cannot hang my stocking in the fireplace, but I shall put my wooden shoe on the hearth for him. He will not forget me, I am sure."

"Do not think of it this year, my dear child," replied her mother. "We must be glad if we have bread enough to eat."

But Piccola could not believe that the good saint would forget her. On Christmas Eve she put her little wooden patten on the hearth before the fire, and went to sleep to dream of Saint Nicholas.

As the poor mother looked at the little shoe, she thought how unhappy her dear child would be to find it empty in the morning, and wished that she had something, even if it were only a tiny cake, for a Christmas gift. There was nothing in the house but a few sous, and these must be saved to buy bread.

When the morning dawned Piccola awoke and ran to her shoe.

Saint Nicholas had come in the night. He had not forgotten the little child who had thought of him with such faith.

See what he had brought her. It lay in the wooden patten, looking up at her with its two

bright eyes, and chirping contentedly as she stroked its soft feathers.

A little swallow, cold and hungry, had flown into the chimney and down to the room, and had crept into the shoe for warmth.

Piccola danced for joy, and clasped the shivering swallow to her breast.

She ran to her mother's bedside. "Look, look!" she cried. "A Christmas gift, a gift from the good Saint Nicholas!" And she danced again in her little bare feet.

Then she fed and warmed the bird, and cared for it tenderly all winter long; teaching it to take crumbs from her hand and her lips, and to sit on her shoulder while she was working.

In the spring she opened the window for it to fly away, but it lived in the woods near by all summer, and came often in the early morning to sing its sweetest songs at her door.

THE WOODEN SHOES OF LITTLE WOLFF
FRANÇOIS COPPÉE (ADAPTED)

Once upon a time,—so long ago that the world
has forgotten the date,—in a city of the North of
Europe,—the name of which is so hard to pro-
nounce that no one remembers it,—there was a
little boy, just seven years old, whose name was
Wolff. He was an orphan and lived with his aunt,
a hard-hearted, avaricious old woman, who
never kissed him but once a year, on New Year's
Day; and who sighed with regret every time she
gave him a bowlful of soup.

The poor little boy was so sweet-tempered that
he loved the old woman in spite of her bad treat-
ment, but he could not look without trembling at
the wart, decorated with four gray hairs, which
grew on the end of her nose.

As Wolff's aunt was known to have a house of
her own and a woolen stocking full of gold, she
did not dare to send her nephew to the school
for the poor. But she wrangled so that the
schoolmaster of the rich boys' school was forced
to lower his price and admit little Wolff among
his pupils. The bad schoolmaster was vexed to
have a boy so meanly clad and who paid so little,
and he punished little Wolff severely without
cause, ridiculed him, and even incited against
him his comrades, who were the sons of rich
citizens. They made the orphan their drudge and
mocked at him so much that the little boy was

as miserable as the stones in the street, and hid himself away in corners to cry—when the Christmas season came.

On the Eve of the great Day the schoolmaster was to take all his pupils to the midnight mass, and then to conduct them home again to their parents' houses.

Now as the winter was very severe, and a quantity of snow had fallen within the past few days, the boys came to the place of meeting warmly wrapped up, with fur-lined caps drawn down over their ears, padded jackets, gloves and knitted mittens, and good strong shoes with thick soles. Only little Wolff presented himself shivering in his thin everyday clothes, and wearing on his feet socks and wooden shoes.

His naughty comrades tried to annoy him in every possible way, but the orphan was so busy warming his hands by blowing on them, and was suffering so much from chilblains, that he paid no heed to the taunts of the others. Then the band of boys, marching two by two, started for the parish church.

It was comfortable inside the church, which was brilliant with lighted tapers. And the pupils, made lively by the gentle warmth, the sound of the organ, and the singing of the choir, began to chatter in low tones. They boasted of the midnight treats awaiting them at home. The son of

the Mayor had seen, before leaving the house, a
monstrous goose larded with truffles so that it
looked like a black-spotted leopard. Another boy
told of the fir tree waiting for him, on the
branches of which hung oranges, sugar-plums,
and punchinellos. Then they talked about what
the Christ Child would bring them, or what he
would leave in their shoes which they would
certainly be careful to place before the fire when
they went to bed. And the eyes of the little
rogues, lively as a crowd of mice, sparkled with
delight as they thought of the many gifts they
would find on waking,—the pink bags of burnt
almonds, the bonbons, lead soldiers standing in
rows, menageries, and magnificent jumping-
jacks, dressed in purple and gold.

Little Wolff, alas! knew well that his miserly old
aunt would send him to bed without any supper;
but as he had been good and industrious all the
year, he trusted that the Christ Child would not
forget him, so he meant that night to set his
wooden shoes on the hearth.

The midnight mass was ended. The worshipers
hurried away, anxious to enjoy the treats awaiting them in their homes. The band of pupils, two
by two, following the schoolmaster, passed out of
the church.

Now, under the porch, seated on a stone bench,
in the shadow of an arched niche, was a child
asleep,—a little child dressed in a white garment

and with bare feet exposed to the cold. He was not a beggar, for his dress was clean and new, and —beside him upon the ground, tied in a cloth, were the tools of a carpenter's apprentice.

Under the light of the stars, his face, with its closed eyes, shone with an expression of divine sweetness, and his soft, curling blond hair seemed to form an aureole of light about his forehead. But his tender feet, blue with the cold on this cruel night of December, were pitiful to see!

The pupils so warmly clad and shod, passed with indifference before the unknown child. Some, the sons of the greatest men in the city, cast looks of scorn on the barefooted one. But little Wolff, coming last out of the church, stopped deeply moved before the beautiful, sleeping child.

"Alas!" said the orphan to himself, "how dreadful! This poor little one goes without stockings in weather so cold! And, what is worse, he has no shoe to leave beside him while he sleeps, so that the Christ Child may place something in it to comfort him in all his misery."

And carried away by his tender heart, little Wolff drew off the wooden shoe from his right foot, placed it before the sleeping child; and as best as he was able, now hopping, now limping, and

wetting his sock in the snow, he returned to his aunt.

"You good-for-nothing!" cried the old woman, full of rage as she saw that one of his shoes was gone. "What have you done with your shoe, little beggar?"

Little Wolff did not know how to lie, and, though shivering with terror as he saw the gray hairs on the end of her nose stand upright, he tried, stammering, to tell his adventure.

But the old miser burst into frightful laughter. "Ah! the sweet young master takes off his shoe for a beggar! Ah! master spoils a pair of shoes for a barefoot! This is something new, indeed! Ah! well, since things are so, I will place the shoe that is left in the fireplace, and to-night the Christ Child will put in a rod to whip you when you wake. And to-morrow you shall have nothing to eat but water and dry bread, and we shall see if the next time you will give away your shoe to the first vagabond that comes along."

And saying this the wicked woman gave him a box on each ear, and made him climb to his wretched room in the loft. There the heartbroken little one lay down in the darkness, and, drenching his pillow with tears, fell asleep.

But in the morning, when the old woman, awakened by the cold and shaken by her cough, descended to the kitchen, oh! wonder of wonders! she saw the great fireplace filled with bright toys, magnificent boxes of sugar-plums, riches of all sorts, and in front of all this treasure, the wooden shoe which her nephew had given to the vagabond, standing beside the other shoe which she herself had placed there the night before, intending to put in it a handful of switches.

And as little Wolff, who had come running at the cries of his aunt, stood in speechless delight before all the splendid Christmas gifts, there came great shouts of laughter from the street.

The old woman and the little boy went out to learn what it was all about, and saw the gossips gathered around the public fountain. What could have happened? Oh, a most amusing and extraordinary thing! The children of all the rich men of the city, whose parents wished to surprise them with the most beautiful gifts, had found nothing but switches in their shoes!

Then the old woman and little Wolff remembered with alarm all the riches that were in their own fireplace, but just then they saw the pastor of the parish church arriving with his face full of perplexity.

Above the bench near the church door, in the
very spot where the night before a child, dressed
in white, with bare feet exposed to the great
cold, had rested his sleeping head, the pastor
had seen a golden circle wrought into the old
stones. Then all the people knew that the beautiful, sleeping child, beside whom had lain the
carpenter's tools, was the Christ Child himself,
and that he had rewarded the faith and charity
of little Wolff.

SAINT CHRISTOPHER
WILLIAM CAXTON

Christopher was a Canaanite, and he was of a right great stature, twelve cubits in height, and had a terrible countenance. And it is said that as he served and dwelled with the King of Canaan, it came in his mind that he would seek the greatest prince that was in the world, and him would he serve and obey.

So he went forth and came to a right great king, whom fame said was the greatest of the world. And when the king saw him he received him into his service, and made him to dwell in his court.

Upon a time a minstrel sang before him a song in which he named oft the devil. And the king, who was a Christian, when he heard him name the devil, made anon the sign of the cross.

And when Christopher saw that he marveled, and asked what the sign might mean. And because the king would not say, he said: "If thou tell me not, I shall no longer dwell with thee."

And then the King told him, saying: "Always when I hear the devil named make I this sign lest he grieve or annoy me."

Then said Christopher to him: "Fearest thou the devil? Then is the devil more mighty and greater than thou art. I am then deceived, for I had

supposed that I had found the most mighty and the most greatest lord in all the world! Fare thee well, for I will now go seek the devil to be my lord and I his servant."

So Christopher departed from this king and hastened to seek the devil. And as he went by a great desert he saw a company of knights, and one of them, a knight cruel and horrible, came to him and demanded whither he went.

And Christopher answered: "I go to seek the devil for to be my master."

Then said the knight: "I am he that thou seekest."

And then Christopher was glad and bound himself to be the devil's servant, and took him for his master and lord.

Now, as they went along the way they found there a cross, erect and standing. And anon as the devil saw the cross he was afeared and fled. And when Christopher saw that he marveled and demanded why he was afeared, and why he fled away. And the devil would not tell him in no wise.

Then Christopher said to him: "If thou wilt not tell me, I shall anon depart from thee and shall serve thee no more."

Wherefore the devil was forced to tell him and said: "There was a man called Christ, which was hanged on the cross, and when I see his sign I am sore afraid and flee from it."

To whom Christopher said: "Then he is greater and more mightier than thou, since thou art afraid of his sign, and I see well that I have labored in vain, and have not founden the greatest lord of the world. I will serve thee no longer, but I will go seek Christ."

And when Christopher had long sought where he should find Christ, at last he came into a great desert, to a hermit that dwelt there. And he inquired of him where Christ was to be found.

Then answered the hermit: "The king whom thou desirest to serve, requireth that thou must often fast."

Christopher said: "Require of me some other thing and I shall do it, but fast I may not."

And the hermit said: "Thou must then wake and make many prayers."

And Christopher said: "I do not know how to pray, so this I may not do."

And the hermit said: "Seest thou yonder deep and wide river, in which many people have perished? Because thou art noble, and of high stature and strong of limb, so shalt thou live by the river and thou shalt bear over all people who pass that way. And this thing will be pleasing to our Lord Jesu Christ, whom thou desirest to serve, and I hope he shall show himself to thee."

Then said Christopher: "Certes, this service may I well do, and I promise Him to do it."

Then went Christopher to this river, and built himself there a hut. He carried a great pole in his hand, to support himself in the water, and bore over on his shoulders all manner of people to the other side. And there he abode, thus doing many days.

And on a time, as he slept in his hut, he heard the voice of a child which called him:—

"Christopher, Christopher, come out and bear me over."

Then he awoke and went out, but he found no man. And when he was again in his house he heard the same voice, crying:—

"Christopher, Christopher, come out and bear me over."

And he ran out and found nobody.

And the third time he was called and ran thither, and he found a Child by the brink of the river, which prayed him goodly to bear him over the water.

And then Christopher lifted up the Child on his shoulders, and took his staff, and entered into the river for to pass over. And the water of the river arose and swelled more and more; and the Child was heavy as lead, and always as Christopher went farther the water increased and grew more, and the Child more and more waxed heavy, insomuch that Christopher suffered great anguish and was afeared to be drowned.

And when he was escaped with great pain, and passed over the water, and set the Child aground, he said:—

"Child, thou hast put me in great peril. Thou weighest almost as I had all the world upon me. I might bear no greater burden."

And the Child answered: "Christopher, marvel thee nothing, for thou hast not only borne all the world upon thee, but thou hast borne Him that created and made all the world, upon thy shoulders. I am Jesu Christ the King whom thou servest. And that thou mayest know that I say

the truth, set thy staff in the earth by thy house, and thou shalt see to-morn that it shall bear flowers and fruit."

And anon the Child vanished from his eyes.

And then Christopher set his staff in the earth, and when he arose on the morn, he found his staff bearing flowers, leaves, and dates.

THE STRANGER CHILD (A LEGEND)
COUNT FRANZ POCCI (TRANSLATED)

There once lived a laborer who earned his daily
bread by cutting wood. His wife and two children, a boy and girl, helped him with his work.
The boy's name was Valentine, and the girl's,
Marie. They were obedient and pious and the joy
and comfort of their poor parents.

One winter evening, this good family gathered
about the table to eat their small loaf of bread,
while the father read aloud from the Bible. Just
as they sat down there came a knock on the
window, and a sweet voice called:—

"O let me in! I am a little child, and I have nothing to eat, and no place to sleep in. I am so cold
and hungry! Please, good people, let me in!"

Valentine and Marie sprang from the table and
ran to open the door, saying:—

"Come in, poor child, we have but very little
ourselves, not much more than thou hast, but
what we have we will share with thee."

The stranger Child entered, and going to the fire
began to warm his cold hands.

The children gave him a portion of their bread,
and said:—

"Thou must be very tired; come, lie down in our bed, and we will sleep on the bench here before the fire."

Then answered the stranger Child: "May God in Heaven reward you for your kindness."

They led the little guest to their small room, laid him in their bed, and covered him closely, thinking to themselves:—

"Oh! how much we have to be thankful for! We have our nice warm room and comfortable bed, while this Child has nothing but the sky for a roof, and the earth for a couch."

When the parents went to their bed, Valentine and Marie lay down on the bench before the fire, and said one to the other:—

"The stranger Child is happy now, because he is so warm! Good-night!"

Then they fell asleep.

They had not slept many hours, when little Marie awoke, and touching her brother lightly, whispered:—

"Valentine, Valentine, wake up! wake up! Listen to the beautiful music at the window."

Valentine rubbed his eyes and listened. He heard the most wonderful singing and the sweet notes of many harps.

"Blessed Child,
Thee we greet,
With sound of harp
And singing sweet.

"Sleep in peace,
Child so bright,
We have watched thee
All the night.

"Blest the home
That holdeth Thee,
Peace, and love,
Its guardians be."

The children listened to the beautiful singing, and it seemed to fill them with unspeakable happiness. Then creeping to the window they looked out.

They saw a rosy light in the east, and, before the house in the snow, stood a number of little children holding golden harps and lutes in their hands, and dressed in sparkling, silver robes.

Full of wonder at this sight, Valentine and Marie continued to gaze out at the window, when they heard a sound behind them, and turning saw the stranger Child standing near. He was clad in

a golden garment, and wore a glistening, golden crown upon his soft hair. Sweetly he spoke to the children:—

"I am the Christ Child, who wanders about the world seeking to bring joy and good things to loving children. Because you have lodged me this night I will leave with you my blessing."

As the Christ Child spoke He stepped from the door, and breaking off a bough from a fir tree that grew near, planted it in the ground, saying:—

"This bough shall grow into a tree, and every year it shall bear Christmas fruit for you."

Having said this He vanished from their sight, together with the silver-clad, singing children— the angels.

And, as Valentine and Marie looked on in wonder, the fir bough grew, and grew, and grew, into a stately Christmas Tree laden with golden apples, silver nuts, and lovely toys. And after that, every year at Christmas time, the Tree bore the same wonderful fruit.

And you, dear boys and girls, when you gather around your richly decorated trees, think of the two poor children who shared their bread with a stranger child, and be thankful.

THE THREE KINGS OF COLOGNE
A LEGEND OF THE MIDDLE AGES
JOHN OF HILDESHEIM

THE STAR

Now, when the Children of Israel were gone out
of Egypt, and had won and made subject to
them Jerusalem and all the land lying about,
there was in the Kingdom of Ind a tall hill called
the Hill of Vaws, or the Hill of Victory. On this
hill were stationed sentinels of Ind, who watched
day and night against the Children of Israel, and
afterward against the Romans.

And if an enemy approached, the keepers of the
Hill of Vaws made a great fire to warn the inhabitants of the land so that the men might make
ready to defend themselves.

Now in the time when Balaam prophesied of the
Star that should betoken the birth of Christ, all
the great lords and the people of Ind and in the
East desired greatly to see this Star of which he
spake; and they gave gifts to the keepers of the
Hill of Vaws, and bade them, if they saw by night
or by day any star in the air, that had not been
seen aforetime, that they, the keepers, should
send anon word to the people of Ind.

And thus was it that for so long a time the fame
of this Star was borne throughout the lands of
the East. And the more the Star was sought for,

and the more its fame increased, so much the more all the people of the Land of Ind desired to see it. So they ordained twelve of the wisest and greatest of the clerks of astronomy, that were in all that country about, and gave them great hire to keep watch upon the Hill of Vaws for the Star that was prophesied of Balaam.

Now, when Christ was born in Bethlehem of Judea, His Star began to rise in the manner of a sun, bright shining. It ascended above the Hill of Vaws, and all that day in the highest air it abode without moving, insomuch that when the sun was hot and most high there was no difference in shining betwixt them.

But when the day of the nativity was passed the Star ascended up into the firmament, and it had right many long streaks and beams, more burning and brighter than a brand of fire; and, as an eagle flying and beating the air with his wings, right so the streaks and beams of the Star stirred about.

Then all the people, both man and woman, of all that country about when they saw this marvelous Star, were full of wonder thereat; yet they knew well that it was the Star that was prophesied of Balaam, and long time was desired of all the people in that country.

Now, when the three worshipful kings, who at that time reigned in Ind, Chaldea, and Persia,

were informed by the astronomers of this Star, they were right glad that they had grace to see the Star in their days.

Wherefore these three worshipful kings, Melchior, Balthazar, and Jasper (in the same hour the Star appeared to all three), though each of them was far from the other, and none knew of the others' purpose, decided to go and seek and worship the Lord and King of the Jews, that was new born, as the appearance of the Star announced.

So each king prepared great and rich gifts, and trains of mules, camels, and horses charged with treasure, and together with a great multitude of people they set forth on their journeys.

THE CHILD

Now, when these three worshipful kings were passed forth out of their kingdoms, the Star went before each king and his people. When they stood still and rested, the Star stood still; and when they went forward again, the Star always went before them in virtue and strength and gave light all the way.

And, as it is written, in the time that Christ was born, there was peace in all the world, wherefore in all the cities and towns through which they went there was no gate shut neither by night nor by day; and all the people of those same cities

and towns marveled wonderfully as they saw
kings and vast multitudes go by in great haste;
but they knew not what they were, nor whence
they came, nor whither they should go.

Furthermore these three kings rode forth over
hills, waters, valleys, plains, and other divers
and perilous places without hindrance, for all
the way seemed to them plain and even. And
they never took shelter by night nor by day, nor
ever rested, nor did their horses and other
beasts ever eat or drink till they had come to
Bethlehem. And all this time it did seem to them
as one day.

But when the three blessed kings had come near
to Jerusalem, then a great cloud of darkness hid
the Star from their sight. And when Melchior
and his people were come fast by the city, they
abode in fog and darkness. Then came
Balthazar, and he abode under the same cloud
near unto Melchior. Thereupon appeared Jasper
with all his host.

So these three glorious kings, each with his host
and burdens and beasts, met together in the
highway without the city of Jerusalem. And,
notwithstanding that none of them ever before
had seen the other, nor knew him, nor had
heard of his coming, yet at their meeting each
one with great reverence and joy kissed the
other. So afterward, when they had spoken
together and each had told his purpose and the

cause of his journey, they were much more glad
and fervent. So they rode forth, and at the upris-
ing of the sun, they came into Jerusalem. And
yet the Star appeared not.

So then these three worshipful kings, when they
were come into the city, asked of the people
concerning the Child that was born; and when
Herod heard this he was troubled and all
Jerusalem with him, and he privately summoned to him these three kings and learned of
them the time when the Star appeared. He then
sent them forth, bidding them find the young
Child and return to him.

Now when these three kings were passed out of
Jerusalem the Star appeared to them again as it
did erst, and went before them till they were
come to Bethlehem.

Now, the nearer the kings came to the place
where Christ was born, the brighter shined the
Star, and they entered Bethlehem the sixth hour
of the day. And they rode through the streets till
they came before a little house. There the Star
stood still, and then descended and shone with
so great a light that the little house was full of
radiance; till anon the Star went upward again
into the air, and stood still always above the
same place.

And the three kings went into the little house
and found the Child with his mother, and they

fell down and worshiped him, and offered him gifts.

And you shall understand that these three kings had brought great gifts from their own lands, rich ornaments and divers golden vessels, and many jewels and precious stones, and both gold and silver,—these they had brought to offer to the King of the Jews. But when they found the Lord in a little-house, in poor clothes, and when they saw that the Star gave so great and holy a light in all the place that it seemed as though they stood in a furnace of fire, then were they so sore afraid, that of all the rich jewels and ornaments they had brought with them, they chose from their treasures what came first to their hands. For Melchior took a round apple of gold in his hand, and thirty gilt pennies, and these he offered unto our Lord; and Balthazar took out of his treasury incense; and Jasper took out myrrh, and that he offered with weeping and tears.

And now after these three kings had worshiped the Lord, they abode in Bethlehem for a little space, and as they abode, there came a command to them, in their sleep, that they should not return to Herod; and so by another way they went home to their kingdoms. But the Star that had gone before appeared no more.

So these three kings, who had suddenly met together in the highway before Jerusalem, went

home together with great joy and honor. And when, after many days' journey over perilous places, they had come to the Hill of Vaws, they made there a fair chapel in worship of the Child they had sought. Also they agreed to meet together at the same place once in the year, and they ordained that the Hill of Vaws should be the place of their burial.

So when the three worshipful kings had done what they would, they took leave of each other, and each one with his people rode to his own land rejoicing.

HOW THEY CAME TO COLOGNE

Now, after many years, a little before the feast of Christmas, there appeared a wonderful Star above the cities where these three kings dwelt, and they knew thereby that their time was come when they should pass from earth. Then with one consent they built, at the Hill of Vaws, a fair and large tomb, and there the three Holy Kings, Melchior, Balthazar, and Jasper died, and were buried in the same tomb by their sorrowing people.

Now after much time had passed away, Queen Helen, the mother of the Emperor Constantine, began to think greatly of the bodies of these three kings, and she arrayed herself, and, accompanied by many attendants, went into the Land of Ind.

And you shall understand that after she had found the bodies of Melchior, Balthazar, and Jasper, Queen Helen put them into one chest and ornamented it with great riches, and she brought them into Constantinople, with joy and reverence, and laid them in a church that is called Saint Sophia; and this church the Emperor Constantine did make,—he alone, with a little child, set up all the marble pillars thereof.

Now, after the death of the Emperor Constantine a persecution against the Christian faith arose, and in this persecution the bodies of the three worshipful kings were set at naught. Then came the Emperor Mauricius of Rome, and, through his counsel, the bodies of these three kings were carried to Italy, and there they were laid in a fair church in the city of Milan.

Then afterward, in the process of time, the city of Milan rebelled against the Emperor Frederick the First, and he, being sore beset, sent to Rainald, Archbishop of Cologne, asking for help.

This Archbishop with his army did take the city of Milan, and delivered it to the Emperor. And for this service did the Emperor grant, at the Archbishop's great entreaty, that he should carry forth to Cologne the bodies of the three blessed kings.

Then the Archbishop, with great solemnity and in procession, did carry forth from the city of Milan the bodies of the three kings, and brought them unto Cologne and there placed them in the fair church of Saint Peter. And all the people of the country roundabout, with all the reverence they might, received these relics, and there in the city of Cologne they are kept and beholden of all manner of nations unto this day.

Thus endeth the legend of these three blessed kings,—Melchior, Balthazar, and Jasper.

THE THREE PURSES - A LEGEND
WILLIAM S. WALSH

When Saint Nicholas was Bishop of Myra, there were among his people three beautiful maidens, daughters of a nobleman. Their father was so poor that he could not afford to give them dowries, and as in that land no maid might marry without a dowry, so these three maidens could not wed the youths who loved them.

At last the father became so very poor that he no longer had money with which to buy food or clothes for his daughters, and he was overcome by shame and sorrow. As for the daughters they wept continually, for they were both cold and hungry.

One day Saint Nicholas heard of the sad state of this noble family. So at night, when the maidens were asleep, and the father was watching, sorrowful and lonely, the good saint took a handful of gold, and, tying it in a purse, set off for the nobleman's house. Creeping to the open window he threw the purse into the chamber, so that it fell on the bed of the sleeping maidens.

The father picked up the purse, and when he opened it and saw the gold, he rejoiced greatly, and awakened his daughters. He gave most of the gold to his eldest child for a dowry, and thus she was enabled to wed the young man whom she loved.

A few days later Saint Nicholas filled another
purse with gold, and, as before, went by night to
the nobleman's house, and tossed the purse
through the open window. Thus the second
daughter was enabled to marry the young man
whom she loved.

Now, the nobleman felt very grateful to the unknown one who threw purses of gold into his
room and he longed to know who his benefactor
was and to thank him. So the next night he
watched beneath the open window. And when all
was dark, lo! good Saint Nicholas came for the
third time, carrying a silken purse filled with
gold, and as he was about to throw it on the
youngest maiden's bed, the nobleman caught
him by his robe, crying:—

"Oh good Saint Nicholas! why do you hide yourself thus?"

And he kissed the saint's hands and feet, but
Saint Nicholas, overcome with confusion at
having his good deed discovered, begged the
nobleman to tell no man what had happened.

Thus the nobleman's third daughter was enabled to marry the young man whom she loved;
and she and her father and her two sisters lived
happily for the remainder of their lives.

THE THUNDER OAK
A SCANDINAVIAN LEGEND
WILLIAM S. WALSH AND OTHER SOURCES

When the heathen raged through the forests of
the ancient Northland there grew a giant tree
branching with huge limbs toward the clouds. It
was the Thunder Oak of the war-god Thor.

Thither, under cover of night, heathen priests
were wont to bring their victims—both men and
beasts—and slay them upon the altar of the
thunder-god. There in the darkness was
wrought many an evil deed, while human blood
was poured forth and watered the roots of that
gloomy tree, from whose branches depended the
mistletoe, the fateful plant that sprang from the
blood-fed veins of the oak. So gloomy and terror-
ridden was the spot on which grew the tree that
no beasts of field or forest would lodge beneath
its dark branches, nor would birds nest or perch
among its gnarled limbs.

Long, long ago, on a white Christmas Eve, Thor's
priests held their winter rites beneath the Thunder Oak. Through the deep snow of the dense
forest hastened throngs of heathen folk, all
intent on keeping the mystic feast of the mighty
Thor. In the hush of the night the folk gathered
in the glade where stood the tree. Closely they
pressed around the great altar-stone under the
overhanging boughs where stood the white-

robed priests. Clearly shone the moonlight on all.

Then from the altar flashed upward the sacrificial flames, casting their lurid glow on the straining faces of the human victims awaiting the blow of the priest's knife.

But the knife never fell, for from the silent avenues of the dark forest came the good Saint Winfred and his people. Swiftly the saint drew from his girdle a shining axe. Fiercely he smote the Thunder Oak, hewing a deep gash in its trunk. And while the heathen folk gazed in horror and wonder, the bright blade of the axe circled faster and faster around Saint Winfred's head, and the flakes of wood flew far and wide from the deepening cut in the body of the tree.

Suddenly there was heard overhead the sound of a mighty, rushing wind. A whirling blast struck the tree. It gripped the oak from its foundations. Backward it fell like a tower, groaning as it split into four pieces.

But just behind it, unharmed by the ruin, stood a young fir tree, pointing its green spire to heaven.

Saint Winfred dropped his axe, and turned to speak to the people. Joyously his voice rang out through the crisp, winter air:—

"This little tree, a young child of the forest, shall be your holy tree to-night. It is the tree of peace, for your houses are built of fir. It is the sign of endless life, for its leaves are forever green. See how it points upward to heaven! Let this be called the tree of the Christ Child. Gather about it, not in the wildwood, but in your own homes. There it will shelter no deeds of blood, but loving gifts and rites of kindness. So shall the peace of the White Christ reign in your hearts!"

And with songs of joy the multitude of heathen folk took up the little fir tree and bore it to the house of their chief, and there with good will and peace they kept the holy Christmastide.

THE CHRISTMAS TREE
SAMUEL T. COLERIDGE

There is a Christmas custom here which pleased and interested me. The children make little presents to their parents, and to each other; and the parents to the children. For three or four months before Christmas the girls are all busy; and the boys save up their pocket money, to make or purchase these presents. What the present is to be is cautiously kept secret, and the girls have a world of contrivances to conceal it—such as working when they are out on visits, and the others are not with them; getting up in the morning before daylight; and the like. Then, on the evening before Christmas day, one of the parlours is lighted up by the children, into which the parents must not go. A great yew bough is fastened on the table at a little distance from the wall, a multitude of little tapers are fastened in the bough, but so as not to catch it till they are nearly burnt out, and coloured paper hangs and flutters from the twings. Under this bough, the children lay out in great order the presents they mean for their parents, still concealing in their pockets what they intend for each other. Then the parents are introduced, and each presents his little gift, and then bring out the rest one by one from their pockets, and present them with kisses and embraces. Where I witnessed this scene there were eight or nine children, and the eldest daughter and the mother wept aloud for joy and tenderness; and

the tears ran down the face of the father, and he clasped all his children so tight to his breast, it seemed as if he did it to stifle the sob that was rising within him. I was very much affected. The shadow of the bough and its appendages on the wall, and arching over on the ceiling, made a pretty picture, and then the raptures of the very little ones, when at last the twings and their needles began to take fire and snap! — Oh, it was a delight for them! On the next day, in the great parlour, the parents lay out on the table the presents for the children; a scene of more sober joy success, as on this day, after an old custom, the mother says privately to each of her daughters, and the father to his sons, that which he has observed most praiseworthy, and that which was most faulty in their conduct. Formerly, and still in all the smaller towns and villages throughout North Germany, these presents were sent by all the parents to some one fellow, who in high buskins, a white robe, a mask, and an enormous flax wig, personate Knecht Rupert, the servant Rupert. On Christmas night he goes round to every house, and says that Jesus Christ his master sent him thither, the parents and elder children receive him with great pomp of reverence, while the little ones are most terribly frightened. He then inquires for the children, and, according to the character which he hears from the parent, he gives them the intended presents, as if they came out of heaven from Jesus Christ. Or, if they should have been bad children, he gives the

parents a rod, and in the name of his master recommends them to use it frequently. About seven or eight years old the children are let into the secret, and it is curious to observe how faithfully they keep it.

THE GIFT OF THE MAGI
O. HENRY

One dollar and eighty-seven cents. That was all.
And sixty cents of it was in pennies. Pennies
saved one and two at a time by bulldozing the
grocer and the vegetable man and the butcher
until one's cheeks burned with the silent impu-
tation of parsimony that such close dealing
implied. Three times Della counted it. One dollar
and eighty- seven cents. And the next day would
be Christmas.

There was clearly nothing to do but flop down on
the shabby little couch and howl. So Della did it.
Which instigates the moral reflection that life is
made up of sobs, sniffles, and smiles, with
sniffles predominating.

While the mistress of the home is gradually
subsiding from the first stage to the second, take
a look at the home. A furnished flat at $8 per
week. It did not exactly beggar description, but it
certainly had that word on the lookout for the
mendicancy squad.

In the vestibule below was a letter-box into
which no letter would go, and an electric button
from which no mortal finger could coax a ring.
Also appertaining thereunto was a card bearing
the name "Mr. James Dillingham Young."

The "Dillingham" had been flung to the breeze
during a former period of prosperity when its

possessor was being paid $30 per week. Now, when the income was shrunk to $20, though, they were thinking seriously of contracting to a modest and unassuming D. But whenever Mr. James Dillingham

Young came home and reached his flat above he was called "Jim" and greatly hugged by Mrs. James Dillingham Young, already introduced to you as Della. Which is all very good.

Della finished her cry and attended to her cheeks with the powder rag. She stood by the window and looked out dully at a gray cat walk-ing a gray fence in a gray backyard. Tomorrow would be Christmas Day, and she had only $1.87 with which to buy Jim a present. She had been saving every penny she could for months, with this result. Twenty dollars a week doesn't go far. Expenses had been greater than she had calculated. They always are. Only $1.87 to buy a present for Jim. Her Jim. Many a happy hour she had spent planning for something nice for him. Something fine and rare and sterling— something just a little bit near to being worthy of the honor of being owned by Jim.

There was a pier-glass between the windows of the room. Perhaps you have seen a pier-glass in an $8 flat. A very thin and very agile person may, by observing his reflection in a rapid se-quence of longitudinal strips, obtain a fairly

accurate conception of his looks. Della, being slender, had mastered the art.

Suddenly she whirled from the window and stood before the glass. Her eyes were shining brilliantly, but her face had lost its color within twenty seconds. Rapidly she pulled down her hair and let it fall to its full length.

Now, there were two possessions of the James Dillingham Youngs in which they both took a mighty pride. One was Jim's gold watch that had been his father's and his grandfather's. The other was Della's hair. Had the queen of Sheba lived in the flat across the airshaft, Della would have let her hair hang out the window some day to dry just to depreciate Her Majesty's jewels and gifts. Had King Solomon been the janitor, with all his treasures piled up in the basement, Jim would have pulled out his watch every time he passed, just to see him pluck at his beard from envy.

So now Della's beautiful hair fell about her rippling and shining like a cascade of brown waters. It reached below her knee and made itself almost a garment for her. And then she did it up again nervously and quickly. Once she faltered for a minute and stood still while a tear or two splashed on the worn red carpet.

On went her old brown jacket; on went her old brown hat. With a whirl of skirts and with the

brilliant sparkle still in her eyes, she fluttered out the door and down the stairs to the street.

Where she stopped the sign read: "Mne. Sofronie. Hair Goods of All Kinds." One flight up Della ran, and collected herself, panting. Madame, large, too white, chilly, hardly looked the "Sofronie."

"Will you buy my hair?" asked Della.

"I buy hair," said Madame. "Take yer hat off and let's have a sight at the looks of it."

Down rippled the brown cascade.

"Twenty dollars," said Madame, lifting the mass with a practised hand.

"Give it to me quick," said Della.

Oh, and the next two hours tripped by on rosy wings. Forget the hashed metaphor. She was ransacking the stores for Jim's present.

She found it at last. It surely had been made for Jim and no one else. There was no other like it in any of the stores, and she had turned all of them inside out. It was a platinum fob chain simple and chaste in design, properly proclaiming its value by substance alone and not by meretricious ornamentation—as all good things

should do. It was even worthy of The Watch. As soon as she saw it she knew that it must be Jim's. It was like him. Quietness and value—the description applied to both.

Twenty-one dollars they took from her for it, and she hurried home with the 87 cents. With that chain on his watch Jim might be properly anxious about the time in any company. Grand as the watch was, he sometimes looked at it on the sly on account of the old leather strap that he used in place of a chain.

When Della reached home her intoxication gave way a little to prudence and reason. She got out her curling irons and lighted the gas and went to work repairing the ravages made by generosity added to love. Which is always a tremendous task, dear friends—a mammoth task.

Within forty minutes her head was covered with tiny, close-lying curls that made her look wonderfully like a truant schoolboy. She looked at her reflection in the mirror long, carefully, and critically.

"If Jim doesn't kill me," she said to herself, "before he takes a second look at me, he'll say I look like a Coney Island chorus girl. But what could I do—oh! what could I do with a dollar and eighty-seven cents?"

At 7 o'clock the coffee was made and the frying-pan was on the back of the stove hot and ready to cook the chops.

Jim was never late. Della doubled the fob chain in her hand and sat on the corner of the table near the door that he always entered. Then she heard his step on the stair away down on the first flight, and she turned white for just a moment. She had a habit for saying little silent prayer about the simplest everyday things, and now she whispered: "Please God, make him think I am still pretty."

The door opened and Jim stepped in and closed it. He looked thin and very serious. Poor fellow, he was only twenty-two—and to be burdened with a family! He needed a new overcoat and he was without gloves.

Jim stopped inside the door, as immovable as a setter at the scent of quail. His eyes were fixed upon Della, and there was an expression in them that she could not read, and it terrified her. It was not anger, nor surprise, nor disapproval, nor horror, nor any of the sentiments that she had been prepared for. He simply stared at her fixedly with that peculiar expression on his face.

Della wriggled off the table and went for him. "Jim, darling," she cried, "don't look at me that way. I had my hair cut off and sold because I

couldn't have lived through Christmas without
giving you a present. It'll grow out again—you
won't mind, will you? I just had to do it. My hair
grows awfully fast. Say `Merry Christmas!' Jim,
and let's be happy. You don't know what a
nice— what a beautiful, nice gift I've got for you."

"You've cut off your hair?" asked Jim, labori-
ously, as if he had not arrived at that patent fact
yet even after the hardest mental labor.

"Cut it off and sold it," said Della. "Don't you like
me just as well, anyhow? I'm me without my
hair, ain't I?"

Jim looked about the room curiously.

"You say your hair is gone?" he said, with an air
almost of idiocy.

"You needn't look for it," said Della. "It's sold, I
tell you—sold and gone, too. It's Christmas Eve,
boy. Be good to me, for it went for you. Maybe
the hairs of my head were numbered," she went
on with sudden serious sweetness, "but nobody
could ever count my love for you. Shall I put the
chops on, Jim?"

Out of his trance Jim seemed quickly to wake.
He enfolded his Della. For ten seconds let us
regard with discreet scrutiny some inconsequen-
tial object in the other direction. Eight dollars a

week or a million a year—what is the difference? A mathematician or a wit would give you the wrong answer. The magi brought valuable gifts, but that was not among them. This dark assertion will be illuminated later on.

Jim drew a package from his overcoat pocket and threw it upon the table.

"Don't make any mistake, Dell," he said, "about me. I don't think there's anything in the way of a haircut or a shave or a shampoo that could make me like my girl any less. But if you'll unwrap that package you may see why you had me going a while at first."

White fingers and nimble tore at the string and paper. And then an ecstatic scream of joy; and then, alas! a quick feminine change to hysterical tears and wails, necessitating the immediate employment of all the comforting powers of the lord of the flat.

For there lay The Combs—the set of combs, side and back, that Della had worshipped long in a Broadway window. Beautiful combs, pure tortoise shell, with jewelled rims—just the shade to wear in the beautiful vanished hair. They were expensive combs, she knew, and her heart had simply craved and yearned over them without the least hope of possession. And now, they were hers, but the tresses that should have adorned the coveted adornments were gone.

But she hugged them to her bosom, and at length she was able to look up with dim eyes and a smile and say: "My hair grows so fast, Jim!"

And them Della leaped up like a little singed cat and cried, "Oh, oh!"

Jim had not yet seen his beautiful present. She held it out to him eagerly upon her open palm. The dull precious metal seemed to flash with a reflection of her bright and ardent spirit.

"Isn't it a dandy, Jim? I hunted all over town to find it. You'll have to look at the time a hundred times a day now. Give me your watch. I want to see how it looks on it."
Instead of obeying, Jim tumbled down on the couch and put his hands under the back of his head and smiled.

"Dell," said he, "let's put our Christmas presents away and keep 'em a while. They're too nice to use just at present. I sold the watch to get the money to buy your combs. And now suppose you put the chops on."

The magi, as you know, were wise men—wonderfully wise men—who brought gifts to the Babe in the manger. They invented the art of giving Christmas presents. Being wise, their gifts were no doubt wise ones, possibly bearing the privilege of exchange in case of duplication. And

here I have lamely related to you the uneventful chronicle of two foolish children in a flat who most unwisely sacrificed for each other the greatest treasures of their house. But in a last word to the wise of these days let it be said that of all who give gifts these two were the wisest. O all who give and receive gifts, such as they are wisest. Everywhere they are wisest. They are the magi.

THE HOLY NIGHT
SELMA LAGERLOF

There was a man who went out in the dark night to borrow live coals to kindle a fire. He went from hut to hut and knocked. "Dear friends, help me!" said he. "My wife has just given birth to a child, and I must make a fire to warm her and the little one."

But it was way in the night, and all the people were asleep. No one replied.

The man walked and walked. At last he saw the gleam of a fire a long way off. Then he went in that direction and saw that the fire was burning in the open. A lot of sheep were sleeping around the fire, and an old shepherd sat and watched over the flock.

When the man who wanted to borrow fire came up to the sheep, he saw that three big dogs lay asleep at the shepherd's feet. All three awoke when the man approached and opened their great jaws, as though they wanted to bark; but not a sound was heard. The man noticed that the hair on their backs stood up and that their sharp, white teeth glistened if in the firelight. They dashed toward him.

He felt that one of them bit at his leg and one at this hand and that one clung to this throat. But their jaws and teeth wouldn't obey them, and the man didn't suffer the least harm.

Now the man wished to go farther, to get what he needed. But the sheep lay back to back and so close to one another that he couldn't pass them. Then the man stepped upon their backs and walked over them and up to the fire. And not one of the animals awoke or moved.

When the man had almost reached the fire, the shepherd looked up. He was a surly old man, who was unfriendly and harsh toward human beings. And when he saw the strange man coming, he seized the long, spiked staff, which he always held in his hand when he tended his flock, and threw it at him. The staff came right toward the man, but, before it reached him, it turned off to one side and whizzed past him, far out in the meadow.

Now the man came up to the shepherd and said to him: "Good man, help me, and lend me a little fire! My wife has just given birth to a child, and I must make a fire to warm her and the little one." The shepherd would rather have said no, but when he pondered that the dogs couldn't hurt the man, and the sheep had not run from him, and that the staff had not wished to strike him, he was a little afraid, and dared not deny the man that which he asked.

"Take as much as you need!" he said to the man.

But then the fire was nearly burnt out. There were no logs or branches left, only a big heap of live coals, and the stranger had neither spade nor shovel wherein he could carry the red-hot coals.

When the shepherd saw this, he said again: "Take as much as you need!" And he was glad that the man wouldn't be able to take away any coals.

But the man stopped and picked coals from the ashes with his bare hands, and laid them in his mantle. And he didn't burn his hands when he touched them, nor did the coals scorch his mantle; but he carried them away as if they had been nuts or apples.

And when the shepherd, who was such a cruel and hardhearted man, saw all this, he began to wonder to himself. What kind of a night is this, when the dogs do not bite, the sheep are not scared, the staff does not kill, or the fire scorch?

He called the stranger back and said to him: "What kind of a night is this? And how does it happen that all things show you compassion?"

Then said the man: "I cannot tell you if you yourself do not see it." And he wished to go his

way, that he might soon make a fire and warm his wife and child.

But the shepherd did not wish to lose sight of the man before he had found out what all this might portend. He got up and followed the man till they came to the place where he lived.

Then the shepherd saw the man didn't have so much as a hut to dwell in, but that his wife and babe were lying in a mountain grotto, where there was nothing except the cold and naked stone walls.

But the shepherd thought that perhaps the poor innocent child might freeze to death there in the grotto; and, although he was a hard man, he was touched, and thought he would like to help it. And he loosened the knapsack from his shoulder, took from it a soft white sheepskin, gave it to the strange man, and said that he should let the child sleep on it.

But just as soon as he showed that he, too, could be merciful, his eyes were opened, and he saw what he had not been able to see before, and heard what he could not have heard before.

He saw that all around him stood a ring of little silver-winged angels, and each held a stringed instrument, and all sang in loud tones that tonight the Saviour was born who should redeem the world from its sins.

Then he understood how all things were so
happy this night that they didn't want to do
anything wrong.

And it was not only around the shepherd that
there were angels, but he saw them everywhere.
They sat inside the grotto, they sat outside on
the mountain, and they flew under the heavens.
They came marching in great companies, and,
as they passed, they paused and cast a glance at
the child.

There was such jubilation and such gladness
and songs and play! And all this he saw in the
dark night whereas before he could not have
made out anything. He was so happy because
his eyes had been opened that he fell upon his
knees and thanked God.

What that shepherd saw, we might also see, for
the angels fly down from heaven every Christmas Eve, if we could only see them.

You must remember this, for it is as true, as
true as that I see you and you see me. It is not
revealed by the light of lamps or candles, and it
does not depend upon sun and moon; but that
which is needful is that we have such eyes as
can see God's glory.

CHRISTMAS EVERY DAY
WILLIAM DEAN HOWELLS

The Little girl came into her papa's study, as she always did Saturday morning before breakfast, and asked for a story. He tried to beg off that morning, for he was very busy, but she would not let him. So he began:

"Well, once there was a little pig—" She put her hand over his mouth and stopped him at the word. She said she had heard little pig-stories till she was perfectly sick of them.

"Well, what kind of story shall I tell, then?"

"About Christmas. It's getting to be the season. It's past Thanksgiving already."

"It seems to me," her papa argued, "that I've told as often about Christmas as I have about little pigs."

"No difference, Christmas is more interesting."

"Well!" Her papa roused himself from his writing by a great effort. "Well, then, I'll tell you about the little girl that wanted it Christmas every day in the year. How would you like that."

"First-rate" said the little girl; and she nestled into comfortable shape in his lap, ready for

listening. "Very well, then, this little pig— Oh, what are you pounding me for?"

"Because you said little pig instead of little girl."

"I should like to know what's the difference between a little pig and a little girl that wanted it Christmas every day."

"Papa," said the little girl, warningly, "if you don't go on, I'll give it to you!" And at this her papa darted off like lightning, and began to tell the story as fast as he could.

Well, once there was a little girl who liked Christmas so much that she wanted it to be Christmas every day in the year; and as soon as Thanksgiving was over she began to send postal-cards to the old Christmas Fairy to ask if she mightn't have it. But the old Fairy never answered any of the postals; and after a while the little girl found out that the Fairy was pretty particular, and wouldn't notice anything but letters— not even correspondence cards in envelopes; but real letters on sheets of paper, and sealed outside with a monogram—or your initial, anyway. So, then, she began to send her letters; and in about three weeks—or just the day before Christmas, it was—she got a letter from the Fairy, saying she might have it Christmas every day for a year, and then they would see about having it longer.

The little girl was a good deal excited already, preparing for the old-fashioned, once-a-year Christmas that was coming the next day, and perhaps the Fairy's promise didn't make such an impression on her as it would have made at some other time. She just resolved to keep it to herself, and surprise everybody with it as it kept coming true; and then it slipped out of her mind altogether.

She had a splendid Christmas. She went to bed early, so as to let Santa Claus have a chance at the stockings, and in the morning she was up the first of anybody and went and felt them, and found hers all lumpy with packages of candy, and oranges and grapes, and pocketbooks and rubber balls, and all kinds of small presents, and her big brother's with nothing but the tongs in them, and her young lady sister's with a new silk umbrella, and her papa's and mamma's with potatoes and pieces of coal wrapped up in tissue-paper, just as they always had every Christmas. Then she waited around till the rest of the family were up, and she was the first to burst into the library, when the doors were opened, and look at the large presents laid out on the library-table-books, and portfolios, and boxes of stationery, and breastpins, and dolls, and little stoves, and dozens of handkerchiefs, and inkstands, and skates, and snow-shovels, and photograph-frames, and little easels, and boxes of water-colors, and Turkish paste, and nougat, and candied cherries, and dolls' houses, and

waterproofs — and the big Christmas-tree, lighted and standing in a waste-basket in the middle.

She had a splendid Christmas all day. She ate so much candy that she did not want any breakfast; and the whole forenoon the presents kept pouring in that the expressman had not had time to deliver the night before; and she went round giving the presents she had got for other people, and came home and ate turkey and cranberry for dinner, and plum-pudding and nuts and raisins and oranges and more candy, and then went out and coasted, and came in with a stomach-ache, crying; and her papa said he would see if his house was turned into that sort of fool's paradise another year; and they had a light supper, and pretty early everybody went to bed cross.

Here the little girl pounded her papa in the back, again.

"Well, what now? Did I say pigs?"

"You made them act like pigs."

"Well, didn't they?"

"No matter; you oughtn't to put it into a story."

"Very well, then, I'll take it all out."

Her father went on:

The little girl slept very heavily, and she slept very late, but she was wakened at last by the other children dancing round the bed with their stockings full of presents in their hands.

"What is it?" said the little girl, and she rubbed her eyes and tried to rise up in bed. "Christmas! Christmas! Christmas!" they all shouted, and waved their stockings.

"Nonsense! It was Christmas yesterday."

Her brothers and sisters just laughed. "We don't know about that. It's Christmas to-day, anyway. You come into the library and see."

Then all at once it flashed on the little girl that the Fairy was keeping her promise, and her year of Christmases was beginning. She was dreadfully sleepy, but she sprang up like a lark—a lark that had overeaten itself and gone to bed cross— and darted into the library. There it was again! Books, and portfolios, and boxes of stationery, and breastpins—

"You needn't go over it all, papa; I guess I can remember just what was there," said the little girl.

Well, and there was the Christmas-tree blazing away, and the family picking out their presents, but looking pretty sleepy, and her father perfectly puzzled, and her mother ready to cry. "I'm

sure I don't see how I'm to dispose of all these things," said her mother, and her father said it seemed to him they had had something just like it the day before, but he supposed he must have dreamed it. This struck the little girl as the best kind of a joke; and so she ate so much candy she didn't want any breakfast, and went round carrying presents, and had turkey and cranberry for dinner, and then went out and coasted, and came in with a—

"Papa!"

"Well, what now?"

"What did you promise, you forgetful thing."

"Oh! oh yes!"

Well, the next day, it was just the same thing over again, but everybody getting crosser; and at the end of a week's time so many people had lost their tempers that you could pick up lost tempers anywhere; they perfectly strewed the ground. Even when people tried to recover their tempers they usually got somebody else's, and it made the most dreadful mix.

The little girl began to get frightened, keeping the secret all to herself; she wanted to tell her mother, but she didn't dare to; and she was ashamed to ask the Fairy to take back her gift, it seemed ungrateful and ill-bred, and she thought

she would try to stand it, but she hardly knew
how she could, for a whole year. So it went on
and on, and it was Christmas on St. Valentine's
Day and Washington's Birthday, just the same
as any day, and it didn't skip even the First of
April, though everything was counterfeit that
day, and that was some little relief.

After a while coal and potatoes began to be awfully scarce, so many had been wrapped up in
tissue-paper to fool papas and mammas with.
Turkeys got to be about a thousand dollars
apiece—

"Papa!"

"Well, what?"

"You're beginning to fib."

"Well, two thousand, then."

And they got to passing off almost anything for
turkeys— half-grown humming-birds, and even
rocs out of the Arabian Nights—the real turkeys
were so scarce. And cranberries— well, they
asked a diamond apiece for cranberries. All the
woods and orchards were cut down for Christmas-trees, and where the woods and orchards
used to be it looked just like a stubble-held, with
the stumps. After a while they had to make
Christmas-trees out of rags, and stuff them with
bran, like old-fashioned dolls; but there were

plenty of rags, because People got so poor, buy-
ing presents for one another, that they couldn't
get any new clothes, and they just wore their old
ones to tatters. They got so poor that everybody
had to go to the poor-house, except the confec-
tioners, and the fancy-store keepers, and the
picture-book sellers, and the expressmen; and
they all got so rich and proud that they would
hardly wait upon a person when he came to buy.
It was perfectly shameful!

Well, after it had gone on about three or four
months, the little girl, whenever she came into
the room in the morning and saw those great
ugly, lumpy stockings dangling at the fireplace,
and the disgusting presents around everywhere,
used to just sit down and burst out crying. In six
months she was perfectly exhausted; she
couldn't even cry any more; she just lay on the
lounge and rolled her eyes and panted. About
the beginning of October she took to sitting
down on dolls wherever she found them—French
dolls, or any kind—she hated the sight of them
so; and by Thanksgiving she was crazy, and just
slammed her presents across the room.

By that time people didn't carry presents around
nicely any more. They flung them over the fence,
or through the window, or anything; and, instead of running their tongues out and taking
great pains to write "For dear Papa," or
"Mamma," or "Brother," or "Sister," or "Susie," or
"Sammie," or "Billie," or "Bobbie," or "Jimmie,"

or "Jennie," or whoever it was, and troubling to get the spelling right, and then signing their names, and "Xmas, 18__," they used to write in the gift-books, "Take it, you horrid old thing!" and then go and bang it against the front door. Nearly everybody had built barns to hold their presents, but pretty soon the barns overflowed, and then they used to let them lie out in the rain, or anywhere. Sometimes the police used to come and tell them to shovel their presents off the sidewalk, or they would arrest them.

"I thought you said everybody had gone to the poor-house," interrupted the little girl.

"They did go, at first" said her papa; "but after a while the poor-houses got so full that they had to send the people back to their own houses. They tried to cry, when they got back, but they couldn't make the least sound."

"Why couldn't they?"

"Because they had lost their voices, saying 'Merry Christmas' so much. Did I tell you how it was on the Fourth of July?"

"No; how was it?" And the little girl nestled closer, in expectation of something uncommon.

Well, the night before, the boys stayed up to celebrate, as they always do, and fell asleep before twelve o'clock, as usual, expecting to be

wakened by the bells and cannon. But it was
nearly eight o'clock before the first boy in the
United States woke up, and then he found out
what the trouble was. As soon as he could get
his clothes on he ran out of the house and
smashed a big cannon-torpedo down on the
pavement; but it didn't make any more noise
than a damp wad of paper; and after he tried
about twenty or thirty more, he began to pick
them up and look at them.

Every single torpedo was a big raisin! Then he
just streaked it upstairs, and examined his
firecrackers and toy pistol and two-dollar collection of fireworks, and found that they were nothing but sugar and candy painted up to look like
fireworks! Before ten o'clock every boy in the
United States found out that his Fourth of July
things had turned into Christmas things; and
then they just sat down and cried—they were so
mad. There are about twenty million boys in the
United States, and so you can imagine what a
noise they made. Some men got together before
night, with a little powder that hadn't turned
into purple sugar yet, and they said they would
fire off one cannon, anyway. But the cannon
burst into a thousand pieces, for it was nothing
but rock-candy, and some of the men nearly got
killed. The Fourth of July orations all turned
into Christmas carols, and when anybody tried
to read the Declaration, instead of saying, "When
in the course of human events it becomes necessary," he was sure to sing, "God rest you, merry

gentlemen." It was perfectly awful.

The little girl drew a deep sigh of satisfaction.

"And how was it at Thanksgiving?"

Her papa hesitated. "Well, I'm almost afraid to tell you. I'm afraid you'll think it's wicked."

"Well, tell, anyway," said the little girl.

Well, before it came Thanksgiving it had leaked out who had caused all these Christmases. The little girl had suffered so much that she had talked about it in her sleep; and after that hardly anybody would play with her. People just perfectly despised her, because if it had not been for her greediness it wouldn't have happened; and now, when it came Thanksgiving, and she wanted them to go to church, and have squash-pie and turkey, and show their gratitude, they said that all the turkeys had been eaten up for her old Christmas dinners, and if she would stop the Christmases, they would see about the grati-tude. Wasn't it dreadful? And the very next day the little girl began to send letters to the Christ-mas Fairy, and then telegrams, to stop it. But it didn't do any good; and then she got to calling at the Fairy's house, but the girl that came to the door always said, "Not at home," or "Engaged," or "At dinner," or something like that; and so it went on till it came to the old once-a-year

Christmas Eve. The little girl fell asleep, and when she woke up in the morning—

"She found it was all nothing but a dream," suggested the little girl.

"No, indeed!" said her papa. "It was all every bit true!"

"Well, what did she find out, then?"

"Why, that it wasn't Christmas at last, and wasn't ever going to be, any more. Now it's time for breakfast."

The little girl held her papa fast around the neck.

"You sha'n't go if you're going to leave it so!"

"How do you want it left?"

"Christmas once a year."

"Alright," said her papa; and he went on again.

Well, there was the greatest rejoicing all over the country, and it extended clear up into Canada. The people met together everywhere, and kissed and cried for joy. The city carts went around and gathered up all the candy and raisins and nuts, and dumped them into the river; and it made the

fish perfectly sick; and the whole United States, as far out as Alaska, was one blaze of bonfires, where the children were burning up their gift-books and presents of all kinds. They had the greatest time!

The little girl went to thank the old Fairy because she had stopped its being Christmas, and she said she hoped she would keep her promise and see that Christmas never, never came again. Then the Fairy frowned, and asked her if she was sure she knew what she meant; and the little girl asked her, Why not? and the old Fairy said that now she was behaving just as greedily as ever, and she'd better look out. This made the little girl think it all over carefully again, and she said she would be willing to have it Christmas about once in a thousand years; and then she said a hundred, and then she said ten, and at last she got down to one. Then the Fairy said that was the good old way that had pleased people ever since Christmas began, and she agreed. Then the little girl said, "What're your shoes made of?" And the Fairy said, "Leather." And the little girl said, "Bargain's done forever," and skipped off, and hippity-hopped the whole way home, she was so glad.

"How will that do?" asked the papa.

"First-rate!" said the little girl; but she hated to have the story stop, and was rather sober.

However, her mamma put her head in at the door, and asked her papa, "Are you never coming to breakfast! What have you been telling that child?"

"Oh, just a moral tale."

The little girl caught him around the neck again.

"We know! Don't you tell what, papa! Don't you tell what!"

THE GOBLIN AND THE HUCKSTER
HANS CHRISTIAN ANDERSEN

THERE was once a regular student, who lived in a garret, and had no possessions. And there was also a regular huckster, to whom the house belonged, and who occupied the ground floor. A goblin lived with the huckster, because at Christmas he always had a large dish full of jam, with a great piece of butter in the middle. The huckster could afford this; and therefore the goblin remained with the huckster, which was very cunning of him.

One evening the student came into the shop through the back door to buy candles and cheese for himself, he had no one to send, and therefore he came himself; he obtained what he wished, and then the huckster and his wife nodded good evening to him, and she was a woman who could do more than merely nod, for she had usually plenty to say for herself. The student nodded in return as he turned to leave, then suddenly stopped, and began reading the piece of paper in which the cheese was wrapped. It was a leaf torn out of an old book, a book that ought not to have been torn up, for it was full of poetry. "Yonder lies some more of the same sort," said the huckster: "I gave an old woman a few coffee berries for it; you shall have the rest for sixpence, if you will."

"Indeed I will," said the student; "give me the
book instead of the cheese; I can eat my bread
and butter without cheese. It would be a sin to
tear up a book like this. You are a clever man;
and a practical man; but you understand no
more about poetry than that cask yonder."

This was a very rude speech, especially against
the cask; but the huckster and the student both
laughed, for it was only said in fun. But the
goblin felt very angry that any man should venture to say such things to a huckster who was a
householder and sold the best butter. As soon as
it was night, and the shop closed, and every one
in bed except the student, the goblin stepped
softly into the bedroom where the huckster's
wife slept, and took away her tongue, which of
course, she did not then want. Whatever object
in the room he placed his tongue upon immediately received voice and speech, and was able to
express its thoughts and feelings as readily as
the lady herself could do. It could only be used
by one object at a time, which was a good thing,
as a number speaking at once would have
caused great confusion. The goblin laid the
tongue upon the cask, in which lay a quantity of
old newspapers.

"Is it really true," he asked, that you do not
know what poetry is?"

"Of course I know," replied the cask: "poetry is something that always stand in the corner of a newspaper, and is sometimes cut out; and I may venture to affirm that I have more of it in me than the student has, and I am only a poor tub of the huckster's."

Then the goblin placed the tongue on the coffee mill; and how it did go to be sure! Then he put it on the butter tub and the cash box, and they all expressed the same opinion as the waste-paper tub; and a majority must always be respected.

"Now I shall go and tell the student," said the goblin; and with these words he went quietly up the back stairs to the garret where the student lived. He had a candle burning still, and the goblin peeped through the keyhole and saw that he was reading in the torn book, which he had brought out of the shop. But how light the room was! From the book shot forth a ray of light which grew broad and full, like the stem of a tree, from which bright rays spread upward and over the student's head. Each leaf was fresh, and each flower was like a beautiful female head; some with dark and sparkling eyes, and others with eyes that were wonderfully blue and clear. The fruit gleamed like stars, and the room was filled with sounds of beautiful music. The little goblin had never imagined, much less seen or heard of, any sight so glorious as this. He stood still on tiptoe, peeping in, till the light went out in the garret. The student no doubt

had blown out his candle and gone to bed; but the little goblin remained standing there never-theless, and listening to the music which still sounded on, soft and beautiful, a sweet cradle-song for the student, who had lain down to rest."

"This is a wonderful place," said the goblin; "I never expected such a thing. I should like to stay here with the student;" and the little man thought it over, for he was a sensible little spirit. At last he sighed, "but the student has no jam!" So he went down stairs again into the huckster's shop, and it was a good thing he got back when he did, for the cask had almost worn out the lady's tongue; he had given a description of all that he contained on one side, and was just about to turn himself over to the other side to describe what was there, when the goblin en-tered and restored the tongue to the lady. But from that time forward, the whole shop, from the cash box down to the pinewood logs, formed their opinions from that of the cask; and they all had such confidence in him, and treated him with so much respect, that when the huckster read the criticisms on theatricals and art of an evening, they fancied it must all come from the cask.

But after what he had seen, the goblin could no longer sit and listen quietly to the wisdom and understanding down stairs; so, as soon as the evening light glimmered in the garret, he took courage, for it seemed to him as if the rays of

light were strong cables, drawing him up, and obliging him to go and peep through the keyhole; and, while there, a feeling of vastness came over him such as we experience by the ever-moving sea, when the storm breaks forth; and it brought tears into his eyes. He did not himself know why he wept, yet a kind of pleasant feeling mingled with his tears. "How wonderfully glorious it would be to sit with the student under such a tree;" but that was out of the question, he must be content to look through the keyhole, and be thankful for even that.

There he stood on the old landing, with the autumn wind blowing down upon him through the trap-door. It was very cold; but the little creature did not really feel it, till the light in the garret went out, and the tones of music died away. Then how he shivered, and crept down stairs again to his warm corner, where it felt home-like and comfortable. And when Christmas came again, and brought the dish of jam and the great lump of butter, he liked the huckster best of all.

Soon after, in the middle of the night, the goblin was awoke by a terrible noise and knocking against the window shutters and the house doors, and by the sound of the watchman's horn; for a great fire had broken out, and the whole street appeared full of flames. Was it in their house, or a neighbor's? No one could tell, for terror had seized upon all. The huckster's

wife was so bewildered that she took her gold ear-rings out of her ears and put them in her pocket, that she might save something at least. The huckster ran to get his business papers, and the servant resolved to save her blue silk mantle, which she had managed to buy. Each wished to keep the best things they had. The goblin had the same wish; for, with one spring, he was up stairs and in the student's room, whom he found standing by the open window, and looking quite calmly at the fire, which was raging at the house of a neighbor opposite. The goblin caught up the wonderful book which lay on the table, and popped it into his red cap, which he held tightly with both hands. The greatest treasure in the house was saved; and he ran away with it to the roof, and seated himself on the chimney. The flames of the burning house opposite illuminated him as he sat, both hands pressed tightly over his cap, in which the treasure lay; and then he found out what feelings really reigned in his heart, and knew exactly which way they tended. And yet, when the fire was extinguished, and the goblin again began to reflect, he hesitated, and said at last, "I must divide myself between the two; I cannot quite give up the huckster, because of the jam." And this is a representation of human nature. We are like the goblin; we all go to visit the huckster "because of the jam."

HIS CHRISTMAS MIRACLE
CHARLES EGBERT CRADDOCK

HE yearned for a sign from the heavens. Could one intimation be vouchsafed him, how it would confirm his faltering faith! Jubal Kennedy was of the temperament impervious to spiritual subtleties, fain to reach conclusions with the line and rule of mathematical demonstration. Thus, all unreceptive, he looked through the mountain gap, as through some stupendous gateway, on the splendors of autumn: the vast landscape glamorous in a transparent amethystine haze; the foliage of the dense primeval wilderness in the October richness of red and russet; the 'hunter's moon,' a full sphere of illuminated pearl, high in the blue east while yet the dull vermilion sun swung westering above the massive purple heights. He knew how the sap was sinking; that the growths of the year had now failed; presently all would be shrouded in snow, but only to rise again in the reassurance of vernal quickening, to glow anew in the fullness of bloom, to attain eventually the perfection of fruition. And still he was deaf to the reiterated analogy of death, and blind to the immanent obvious prophecy of resurrection and the life to come.

His thoughts, as he stood on this jutting crag in Sunrise Gap, were with a recent 'experience meeting' at which he had sought to canvass his spiritual needs. His demand of a sign from the

heavens as evidence of the existence of the God
of revelation, as assurance of the awakening of
divine grace in the human heart, as actual proof
that wistful mortality is inherently endowed with
immortality, had electrified this symposium.
Though it was fashionable, so to speak, in this
remote cove among the Great Smoky Mountains,
to be repentant in rhetorical involutions and a
self-accuser in fine-spun interpretations of sin,
doubt, or more properly an eager questioning, a
desire to possess the sacred mysteries of religion, was unprecedented. Kennedy was a proud
man, reticent, reserved. Although the old parson, visibly surprised and startled, had gently
invited his full confidence, Kennedy had hastily
swallowed his words, as best he might, perceiv-
ing that the congregation had wholly misinter-
preted their true intent and that certain gossips
had an unholy relish of the sensation they had
caused.

Thereafter he indulged his poignant longings for
the elucidation of the veiled truths only when, as
now, he wandered deep in the woods with his
rifle on his shoulder. He could not have said
today that he was nearer an inspiration, a hope,
a 'leading,' than heretofore, but as he stood on
the crag it was with the effect of a dislocation
that he was torn from the solemn theme by an
interruption at a vital crisis.

The faint vibrations of a violin stirred the rever-
ent hush of the landscape in the blended light of

the setting sun and the 'hunter's moon.' Presently the musician came into view, advancing
slowly through the aisles of the red autumn
forest. A rapt figure it was, swaying in respon-
sive ecstasy with the rhythmic cadence. The
head, with its long, blowsy yellow hair, was
bowed over the dark polished wood of the instrument; the eyes were half closed; the right arm,
despite the eccentric patches on the sleeve of the
old brown-jeans coat, moved with free, elastic
gestures in all the liberties of a practiced bowing. If he saw the hunter motionless on the brink
of the crag, the fiddler gave no intimation. His
every faculty was as if enthralled by the swinging iteration of the sweet melancholy melody,
rendered with a breadth of effect, an inspiration,
it might almost have seemed, incongruous with
the infirmities of the crazy old fiddle. He was like
a creature under the sway of a spell, and apparently drawn by this dulcet lure of the enchant-
ment of sound was the odd procession that
trailed silently after him through these deep
mountain fastnesses.

A woman came first, arrayed in a ragged purple
skirt and a yellow blouse open at the throat,
displaying a slender white neck which upheld a
face of pensive, inert beauty. She clasped in her
arms a delicate infant, ethereal of aspect with its
flaxen hair, transparently pallid complexion, and
wide blue eyes. It was absolutely quiescent, save
that now and then it turned feebly in its waxen
hands a little striped red-and-yellow pomegran-

ate. A sturdy blond toddler trudged behind, in a checked blue cotton frock, short enough to disclose cherubic pink feet and legs bare to the knee; he carried that treasure of rural juveniles, a cornstalk violin. An old hound, his tail suavely wagging, padded along the narrow path; and last of all came, with frequent pause to crop the wayside herbage, a large cow, brindled red and white.

'The whole fambly!' muttered Kennedy. Then, aloud, 'Why don't you uns kerry the baby, Basil Beddell, an' give yer wife a rest?'

At the prosaic suggestion the crystal realm of dreams was shattered. The bow, with a quavering discordant scrape upon the strings, paused. Then Bedell slowly mastered the meaning of the interruption.

'Kerry the baby? Why, Aurely won't let none but herself tech that baby.' He laughed as he tossed the tousled yellow hair from his face, and looked over his shoulder to speak to the infant. 'It air sech a plumb special delightsome peach, it air, — it air!'

The pale face of the child lighted up with a smile of recognition and a faint gleam of mirth.

'I jes' kem out ennyhows ter drive up the cow,' Basil added.

'Big job,' sneered Kennedy. "Pears-like it takes the whole fambly to do it.'

Such slothful mismanagement was calculated to affront an energetic spirit. Obviously, at this hour the woman should be at home cooking the supper.

'I follered along ter listen ter the fiddle, — ef ye hev enny call ter know.' Mrs. Bedell replied to his unspoken thought, as if by divination.

But indeed such strictures were not heard for the first time. They were in some sort the penalty of the disinterested friendship which Kennedy had harbored for Basil since their childhood. He wished that his compeer might prosper in such simple wise as his own experience had proved to be amply possible. Kennedy's earlier incentive to husbandry had been his intention to marry, but the object of his affections had found him 'too mortal solemn,' and without a word of warning had married another man in a distant cove. The element of treachery in this event had gone far to reconcile the jilted lover to his future, bereft of her companionship, but the habit of industry thus formed had continued of its own momentum. It had resulted in forehanded thrift; he now possessed a comfortable holding, — cattle, house, ample land; and he had all the intolerance of the ant for the cricket. As Bedell lifted the bow once more, every

wincing nerve was enlisted in arresting it in mid-air.

'Mighty long tramp fur Bobbie, thar, — why'n't ye kerry him?'

The imperturbable calm still held fast on the musician's face. 'Bob,' he addressed the toddler, 'will you uns let daddy kerry ye like a baby?'

He swooped down as if to lift the child, the violin and bow in his left hand. The hardy youngster backed off precipitately.

'Don't ye DARE ter do it' he virulently admonished his parent, a resentful light in his big blue eyes. Then, as Bedell sang a stave in a full rich voice,

'Bye-oh, Baby!' Bob vociferated anew,

'Don't you BEGIN ter dare do it!' every inch a man though a little one.

'That's the kind of fambly I hev got,' Basil commented easily. 'Wife an' boy an' baby all walk over me, — plumb stomp on me! Jes' enough lef' of me ter play the fiddle a leetle once in a while.'

'Mighty nigh all the while, I be afeared,' Kennedy corrected the phrase. 'How did yer corn crap turn out?' he asked, as he too fell into line and

the procession moved on once more along the narrow path.

'Well enough,' said Basil; 'we uns hev got a sufficiency.' Then, as if afraid of seeming boastful he qualified, 'Ye know I hain't got but one muel ter feed, an' the cow thar. My sheep gits thar pastur' on the volunteer grass 'mongst the rocks, an' I hev jes' got a few head ennyhows.'

'But WHY hain't ye got more, Basil? Why 'n't ye work more and quit wastin' yer time on that old fool fiddle?'

The limits of patience were reached. The musician fired up. "Kase,' he retorted, 'I make enough. I hev got grace enough ter be thankful fur sech ez be vouchsafed ter me. *I* ain't wantin' no meracle.'

Kennedy flushed, following in silence while the musician annotated his triumph by a series of gay little harmonics, and young Hopeful, trudging in the rear, executed a soundless fantasia on the cornstalk fiddle with great brilliancy of technique.

'You uns air talkin' 'bout what I said at the meetin' las' month,' Kennedy observed at length.

'An' so be all the mounting,' Aurelia interpolated with a sudden fierce joy of reproof.

Kennedy winced visibly.

'The folks all 'low ez ye be no better than an onbeliever.' Aurelia was bent on driving the blade home. 'The idee of axin' fur a meracle at this late day, — so ez YE kin be satisfied in yer mind ez ye hev got grace! Providence, though merciful, air OBLEEGED ter know ez sech air plumb scandalous an' redic'lous.'

'Why, Aurely, hesh up,' exclaimed her husband, startled from his wonted leniency. 'I hev never hearn ye talk in sech a key, — yer voice sounds plumb out o' tune. I be plumb sorry, Jube, ez I spoke ter you uns 'bout a meracle at all. But I was consider'ble nettled by yer words, ye see, — 'kase I know I be a powerful, lazy, shif'less cuss — '

'Ye know a lie, then,' his helpmeet interrupted promptly.

'Why, Aurely, hesh up, — ye — ye — WOMAN, ye!' he concluded injuriously. Then resuming his remarks to Kennedy. 'I know I DO fool away a deal of my time with the fiddle — '

'The sound of it is like bread ter me, — I couldn't live without it,' interposed the unconquered Aurelia. 'Sometimes it minds me o' the singin' o' runnin' water in a lonesome place.

Then agin it minds me o' seein' sunshine in a dream. An' sometimes it be sweet an' high an' fur off, like a voice from the sky, tellin' what no mortial ever knowed before, — an' THEN it minds me o' the tune them angels sung ter the shepherds abidin' in the fields. I COULD N'T live without it.'

'Woman, hold yer jaw!' Basil proclaimed comprehensively. Then, renewing his explanation to Kennedy, 'I kin see that I don't purvide fur my fambly ez I ought ter do, through hatin' work and lovin' to play the fiddle.'

'I ain't goin' ter hear my home an' hearth reviled.' Aurelia laid an imperative hand on her husband's arm. 'Ye know ye could n't make more out'n sech ground, — though I ain't faultin' our land, neither. We uns hev enough an' ter spare, all we need an' more than we deserve. We don't need ter ax a meracle from the skies ter stay our souls on faith, nor a sign ter prove our grace.'

'Now, now, stop, Aurely! — I declar', Jube, I dunno what made me lay my tongue ter sech n word ez that thar miser'ble benighted meracle! I be powerful sorry I hurt yer feelin's, Jube; folks seekin' salvation git mightily mis-put sometimes, an' — '

'I don't want ter hear none o' yer views on religion,' Kennedy interrupted gruffly. An apology

often augments the sense of injury. In this instance it also annulled the provocation, for his
own admission put Bedell hopelessly in the
wrong. 'Ez a friend I war argufyin' with ye agin'
yer waste o' time with that old fool fiddle. Ye hev
got wife an' children, an' yit not so well off in
this worl's gear ez me, a single man. I misdoubts
ef ye hev hunted a day since the craps war laid
by, or hev got a pound o' jerked venison stored
up fer winter. But this air yer home,' — he
pointed upward at a little clearing beginning, as
they approached, to be visible amidst the forest,
— 'an' ef ye air satisfied with sech ez it be, that
comes from laziness stiddier a contented sperit.'

With this caustic saying he suddenly left them,
the procession standing silently staring after
him as he took his way through the woods in the
dusky red shadows of the autumnal gloaming.

Aurelia's vaunted home was indeed a poor place,
— not even the rude though substantial log-
cabin common to the region. It was a flimsy
shanty of boards, and except for its rickety
porch was more like a box than a house. It had
its perch on a jutting eminence, where it seemed
the familiar of the skies, so did the clouds and
winds circle about it. Through the great gateway
of Sunrise Gap it commanded a landscape of a
scope that might typify a world, in its multitude
of mountain ranges, in the intricacies of its
intervening valleys, in the glittering coils of its
water-courses. Basil would sometimes sink into

deep silences, overpowered by the majesty of nature in this place. After a long hiatus the bow would tremble and falter on the strings as if overawed for a time; presently the theme would strengthen, expand, resound with large meaning, and then he would send forth melodies that he had never before played or heard, his own dream, the reflection of that mighty mood of nature in the limpid pool of his recepti
ve mind.

Around were rocks, crags, chasms, — the fields which nourished the family lay well from the verge, within the purlieus of the limited mountain plateau. He had sought to persuade himself that it was to save all the arable land for tillage that he had placed his house and door-yard here, but both he and Aurelia were secretly aware of the subterfuge; he would fain be always within the glamour of the prospect through Sunrise Gap!

Their interlocutor had truly deemed that the woman should have been earlier at home cooking the supper. Dusk had deepened to darkness long before the meal smoked upon the board. The spinning-wheel had begun to whir for her evening stent when other hill-folks had betaken themselves to bed. Basil pulled his pipe before the fire; the flicker and flare pervaded every nook of his bright little house. Strings of red-pepper-pods flaunted in festoons from the beams; the baby slumbered under a gay quilt in

his rude cradle, never far from his mother's hand, but the bluff little boy was still up and about, although his aspect, round and burly, in a scanty nightgown, gave token of recognition of the fact that bed was his appropriate place. His shrill plaintive voice rose ever and anon wakefully.

'I wanter hear a bear tale, — I wanter hear a bear tale.'

Thus Basil must needs knock the ashes from his pipe the better to devote himself to the narration, — a prince of raconteurs, to judge by the spell-bound interest of the youngster who stood at his knee and hung on his words. Even Aurelia checked the whir of her wheel to listen smilingly. She broke out laughing in appreciative pleasure when Basil took up the violin to show how a jovial old bear, who intruded into this very house one day when all the family were away at the church in the cove, and who mistook the instrument for a banjo, addressed himself to picking out this tune, singing the while a quaint and ursine lay. Basil embellished the imitation with a masterly effect of realistic growls.

'Ef ye keep goin' at that gait, Basil,' Aurelia admonished him, 'daylight will ketch us all wide awake around the fire, — no wonder the child won't go to bed.' She seemed suddenly impressed with the pervasive cheer.

'What a fool that man, Jube Kennedy, must be!
How COULD ennybody hev a sweeter darling-er
home than we uns hev got hyar in Sunrise Gap!'

On the languorous autumn a fierce winter ensued. The cold came early. The deciduous
growths of the forests were leafless ere Novem-
ber waned, rifled by the riotous marauding
winds. December set in with the gusty snow
flying fast. Drear were the gray skies; ghastly the
sheeted ranges. Drifts piled high in bleak ravines, and the grim gneissoid crags were begirt
with gigantic icicles. But about the little house
in Sunrise Gap that kept so warm a heart, the
holly trees showed their glad green leaves and
the red berries glowed with a mystic significance.

As the weeks wore on, the place was often in
Kennedy's mind, although he had not seen it
since that autumn afternoon when he had be-
stirred himself to rebuke its owner concerning
the inadequacies of the domestic provision. His
admonition had been kindly meant and had not
deserved the retort, the flippant ridicule of his
spiritual yearnings. Though he still winced from
the recollection, he was sorry that he had re-
sisted the importunacy of Basil's apology. He
realized that Aurelia had persisted to the limit of
her power in the embitterment of the contro-
versy, but even Aurelia he was disposed to forgive as time passed on. When Christmas Day
dawned, the vague sentiment began to assume

the definiteness of a purpose, and noontide
found him on his way to Sunrise Gap.

There was now no path through the woods; the
snow lay deep over all, unbroken save at long
intervals when queer footprints gave token of the
stirring abroad of the sylvan gentry, and he felt
an idle interest in distinguishing the steps of
wolf and fox, of opossum and weasel. In the
intricacies of the forest aisles, amid laden
boughs of pine and fir, there was a suggestion of
darkness, but all the sky held not enough light
to cast the shadow of a bole on the white blank
spaces of the snow-covered ground. A vague
blue haze clothed the air; yet as he drew near
the mountain brink, all was distinct in the vast
landscape. The massive ranges and alternating
valleys in infinite repetition.

He wondered when near the house that he had
not heard the familiar barking of the old hound;
then he remembered that the sound of his
horse's hoofs was muffled by the snow. He was
glad to be unheralded. He would like to surprise
Aurelia into geniality before her vicarious rancor
for Basil's sake should be roused anew. As he
emerged from the thick growths of the holly,
with the icy scintillations of its clustering green
leaves and red berries, he drew rein so suddenly
that the horse was thrown back on his
haunches. The rider sat as if petrified in the
presence of an awful disaster.

The house was gone! Kennedy stared bewildered.
Slowly the realization of what had chanced here
began to creep through his brain. Evidently
there had been a gigantic landslide. The cliff-like
projection was broken sheer off, — hurled into
the depths of the valley. Some action of subterranean waters, throughout the ages, doubtless,
had been undermining the great crags till the
rocky crust of the earth had collapsed. He could
see even now how the freeze had fractured out-
cropping ledges where the ice had gathered in
the fissures. A deep abyss that he remembered
as being at a considerable distance from the
mountain's brink, once spanned by a foot-
bridge, now showed the remnant of its jagged,
shattered walls at the extreme verge of the precipice.

A cold chill of horror benumbed his senses.
Basil, the wife, the children, — where were they?
A terrible death, surely, to be torn from the
warm securities of the hearth-stone, without a
moment's warning and hurled into the midst of
this frantic turmoil of nature, down to the
depths of the gap, — a thousand feet below! And
at what time had this dread fate befallen his
friend? He remembered that at the cross-roads'
store, when he had paused on his way to warm
himself that morning, some gossip was detailing
the phenomenon of unseasonable thunder during the previous night, while others protested
that it must have been only the clamors of
'Christmas guns' firing all along the country-

side. 'A turrible clap, it was,' the raconteur had
persisted. 'Sounded ez ef all creation hed split
apart.' Perhaps, therefore, the catastrophe might
be recent. Kennedy could scarcely command his
muscles as he dismounted and made his way
slowly and cautiously to the verge.

Any deviation from the accustomed routine of
nature has an unnerving effect unparalleled by
disaster in other sort: no individual danger or
doom, the aspect of death by drowning, or gun-
shot or disease, can so abash the reason and
stultify normal expectation. Kennedy was
scarcely conscious that he saw the vast disorder
of the land-slide, scattered from the precipice on
the mountain's brink to the depths of the Gap —
inverted roots of great pines thrust out in mid-
air, foundations of crags riven asunder and
hurled in monstrous fragments along the steep
slant, unknown streams newly liberated from
the caverns of the range and cascading from the
crevices of the rocks. In effect he could not believe his own eyes. His mind realized the percep-
tion of his senses only when his heart suddenly
plunged with a wild hope — he had discerned
amongst the turmoil a shape of line and rule,
the little box-like hut! Caught as it was in the
boughs of a cluster of pines and firs, uprooted
and thrust out at an incline a little less than
vertical, the inmates might have been spared
such shock of the fall as would otherwise have
proved fatal. Had the house been one of the
substantial log-cabins of the region its timbers

must have been torn from one another, the daubing and chinking scattered as mere atoms. But the more flimsy character of the little dwelling had thus far served to save it, — the interdependent 'framing' of its structure held fast; the upright studding and boards, nailed stoutly on, rendered it indeed the box that it looked. It was, so to speak, built in one piece, and no part was subjected to greater strain than another. But should the earth cave anew, should the tough fibres of one of those gigantic roots tear out from the loosened friable soil, should the elastic supporting branches barely sway in some errant gust of wind, the little box would fall hundreds of feet, cracked like a nut, shattering against the rocks of the levels below.

He wondered if the inmates yet lived, — he pitied them still more if they only existed to realize their peril, to await in an anguish of fear their ultimate doom. Perhaps — he knew he was but trifling with despair — some rescue might be devised.

Such a weird cry he set up on the brink of the mountain! — full of horror, grief, and that poignant hope. The echoes of the Gap seemed reluctant to repeat the tones, dull, slow, muffled in snow. But a sturdy halloo responded from the window, uppermost now, for the house lay on its side amongst the boughs. Kennedy thought he saw the pallid simulacrum of a face.

'This be Jube Kennedy,' he cried, reassuringly. 'I
be goin' ter fetch help, — men, ropes, and a
windlass.'

'Make haste then, — we uns be nigh friz.'

'Ye air in no danger of fire, then?' asked the
practical man.

'We hev hed none, — before we war flunged off 'n
the bluff we hed squinched the fire ter pledjure
Bob, ez he war afeard Santy Claus would scorch
his feet comin' down the chimbley, — powerfull
lucky fur we uns; the fire would hev burnt the
house bodaciously.'

Kennedy hardly stayed to hear. He was off in a
moment, galloping at frantic speed along the
snowy trail scarcely traceable in the sad light of
the gray day; taking short cuts through the
densities of the laurel; torn by jagged rocks and
tangles of thorny growths and broken branches
of great trees; plunging now and again into deep
drifts above concealed icy chasms, and rescuing
with inexpressible difficulty the floundering
struggling horse; reaching again the open
sheeted roadway, bruised, bleeding, exhausted,
yet furiously plunging forward, rousing the
sparsely settled country-side with imperative
insistence for help in this matter of life or death!

Death, indeed, only, — for the enterprise was pronounced impossible by those more experienced than Kennedy. Among the men now on the bluff were several who had been employed in the silver mines of this region, and they demonstrated conclusively that a rope could not be worked clear of the obstructions of the face of the rugged and shattered cliffs; that a human being, drawn from the cabin; strapped in a chair, must needs be torn from it and flung into the abyss below, or beaten to a frightful death against the jagged rocks in the transit.

'But not ef the chair war ter be steadied by a guy-rope from — say — from that thar old pine tree over thar,' Kennedy insisted, indicating the long bole of a partially uprooted and inverted tree on the steeps. 'The chair would swing cl'ar of the bluff then.'

'But, Jube, it is onpossible ter git a guy-rope over ter that tree, — more than a man's life is wuth ter try it.'

A moment ensued of absolute silence, — space, however, for a hard-fought battle. The aspect of that mad world below, with every condition of creation reversed; a mistake in the adjustment of the winch and gear by the excited, reluctant, disapproving men; an overstrain on the fibres of the long-used rope; a slip on the treacherous ice; the dizzy whirl of the senses that even a glance downward at those drear depths set astir in the

brain, — all were canvassed within his mental processes, all were duly realized in their entirety ere he said with a spare dull voice and dry lips, —

'Fix ter let me down ter that thar leanin' pine, boys, — I'll kerry a guy-rope over thar.'

At one side the crag beetled, and although it was impossible thence to reach the cabin with a rope it would swing clear of obstructions here, and might bring the rescuer within touch of the pine, where could be fastened the guy-rope; the other end would be affixed to the chair which could be lowered to the cabin only from the rugged face of the cliff. Kennedy harbored no self-deception; he more than doubled the outcome of the enter-prise. He quaked and turned pale with dread as with the great rope knotted about his armpits and around his waist he was swung over the brink at the point where the crag jutted forth, — lower and lower still; now nearing the slanting inverted pine, caught amidst the debris of earth and rock; now failing to reach its boughs; once more swinging back to a great distance, so did the length of the rope increase the scope of the pendulum; now nearing the pine again, and at last fairly lodged on the icy bole, knotting and coiling about it the end of the guy-rope, on which he had come and on which he must needs return.

It seemed, through the inexpert handling of the little group, a long time before the stout arm-chair was secured to the cables, slowly lowered, and landed at last on the outside of the hut. Many an anxious glance was cast at the slate-gray sky. An inopportune flurry of snow, a flaw of wind, — and even now all would be lost. Dusk too impended and as the rope began to coil on the windlass at the signal to hoist every eye was strained to discern the identity of the first voyag-ers in this aerial journey, — the two children, securely lashed to the chair. This was well, — all felt that both parents might best wait, might risk the added delay. The chair came swinging easily, swiftly, along the gradations of the rise, the guy-rope holding it well from the chances of contact with the jagged projections of the face of the cliff, and the first shout of triumph rang sonorously from the summit.

When next the chair rested on the chair beside the window, a thrill of anxiety and anger went through Kennedy's heart to note, from his perch on the leaning pine, a struggle between husband and wife as to who should be first. Each was eager to take the many risks incident to the long wait in this precarious lodgment. The man was the stronger. Aurelia was forced into the chair, tied fast, pushed off, waving her hand to her husband, shedding floods of tears, looking at him for the last time, as she fancied, and calling out dismally, 'Far'well, Basil, far' well.'

Even this lugubrious demonstration could not damp the spirits of the men, working like mad at the windlass. They were jovial enough for bursts of laughter when it became apparent that Basil had utilized the ensuing interval to tie together, in preparation for the ascent with himself, the two objects which he next most treasured, his violin and his old hound. The trusty chair bore all aloft, and Basil was received with welcoming acclamations.

Before the rope was wound anew and for the last time, the aspect of the group on the cliff had changed. It had grown eerie, indistinct. The pines and firs showed no longer their sempervirent green, but were black amid the white tufted lines on their branches, that still served to accentuate their symmetry. The vale had disappeared in a sinister abyss of gloom, though Kennedy would not look down at its menace, but upward, always upward. Thus he saw, like some radiant and splendid star, the first torch whitely aglow on the brink of the precipice. It opened long avenues of light adown the snowy landscape, — soft blue shadows trailed after it, like half-descried draperies of elusive hovering beings. Soon the torch was duplicated- another and then another began to glow. Now several drew together, and like a constellation glimmered crown-like on the brow of the night, as he felt the rope stir with the signal to hoist.

Upward, always upward, his eyes on that radiant stellular coronal, as it shone white and splendid in the snowy night. And now it had lost its mystic glamour, — disintegrated by gradual approach he could see the long handles of the pine-knots; the red verges of the flame; the blue and yellow tones of the focus; the trailing wreaths of dun-tinted smoke that rose from them. Then became visible the faces of the men who held them, all crowding eagerly to the verge. But it was in a solemn silence that he was received; a drear cold darkness, every torch being struck downward into the snow- a frantic haste in unharnessing him from the ropes, for he was almost frozen. He was hardly apt enough to interpret this as an emotion too deep for words, but now and again, as he was disentangled, he felt about his shoulders a furtive hug, and more than one pair of the ministering hands must needs pause to wring his own hands hard. They practically carried him to a fire that had been built in a sheltered place in one of those grottoes of the region, locally called 'Rockhouses.' Its cavernous portal gave upon a dark interior, and not until they had turned a corner in a tunnel-like passage was revealed an arched space in a rayonnant suffusion of light, the fire itself obscured by the figures about it. His eyes were caught first by the aspect of a youthful mother with a golden-haired babe on her breast; close by showed the head and horns of a cow; the mule was mercifully sheltered too, and stood near, munching his fodder; a cluster of sheep

pressed after the steps of half a dozen men, that somehow in the clear-obscure reminded him of the shepherds of old summoned by good tidings of great Joy.

A sudden figure started up with streaming white hair and patriarchal beard.

'Will ye deny ez ye hev hed a sign from the heavens, Jubal Kennedy?' the old circuit-rider straitly demanded. 'How could ye hev strengthened yer heart fur sech a deed onless the grace o' God prevailed mightily within ye? Inasmuch as ye hev done it unto one o' the least o' these my brethren, ye hev done it unto me.'That ain't the KIND o' sign, parson,' Kennedy faltered. 'I be lookin' fur a meracle in the yearth or in the air, that I kin view or hear.'

'The kingdom o' Christ is a spiritual kingdom,' said the parson solemnly. 'The kingdom o' Christ is a SPIRITUAL kingdom, an' great are the wonders that are wrought therein.'

CHRISTMAS: A DEFINITION
CLEMENT A. MILES

Christmas is a microcosm of world religion. It reflects almost every phase of thought and feeling from crude magic and superstition to the speculative mysticism of Eckhart, from the mere delight in physical indulgence to the exquisite spirituality of St. Frances.

Ascetic and bon-vivant, mystic and materialist, learned and simple, noble and peasant, all have found something in it on which to lay hold. it is a river into which have flowed tributaries from every side, from Oriental religion, from Greek and Roman civilization, from celtic, Teutonic, Slav and probably pre-Aryan society, all mingling their waters so that it is often hard to discover the far-away springs.

At no time has so much been made of children as today, and because Christmas is their feast its luster continues unabated in an age upon which dogmatic Christanity has largely lost its hold, which laughs at the pagan superstitions of its forefathers.

Christmas is the feast of the beginnings, of instinctive happy childhood; the Christian idea of the Immortal Babe renewing weary, stained humanity. It blends with the thought of the New Year, with its hope and promise, laid in the cradle of Time.

LITTLE WOMEN
LOUIS MAY ALCOTT

PLAYING PILGRIMS

"Christmas won't be Christmas without any presents," grumbled Jo, lying on the rug.

"It's so dreadful to be poor! sighed Meg," looking down at her old dress.

"I don't think it's fair for some girls to have plenty of pretty things, and other girls nothing at all," added little Amy, with an injured sniff.

"We've got Father and Mother, and each other," said Beth contentedly from her corner.

The four young faces on which the firelight shone brightened at the cheerful words, but darkened again as Jo said sadly, "We haven't got Father, and shall not have him for a long time." She didn't say perhaps never, but each silently added it, thinking of Father far away, where the fighting was.

Nobody spoke for a minute; then Meg said in an altered tone, "You know the reason Mother proposed not having any presents this Christmas was because it is going to be a hard winter for everyone; and she thinks we ought not to spend money for pleasure, when our men are suffering so in the army. We can't do much, but we can make our little sacrifices, and ought to do it

gladly. But I am afraid I don't." And Meg shook her head, as she thought regretfully of all the pretty things she wanted.

"But I don't think the little we should spend would do any good. We've each got a dollar, and the army wouldn't be much helped by our giving that. I agree not to expect anything from Mother or you, but I do want to buy UNDINE AND SINTRAM for myself. I've wanted it so long," said Jo, who was a bookworm.

"I planned to spend mine in new music," said Beth, with a little sigh, which no one heard but the hearth brush and kettle holder.

"I shall get a nice box of Faber's drawing pencils. I really need them," said Amy decidedly.

"Mother didn't say anything about our money, and she won't wish us to give up everything. Let's each buy what we want, and have a little fun. I'm sure we work hard enough to earn it," cried Jo, examining the heels of her shoes in a gentlemanly manner.

"I know I do — teaching those tiresome children nearly all day, when I'm longing to enjoy myself at home," began Meg, in the complaining tone again.

"You don't have half such a hard time as I do," said Jo. "How would you like to be shut up for

hours with a nervous, fussy old lady, who keeps
you trotting, is never satisfied, and worries you
till you you're ready to fly out the window or
cry?"

"It's naughty to fret, but I do think washing
dishes and keeping things tidy is the worst work
in the world. It makes me cross, and my hands
get so stiff, I can't practice well at all." And Beth
looked at her rough hands with a sigh that any
one could hear that time.

"I don't believe any of you suffer as I do," cried
Amy, "for you don't have to go to school with
impertinent girls, who plague you if you don't
know your lessons, and laugh at your dresses,
and label your father if he isn't rich, and insult
you when your nose isn't nice."

"If you mean libel, I'd say so, and not talk about
labels, as if Papa was a pickle bottle," advised
Jo, laughing.

"I know what I mean, and you needn't be satiri-
cal about it. It's proper to use good words, and
improve your vocabulary," returned Amy, with
dignity.

"Don't peck at one another, children. Don't you
wish we had the money Papa lost when we were
little, Jo? Dear me! How happy and good we'd
be, if we had no worries!" said Meg, who could
remember better times.

"You said the other day you thought we were a deal happier than the King children, for they were fighting and fretting all the time, in spite of their money."

"So I did, Beth. Well, I think we are. For though we do have to work, we make fun of ourselves, and are a pretty jolly set, as Jo would say."

"Jo does use such slang words!" observed Amy, with a reproving look at the long figure stretched on the rug.

Jo immediately sat up, put her hands in her pockets, and began to whistle.

"Don't, Jo. It's so boyish!"

"That's why I do it."

"I detest rude, unladylike girls!"

"I hate affected, niminy-piminy chits!"

"Birds in their little nests agree," sang Beth, the peacemaker, with such a funny face that both sharp voices softened to a laugh, and the pecking ended for that time.

"Really, girls, you are both to be blamed," said Meg, beginning to lecture in her elder-sisterly fashion. "You are old enough to leave off boyish

tricks, and to behave better, Josephine. It didn't matter so much when you were a little girl, but now you are so tall, and turn up your hair, you should remember that you are a young lady."

"I'm not! And if turning up my hair makes me one, I'll wear it in two tails till I'm twenty," cried Jo, pulling off her net, and shaking down a chestnut mane. "I hate to think I've got to grow up, and be Miss March, and wear long gowns, and look as prim as a China Aster! It's bad enough to be a girl, anyway, when I like boy's games and work and manners! I can't get over my disappointment in not being a boy. And it's worse than ever now, for I'm dying to go and fight with Papa. And I can only stay home and knit, like a poky old woman!"

And Jo shook the blue army sock till the needles rattled like castanets, and her ball bounded across the room.

"Poor Jo! It's too bad, but it can't be helped. So you must try to be contented with making your name boyish, and playing brother to us girls," said Beth, stroking the rough head with a hand that all the dish washing and dusting in the world could not make ungentle in its touch.

"As for you, Amy," continued Meg, "you are altogether to particular and prim. Your airs are funny now, but you'll grow up an affected little goose, if you don't take care. I like your nice

manners and refined ways of speaking, when
you don't try to be elegant. But your absurd
words are as bad as Jo's slang."

"If Jo is a tomboy and Amy a goose, what am I,
please?" asked Beth, ready to share the lecture.

"You're a dear, and nothing else," answered Meg
warmly, and no one contradicted her, for the
'Mouse' was the pet of the family.

As young readers like to know 'how people look',
we will take this moment to give them a little
sketch of the four sisters, who sat knitting away
in the twilight, while the December snow fell
quietly without, and the fire crackled cheerfully
within. It was a comfortable room, though the
carpet was faded and the furniture very plain,
for a good picture or two hung on the walls,
books filled the recesses, chrysanthemums and
Christmas roses bloomed in the windows, and a
pleasant atmosphere of home peace pervaded it.

Margaret, the eldest of the four, was sixteen, and
very pretty, being plump and fair, with large
eyes, plenty of soft brown hair, a sweet mouth,
and white hands, of which she was rather vain.
Fifteen-year-old Jo was very tall, thin, and
brown, and reminded one of a colt, for she never
seemed to know what to do with her long limbs,
which were very much in her way. She had a
decided mouth, a comical nose, and sharp, gray
eyes, which appeared to see everything, and

were by turns fierce, funny, or thoughtful. Her long, thick hair was her one beauty, but it was usually bundled into a net, to be out of her way. Round shoulders had Jo, big hands and feet, a fly-away look to her clothes, and the uncomfortable appearance of a girl who was rapidly shooting up into a woman and didn't like it. Elizabeth, or Beth, as everyone called her, was a rosy, smooth-haired, bright-eyed girl of thirteen, with a shy manner, a timid voice, and a peaceful expression which was seldom disturbed. Her father called her 'Little Miss Tranquillity', and the name suited her excellently, for she seemed to live in a happy world of her own, only venturing out to meet the few whom she trusted and loved. Amy, though the youngest, was a most important person, in her own opinion at least. A regular snow maiden, with blue eyes, and yellow hair curling on her shoulders, pale and slender, and always carrying herself like a young lady mindful of her manners. What the characters of the four sisters were we will leave to be found out.

The clock struck six and, having swept up the hearth, Beth put a pair of slippers down to warm. Somehow the sight of the old shoes had a good effect upon the girls, for Mother was coming, and everyone brightened to welcome her. Meg stopped lecturing, and lighted the lamp, Amy got out of the easy chair without being asked, and Jo forgot how tired she was as she sat up to hold the slippers nearer to the blaze.

"They are quite worn out. Marmee must have a new pair."

"I thought I'd get her some with my dollar," said Beth.

"No, I shall!" cried Amy.

"I'm the oldest," began Meg, but Jo cut in with a decided, "I'm the man of the family now Papa is away, and I shall provide the slippers, for he told me to take special care of Mother while he was gone."

"I'll tell you what we'll do," said Beth, "let's each get her something for Christmas, and not get anything for ourselves."

"That's like you, dear! What will we get?" exclaimed Jo.

Everyone thought soberly for a minute, then Meg announced, as if the idea was suggested by the sight of her own pretty hands, "I shall give her a nice pair of gloves."

"Army shoes, best to be had," cried Jo.

"Some handkerchiefs, all hemmed," said Beth.

"I'll get a little bottle of cologne. She likes it, and it won't cost much, so I'll have some left to buy my pencils," added Amy.

"How will we give the things?" asked Meg.

"Put them on the table, and bring her in and see her open the bundles. Don't you remember how we used to do on our birthdays?" answered Jo.

"I used to be so frightened when it was my turn to sit in the chair with the crown on, and see you all come marching round to give the presents, with a kiss. I liked the things and the kisses, but it was dreadful to have you sit looking at me while I opened the bundles," said Beth, who was toasting her face and the bread for tea at the same time.

"Let Marmee think we are getting things for ourselves, and then surprise her. We must go shopping tomorrow afternoon, Meg. There is so much to do about the play for Christmas night," said Jo, marching up and down, with her hands behind her back, and her nose in the air.

"I don't mean to act any more after this time. I'm getting too old for such things," observed Meg, who was as much a child as ever about 'dressing-up' frolics.

"You won't stop, I know, as long as you can trail round in a white gown with your hair down, and wear gold-paper jewelry. You are the best actress we've got, and there'll be an end of everything if you quit the boards," said Jo. "We ought to rehearse tonight. Come here, Amy, and do the

fainting scene, for you are as stiff as a poker in that."

"I can't help it. I never saw anyone faint, and I don't choose to make myself all black and blue, tumbling flat as you do. If I can go down easily, I'll drop. If I can't, I shall fall into a chair and be graceful. I don't care if Hugo does come at me with a pistol," returned Amy, who was not gifted with dramatic power, but was chosen because she was small enough to be borne out shrieking by the villain of the piece.

"Do it this way. Clasp your hands so, and stagger across the room, crying frantically, 'Roderigo' Save me! Save me!" and away went Jo, with a melodramatic scream which was truly thrilling.

Amy followed, but she poked her hands out stiffly before her, and jerked herself along as if she went by machinery, and her Ow! was more suggestive of pins being run into her than of fear and anguish. Jo gave a despairing groan, and Meg laughed outright, while Beth let her bread burn as she watched the fun with interest.

"It's no use! Do the best you can when the time comes, and if the audience laughs, don't blame me. Come on, Meg."

Then things went smoothly, for Don Pedro defied the world in a speech of two pages without a single break. Hagar, the witch, chanted an awful

incantation over her kettleful of simmering toads, with weird effect. Roderigo rent his chains asunder manfully, and Hugo died in agonies of remorse and arsenic, with a wild, "Ha! Ha!"

"It's the best we've had yet," said Meg, as the dead villain sat up and rubbed his elbows.

"I don't see how you can write and act such splendid things, Jo. You're a regular Shakespeare!" exclaimed Beth, who firmly believed that her sisters were gifted with wonderful genius in all things.

"Not quite," replied Jo modestly. "I do think THE WITCHES CURSE, an Operatic Tragedy is rather a nice thing, but I'd like to try MacBETH, if we only had a trapdoor for Banquo. I always wanted to do the killing part. 'Is that a dagger that I see before me?'" muttered Jo, rolling her eyes and clutching at the air, as she had seen a famous tragedian do.

"No, it's the toasting fork, with Mother's shoe on it instead of the bread." "Beth's stage-struck!" cried Meg, and the rehearsal ended in a general burst of laughter.

"Glad to find you so merry, my girls," said a cheery voice at the door, and actors and audience turned to welcome a tall, motherly lady with a 'can I help you' look about her which was truly delightful. She was not elegantly dressed,

but a noble-looking woman, and the girls thought the gray cloak and unfashionable bonnet covered the most splendid mother in the world.

"Well, dearies, how have you got on today? There was so much to do, getting the boxes ready to go tomorrow, that I didn't come home to dinner. Has anyone called, Beth? How is your cold, Meg? Jo, you look tired to death. Come and kiss me, baby."

While making these maternal inquiries Mrs. March got her wet things off, her warm slippers on, and sitting down in the easy chair, drew Amy to her lap, preparing to enjoy the happiest hour of her busy day. The girls flew about, trying to make things comfortable, each in her own way. Meg arranged the tea table, Jo brought wood and set chairs, dropping, over-turning, and clattering everything she touched. Beth trotted to and fro between parlor kitchen, quiet and busy, while Amy gave directions to everyone, as she sat with her hands folded.

As they gathered about the table, Mrs. March said, with a particularly happy face, "I've got a treat for you after supper."

A quick, bright smile went round like a streak of sunshine. Beth clapped her hands, regardless of the biscuit she held, and Jo tossed up her nap-

kin, crying, "A letter! A letter! Three cheers for Father!"

"Yes, a nice long letter. He is well, and thinks he shall get through the cold season better than we feared. He sends all sorts of loving wishes for Christmas, and an especial message to you girls," said Mrs. March, patting her pocket as if she had got a treasure there.

"Hurry and get done! Don't stop to quirk your little finger and simper over your plate, Amy," cried Jo, choking on her tea and dropping her bread, butter side down, on the carpet in her haste to get at the treat.

Beth ate no more, but crept away to sit in her shadowy corner and brood over the delight to come, till the others were ready.

"I think it was so splendid in Father to go as chaplain when he was too old to be drafted, and not strong enough for a soldier," said Meg warmly.

"Don't I wish I could go as a drummer, a vivan— what's its name? Or a nurse, so I could be near him and help him," exclaimed Jo, with a groan.

"It must be very disagreeable to sleep in a tent, and eat all sorts of bad-tasting things, and drink out of a tin mug," sighed Amy.

"When will he come home, Marmee?" asked
Beth, with a little quiver in her voice.

"Not for many months, dear, unless he is sick.
He will stay and do his work faithfully as long as
he can, and we won't ask for him back a minute
sooner than he can be spared. Now come and
hear the letter."

They all drew to the fire, Mother in the big chair
with Beth at her feet, Meg and Amy perched on
either arm of the chair, and Jo leaning on the
back, where no one would see any sign of emotion if the letter should happen to be touching.
Very few letters were written in those hard times
that were not touching, especially those which
fathers sent home. In this one little was said of
the hardships endured, the dangers faced, or the
homesickness conquered. It was a cheerful,
hopeful letter, full of lively descriptions of camp
life, marches, and military news, and only at the
end did the writer's heart over-flow with fatherly
love and longing for the little girls at home.

*Give them all of my dear love and a kiss. Tell
them I think of them by day, pray for them by
night, and find my best comfort in their affection
at all times. A year seems very long to wait before
I see them, but remind them that while we wait
we may all work, so that these hard days need
not be wasted. I know they will remember all I
said to them, that they will be loving children to*

you, will do their duty faithfully, fight their bosom enemies bravely, and conquer themselves so beautifully that when I come back to them I may be fonder and prouder than ever of my little women.

Everybody sniffed when they came to that part. Jo wasn't ashamed of the great tear that dropped off the end of her nose, and Amy never minded the rumpling of her curls as she hid her face on her mother's shoulder and sobbed out, "I am a selfish girl! But I'll truly try to be better, so he mayn't be disappointed in me by-and-by."

"We all will," cried Meg. "I think too much of my looks and hate to work, but won't any more, if I can help it."

"I'll try and be what he loves to call me, 'a little woman' and not be rough and wild, but do my duty here instead of wanting to be somewhere else," said Jo, thinking that keeping her temper at home was a much harder task than facing a rebel or two down South.

Beth said nothing, but wiped away her tears with the blue army sock and began to knit with all her might, losing no time in doing the duty that lay nearest her, while she resolved in her quiet little soul to be all that Father hoped to find her when the year brought round the happy coming home.

Mrs. March broke the silence that followed Jo's words, by saying in her cheery voice, "Do you remember how you used to play Pilgrims Progress when you were little things? Nothing delighted you more than to have me tie my piece bags on your backs for burdens, give you hats and sticks and rolls of paper, and let you travel through the house from the cellar, which was the City of Destruction, up, up, to the housetop, where you had all the lovely things you could collect to make a Celestial City."

"What fun it was, especially going by the lions, fighting Apollyon, and passing through the valley where the hob-goblins were," said Jo.

"I liked the place where the bundles fell off and tumbled downstairs," said Meg.

"I don't remember much about it, except that I was afraid of the cellar and the dark entry, and always liked the cake and milk we had up at the top. If I wasn't too old for such things, I'd rather like to play it over again," said Amy, who began to talk of renouncing childish things at the mature age of twelve.

"We never are too old for this, my dear, because it is a play we are playing all the time in one way or another. Out burdens are here, our road is before us, and the longing for goodness and happiness is the guide that leads us through many troubles and mistakes to the peace which

is a true Celestial City. Now, my little pilgrims, suppose you begin again, not in play, but in earnest, and see how far on you can get before Father comes home."

"Really, Mother? Where are our bundles?" asked Amy, who was a very literal young lady. "Each of you told what your burden was just now, except Beth. I rather think she hasn't got any," said her mother.

"Yes, I have. Mine is dishes and dusters, and envying girls with nice pianos, and being afraid of people."

Beth's bundle was such a funny one that everybody wanted to laugh, but nobody did, for it would have hurt her feelings very much.

"Let us do it," said Meg thoughtfully. "It is only another name for trying to be good, and the story may help us, for though we do want to be good, it's hard work and we forget, and don't do our best."

"We were in the Slough of Despond tonight, and Mother came and pulled us out as Help did in the book. We ought to have our roll of directions, like Christian. What shall we do about that?" asked Jo, delighted with the fancy which lent a little romance to the very dull task of doing her duty.

"Look under your pillows Christmas morning, and you will find your guidebook," replied Mrs. March.

They talked over the new plan while old Hannah cleared the table, then out came the four little work baskets, and the needles flew as the girls made sheets for Aunt March. It was uninteresting sewing, but tonight no one grumbled. They adopted Jo's plan of dividing the long seams into four parts, and calling the quarters Europe, Asia, Africa, and America, and in that way got on capitally, especially when they talked about the different countries as they stitched their way through them.

At nine they stopped work, and sang, as usual, before they went to bed. No one but Beth could get much music out of the old piano, but she had a way of softly touching the yellow keys and making a pleasant accompaniment to the simple songs they sang. Meg had a voice like a flute, and she and her mother led the little choir. Amy chirped like a cricket, and Jo wandered through the airs at her own sweet will, always coming out at the wrong place with a croak or a quaver that spoiled the most pensive tune. They had always done this from the time they could lisp... Crinkle, crinkle, 'ittle 'tar, and it had become a household custom, for the mother was a born singer. The first sound in the morning was her voice as she went about the house singing like a

lark, and the last sound at night was the same cheery sound, for the girls never grew too old for that familiar lullaby.

A MERRY CHRISTMAS

Jo was the first to wake in the gray dawn of Christmas morning. No stockings hung at the fireplace, and for a moment she felt as much disappointed as she did long ago, when her little sock fell down because it was crammed so full of goodies. Then she remembered her mother's promise and, slipping her hand under her pillow, drew out a little crimson-covered book. She knew it very well, for it was that beautiful old story of the best life ever lived, and Jo felt that it was a true guidebook for any pilgrim going on a long journey. She woke Meg with a Merry Christmas, and bade her see what was under her pillow. A green-covered book appeared, with the same picture inside, and a few words written by their mother, which made their one present very precious in their eyes. Presently Beth and Amy woke to rummage and find their little books also, one dove-colored, the other blue, and all sat looking at and talking about them, while the east grew rosy with the coming day.

In spite of her small vanities, Margaret had a sweet and pious nature, which unconsciously influenced her sisters, especially Jo, who loved her very tenderly, and obeyed her because her advice was so gently given.

"Girls," said Meg seriously, looking from the
tumbled head beside her to the two little night-
capped ones in the room beyond, "Mother wants
us to read and love and mind these books, and
we must begin at once. We used to be faithful
about it, but since Father went away and all this
war trouble unsettled us, we have neglected
many things. You can do as you please, but I
shall keep my book on the table here and read a
little every morning as soon as I wake, for I know
it will do me good and help me through the day."

Then she opened her new book and began to
read. Jo put her arm round her and, leaning
cheek to cheek, read also, with the quiet expression so seldom seen on her restless face.

"How good Meg is! Come, Amy, let's do as they
do. I'll help you with the hard words, and they'll
explain things if we don't understand," whispered Beth, very much impressed by the pretty
books and her sisters, example.

"I'm glad mine is blue," said Amy. And then the
rooms were every still while the pages were softly
turned, and the winter sunshine crept in to
touch the bright heads and serious faces with a
Christmas greeting.

"Where is Mother?" asked Meg, as she and Jo
ran down to thank her for their gifts, half an
hour later.

"Goodness only knows. Some poor creature came a-beggin', and your ma went straight off to see what was needed. There never was such a woman for givin' away vittles and drink, clothes and firin'," replied Hannah, who had lived with the family since Meg was born, and was considered by them all more as a friend than a servant.

"She will be back soon, I think, so fry your cakes, and have everything ready," said Meg, looking over the presents which were collected in a basket and kept under the sofa, ready to be produced at the proper time. "Why, where is Amy's bottle of cologne?" she added, as the little flask did not appear.

"She took it out a minute ago, and went off with it to put a ribbon on it, or some such notion," replied Jo, dancing about the room to take the first stiffness off the new army slippers.

"How nice my handkerchiefs look, don't they? Hannah washed and ironed them for me, and I marked them all myself," said Beth, looking proudly at the somewhat uneven letters which had cost her such labor.

"Bless the child! She's gone and put 'Mother' on them instead of 'M. March'. How funny!" cried Jo, taking one up.

"Isn't that right? I thought it was better to do it so, because Meg's initials are M.M., and I don't want anyone to use these but Marmee," said Beth, looking troubled.

"It's all right, dear, and a very pretty idea, quite sensible too, for no one can ever mistake now. It will please her very much, I know," said Meg, with a frown for Jo and a smile for Beth.

"There's Mother. Hide the basket, quick!" cried Jo, as a door slammed and steps sounded in the hall.

Amy came in hastily, and looked rather abashed when she saw her sisters all waiting for her.

"Where have you been, and what are you hiding behind you?" asked Meg, surprised to see, by her hood and cloak, that lazy Amy had been out so early.

"Don't laugh at me, Jo! I didn't mean anyone should know till the time came. I only meant to change the little bottle for a big gone, and I gave all my money to get it, and I'm truly trying not to be selfish any more."

As she spoke, Amy showed the handsome flask which replaced the cheap one, and looked so earnest and humble in her little effort to forget herself that Meg hugged her on the spot, and Jo pronounced her 'a trump,' while Beth ran to the

window, and picked her finest rose to ornament the stately bottle.

"You see I felt ashamed of my present, after reading and talking about being good this morning, so I ran round the corner and changed it the minute I was up, and I'm so glad, for mine is the handsomest now."

Another bang of the street door sent the basket under the sofa, and the girls to the table, eager for breakfast.

"Merry Christmas, Marmee! Many of them! Thank you for our books. We read some, and mean to every day," they all cried in chorus.

"Merry Christmas, little daughters! I'm glad you began at once, and hope you will keep on. But I want to say one word before we sit down. Not far away from here lies a poor woman with a little newborn baby. Six children are huddled into one bed to keep from freezing, for they have no fire. There is nothing to eat over there, and the oldest boy came to tell me they were suffering hunger and cold. My girls, will you give them your breakfasts a Christmas present?"

They were all unusually hungry, having waited nearly an hour, and for a minute no one spoke, only a minute, for Jo exclaimed impetuously, "I'm so glad you came before we began!"

"May I go and help carry the things to the poor little children?" asked Beth eagerly.

"I shall take the cream and the muffins," added Amy, heroically giving up the article she most liked.

Meg was already covering the buckwheat's, and piling the bread into one big plate.

"I thought you'd do it," said Mrs. March, smiling as if satisfied. "You shall all go and help me, and when we come back we will have bread and milk for breakfast, and make it up at dinnertime."

They were soon ready, and the procession set out. Fortunately it was early, and they went through back streets, so few people saw them, and no one laughed at the queer party.

A poor, bare, miserable room it was, with broken windows, no fire, ragged bedclothes, a sick mother, wailing baby, and a group of pale, hungry children cuddled under one old quilt, trying to keep warm.

How the big eyes stared and the blue lips smiled as the girls went in.

"Ach, mein Gott! It is good angels come to us!" said the poor woman, crying for joy.

"Funny angels in hoods and mittens," said Jo, and set them to laughing.

In a few minutes it really did seem as if kind spirits had been at work there. Hannah, who had carried wood, made a fire, and stopped up the broken panes with old hats and her own cloak. Mrs. March gave the mother tea and gruel, and comforted her with promises of help, while she dressed the little baby as tenderly as if it had been her own. The girls meantime spread the table, set the children round the fire, and fed them like so many hungry birds, laughing, talking, and trying to understand the funny broken English.

"Das ist gut! Die Engel-kinder!" cried the poor things as they ate and warmed their purple hands at the comfortable blaze.

The girls had never been called angel children before, and thought it very agreeable, especially Jo, who had been considered 'Sancho' ever since she was born. That was a very happy breakfast, though they didn't get any of it. And when they went away, leaving comfort behind, I think there were not in all the city four merrier people than the hungry little girls who gave away their breakfasts and contented themselves with bread and milk on Christmas morning.

"That's loving our neighbor better than ourselves, and I like it," said Meg, as they set out

their presents while their mother was upstairs collecting clothes for the poor Hummels.

Not a very splendid show, but there was a great deal of love done up in the few little bundles, and the tall vase of red roses, white chrysanthemums, and trailing vines, which stood in the middle, gave quite an elegant air to the table.

"She's coming! Strike up, Beth! Open the door, Amy! Three cheers for Marmee!" cried Jo, prancing about while Meg went to conduct Mother to the seat of honor.

Beth played her gayest march, Amy threw open the door, and Meg enacted escort with great dignity. Mrs. March was both surprised and touched, and smiled with her eyes full as she examined her presents and read the little notes which accompanied them. The slippers went on at once, a new handkerchief was slipped into her pocket, well scented with Amy's cologne, the rose was fastened in her bosom, and the nice gloves were pronounced a perfect fit.

There was a good deal of laughing and kissing and explaining, in the simple, loving fashion which makes these home festivals so pleasant at the time, so sweet to remember long afterward, and then all fell to work.

The morning charities and ceremonies took so much time that the rest of the day was devoted

to preparations for the evening festivities. Being still too young to go often to the theater, and not rich enough to afford any great outlay for private performances, the girls put their wits to work, and necessity being the mother of invention, made whatever they needed. Very clever were some of their productions, pasteboard guitars, antique lampshade of old-fashioned butter boats covered with silver paper, gorgeous robes of old cotton, glittering with tin spangles from a pickle factory, and armor covered with the same useful diamond shaped bits left in sheets when the lids of preserve pots were cut out. The big chamber was the scene of many innocent revels.

No gentleman were admitted, so Jo played male parts to her heart's content and took immense satisfaction in a pair of russet leather boots given her by a friend, who knew a lady who knew an actor. These boots, an old foil, and a slashed doublet once used by an artist for some picture, were Jo's chief treasures and appeared on all occasions. The smallness of the company made it necessary for the two principal actors to take several parts apiece, and they certainly deserved some credit for the hard work they did in learning three or four different parts, whisking in and out of various costumes, and managing the stage besides. It was excellent drill for their memories, a harmless amusement, and employed many hours which otherwise would have been idle, lonely, or spent in less profitable society.

On Christmas night, a dozen girls piled onto the
bed which was the dress circle, and sat before
the blue and yellow chintz curtains in a most
flattering state of expectancy. There was a good
deal of rustling and whispering behind the curtain, a trifle of lamp smoke, and an occasional
giggle from Amy, who was apt to get hysterical in
the excitement of the moment. Presently a bell
sounded, the curtains flew apart, and the OPER-
ATIC TRAGEDY began.

A gloomy wood, according to the one playbill,
was represented by a few shrubs in pots, green
baize on the floor, and a cave in the distance.
This cave was made with a clothes horse for a
roof, bureaus for walls, and in it was a small
furnace in full blast, with a black pot on it and
an old witch bending over it. The stage was dark
and the glow of the furnace had a fine effect,
especially as real steam issued from the kettle
when the witch took off the cover. A moment was
allowed for the first thrill to subside, then Hugo,
the villain, stalked in with a clanking sword at
his side, a slouching hat, black beard, mysterious cloak, and the boots. After pacing to and fro
in much agitation, he struck his forehead, and
burst out in a wild strain, singing of his hatred
to Roderigo, his love for Zara, and his pleasing
resolution to kill the one and win the other. The
gruff tones of Hugo's voice, with an occasional
shout when his feelings overcame him, were very
impressive, and the audience applauded the

moment he paused for breath. Bowing with the
air of one accustomed to public praise, he stole
to the cavern and ordered Hagar to come forth
with a commanding, What ho, minion! I need
thee!

Out came Meg, with gray horsehair hanging
about her face, a red and black robe, a staff, and
cabalistic signs upon her cloak. Hugo demanded
a potion to make Zara adore him, and destroy
Roderigo. Hagar, in a fine dramatic melody,
promised both, and proceeded to call up the
spirit who would bring the love philter.

"Hither, hither, from thy home,
Airy sprite, I bid thee come!
Born of roses, fed on dew
Charms and potions canst thou brew,
Bring me here, with elfin speed,
The fragrant philter which I need.
Make it sweet and swift and strong,
Spirit, answer now my song!"

A soft strain of music sounded, and then at the
back of the cave appeared a little figure in
cloudy white, with glittering wings, golden hair,
and a garland of roses on its head. Waving a
wand, it sang . . .

"Hither I come,
From my airy home,
Afar in the silver moon.
Take the magic spell,

And use it well,
Or its power will vanish soon!"

And dropping a small, gilded bottle at the witch's feet, the spirit vanished. Another chant from Hagar produced another apparition, not a lovely one, for with a bang an ugly black imp appeared and, having croaked a reply, tossed a dark bottle at Hugo and disappeared with a mocking laugh. Having warbled his thanks and put the potions in his boots, Hugo departed, and Hagar informed the audience that as he had killed a few of her friends in times past, she had cursed him, and intends to thwart his plans, and be revenged on him. Then the curtain fell, and the audience reposed and ate candy while discussing the merits of the play.

A good deal of hammering went on before the curtain rose again, but when it became evident what a masterpiece of stage carpentry had been got up, no one murmured at the delay. It was truly superb. A tower rose to the ceiling, halfway up appeared a window with a lamp burning in it, and behind the white curtain appeared Zara in a lovely blue and silver dress, waiting for Roderigo. He came in gorgeous array, with plumed cap, red cloak, chestnut love locks, a guitar, and the boots, of course. Kneeling at the foot of the tower, he sang a serenade in melting tones. Zara replied and, after a musical dialogue, consented to fly. Then came the grand effect of the play. Roderigo produced a rope ladder, with five steps

to it, threw up one end, and invited Zara to
descend. Timidly she crept from her lattice, put
her hand on Roderigo's shoulder, and was about
to leap gracefully down when Alas! Alas for Zara!
she forgot her train. It caught in the window, the
tower tottered, leaned forward, fell with a crash,
and buried the unhappy lovers in the ruins.

A universal shriek arose as the russet boots
waved wildly from the wreck and a golden head
emerged, exclaiming, I told you so! I told you so!
With wonderful presence of mind, Don Pedro,
the cruel sire, rushed in, dragged out his daughter, with a hasty aside . . .

"Don't laugh! Act as if it was all right!" and,
ordering Roderigo up, banished him from the
kingdom with wrath and scorn. Though decidedly shaken by the fall from the tower upon him,
Roderigo defied the old gentleman and refused to
stir. This dauntless example fired Zara. She also
defied her sire, and he ordered them both to the
deepest dungeons of the castle. A stout little
retainer came in with chains and led them away,
looking very much frightened and evidently
forgetting the speech he ought to have made.

Act third was the castle hall, and here Hagar
appeared, having come to free the lovers and
finish Hugo. She hears him coming and hides,
sees him put the potions into two cups of wine
and bid the timid little servant, "Bear them to
the captives in their cells, and tell them I shall

come anon." The servant takes Hugo aside to tell him something, and Hagar changes the cups for two others which are harmless. Ferdinando, the 'minion', carries them away, and Hagar puts back the cup which holds the poison meant for Roderigo. Hugo, getting thirsty after a long warble, drinks it, loses his wits, and after a good deal of clutching and stamping, falls flat and dies, while Hagar informs him what she has done in a song of exquisite power and melody.

This was a truly thrilling scene, though some persons might have thought that the sudden tumbling down of a quantity of long red hair rather marred the effect of the villain's death. He was called before the curtain, and with great propriety appeared, leading Hagar, whose singing was considered more wonderful than all the rest of the performance put together.

Act fourth displayed the despairing Roderigo on the point of stabbing himself because he has been told that Zara has deserted him. Just as the dagger is at his heart, a lovely song is sung under his window, informing him that Zara is true but in danger, and he can save her if he will. A key is thrown in, which unlocks the door, and in a spasm of rapture he tears off his chains and rushes away to find and rescue his lady love.

Act fifth opened with a stormy scene between Zara and Don Pedro. He wishes her to go into a

convent, but she won't hear of it, and after a touching appeal, is about to faint when Roderigo dashes in and demands her hand. Don Pedro refuses, because he is not rich. They shout and gesticulate tremendously but cannot agree, and Rodrigo is about to bear away the exhausted Zara, when the timid servant enters with a letter and a bag from Hagar, who has mysteriously disappeared. The latter informs the party that she bequeaths untold wealth to the young pair and an awful doom to Don Pedro, if he doesn't make them happy. The bag is opened, and several quarts of tin money shower down upon the stage till it is quite glorified with the glitter. This entirely softens the stern sire. He consents without a murmur, all join in a joyful chorus, and the curtain falls upon the lovers kneeling to receive Don Pedro's blessing in attitudes of the most romantic grace.

Tumultuous applause followed but received an unexpected check, for the cot bed, on which the dress circle was built, suddenly shut up and extinguished the enthusiastic audience. Roderigo and Don Pedro flew to the rescue, and all were taken out unhurt, though many were speechless with laughter. The excitement had hardly subsided when Hannah appeared, with Mrs. March's compliments, and would the ladies walk down to supper.

This was a surprise even to the actors, and when they saw the table, they looked at one another in

rapturous amazement. It was like Marmee to get up a little treat for them, but anything so fine as this was unheard of since the departed days of plenty. There was ice cream, actually two dishes of it, pink and white, and cake and fruit and distracting French bonbons and, in the middle of the table, four great bouquets of hot house flowers.

It quite took their breath away, and they stared first at the table and then at their mother, who looked as if she enjoyed it immensely.

"Is it fairies?" asked Amy.

"Santa Claus," said Beth.

"Mother did it." And Meg smiled her sweetest, in spite of her gray beard and white eyebrows.

"Aunt March had a good fit and sent the supper," cried Jo, with a sudden inspiration.

"All wrong. Old Mr. Laurence sent it," replied Mrs. March.

"The Laurence boy's grandfather! What in the world put such a thing into his head? We don't know him!" exclaimed Meg.

"Hannah told one of his servants about your breakfast party. He is an odd old gentleman, but that pleased him. He knew my father years ago,

and he sent me a polite note this afternoon, saying he hoped I would allow him to express his friendly feeling toward my children by sending them a few trifles in honor of the day. I could not refuse, and so you have a little feast at night to makeup for the bread-and-milk breakfast."

"That boy put it into his head, I know he did! He's a capital fellow, and I wish we could get acquainted. He looks as if he'd like to know us but he's bashful, and Meg is so prim she won't let me speak to him when we pass," said Jo, as the plates went round, and the ice began to melt out of sight, with ohs and ahs of satisfaction.

"You mean the people who live in the big house next door, don't you?" asked one of the girls. "My mother knows old Mr. Laurence, but says he's very proud and doesn't like to mix with his neighbors. He keeps his grandson shut up, when he isn't riding or walking with his tutor, and makes him study very hard. We invited him to our party, but he didn't come. Mother says he's very nice, though he never speaks to us girls."

"Our cat ran away once, and he brought her back, and we talked over the fence, and were getting on capitally, all about cricket, and so on, when he saw Meg coming, and walked off. I mean to know him some day, for he needs fun, I'm sure he does," said Jo decidedly.

"I like his manners, and he looks like a little gentleman, so I've no objection to your knowing him, if a proper opportunity comes. He brought the flowers himself, and I should have asked him in, if I had been sure what was going on upstairs. He looked so wistful as he went away, hearing the frolic and evidently having none of his own."

"It's a mercy you didn't, Mother!" laughed Jo, looking at her boots. "But we'll have another play sometime that he can see. Perhaps he'll help act. Wouldn't that be jolly?"

"I never had such a fine bouquet before! How pretty it is!" And Meg examined her flowers with great interest.

"They are lovely. But Beth's roses are sweeter to me," said Mrs. March, smelling the half-dead posy in her belt.

Beth nestled up to her, and whispered softly, "I wish I could send my bunch to Father. I'm afraid he isn't having such a merry Christmas as we are."

WHY THE EVERGREEN TREES NEVER LOSE THEIR LEAVES
FLORENCE HOLBROOK

WINTER was coming, and the birds had flown far to the south, where the air was warm and they could find berries to eat. One little bird had broken its wing and could not fly with the others. It was alone in the cold world of frost and snow. The forest looked warm, and it made its way to the trees as well as it could, to ask for help.

First it came to a birch tree. "Beautiful birch tree," it said, "my wing is broken, and my friends have flown away. May I live among your branches till they come back to me?"

"No, indeed," answered the birch tree, drawing her fair green leaves away. "We of the great forest have our own birds to help. I can do nothing for you."

"The birch is not very strong," said the little bird to itself, "and it might be that she could not hold me easily. I will ask the oak." So the bird said: "Great oak tree, you are so strong, will you not let me live on your boughs till my friends come back in the springtime?"

"In the springtime!" cried the oak. "That is a long way off. How do I know what you might do in all that time? Birds are always looking for

something to eat, and you might even eat up some of my acorns."

"It may be that the willow will be kind to me," thought the bird, and it said: "Gentle willow, my wing is broken, and I could not fly to the south with the other birds. May I live on your branches till the springtime?"

The willow did not look gentle then, for she drew herself up proudly and said: "Indeed, I do not know you, and we willows never talk to people whom we do not know. Very likely there are trees somewhere that will take in strange birds. Leave me at once."

The poor little bird did not know what to do. Its wing was not yet strong, but it began to fly away as well as it could. Before it had gone far a voice was heard. "Little bird," it said, "where are you going?"

"Indeed, I do not know," answered the bird sadly. "I am very cold."

"Come right here, then," said the friendly spruce tree, for it was her voice that had called.

"You shall live on my warmest branch all winter if you choose."

"Will you really let me?" asked the little bird eagerly.

"Indeed, I will," answered the kind-hearted spruce tree. "If your friends have flown away, it is time for the trees to help you. Here is the branch where my leaves are thickest and softest."

"My branches are not very thick," said the friendly pine tree, "but I am big and strong, and I can keep the North Wind from you and the spruce."

"I can help, too," said a little juniper tree. "I can give you berries all winter long, and every bird knows that juniper berries are good."

So the spruce gave the lonely little bird a home; the pine kept the cold North Wind away from it; and the juniper gave it berries to eat. The other trees looked on and talked together wisely.

"I would not have strange birds on my boughs," said the birch.

"I shall not give my acorns away for any one," said the oak.

"I never have anything to do with strangers," said the willow, and the three trees drew their leaves closely about them.

In the morning all those shining, green leaves lay on the ground, for a cold North Wind had

come in the night, and every leaf that it touched fell from the tree.

"May I touch every leaf in the forest?" asked the wind in its frolic.

"No," said the Frost King. "The trees that have been kind to the little bird with the broken wing may keep their leaves."

This is why the leaves of the spruce, the pine, and the juniper are always green.

THE STORY OF THE OTHER WISE MAN
HENRY VAN DYKE

Who seeks for heaven alone to save his soul,
May keep the path, but will not reach the goal;
While he who walks in love may wander far,
Yet God will bring him where the blessed are.

You know the story of the Three Wise Men of the East, and how they traveled from far away to offer their gifts at the manger-cradle in Bethlehem. But have you ever heard the story of the Other Wise Man, who also saw the star in its rising, and set out to follow it, yet did not arrive with his brethren in the presence of the young child Jesus? Of the great desire of this fourth pilgrim, and how it was denied, yet accomplished in the denial; of his many wanderings and the probations of his soul; of the long way of his seeking, and the strange way of his finding, the One whom he sought-I would tell the tale as I have heard fragments of it in the Hall of Dreams, in the palace of the Heart of Man.

THE SIGN IN THE SKY

IN the days when Augustus Cæsar was master of many kings and Herod reigned in Jerusalem, there lived in the city of Ecbatana, among the mountains of Persia, a certain man named Artaban, the Median. His house stood close to the outermost of the seven walls which encircled the royal treasury. From his roof he could look

over the rising battlements of black and white and crimson and blue and red and silver and gold, to the hill where the summer palace of the Parthian emperors glittered like a jewel in a sevenfold crown.

Around the dwelling of Artaban spread a fair garden, a tangle of flowers and fruit trees, watered by a score of streams descending from the slopes of Mount Orontes, and made musical by innumerable birds. But all color was lost in the soft and odorous darkness of the late September night, and all sounds were hushed in the deep charm of its silence, save the plashing of the water, like a voice half sobbing and half laughing under the shadows. High above the trees a dim glow of light shone through the curtained arches of the upper chamber, where the master of the house was holding council with his friends.

He stood by the doorway to greet his guests-a tall, dark man of about forty years, with brilliant eyes set near together under his broad brow, and firm lines graven around his fine, thin lips; the brow of a dreamer and the mouth of a soldier, a man of sensitive feeling but inflexible will-one of those who, in whatever age they may live, are born for inward conflict and a life of quest.

His robe was of pure white wool, thrown over a tunic of silk; and a white, pointed cap, with long lapels at the sides, rested on his flowing black

hair. It was the dress of the ancient priesthood of the Magi, called the fire-worshipers.

"Welcome!" he said, in his low, pleasant voice, as one after another entered the room- "welcome, Abdus; peace be with you, Rhodaspes and Tigranes, and with you my father, Abgarus. You are all welcome and this house grows bright with the joy of your presence."

There were nine of the men, differing widely in age, but alike in the richness of their dress of many-colored silks, and in the massive golden collars around their necks, marking them as Parthian nobles, and in the winged circles of gold resting upon their breasts, the sign of the followers of Zoroaster.

They took their places around a small black altar at the end of the room,
where a tiny flame was burning. Artaban, standing beside it, and waving a barsom of thin tamarisk branches above the fire, fed it with dry sticks of pine and fragrant oils. Then he began the ancient chant of the Yasna, and the voices of his companions joined in the beautiful hymn to Ahura-Mazda:

We worship the Spirit Divine,
all wisdom and goodness possessing,

Surrounded by Holy Immortals,
the givers of bounty and blessing.

We joy in the works of His hands,
His truth and His power confessing.

We praise all the things that are pure,
for these are His only Creation;

The thoughts that are true, and the words
and deeds that have won approbation;

These are supported by Him,
and for these we make adoration.

Hear us, O Mazda! Thou livest
in truth and in heavenly gladness;

Cleanse us from falsehood, and keep us
from evil and bondage to badness;

Pour out the light and the joy of Thy life
on our darkness and sadness.

Shine on our gardens and fields,
Shine on our working and weaving;

Shine on the whole race of man,
Believing and unbelieving;

Shine on us now through the night,
Shine on us now in Thy might,

The flame of our holy love
and the song of our worship receiving.

The fire rose with the chant, throbbing as if it were made of musical flame, until it cast a bright illumination through the whole apartment, revealing its simplicity and splendor.

The floor was laid with tiles of dark blue veined with white; pilasters of twisted silver stood out against the blue walls; the clear-story of round-arched windows above them was hung with azure silk; the vaulted ceiling was a pavement of sapphires, like the body of heaven in its clearness, sown with silver stars. From the four corners of the roof hung four golden magic-wheels, called the tongues of the gods. At the eastern end, behind the altar, there were two dark-red pillars of porphyry; above them a lintel of the same stone, on which was carved the figure of a winged archer, with his arrow set to the string and his bow drawn.

The doorway between the pillars, which opened upon the terrace of the roof, was covered with a heavy curtain of the color of a ripe pomegranate, embroidered with innumerable golden rays shooting upward from the floor. In effect the room was like a quiet, starry night, all azure and silver, flushed in the east with rosy promise of the dawn. It was, as the house of a man should be, an expression of the character and spirit of the master.

He turned to his friends when the song was
ended, and invited them to be seated on the
divan at the western end of the room.

"You have come tonight," said he, looking
around the circle, "at my call, as the faithful
scholars of Zoroaster, to renew your worship and
rekindle your faith in the God of Purity, even as
this fire has been rekindled on the altar. We
worship not the fire, but Him of whom it is the
chosen symbol, because it is the purest of all
created things. It speaks to us of one who is
Light and Truth. Is it not so, my father?"

"It is well said, my son," answered the venerable
Abgarus. "The enlightened are never idolaters.
They lift the veil of the form and go in to the
shrine of the reality, and new light and truth are
coming to them continually through the old
symbols."

"Hear me, then, my father and my friends," said
Artaban, very quietly, "while I tell you of the new
light and truth that have come to me through
the most ancient of all signs. We have searched
the secrets of nature together, and studied the
healing virtues of water and fire and the plants.
We have read also the books of prophecy in
which the future is dimly foretold in words that
are hard to understand. But the highest of all
learning is the knowledge of the stars. To trace
their courses is to untangle the threads of the
mystery of life from the beginning to the end. If

we could follow them perfectly, nothing would be hidden from us. But is not our knowledge of them still incomplete? Are there not many stars still beyond our horizon-lights that are known only to the dwellers in the far southland, among the spice-trees of Punt and the gold mines of Ophir?"

There was a murmur of assent among the listeners.

"The stars," said Tigranes, "are the thoughts of the Eternal. They are numberless. But the thoughts of man can be counted, like the years of his life. The wisdom of the Magi is the greatest of all wisdoms on earth, because it knows its own ignorance. And that is the secret of power. We keep men always looking and waiting for a new sunrise. But we ourselves know that the darkness is equal to the light, and that the con-flict between them will never be ended."

"That does not satisfy me," answered Artaban, "for, if the waiting must be endless, if there could be no fulfillment of it, then it would not be wisdom to look and wait. We should become like those new teachers of the Greeks, who say that there is no truth, and that the only wise men are those who spend their lives in discovering and exposing the lies that have been believed in the world. But the new sunrise will certainly dawn in the appointed time. Do not our own books tell us that this will come to pass, and that men will see the brightness of a great light?"

"That is true," said the voice of Abgarus; "every faithful disciple of Zoroaster knows the prophecy of the Avesta and carries the word in his heart. 'In that day Sosiosh the Victorious shall arise out of the number of the prophets in the east country. Around him shall shine a mighty brightness, and he shall make life everlasting, incorruptible, and immortal, and the dead shall rise again.'"

"This is a dark saying," said Tigranes, "and it may be that we shall never understand it. It is better to consider the things that are near at hand, and to increase the influence of the Magi in their own country, rather than to look for one who may be a stranger, and to whom we must resign our power."

The others seemed to approve these words. There was a silent feeling of agreement manifest among them; their looks responded with that indefinable expression which always follows when a speaker has uttered the thought that has been slumbering in the hearts of his listeners. But Artaban turned to Abgarus with a glow on his face, and said:

"My father, I have kept this prophecy in the secret place of my soul. Religion without a great hope would be like an altar without a living fire. And now the flame has burned more brightly, and by the light of it I have read other words which also have come from the fountain of

Truth, and speaking yet more clearly of the rising of the Victorious One in his brightness."

He drew from the breast of his tunic two small rolls of fine linen, with writing upon them, and unfolded them carefully upon his knee.

"In the years that are lost in the past, long before our fathers came into the land of Babylon, there were wise men in Chaldea, from whom the first of the Magi learned the secret of the heavens. And of these Balaam the son of Beor was one of the mightiest. Hear the words of his prophecy: 'There shall come a star out of Jacob, and a scepter shall arise out of Israel.'"

The lips of Tigranes drew downward with contempt, as he said:

"Judah was a captive by the waters of Babylon, and the sons of Jacob in bondage to our kings. The tribes of Israel are scattered through the mountains like lost sheep, and from the remnant that dwells in Judea under the yoke of Rome neither star nor scepter shall arise."

"And yet," answered Artaban, "it was the Hebrew Daniel, the mighty searcher of dreams, the counselor of kings, the wise Belteshazzar, who was most honored and beloved of our great King Cyrus. A prophet of sure things and a reader of the thoughts of God, Daniel proved himself to our people. And these are the words that he

wrote." (Artaban read from the second roll:) "'Know, therefore, and understand that from the going forth of the commandment to restore Jerusalem, unto the Anointed One, the Prince, the time shall be seven and three-score and two weeks.'"

"But, my son," said Abgarus, doubtfully, "these are mystical numbers. Who can interpret them, or who can find the key that shall unlock their meaning?"

Artaban answered: "It has been shown to me and to my three companions among the Magi-Caspar, Melchior, and Balthazar. We have searched the ancient tablets of Chaldea and computed the time. It falls in this year. We have studied the sky, and in the spring of the year we saw two of the greatest stars draw near together in the sign of the Fish, which is the house of the Hebrews. We also saw a new star there, which shone for one night and then vanished. Now again the two great planets are meeting. This night is their conjunction. My three brothers are watching at the ancient Temple of the Seven Spheres, at Borsippa, in Babylonia, and I am watching here. If the star shines again, they will wait ten days for me at the temple, and then we will set out together for Jerusalem, to see and worship the promised one who shall be born King of Israel. I believe the sign will come. I have made ready for the journey. I have sold my house and my possessions, and bought these

three jewels-a sapphire, a ruby, and a pearl-to carry them as tribute to the King. And I ask you to go with me on the pilgrimage, that we may have joy together in finding the Prince who is worthy to be served."

While he was speaking he thrust his hand into the inmost fold of his girdle and drew out three great gems-one blue as a fragment of the night sky, one redder than a ray of sunrise, and one as pure as the peak of a snow mountain at twilight-and laid them on the outspread linen scrolls before him.

But his friends looked on with strange and alien eyes. A veil of doubt and mistrust came over their faces, like a fog creeping up from the marshes to hide the hills. They glanced at each other with looks of wonder and pity, as those who have listened to incredible sayings, the story of a wild vision, or the proposal of an impossible enterprise.

At last Tigranes said: "Artaban, this is a vain dream. It comes from too much looking upon the stars and the cherishing of lofty thoughts. It would be wiser to spend the time in gathering money for the new fire-temple at Chala. No king will ever rise from the broken race of Israel, and no end will ever come to the eternal strife of light and darkness. He who looks for it is a chaser of shadows. Farewell."

And another said: "Artaban, I have no knowledge of these things, and my office as guardian of the royal treasure binds me here. The quest is not for me. But if thou must follow it, fare thee well."

And another said: "In my house there sleeps a new bride, and I cannot leave her nor take her with me on this strange journey. This quest is not for me. But may thy steps be prospered wherever thou goest. So, farewell."

And another said: "I am ill and unfit for hardship, but there is a man among my servants whom I will send with thee when thou goest, to bring me word how thou farest."

But Abgarus, the oldest and the one who loved Artaban the best, lingered after the others had gone, and said, gravely: "My son, it may be that the light of truth is in this sign that has appeared in the skies, and then it will surely lead to the Prince and the mighty brightness. Or it may be that it is only a shadow of the light, as Tigranes has said, and then he who follows it will have only a long pilgrimage and an empty search. But it is better to follow even the shadow of the best than to remain content with the worst. And those who would see wonderful things must often be ready to travel alone. I am too old for this journey, but my heart shall be a companion of the pilgrimage day and night, and I shall know the end of thy quest. Go in peace."

So one by one they went out of the azure chamber with its silver stars, and Artaban was left in solitude.

He gathered up the jewels and replaced them in his girdle. For a long time he stood and watched the flame that flickered and sank upon the altar. Then he crossed the hall, lifted the heavy curtain, and passed out between the dull red pillars of porphyry to the terrace on the roof.

The shiver that thrills through the earth ere she rouses from her night sleep had already begun, and the cool wind that heralds the daybreak was drawing downward from the lofty snow-traced ravines of Mount Orontes. Birds, half awakened, crept and chirped among the rustling leaves, and the smell of ripened grapes came in brief wafts from the arbors.

Far over the eastern plain a white mist stretched like a lake. But where the distant peak of Zagros serrated the western horizon the sky was clear. Jupiter and Saturn rolled together like drops of lambent flame about to blend in one.

As Artaban watched them, behold, an azure spark was born out of the darkness beneath, rounding itself with purple splendors to a crimson sphere, and spiring upward through rays of saffron and orange into a point of white radiance. Tiny and infinitely remote, yet perfect in every part, it pulsated in the enormous vault as

if the three jewels in the Magian's breast had mingled and been transformed into a living heart of light.

He bowed his head. He covered his brow with his hands.

"It is the sign," he said. "The King is coming, and I will go to meet him."

BY THE WATERS OF BABYLON

ALL night long Vasda, the swiftest of Artaban's horses, had been waiting, saddled and bridled, in her stall, pawing the ground impatiently, and shaking her bit as if she shared the eagerness of her master's purpose, though she knew not its meaning.

Before the birds had fully roused to their strong, high, joyful chant of morning song, before the white mist had begun to lift lazily from the plain, the other wise man was in the saddle, riding swiftly along the highroad, which skirted the base of Mount Orontes, westward.

How close, how intimate is the comradeship between a man and his favorite horse on a long journey. It is a silent, comprehensive friendship, an intercourse beyond the need of words.

They drink at the same wayside springs, and sleep under the same guardian stars. They are

conscious together of the subduing spell of nightfall and the quickening joy of daybreak. The master shares his evening meal with his hungry companion, and feels the soft, moist lips caressing the palm of his hand as they close over the morsel of bread. In the gray dawn he is roused from his bivouac by the gentle stir of a warm, sweet breath over his sleeping face, and looks up into the eyes of his faithful fellow-traveler, ready and waiting for the toil of the day. Surely, unless he is a pagan and an unbeliever, by whatever name he calls upon his God, he will thank Him for this voiceless sympathy, this dumb affection, and his morning prayer will embrace a double blessing-God bless us both, and keep our feet from falling and our souls from death!

And then, through the keen morning air, the swift hoofs beat their spirited music along the road, keeping time to the pulsing of two hearts that are moved with the same eager desire-to conquer space, to devour the distance, to attain the goal of the journey.

Artaban must indeed ride wisely and well if he would keep the appointed hour with the other Magi; for the route was a hundred and fifty parasangs, and fifteen was the utmost that he could travel in a day. But he knew Vasda's strength, and pushed forward without anxiety, making the fixed distance every day, though he must travel late into the night, and in the morning long before sunrise.

He passed along the brown slopes of Mount Orontes, furrowed by the rocky courses of a hundred torrents.

He crossed the level plains of the Nisæans, where the famous herds of horses, feeding in the wide pastures, tossed their heads at Vasda's approach, and galloped away with a thunder of many hoofs, and flocks of wild birds rose suddenly from the swampy meadows, wheeling in great circles with a shining flutter of innumerable wings and shrill cries of surprise.

He traversed the fertile fields of Concabar, where the dust from the threshing-floors filled the air with a golden mist, half hiding the huge temple of Astarte with its four hundred pillars.

At Baghistan, among the rich gardens watered by fountains from the rock, he looked up at the mountain thrusting its immense rugged brow out over the road, and saw the figure of King Darius trampling upon his fallen foes, and the proud list of his wars and conquests graven high upon the face of the eternal cliff.

Over many a cold and desolate pass, crawling painfully across the wind-swept shoulders of the hills; down many a black mountain-gorge, where the river roared and raced before him like a savage guide; across many a smiling vale, with terraces of yellow limestone full of vines and fruit-trees; through the oak-groves of Carine and

the dark Gates of Zagros, walled in by preci-
pices; into the ancient city of Chala, where the
people of Samaria had been kept in captivity
long ago; and out again by the mighty portal,
riven through the encircling hills, where he saw
the image of the High Priest of the Magi sculp-
tured on the wall of rock, with hand uplifted as
if to bless the centuries of pilgrims; past the
entrance of the narrow defile, filled from end to
end with orchards of peaches and figs, through
which the river Gyndes foamed down to meet
him; over the broad rice-fields, where the autumnal vapors spread their deathly mists; following along the course of the river, under
tremulous shadows of poplar and tamarind,
among the lower hills; and out upon the flat
plain, where the road ran straight as an arrow
through the stubble-fields and parched meadows; past the city of Ctesiphon, where the
Parthian emperors reigned, and the vast me-
tropolis of Seleucia which Alexander built;
across the swirling floods of Tigris and the many
channels of Euphrates, flowing yellow through
the corn-lands-Artaban pressed onward until he
arrived, at nightfall of the tenth day, beneath the
shattered walls of populous Babylon.

Vasda was almost spent, and he would gladly
have turned into the city to find rest and refreshment for himself and for her. But he knew
that it was three hours' journey yet to the
Temple of the Seven Spheres, and he must reach
the place by midnight if he would find his com-

rades waiting. So he did not halt, but rode steadily across the stubble-fields.

A grove of date-palms made an island of gloom in the pale yellow sea. As she passed into the shadow Vasda slackened her pace, and began to pick her way more carefully.

Near the farther end of the darkness an access of caution seemed to fall upon her. She scented some danger or difficulty; it was not in her heart to fly from it-only to be prepared for it, and to meet it wisely, as a good horse should do. The grove was close and silent as the tomb; not a leaf rustled, not a bird sang.

She felt her steps before her delicately, carrying her head low, and sighing now and then with apprehension. At last she gave a quick breath of anxiety and dismay, and stood stock-still, quivering in every muscle, before a dark object in the shadow of the last palm-tree.

Artaban dismounted. The dim starlight revealed the form of a man lying across the road. His humble dress and the outline of his haggard face showed that he was probably one of the poor Hebrew exiles who still dwelt in great numbers in the vicinity. His pallid skin, dry and yellow as parchment, bore the mark of the deadly fever which ravaged the marshlands in autumn. The chill of death was in his lean hand, and, as

Artaban released it, the arm fell back inertly upon the motionless breast.

He turned away with a thought of pity, consigning the body to that strange burial which the Magians deem most fitting-the funeral of the desert, from which the kites and vultures rise on dark wings, and the beasts of prey slink furtively away, leaving only a heap of white bones in the sand.

But, as he turned, a long, faint, ghostly sigh came from the man's lips. The brown, bony fingers closed convulsively on the hem of the Magian's robe and held him fast.

Artaban's heart leaped to his throat, not with fear, but with a dumb resentment at the importunity of this blind delay.

How could he stay here in the darkness to minister to a dying stranger? What claim had this unknown fragment of human life upon his compassion or his service? If he lingered but for an hour he could hardly reach Borsippa at the appointed time. His companions would think he had given up the journey. They would go without him. He would lose his quest.

But if he went on now, the man would surely die. If he stayed, life might be restored. His spirit throbbed and fluttered with the urgency of the crisis. Should he risk the great reward of his

divine faith for the sake of a single deed of human love? Should he turn aside, if only for a moment, from the following of the star, to give a cup of cold water to a poor, perishing Hebrew?

"God of truth and purity," he prayed, "direct me in the holy path, the way of wisdom which Thou only knowest."

Then he turned back to the sick man. Loosening the grasp of his hand, he carried him to a little mound at the foot of the palm-tree.

He unbound the thick folds of the turban and opened the garment above the sunken breast. He brought water from one of the small canals near by, and moistened the sufferer's brow and mouth. He mingled a draught of one of those simple but potent remedies which he carried always in his girdle-for the Magians were physicians as well as astrologers-and poured it slowly between the colorless lips. Hour after hour he labored as only a skillful healer of disease can do; and, at last, the man's strength returned; he sat up and looked about him.

"Who art thou?" he said, in the rude dialect of the country, "and why hast thou sought me here to bring back my life?"

"I am Artaban the Magian, of the city of Ecbatana, and I am going to Jerusalem in search of one who is to be born King of the Jews,

a great Prince and Deliverer of all men. I dare
not delay any longer upon my journey, for the
caravan that has waited for me may depart
without me. But see, here is all that I have left of
bread and wine, and here is a potion of healing
herbs. When thy strength is restored thou canst
find the dwellings of the Hebrews among the
houses of Babylon."

The Jew raised his trembling hands solemnly to
heaven.

"Now may the God of Abraham and Isaac and
Jacob bless and prosper the journey of the merciful, and bring him in peace to his desired
haven. But stay; I have nothing to give thee in
return-only this: that I can tell thee where the
Messiah must be sought. For our prophets have
said that he should be born not in Jerusalem,
but in Bethlehem of Judah. May the Lord bring
thee in safety to that place, because thou hast
had pity upon the sick."

It was already long past midnight. Artaban rode
in haste, and Vasda, restored by the brief rest,
ran eagerly through the silent plain and swam
the channels of the river. She put forth the remnant of her strength, and fled over the ground
like a gazelle.

But the first beam of the sun sent her shadow
before her as she entered upon the final stadium
of the journey, and the eyes of Artaban, anx-

iously scanning the great mound of Nimrod and the Temple of the Seven Spheres, could discern no trace of his friends.

The many-colored terraces of black and orange and red and yellow and green and blue and white, shattered by the convulsions of nature, and crumbling under the repeated blows of human violence, still glittered like a ruined rainbow in the morning light.

Artaban rode swiftly around the hill. He dismounted and climbed to the highest terrace, looking out toward the west.

The huge desolation of the marshes stretched away to the horizon and the border of the desert. Bitterns stood by the stagnant pools and jackals skulked through the low bushes; but there was no sign of the caravan of the wise men, far or near.

At the edge of the terrace he saw a little cairn of broken bricks, and under them a piece of parchment. He caught it up and read: "We have waited past the midnight, and can delay no longer. We go to find the King. Follow us across the desert."

Artaban sat down upon the ground and covered his head in despair.

"How can I cross the desert," said he, "with no food and with a spent horse? I must return to

Babylon, sell my sapphire, and buy a train of camels, and provision for the journey. I may never overtake my friends. Only God the merciful knows whether I shall not lose the sight of the King because I tarried to show mercy."

FOR THE SAKE OF A LITTLE CHILD

THERE was a silence in the Hall of Dreams, where I was listening to the story of the Other Wise Man. And through the silence I saw, but very dimly, his figure passing over the dreary undulations of the desert, high upon the back of his camel, rocking steadily onward like a ship over the waves.

The land of death spread its cruel net around him. The stony wastes bore no fruit but briers and thorns. The dark ledges of rock thrust themselves above the surface here and there, like the bones of perished monsters. Arid and inhospitable mountain ranges rose before him, furrowed with dry channels of ancient torrents, white and ghastly as scars on the face of nature. Shifting hills of treacherous sand were heaped like tombs along the horizon. By day, the fierce heat pressed its intolerable burden on the quivering air; and no living creature moved, on the dumb, swooning earth, but tiny jerboas scuttling through the parched bushes, or lizards vanishing in the clefts of the rock. By night the jackals prowled and barked in the distance, and the lion made the black ravines echo with his hollow

roaring, while a bitter, blighting chill followed the fever of the day. Through heat and cold, the Magian moved steadily onward.

Then I saw the gardens and orchards of Damascus, watered by the streams of Abana and Pharpar, with their sloping swards inlaid with bloom, and their thickets of myrrh and roses. I saw also the long, snowy ridge of Hermon, and the dark groves of cedars, and the valley of the Jordan, and the blue waters of the Lake of Galilee, and the fertile plain of Esdraelon, and the hills of Ephraim, and the highlands of Judah. Through all these I followed the figure of Artaban moving steadily onward, until he arrived at Bethlehem. And it was the third day after the three wise men had come to that place and had found Mary and Joseph, with the young child, Jesus, and had laid their gifts of gold and frankincense and myrrh at his feet.

Then the other wise man drew near, weary, but full of hope, bearing his ruby and his pearl to offer to the King. "For now at last," he said, "I shall surely find him, though it be alone, and later than my brethren. This is th   place of which the Hebrew exile told me that the prophets had spoken, and here I shall behold the rising of the great light. But I must inquire about the visit of my brethren, and to what house the star directed them, and to whom they presented their tribute."

The streets of the village seemed to be deserted, and Artaban wondered whether the men had all gone up to the hill-pastures to bring down their sheep. From the open door of a low stone cottage he heard the sound of a woman's voice singing softly. He entered and found a young mother hushing her baby to rest. She told him of the strangers from the far East who had appeared in the village three days ago, and how they said that a star had guided them to the place where Joseph of Nazareth was lodging with his wife and her new-born child, and how they had paid reverence to the child and given him many rich gifts.

"But the travelers disappeared again," she continued, "as suddenly as they had come. We were afraid at the strangeness of their visit. We could not understand it. The man of Nazareth took the babe and his mother and fled away that same night secretly, and it was whispered that they were going far away to Egypt. Ever since, there has been a spell upon the village; something evil hangs over it. They say that the Roman soldiers are coming from Jerusalem to force a new tax from us, and the men have driven the flocks and herds far back among the hills, and hidden themselves to escape it."

Artaban listened to her gentle, timid speech, and the child in her arms looked up in his face and smiled, stretching out its rosy hands to grasp at the winged circle of gold on his breast. His heart

warmed to the touch. It seemed like a greeting of love and trust to one who had journeyed long in loneliness and perplexity, fighting with his own doubts and fears, and following a light that was veiled in clouds.

"Might not this child have been the promised Prince?" he asked within himself, as he touched its soft cheek. "Kings have been born ere now in lower houses than this, and the favorite of the stars may rise even from a cottage. But it has not seemed good to the God of wisdom to reward my search so soon and so easily. The one whom I seek has gone before me; and now I must follow the King to Egypt."

The young mother laid the babe in its cradle, and rose to minister to the wants of the strange guest that fate had brought into her house. She set food before him, the plain fare of peasants, but willingly offered, and therefore full of refreshment for the soul as well as for the body. Artaban accepted it gratefully; and, as he ate, the child fell into a happy slumber, and murmured sweetly in its dreams, and a great peace filled the quiet room.

But suddenly there came the noise of a wild confusion and uproar in the streets of the village, a shrieking and wailing of women's voices, a clangor of brazen trumpets and a clashing of swords, and a desperate cry: "The soldiers! the soldiers of Herod! They are killing our children."

The young mother's face grew white with terror. She clasped her child to her bosom, and crouched motionless in the darkest corner of the room, covering him with the folds of her robe, lest he should wake and cry.

But Artaban went quickly and stood in the doorway of the house. His broad shoulders filled the portal from side to side, and the peak of his white cap all but touched the lintel.

The soldiers came hurrying down the street with bloody hands and dripping swords. At the sight of the stranger in his imposing dress they hesitated with surprise. The captain of the band approached the threshold to thrust him aside. But Artaban did not stir. His face was as calm as though he were watching the stars, and in his eyes there burned that steady radiance before which even the half-tamed hunting leopard shrinks, and the fierce bloodhound pauses in his leap. He held the soldier silently for an instant, and then said in a low voice:

"I am all alone in this place, and I am waiting to give this jewel to the prudent captain who will leave me in peace."

He showed the ruby, glistening in the hollow of his hand like a great drop of blood.

The captain was amazed at the splendor of the gem. The pupils of his eyes expanded with de-

sire, and the hard lines of greed wrinkled around his lips. He stretched out his hand and took the ruby.

"March on!" he cried to his men, "there is no child here. The house is still."

The clamor and the clang of arms passed down the street as the headlong fury of the chase sweeps by the secret covert where the trembling deer is hidden. Artaban re-entered the cottage. He turned his face to the east and prayed:

"God of truth, forgive my sin! I have said the thing that is not, to save the life of a child. And two of my gifts are gone. I have spent for man that which was meant for God. Shall I ever be worthy to see the face of the King?"

But the voice of the woman, weeping for joy in the shadow behind him, said very gently:

"Because thou hast saved the life of my little one, may the Lord bless thee and keep thee; the Lord make His face to shine upon thee and be gracious unto thee; the Lord lift up His countenance upon thee and give thee peace."

IN THE HIDDEN WAY OF SORROW

THEN again there was a silence in the Hall of Dreams, deeper and more mysterious than the

first interval, and I understood that the years of Artaban were flowing very swiftly under the stillness of that clinging fog, and I caught only a glimpse, here and there, of the river of his life shining through the shadows that concealed its course.

I saw him moving among the throngs of men in populous Egypt, seeking everywhere for traces of the household that had come down from Bethlehem, and finding them under the spreading sycamore-trees of Heliopolis, and beneath the walls of the Roman fortress of New Babylon beside the Nile-traces so faint and dim that they vanished before him continually, as footprints on the hard river-sand glisten for a moment with moisture and then disappear.

I saw him again at the foot of the pyramids, which lifted their sharp points into the intense saffron glow of the sunset sky, changeless monuments of the perishable glory and the imperishable hope of man. He looked up into the vast countenance of the crouching Sphinx and vainly tried to read the meaning of the calm eyes and smiling mouth. Was it, indeed, the mockery of all effort and all aspiration, as Tigranes had said-the cruel jest of a riddle that has no answer, a search that never can succeed? Or was there a touch of pity and encouragement in that inscrutable smile-a promise that even the defeated should attain a victory, and the disappointed should discover a prize, and the igno-

rant should be made wise, and the blind should see, and the wandering should come into the haven at last?

I saw him again in an obscure house of Alexandria, taking counsel with a Hebrew rabbi. The venerable man, bending over the rolls of parchment on which the prophecies of Israel were written, read aloud the pathetic words which foretold the sufferings of the promised Messiah-the despised and rejected of men, the man of sorrows and the acquaintance of grief.

"And remember, my son," said he, fixing his deep-set eyes upon the face of Artaban, "the King whom you are seeking is not to be found in a palace, nor among the rich and powerful. If the light of the world and the glory of Israel had been appointed to come with the greatness of earthly splendor, it must have appeared long ago. For no son of Abraham will ever again rival the power which Joseph had in the palaces of Egypt, or the magnificence of Solomon throned between the lions in Jerusalem. But the light for which the world is waiting is a new light, the glory that shall rise out of patient and triumphant suffering. And the kingdom which is to be established forever is a new kingdom, the royalty of perfect and unconquerable love.
"I do not know how this shall come to pass, nor how the turbulent kings and peoples of earth shall be brought to acknowledge the Messiah and pay homage to Him. But this I know. Those

who seek Him will do well to look among the poor and the lowly, the sorrowful and the oppressed."

So I saw the other wise man again and again, traveling from place to place, and searching among the people of the dispersion, with whom the little family from Bethlehem might, perhaps, have found a refuge. He passed through countries where famine lay heavy upon the land, and the poor were crying for bread. He made his dwelling in plague-stricken cities where the sick were languishing in the bitter companionship of helpless misery. He visited the oppressed and the afflicted in the gloom of subterranean prisons, and the crowded wretchedness of slave-markets, and the weary toil of galley-ships. In all this populous and intricate world of anguish, though he found none to worship, he found many to help. He fed the hungry, and clothed the naked, and healed the sick, and comforted the captive; and his years went by more swiftly than the weaver's shuttle that flashes back and forth through the loom while the web grows and the invisible pattern is completed.

It seemed almost as if he had forgotten his quest. But once I saw him for a moment as he stood alone at sunrise, waiting at the gate of a Roman prison. He had taken from a secret resting-place in his bosom the pearl, the last of his jewels. As he looked at it, a mellower luster, soft and iridescent light, full of shifting gleams of

azure and rose, trembled upon its surface. It seemed to have absorbed some reflection of the colors of the lost sapphire and ruby. So the profound, secret purpose of a noble life draws into itself the memories of past joy and past sorrow. All that has helped it, all that has hindered it, is transfused by a subtle magic into its very essence. It becomes more luminous and precious the longer it is carried close to the warmth of the beating heart.

Then, at last, while I was thinking of this pearl, and of its meaning, I heard the end of the story of the Other Wise Man.

A PEARL OF GREAT PRICE

THREE-and-thirty years of the life of Artaban had passed away, and he was still a pilgrim and a seeker after light. His hair, once darker than the cliffs of Zagros, was now white as the wintry snow that covered them. His eyes, that once flashed like flames of fire, were dull as embers smoldering among the ashes.

Worn and weary and ready to die, but still looking for the King, he had come for the last time to Jerusalem. He had often visited the holy city before, and had searched through all its lanes and crowded hovels and black prisons without finding any trace of the family of Nazarenes who had fled from Bethlehem long ago. But now it seemed as if he must make one more effort, and

something whispered in his heart that, at last, he might succeed.

It was the season of the Passover. The city was thronged with strangers. The children of Israel, scattered in far lands all over the world, had returned to the Temple for the great feast, and there had been a confusion of tongues in the narrow streets for many days.

But on this day there was a singular agitation visible in the multitude. The sky was veiled with a portentous gloom, and currents of excitement seemed to flash through the crowd like the thrill which shakes the forest on the eve of a storm. A secret tide was sweeping them all one way. The clatter of sandals, and the soft, thick sound of thousands of bare feet shuffling over the stones, flowed unceasingly along the streets that lead to the Damascus gate.

Artaban joined company with a group of people from his own country, Parthian Jews who had come up to keep the Passover, and inquired of them the cause of the tumult, and where they were going.

"We are going," they answered, "to the place called Golgotha, outside the city walls, where there is to be an execution. Have you not heard what has happened? Two famous robbers are to be crucified, and with them another, called Jesus of Nazareth, a man who has done many

wonderful works among the people, so that they love him greatly. But the priests and elders have said that he must die, because he gave himself out to be the Son of God. And Pilate has sent him to the cross because he said that he was the 'King of the Jews.'"

How strangely these familiar words fell upon the tired heart of Artaban! They had led him for a lifetime over land and sea. And now they came to him darkly and mysteriously like a message of despair. The King had arisen, but He had been denied and cast out. He was about to perish. Perhaps He was already dying. Could it be the same who had been born in Bethlehem, thirty-three years ago, at whose birth the star had appeared in heaven, and of whose coming the prophets had spoken?

Artaban's heart beat unsteadily with that troubled, doubtful apprehension which is the excitement of old age. But he said within himself, "The ways of God are stranger than the thoughts of men, and it may be that I shall find the King, at last, in the hands of His enemies, and shall come in time to offer my pearl for His ransom before He dies."

So the old man followed the multitude with slow and painful steps towards the Damascus gate of the city. Just beyond the entrance of the guard-house a troop of Macedonian soldiers came

down the street, dragging a young girl with torn
dress and disheveled hair. As the Magian paused
to look at her with compassion, she broke suddenly from the hands of her tormentors, and
threw herself at his feet, clasping him around
the knees. She had seen his white cap and the
winged circle on his breast.

"Have pity on me," she cried, "and save me, for
the sake of the God of Purity! I also am a daughter of the true religion which is taught by the
Magi. My father was a merchant of Parthia, but
he is dead, and I am seized for his debts to be
sold as a slave. Save me from worse than death!"

Artaban trembled.

It was the old conflict in his soul, which had
come to him in the palm-grove of Babylon and in
the cottage of Bethlehem-the conflict between
the expectation of faith and the impulse of love.
Twice the gift which he had consecrated to the
worship of religion had been drawn from his
hand to the service of humanity. This was the
third trial, the ultimate probation, the final and
irrevocable choice.

Was it his great opportunity, or his last tempta-
tion? He could not tell. One thing only was clear
in the darkness of his mind-it was inevitable.
And does not the inevitable come from God?

One thing only was sure to his divided heart-to rescue this helpless girl would be a true deed of love. And is not love the light of the soul?

He took the pearl from his bosom. Never had it seemed so luminous, so radiant, so full of tender, living luster. He laid it in the hand of the slave. "This is thy ransom, daughter! It is the last of my treasures which I kept for the King."

While he spoke, the darkness of the sky thickened, and shuddering tremors ran through the earth, heaving convulsively like the breast of one who struggles with mighty grief.

The walls of the houses rocked to and fro. Stones were loosened and crashed into the street. Dust clouds filled the air. The soldiers fled in terror, reeling like drunken men. But Artaban and the girl whom he had ransomed crouched helpless beneath the wall of the Prætorium.

What had he to fear? What had he to live for? He had given away the last remnant of his tribute for the King. He had parted with the last hope of finding Him. The quest was over, and it had failed. But, even in that thought, accepted and embraced, there was peace. It was not resignation. It was not submission. It was something more profound and searching. He knew that all was well, because he had done the best that he could, from day to day. He had been true to the

light that had been given to him. He had looked for more. And if he had not found it, if a failure was all that came out of his life, doubtless that was the best that was possible. He had not seen the revelation of "life everlasting, incorruptible and immortal." But he knew that even if he could live his earthly life over again, it could not be otherwise than it had been.

One more lingering pulsation of the earthquake quivered through the ground. A heavy tile, shaken from the roof, fell and struck the old man on the temple. He lay breathless and pale, with his gray head resting on the young girl's shoulder, and the blood trickling from the wound. As she bent over him, fearing that he was dead, there came a voice through the twilight, very small and still, like music sounding from a distance, in which the notes are clear but the words are lost. The girl turned to see if some one had spoken from the window above them, but she saw no one.

Then the old man's lips began to move, as if in answer, and she heard him say in the Parthian tongue:

"Not so, my Lord! For when saw I thee an hungered, and fed thee? Or thirsty, and gave thee drink? When saw I thee a stranger, and took thee in? Or naked, and clothed thee? When saw I thee sick or in prison, and came unto thee? Three-and-

thirty years have I looked for thee; but I have never seen thy face, nor ministered to thee, my King."

He ceased, and the sweet voice came again. And again the maid heard it, very faintly and far away. But now it seemed as though she understood the words.

"Verily I say unto thee, Inasmuch as thou hast done it unto one of the least of these my brethren, thou hast done it unto me."

A calm radiance of wonder and joy lighted the pale face of Artaban like the first ray of dawn on a snowy mountain-peak. One long, last breath of relief exhaled gently from his lips.

His journey was ended. His treasures were accepted. The Other Wise Man had found the King.

A KIDNAPPED SANTA CLAUS
L. FRANK BAUM

Santa Claus lives in the Laughing Valley, where stands the big, rambling castle in which his toys are manufactured. His workmen, selected from the ryls, knooks, pixies and fairies, live with him, and every one is as busy as can be from one year's end to another.

It is called the Laughing Valley because everything there is happy and gay. The brook chuckles to itself as it leaps rollicking between its green banks; the wind whistles merrily in the trees; the sunbeams dance lightly over the soft grass, and the violets and wild flowers look smilingly up from their green nests. To laugh one needs to be happy; to be happy one needs to be content. And throughout the Laughing Valley of Santa Claus contentment reigns supreme.

On one side is the mighty Forest of Burzee. At the other side stands the huge mountain that contains the Caves of the Daemons. And between them the Valley lies smiling and peaceful.

One would think that our good old Santa Claus, who devotes his days to making children happy, would have no enemies on all the earth; and, as a matter of fact, for a long period of time he encountered nothing but love wherever he might go.

But the Daemons who live in the mountain
caves grew to hate Santa Claus very much, and
all for the simple reason that he made children
happy.

The Caves of the Daemons are five in number. A
broad pathway leads up to the first cave, which
is a finely arched cavern at the foot of the mountain, the entrance being beautifully carved and
decorated. In it resides the Daemon of Selfishness. Back of this is another cavern inhabited
by the Daemon of Envy. The cave of the Daemon of Hatred is next in order, and through this
one passes to the home of the Daemon of Malice—situated in a dark and fearful cave in the
very heart of the mountain. I do not know what
lies beyond this. Some say there are terrible
pitfalls leading to death and destruction, and
this may very well be true. However, from each
one of the four caves mentioned there is a small,
narrow tunnel leading to the fifth cave—a cozy
little room occupied by the Daemon of Repentance. And as the rocky floors of these passages
are well worn by the track of passing feet, I
judge that many wanderers in the Caves of the
Daemons have escaped through the tunnels to
the abode of the Daemon of Repentance, who is
said to be a pleasant sort of fellow who gladly
opens for one a little door admitting you into
fresh air and sunshine again.

Well, these Daemons of the Caves, thinking they
had great cause to dislike old Santa Claus, held

a meeting one day to discuss the matter. "I'm really getting lonesome," said the Daemon of Selfishness. "For Santa Claus distributes so many pretty Christmas gifts to all the children that they become happy and generous, through his example, and keep away from my cave."

"I'm having the same trouble," rejoined the Daemon of Envy. "The little ones seem quite content with Santa Claus, and there are few, indeed, that I can coax to become envious."

"And that makes it bad for me!" declared the Daemon of Hatred. "For if no children pass through the Caves of Selfishness and Envy, none can get to MY cavern."

"Or to mine," added the Daemon of Malice.

"For my part," said the Daemon of Repentance, "it is easily seen that if children do not visit your caves they have no need to visit mine; so that I am quite as neglected as you are." "And all because of this person they call Santa Claus!" exclaimed the Daemon of Envy. "He is simply ruining our business, and something must be done at once."

To this they readily agreed; but what to do was another and more difficult matter to settle. They knew that Santa Claus worked all through the year at his castle in the Laughing Valley, preparing the gifts he was to distribute on Christmas

Eve; and at first they resolved to try to tempt
him into their caves, that they might lead him
on to the terrible pitfalls that ended in destruction.

So the very next day, while Santa Claus was
busily at work, surrounded by his little band of
assistants, the Daemon of Selfishness came to
him and said:

"These toys are wonderfully bright and pretty.
Why do you not keep them for yourself? It's a
pity to give them to those noisy boys and fretful
girls, who break and destroy them so quickly."

"Nonsense!" cried the old graybeard, his bright
eyes twinkling merrily as he turned toward the
tempting Daemon. "The boys and girls are never
so noisy and fretful after receiving my presents,
and if I can make them happy for one day in the
year I am quite content."

So the Daemon went back to the others, who
awaited him in their caves, and said: "I have
failed, for Santa Claus is not at all selfish."

The following day the Daemon of Envy visited
Santa Claus. Said he: "The toy shops are full of
playthings quite as pretty as those you are making. What a shame it is that they should interfere with your business! They make toys by
machinery much quicker than you can make

them by hand; and they sell them for money, while you get nothing at all for your work."

But Santa Claus refused to be envious of the toy shops.

"I can supply the little ones but once a year—on Christmas Eve," he answered; "for the children are many, and I am but one. And as my work is one of love and kindness I would be ashamed to receive money for my little gifts. But throughout all the year the children must be amused in some way, and so the toy shops are able to bring much happiness to my little friends. I like the toy shops, and am glad to see them prosper."

In spite of the second rebuff, the Daemon of Hatred thought he would try to influence Santa Claus. So the next day he entered the busy workshop and said:

"Good morning, Santa! I have bad news for you."

"Then run away, like a good fellow," answered Santa Claus. "Bad news is something that should be kept secret and never told."

"You cannot escape this, however," declared the Daemon; "for in the world are a good many who do not believe in Santa Claus, and these you are

bound to hate bitterly, since they have so wronged you."

"Stuff and rubbish!" cried Santa.

"And there are others who resent your making children happy and who sneer at you and call you a foolish old rattlepate! You are quite right to hate such base slanderers, and you ought to be revenged upon them for their evil words."

"But I don't hate 'em!" exclaimed Santa Claus positively. "Such people do me no real harm, but merely render themselves and their children unhappy. Poor things! I'd much rather help them any day than injure them."

Indeed, the Daemons could not tempt old Santa Claus in any way. On the contrary, he was shrewd enough to see that their object in visiting him was to make mischief and trouble, and his cheery laughter disconcerted the evil ones and showed to them the folly of such an undertaking. So they abandoned honeyed words and determined to use force.

It was well known that no harm can come to Santa Claus while he is in the Laughing Valley, for the fairies, and ryls, and knooks all protect him. But on Christmas Eve he drives his reindeer out into the big world, carrying a sleighload of toys and pretty gifts to the children; and this was the time and the occasion when his enemies

had the best chance to injure him. So the Daemons laid their plans and awaited the arrival of
Christmas Eve.

The moon shone big and white in the sky, and
the snow lay crisp and sparkling on the ground
as Santa Claus cracked his whip and sped away
out of the Valley into the great world beyond.
The roomy sleigh was packed full with huge
sacks of toys, and as the reindeer dashed onward our jolly old Santa laughed and whistled
and sang for very joy. For in all his merry life
this was the one day in the year when he was
happiest—the day he lovingly bestowed the
treasures of his workshop upon the little children.

It would be a busy night for him, he well knew.
As he whistled and shouted and cracked his
whip again, he reviewed in mind all the towns
and cities and farmhouses where he was expected, and figured that he had just enough
presents to go around and make every child
happy. The reindeer knew exactly what was
expected of them, and dashed along so swiftly
that their feet scarcely seemed to touch the
snow-covered ground.

Suddenly a strange thing happened: a rope shot
through the moonlight and a big noose that was
in the end of it settled over the arms and body of
Santa Claus and drew tight. Before he could
resist or even cry out he was jerked from the

seat of the sleigh and tumbled head foremost into a snowbank, while the reindeer rushed onward with the load of toys and carried it quickly out of sight and sound.

Such a surprising experience confused old Santa for a moment, and when he had collected his senses he found that the wicked Daemons had pulled him from the snowdrift and bound him tightly with many coils of the stout rope. And then they carried the kidnapped Santa Claus away to their mountain, where they thrust the prisoner into a secret cave and chained him to the rocky wall so that he could not escape.

"Ha, ha!" laughed the Daemons, rubbing their hands together with cruel glee. "What will the children do now? How they will cry and scold and storm when they find there are no toys in their stockings and no gifts on their Christmas trees! And what a lot of punishment they will receive from their parents, and how they will flock to our Caves of Selfishness, and Envy, and Hatred, and Malice! We have done a mighty clever thing, we Daemons of the Caves!"

Now it so chanced that on this Christmas Eve the good Santa Claus had taken with him in his sleigh Nuter the Ryl, Peter the Knook, Kilter the Pixie, and a small fairy named Wisk—his four favorite assistants. These little people he had often found very useful in helping him to distrib-

ute his gifts to the children, and when their master was so suddenly dragged from the sleigh they were all snugly tucked underneath the seat, where the sharp wind could not reach them.

The tiny immortals knew nothing of the capture of Santa Claus until some time after he had disappeared. But finally they missed his cheery voice, and as their master always sang or whistled on his journeys, the silence warned them that something was wrong.

Little Wisk stuck out his head from underneath the seat and found Santa Claus gone and no one to direct the flight of the reindeer.

"Whoa!" he called out, and the deer obediently slackened speed and came to a halt.

Peter and Nuter and Kilter all jumped upon the seat and looked back over the track made by the sleigh. But Santa Claus had been left miles and miles behind.

"What shall we do?" asked Wisk anxiously, all the mirth and mischief banished from his wee face by this great calamity.

"We must go back at once and find our master," said Nuter the Ryl, who thought and spoke with much deliberation.

"No, no!" exclaimed Peter the Knook, who, cross and crabbed though he was, might always be depended upon in an emergency. "If we delay, or go back, there will not be time to get the toys to the children before morning; and that would grieve Santa Claus more than anything else."

"It is certain that some wicked creatures have captured him," added Kilter thoughtfully, "and their object must be to make the children unhappy. So our first duty is to get the toys distributed as carefully as if Santa Claus were himself present. Afterward we can search for our master and easily secure his freedom."

This seemed such good and sensible advice that the others at once resolved to adopt it. So Peter the Knook called to the reindeer, and the faithful animals again sprang forward and dashed over hill and valley, through forest and plain, until they came to the houses wherein children lay sleeping and dreaming of the pretty gifts they would find on Christmas morning.

The little immortals had set themselves a difficult task; for although they had assisted Santa Claus on many of his journeys, their master had always directed and guided them and told them exactly what he wished them to do. But now they had to distribute the toys according to their own judgment, and they did not understand children as well as did old Santa. So it is no wonder they made some laughable errors.

Mamie Brown, who wanted a doll, got a drum instead; and a drum is of no use to a girl who loves dolls. And Charlie Smith, who delights to romp and play out of doors, and who wanted some new rubber boots to keep his feet dry, received a sewing box filled with colored worsteds and threads and needles, which made him so provoked that he thoughtlessly called our dear Santa Claus a fraud.

Had there been many such mistakes the Daemons would have accomplished their evil purpose and made the children unhappy. But the little friends of the absent Santa Claus labored faithfully and intelligently to carry out their master's ideas, and they made fewer errors than might be expected under such unusual circumstances.

And, although they worked as swiftly as possible, day had begun to break before the toys and other presents were all distributed; so for the first time in many years the reindeer trotted into the Laughing Valley, on their return, in broad daylight, with the brilliant sun peeping over the edge of the forest to prove they were far behind their accustomed hours.

Having put the deer in the stable, the little folk began to wonder how they might rescue their master; and they realized they must discover, first of all, what had happened to him and where he was.

So Wisk the Fairy transported himself to the
bower of the Fairy Queen, which was located
deep in the heart of the Forest of Burzee; and
once there, it did not take him long to find out
all about the naughty Daemons and how they
had kidnapped the good Santa Claus to prevent
his making children happy. The Fairy Queen
also promised her assistance, and then, fortified
by this powerful support, Wisk flew back to
where Nuter and Peter and Kilter awaited him,
and the four counseled together and laid plans
to rescue their master from his enemies.

It is possible that Santa Claus was not as merry
as usual during the night that succeeded his
capture. For although he had faith in the judgment of his little friends he could not avoid a
certain amount of worry, and an anxious look
would creep at times into his kind old eyes as he
thought of the disappointment that might await
his dear little children. And the Daemons, who
guarded him by turns, one after another, did not
neglect to taunt him with contemptuous words
in his helpless condition.

When Christmas Day dawned the Daemon
of Malice was guarding the prisoner, and his
tongue was sharper than that of any of the
others.

"The children are waking up, Santa!" he cried.
"They are waking up to find their stockings
empty! Ho, ho! How they will quarrel, and wail,

and stamp their feet in anger! Our caves will be full today, old Santa! Our caves are sure to be full!"

But to this, as to other like taunts, Santa Claus answered nothing. He was much grieved by his capture, it is true; but his courage did not forsake him. And, finding that the prisoner would not reply to his jeers, the Daemon of Malice presently went away, and sent the Daemon of Repentance to take his place.

This last personage was not so disagreeable as the others. He had gentle and refined features, and his voice was soft and pleasant in tone.

"My brother Daemons do not trust me overmuch," said he, as he entered the cavern; "but it is morning, now, and the mischief is done. You cannot visit the children again for another year."

"That is true," answered Santa Claus, almost cheerfully; "Christmas Eve is past, and for the first time in centuries I have not visited my children."

"The little ones will be greatly disappointed," murmured the Daemon of Repentance, almost regretfully; "but that cannot be helped now. Their grief is likely to make the children selfish and envious and hateful, and if they come to the Caves of the Daemons today I shall get a chance to lead some of them to my Cave of Repentance."

"Do you never repent, yourself?" asked Santa Claus, curiously.

"Oh, yes, indeed," answered the Daemon. "I am even now repenting that I assisted in your capture. Of course it is too late to remedy the evil that has been done; but repentance, you know, can come only after an evil thought or deed, for in the beginning there is nothing to repent of."

"So I understand," said Santa Claus. "Those who avoid evil need never visit your cave."

"As a rule, that is true," replied the Daemon; "yet you, who have done no evil, are about to visit my cave at once; for to prove that I sincerely regret my share in your capture I am going to permit you to escape."

This speech greatly surprised the prisoner, until he reflected that it was just what might be expected of the Daemon of Repentance. The fellow at once busied himself untying the knots that bound Santa Claus and unlocking the chains that fastened him to the wall. Then he led the way through a long tunnel until they both emerged in the Cave of Repentance.

"I hope you will forgive me," said the Daemon pleadingly. "I am not really a bad person, you know; and I believe I accomplish a great deal of good in the world."

With this he opened a back door that let in a flood of sunshine, and Santa Claus sniffed the fresh air gratefully.

"I bear no malice," said he to the Daemon, in a gentle voice; "and I am sure the world would be a dreary place without you. So, good morning, and a Merry Christmas to you!"

With these words he stepped out to greet the bright morning, and a moment later he was trudging along, whistling softly to himself, on his way to his home in the Laughing Valley.

Marching over the snow toward the mountain was a vast army, made up of the most curious creatures imaginable. There were numberless knooks from the forest, as rough and crooked in appearance as the gnarled branches of the trees they ministered to. And there were dainty ryls from the fields, each one bearing the emblem of the flower or plant it guarded. Behind these were many ranks of pixies, gnomes and nymphs, and in the rear a thousand beautiful fairies floated along in gorgeous array.

This wonderful army was led by Wisk, Peter, Nuter, and Kilter, who had assembled it to rescue Santa Claus from captivity and to punish the Daemons who had dared to take him away from his beloved children.

And, although they looked so bright and peace-

ful, the little immortals were armed with powers that would be very terrible to those who had incurred their anger. Woe to the Daemons of the Caves if this mighty army of vengeance ever met them!

But lo! coming to meet his loyal friends appeared the imposing form of Santa Claus, his white beard floating in the breeze and his bright eyes sparkling with pleasure at this proof of the love and veneration he had inspired in the hearts of the most powerful creatures in existence.

And while they clustered around him and danced with glee at his safe return, he gave them earnest thanks for their support. But Wisk, and Nuter, and Peter, and Kilter, he embraced affectionately.

"It is useless to pursue the Daemons," said Santa Claus to the army. "They have their place in the world, and can never be destroyed. But that is a great pity, nevertheless," he continued musingly.

So the fairies, and knooks, and pixies, and ryls all escorted the good man to his castle, and there left him to talk over the events of the night with his little assistants.

Wisk had already rendered himself invisible and flown through the big world to see how the children were getting along on this bright Christmas

morning; and by the time he returned, Peter had finished telling Santa Claus of how they had distributed the toys.

"We really did very well," cried the fairy, in a pleased voice; "for I found little unhappiness among the children this morning. Still, you must not get captured again, my dear master; for we might not be so fortunate another time in carrying out your ideas."

He then related the mistakes that had been made, and which he had not discovered until his tour of inspection. And Santa Claus at once sent him with rubber boots for Charlie Smith, and a doll for Mamie Brown; so that even those two disappointed ones became happy.

As for the wicked Daemons of the Caves, they were filled with anger and chagrin when they found that their clever capture of Santa Claus had come to naught. Indeed, no one on that Christmas Day appeared to be at all selfish, or envious, or hateful. And, realizing that while the children's saint had so many powerful friends it was folly to oppose him, the Daemons never again attempted to interfere with his journeys on Christmas Eve.

CHRISTMAS STORMS AND SUNSHINE
ELIZABETH GASKELL

In the town of —— (no matter where) there circulated two local newspapers (no matter when). Now the Flying Post was long established and respectable — alias bigoted and Tory; the Examiner was spirited and intelligent — alias newfangled and democratic. Every week these newspapers contained articles abusing each other; as cross and peppery as articles could be, and evidently the production of irritated minds, although they seemed to have one stereotyped commencement, — 'Though the article appearing in last week's Post (or Examiner) is below contempt, yet we have been induced,' &c., &c., and every Saturday the Radical shopkeepers shook hands together, and agreed that the Post was done for, by the slashing, clever Examiner; while the more dignified Tories began by regretting that Johnson should think that low paper, only read by a few of the vulgar, worth wasting his wit upon; however the Examiner was at its last gasp.

It was not though. It lived and flourished; at least it paid its way, as one of the heroes of my story could tell. He was chief compositor, or whatever title may be given to the head-man of the mechanical part of a newspaper. He hardly confined himself to that department. Once or twice, unknown to the editor, when the manuscript had fallen short, he had filled up the

vacant space by compositions of his own; an-
nouncements of a forthcoming crop of green
peas in December; a grey thrush having been
seen, or a white hare, or such interesting phe-
nomena; invented for the occasion, I must confess; but what of that? His wife always knew
when to expect a little specimen of her
husband's literary talent by a peculiar cough,
which served as prelude; and, judging from this
encouraging sign, and the high-pitched and
emphatic voice in which he read them, she was
inclined to think, that an 'Ode to an early Rose-
bud,' in the corner devoted to original poetry,
and a letter in the correspondence department,
signed 'Pro Bono Publico,' were her husband's
writing, and to hold up her head accordingly.

I never could find out what it was that occa-
sioned the Hodgsons to lodge in the same house
as the Jenkinses. Jenkins held the same office
in the Tory paper as Hodgson did in the Examiner, and, as I said before, I leave you to give it a
name. But Jenkins had a proper sense of his
position, and a proper reverence for all in authority, from the king down to the editor and
sub-editor. He would as soon have thought of
borrowing the king's crown for a nightcap, or the
king's sceptre for a walking-stick, as he would
have thought of filling up any spare corner with
any production of his own; and I think it would
have even added to his contempt of Hodgson (if
that were possible), had he known of the 'productions of his brain,' as the latter fondly al-

luded to the paragraphs he inserted, when speaking to his wife.

Jenkins had his wife too. Wives were wanting to finish the completeness of the quarrel, which existed one memorable Christmas week, some dozen years ago, between the two neighbours, the two compositors. And with wives, it was a very pretty, a very complete quarrel. To make the opposing parties still more equal, still more well-matched, if the Hodgsons had a baby ('such a baby! — a poor, puny little thing'), Mrs. Jenkins had a cat ('such a cat! a great, nasty, miowling tom-cat, that was always stealing the milk put by for little Angel's supper'). And now, having matched Greek with Greek, I must proceed to the tug of war. It was the day before Christmas; such a cold east wind! such an inky sky! such a blue-black look in people's faces, as they were driven out more than usual, to complete their purchases for the next day's festival.

Before leaving home that morning, Jenkins had given some money to his wife to buy the next day's dinner.

'My dear, I wish for turkey and sausages. It may be a weakness, but I own I am partial to sausages. My deceased mother was. Such tastes are hereditary. As to the sweets — whether plum-pudding or mince-pies — I leave such considerations to you; I only beg you not to mind expense. Christmas comes but once a year.'

And again he had called out from the bottom of the first flight of stairs, just close to the Hodgsons' door ('such ostentatiousness,' as Mrs. Hodgson observed), 'You will not forget the sausages, my dear?'

'I should have liked to have had something above common, Mary,' said Hodgson, as they too made their plans for the next day, 'but I think roast beef must do for us. You see, love, we've a family.'

'Only one, Jem! I don't want more than roast beef though, I'm sure. Before I went to service, mother and me would have thought roast beef a very fine dinner.'

'Well, let's settle it then, roast beef and a plum-pudding; and now, good-by. Mind and take care of little Tom. I thought he was a bit hoarse this morning.'

And off he went to his work.

Now, it was a good while since Mrs. Jenkins and Mrs. Hodgson had spoken to each other, although they were quite as much in possession of the knowledge of events and opinions as though they did. Mary knew that Mrs. Jenkins despised her for not having a real lace cap, which Mrs. Jenkins had; and for having been a servant, which Mrs. Jenkins had not; and the little occasional pinchings which the Hodgsons were

obliged to resort to, to make both ends meet, would have been very patiently endured by Mary, if she had not winced under Mrs. Jenkins's knowledge of such economy. But she had her revenge. She had a child, and Mrs. Jenkins had none. To have had a child, even such a puny baby as little Tom, Mrs. Jenkins would have worn commonest caps, and cleaned grates, and drudged her fingers to the bone. The great unspoken disappointment of her life soured her temper, and turned her thoughts inward, and made her morbid and selfish.

'Hang that cat! he's been stealing again! he's gnawed the cold mutton in his nasty mouth till it's not fit to set before a Christian; and I've nothing else for Jem's dinner. But I'll give it him now I've caught him, that I will!'

So saying, Mary Hodgson caught up her husband's Sunday cane, and despite pussy's cries and scratches, she gave him such a beating as she hoped might cure him of his thievish propensities; when lo! and behold, Mrs. Jenkins stood at the door with a face of bitter wrath.

'Aren't you ashamed of yourself ma'am, to abuse a poor dumb animal, ma'am, as knows no better than to take food when he sees it, ma'am? He only follows the nature which God has given, ma'am; and it's a pity your nature, ma'am, which I've heard, is of the stingy saving species, does not make you shut your cupboard-door a

little closer. There is such a thing as law for
brute animals. I'll ask Mr. Jenkins, but I don't
think them Radicals has done away with that
law yet, for all their Reform Bill, ma'am. My poor
precious love of a Tommy, is he hurt? and is his
leg broke for taking a mouthful of scraps, as
most people would give away to a beggar, — if
he'd take 'em?' wound up Mrs. Jenkins, casting
a contemptuous look on the remnant of a scrag
end of mutton.

Mary felt very angry and very guilty. For she
really pitied the poor limping animal as he crept
up to his mistress, and there lay down to be-
moan himself she wished she had not beaten
him so hard, for it certainly was her own careless way of never shutting the cupboard-door
that had tempted him to his fault. But the sneer
at her little bit of mutton turned her penitence
to fresh wrath, and she shut the door in Mrs.
Jenkins's face, as she stood caressing her cat in
the lobby, with such a bang, that it wakened
little Tom, and he began to cry.

Everything was to go wrong with Mary today.
Now baby was awake, who was to take her
husband's dinner to the office? She took the
child in her arms, and tried to hush him off to
sleep again, and as she sung she cried, she
could hardly tell why, — a sort of reaction from
her violent angry feelings. She wished she had
never beaten the poor cat; she wondered if his
leg was really broken. What would her mother

say if she knew how cross and cruel her little
Mary was getting? If she should live to beat her
child in one of her angry fits?

It was of no use lullabying while she sobbed so;
it must be given up, and she must just carry her
baby in her arms, and take him with her to the
office, for it was long past dinner-time. So she
pared the mutton carefully, although by so doing
she reduced the meat to an infinitesimal quantity, and taking the baked potatoes out of the
oven, she popped them piping hot into her basket with the et-ceteras of plate, butter, salt, and
knife and fork.

It was, indeed, a bitter wind. She bent against it
as she ran, and the flakes of snow were sharp
and cutting as ice. Baby cried all the way,
though she cuddled him up in her shawl. Then
her husband had made his appetite up for a
potato pie, and (literary man as he was) his body
got so much the better of his mind, that he
looked rather black at the cold mutton. Mary
had no appetite for her own dinner when she
arrived at home again. So, after she had tried to
feed baby, and he had fretfully refused to take
his bread and milk, she laid him down as usual
on his quilt, surrounded by play-things, while
she sided away, and chopped suet for the next
day's pudding. Early in the afternoon a parcel
came, done up first in brown paper, then in
such a white, grass-bleached, sweet-smelling

towel, and a note from her dear, dear mother; in which quaint writing she endeavoured to tell her daughter that she was not forgotten at Christmas time; but that learning that Farmer Burton was killing his pig, she had made interest for some of his famous pork, out of which she had manufactured some sausages, and flavoured them just as Mary used to like when she lived at home.

'Dear, dear mother!' said Mary to herself. 'There never was any one like her for remembering other folk. What rare sausages she used to make! Home things have a smack with 'em, no bought things can ever have. Set them up with their sausages! I've a notion if Mrs. Jenkins had ever tasted mother's she'd have no fancy for them town-made things Fanny took in just now.'

And so she went on thinking about home, till the smiles and the dimples came out again at the remembrance of that pretty cottage, which would look green even now in the depth of winter, with its pyracanthus, and its holly-bushes, and the great Portugal laurel that was her mother's pride. And the back path through the orchard to Farmer Burton's; how well she remembered it. The bushels of unripe apples she had picked up there, and distributed among his pigs, till he had scolded her for giving them so much green trash.

She was interrupted — her baby (I call him a baby, because his father and mother did, and because he was so little of his age, but I rather think he was eighteen months old) had fallen asleep some time before among his playthings; an uneasy, restless sleep; but of which Mary had been thankful, as his morning's nap had been too short, and as she was so busy. But now he began to make such a strange crowing noise, just like a chair drawn heavily and gratingly along a kitchen-floor! His eyes were open, but expressive of nothing but pain.

'Mother's darling!' said Mary, in terror, lifting him up. 'Baby, try not to make that noise. Hush, hush, darling; what hurts him?' But the noise came worse and worse.

'Fanny! Fanny!' Mary called in mortal fright, for her baby was almost black with his gasping breath, and she had no one to ask for aid or sympathy but her landlady's daughter, a little girl of twelve or thirteen, who attended to the house in her mother's absence, as daily cook in gentlemen's families. Fanny was more especially considered the attendant of the upstairs lodgers (who paid for the use of the kitchen, 'for Jenkins could not abide the smell of meat cooking'), but just now she was fortunately sitting at her afternoon's work of darning stockings, and hearing Mrs. Hodgson's cry of terror, she ran to her sitting-room, and understood the case at a glance.

"He's got the croup! Oh, Mrs. Hodgson, he'll die as sure as fate. Little brother had it, and he died in no time. The doctor said he could do nothing for him — it had gone too far. He said if we'd put him in a warm bath at first, it might have saved him; but, bless you! he was never half so bad as your baby.' Unconsciously there mingled in her statement some of a child's love of producing an effect; but the increasing danger was clear enough.

'Oh, my baby! my baby! Oh, love, love! don't look so ill; I cannot bear it. And my fire so low! There, I was thinking of home, and picking currants, and never minding the fire. Oh, Fanny! what is the fire like in the kitchen? Speak.'

'Mother told me to screw it up, and throw some slack on as soon as Mrs. Jenkins had done with it, and so I did. It's very low and black. But, oh, Mrs. Hodgson! let me run for the doctor — I cannot abear to hear him, it's so like little brother.'

Through her streaming tears Mary motioned her to go; and trembling, sinking, sick at heart, she laid her boy in his cradle, and ran to fill her kettle.

Mrs. Jenkins, having cooked her husband's snug little dinner, to which he came home; having told him her story of pussy's beating, at which he was justly and dignifiedly indignant,

saying it was all of a piece with that abusive Examiner; having received the sausages, and turkey, and mince pies, which her husband had ordered; and cleaned up the room, and prepared everything for tea, and coaxed and duly bemoaned her cat (who had pretty nearly forgotten his beating, but very much enjoyed the petting); having done all these and many other things, Mrs. Jenkins sat down to get up the real lace cap. Every thread was pulled out separately, and carefully stretched: when, what was that? Outside, in the street, a chorus of piping children's voices sang the old carol she had heard a hundred times in the days of her youth: —

As Joseph was a walking he heard an angel sing,
This night shall be born our heavenly King.
He neither shall be born in housen nor in hall,
Nor in the place of Paradise, but in an ox's stall.
He neither shall be clothed in purple nor in pall,
But all in fair linen, as were babies all:
He neither shall be rocked in silver nor in gold,
But in a wooden cradle that rocks on the mould,'
&c.

She got up and went to the window. There, below, stood the group of grey black little figures, relieved against the snow, which now enveloped everything. 'For old sake's sake,' as she phrased it, she counted out a halfpenny apiece for the singers, out of the copper bag, and threw them down below.

The room had become chilly while she had been counting out and throwing down her money, so she stirred her already glowing fire, and sat down right before it — but not to stretch her lace; like Mary Hodgson, she began to think over long-past days, on softening remembrances of the dead and gone, on words long forgotten, on holy stories heard at her mother's knee.

'I cannot think what's come over me to-night,' said she, half aloud, recovering herself by the sound of her own voice from her train of thought — 'My head goes wandering on them old times. I'm sure more texts have come into my head with thinking on my mother within this last half hour, than I've thought on for years and years. I hope I'm not going to die. Folks say, thinking too much on the dead betokens we're going to join 'em; I should be loth to go just yet — such a fine turkey as we've got for dinner to-morrow, too!'

Knock, knock, knock, at the door, as fast as knuckles could go. And then, as if the comer could not wait, the door was opened, and Mary Hodgson stood there as white as death.

'Mrs. Jenkins! — oh, your kettle is boiling, thank God! Let me have the water for my baby, for the love of God! He's got croup, and is dying!'

Mrs. Jenkins turned on her chair with a wooden inflexible look on her face, that (between our-selves) her husband knew and dreaded for all his pompous dignity.

'I'm sorry I can't oblige you, ma'am; my kettle is wanted for my husband's tea. Don't be afeared, Tommy, Mrs. Hodgson won't venture to intrude herself where she's not desired. You'd better send for the doctor, ma'am, instead of wasting your time in wringing your hands, ma'am — my kettle is engaged.'

Mary clasped her hands together with passion-ate force, but spoke no word of entreaty to that wooden face — that sharp, determined voice; but, as she turned away, she prayed for strength to bear the coming trial, and strength to forgive Mrs. Jenkins.

Mrs. Jenkins watched her go away meekly, as one who has no hope, and then she turned upon herself as sharply as she ever did on any one else.

'What a brute I am, Lord forgive me! What's my husband's tea to a baby's life? In croup, too, where time is everything. You crabbed old vixen, you! — any one may know you never had a child!'

She was down stairs (kettle in hand) before she had finished her self-upbraiding; and when in

Mrs. Hodgson's room, she rejected all thanks (Mary had not the voice for many words), saying, stiffly, 'I do it for the poor babby's sake, ma'am, hoping he may live to have mercy to poor dumb beasts, if he does forget to lock his cupboards.'

But she did everything, and more than Mary, with her young inexperience, could have thought of. She prepared the warm bath, and tried it with her husband's own thermometer (Mr. Jenkins was as punctual as clockwork in noting down the temperature of every day). She let his mother place her baby in the tub, still preserving the same rigid, affronted aspect, and then she went upstairs without a word. Mary longed to ask her to stay, but dared not; though, when she left the room, the tears chased each other down her cheeks faster than ever. Poor young mother! how she counted the minutes till the doctor should come. But, before he came, down again stalked Mrs. Jenkins, with something in her hand.

'I've seen many of these croup-fits, which, I take it, you've not, ma am. Mustard plaisters is very sovereign, put on the throat; I've been up and made one, ma'am, and, by your leave, I'll put it on the poor little fellow.'

Mary could not speak, but she signed her grateful assent.

It began to smart while they still kept silence; and he looked up to his mother as if seeking courage from her looks to bear the stinging pain; but she was softly crying, to see him suffer, and her want of courage reacted upon him, and he began to sob aloud. Instantly Mrs. Jenkins's apron was up, hiding her face: 'Peep-bo, baby,' said she, as merrily as she could. His little face brightened, and his mother having once got the cue, the two women kept the little fellow amused, until his plaister had taken effect.

'He's better, — oh, Mrs. Jenkins, look at his eyes! how different! And he breathes quite softly — '

As Mary spoke thus, the doctor entered. He examined his patient. Baby was really better.

'It has been a sharp attack, but the remedies you have applied have been worth all the Pharmacopoeia an hour later. — I shall send a powder,' &c. &c.

Mrs. Jenkins stayed to hear this opinion; and (her heart wonderfully more easy) was going to leave the room, when Mary seized her hand and kissed it; she could not speak her gratitude. Mrs. Jenkins looked affronted and awkward, and as if she must go upstairs and wash her hand directly.

But, in spite of these sour looks, she came softly down an hour or so afterwards to see how baby was.

The little gentleman slept well after the fright he had given his friends; and on Christmas morning, when Mary awoke and looked at the sweet little pale face lying on her arm, she could hardly realize the danger he had been in.

When she came down (later than usual), she found the household in a commotion. What do you think had happened? Why, pussy had been a traitor to his best friend, and eaten up some of Mr. Jenkins's own especial sausages; and gnawed and tumbled the rest so, that they were not fit to be eaten! There were no bounds to that cat's appetite! he would have eaten his own father if he had been tender enough. And now Mrs. Jenkins stormed and cried — 'Hang the cat!'

Christmas Day, too! and all the shops shut! 'What was turkey without sausages?' gruffly asked Mr. Jenkins.

'Oh, Jem!' whispered Mary, 'hearken what a piece of work he's making about sausages, — I should like to take Mrs. Jenkins up some of mother's; they're twice as good as bought sausages.'

'I see no objection, my dear. Sausages do not involve intimacies, else his politics are what I can no ways respect.'

'But, oh, Jem, if you had seen her last night about baby! I'm sure she may scold me for ever, and I'll not answer. I'd even make her cat welcome to the sausages.' The tears gathered to Mary's eyes as she kissed her boy.

'Better take 'em upstairs, my dear, and give them to the cat's mistress.' And Jem chuckled at his saying.

Mary put them on a plate, but still she loitered.

'What must I say, Jem? I never know.'

'Say — I hope you'll accept of these sausages, as my mother — no, that's not grammar; — say what comes uppermost, Mary, it will be sure to be right.'

So Mary carried them upstairs and knocked at the door; and when told to 'come in,' she looked very red, but went up to Mrs. Jenkins, saying, 'Please take these. Mother made them.' And was away before an answer could be given.

Just as Hodgson was ready to go to church, Mrs. Jenkins came downstairs, and called Fanny. In a minute, the latter entered the Hodgsons' room, and delivered Mr. and Mrs. Jenkins's compli-

ments and they would be particular glad if Mr. and Mrs. Hodgson would eat their dinner with them.

'And carry baby upstairs in a shawl, be sure,' added Mrs. Jenkins's voice in the passage, close to the door, whither she had followed her messenger. There was no discussing the matter, with the certainty of every word being overheard.

Mary looked anxiously at her husband. She remembered his saying he did not approve of Mr. Jenkins's politics.

'Do you think it would do for baby?' asked he.

'Oh, yes,' answered she, eagerly; 'I would wrap him up so warm.'

'And I've got our room up to sixty-five already, for all it's so frosty,' added the voice outside.

Now, how do you think they settled the matter? The very best way in the world. Mr. and Mrs. Jenkins came down into the Hodgsons' room, and dined there. Turkey at the top, roast beef at the bottom, sausages at one side, potatoes at the other. Second course, plum-pudding at the top, and mince pies at the bottom.

And after dinner, Mrs. Jenkins would have baby on her knee; and he seemed quite to take to her; she declared he was admiring the real lace on

her cap, but Mary thought (though she did not say so) that he was pleased by her kind looks and coaxing words. Then he was wrapped up and carried carefully upstairs to tea, in Mrs. Jenkins's room. And after tea, Mrs. Jenkins, and Mary, and her husband, found out each other's mutual liking for music, and sat singing old glees and catches, till I don't know what o'clock, without one word of politics or newspapers.

Before they parted, Mary had coaxed pussy on to her knee; for Mrs. Jenkins would not part with baby, who was sleeping on her lap.

'When you're busy, bring him to me. Do, now, it will be a real favour. I know you must have a deal to do, with another coming; let him come up to me. I'll take the greatest of cares of him; pretty darling, how sweet he looks when he's asleep!'

When the couples were once more alone, the husbands unburdened their minds to their wives.

Mr. Jenkins said to his — 'Do you know, Bur-gess tried to make me believe Hodgson was such a fool as to put paragraphs into the Examiner now and then; but I see he knows his place, and has got too much sense to do any such thing.'

Hodgson said — 'Mary, love, I almost fancy from Jenkins's way of speaking (so much civiler than

I expected), he guesses I wrote that "Pro Bono" and the "Rose-bud," — at any rate, I've no objection to your naming it, if the subject should come uppermost; I should like him to know I'm a literary man.'

Well! I've ended my tale; I hope you don't think it too long; but, before I go, just let me say one thing.

If any of you have any quarrels, or misunderstandings, or coolnesses, or cold shoulders, or shynesses, or tiffs, or miffs, or huffs, with any one else, just make friends before Christmas, — you will be so much merrier if you do.

I ask it of you for the sake of that old angelic song, heard so many years ago by the shepherds, keeping watch by night, on Bethlehem Heights.

FIVE LITTLE PEPPERS AND HOW THEY GREW
MARGARET SIDNEY

In the middle of the night Polly woke up with a start.

"What in the world!" she said, and she bobbed up her head and looked over at her mother, who was still peacefully sleeping and was just going to lie down again, when a second noise out in the kitchen made her pause and lean on her elbow to listen. At this moment she thought she heard a faint whisper, and springing our of bed she ran to Phronsie's crib - it was empty! As quick as a flash she sped out into the kitchen. There, in front of the chimney, were two figures. One was Joel, and the other, unmistakably, was Phronsie!

"What are you doing?" gasped Polly, holding on to a chair.

The two little nightgowns turned round at this.

"Why, I thought it was morning," said Joel, "and I wanted my stocking. Oh!" as he felt the toe, which was generously stuffed, "give it to me, Polly Pepper, and I'll run right back to bed again!"

"Goodness," cried Polly, "and you, too, Phronsie! Why, it's the middle of the night! Did I ever!" and

she had to pinch her mouth together tight to keep from bursting out into a loud laugh. "Oh, dear, I shall laugh! Don't look so scared, Phronsie, there won't anything hurt you." For Phronsie, who, on hearing Joel fumbling around the precious stocking, had been quite willing to hop out of bed and join him, had now, on Polly's saying the dire words, "in the middle of the night," scuttled over to her protecting side like a frightened rabbit.

"It never'll be morning," said Joel, taking up first one cold tow and then the other. "You might let us have 'em now, Polly, do!"

"No," said Polly, sobering down, "you can't have your till Davie wakes up, too. Scamper off to bed, Joel dear, and forget all about 'em - and it'll be morning before you know it."

"Oh, I'd rather go to bed," said Phronsie, trying to tuck up her feet in the little flannel night-gown, which was rather short, "but I don't know the way back, Polly. Take me, Polly, do," and she put up her arms to be carried.

"Oh, I ain't going back alone, either," whimpered Joel, coming up to Polly, too.

"Why, you came down alone, didn't you?" whispered Polly, with a little giggle.

"Yes, but I thought 'twas morning," said Joel, his teeth chattering with something besides the cold.

"Well, you must think of the morning that's coming," said Polly cheerily. "I'll tell you - you wait till I put Phronsie into the crib, and then I'll come back and go halfway up the stairs with you."

"I won't ever come down till it's morning again," said Joel, bouncing along the stairs, when Polly was ready to go with him, at a great rate.

"Better not," laughed Polly softly. "Be careful and not wake Davie nor Ben."

"I'm in," announced Joel, in a loud whisper; and Polly could hear him snuggle down among the warm bedclothes. "Call us when 'tis morning, Polly."

"Yes," said Polly, "I will. Go to sleep."

Phronsie had forgotten stockings and everything else on Polly's return, and was fast asleep in the old crib. The result of it was that the children slept over, when morning did really come; and Polly had to keep her promise, and go to the foot of the stairs and call:

"Merry Christmas! Oh, Ben! and Joel! and Davie!"

"Oh!-oh!-oo-h!" and then the sounds that answered her, as with smothered whoops of expectation they one and all flew into their clothes!

Quick as a flash Joel and Davie were down and dancing around the chimney.

"Mammy! mammy!" screamed Phronsie, hugging her stocking, which Ben lifted her up to unhook from the big nail, "Santy did come, he did!" and then she spun around in the middle of the floor, not stopping to look in it.

"Well, open it, Phronsie," called Davie, deep in the exploring of his own. "Oh, ain't that a splendid windmill, Joe!"

"Yes," said that individual, who, having found a big piece of molasses candy, was so engaged in enjoying a huge bite, that, regardless alike of his other gifts of the smearing his face was getting, he gave himself wholly up to its delights.

"Oh, Joey," cried Polly laughingly, "molasses candy for breakfast!"

"That's prime!" cried Joel, swallowing the last morsel. "Now I'm going to see what's this -Oh,

Dave see here! see here!" he cried in intense excitement, pulling out a nice little parcel which, unrolled, proved to be a bright pair of stout mittens. "See if you've got some - look quick!"

"Yes, I have," said Davie, picking up a parcel about as big. "No, that's molasses candy."

"Just the same as I had," said Joel. "Do look for the mittens. P'r'aps Santa Claus thought you had some - Oh, dear!"

"Here they are!" screamed Davie. "I have got some, Joe, just exactly like yours! See here, Joe!"

"Goody!" said Joel, immediately relieved; for now he could quite enjoy his to see a pair on Davie's hands also. "Look at Phron," he cried, "she hasn't got only half of her things out!"

To tell the truth, Phronsie was so bewildered by her riches that she sat on the floor with the little red stocking in her lap, laughing and cooing to herself amid the few things she had drawn out. When she came to Seraphina's bonnet she was quite overcome. She turned it over and over, and smoothed out the little white feather that had once adorned one of Grandma Bascom's chickens, until the two boys with their stockings, and the others sitting around in a group on the floor watching them, laughed in glee to see her enjoyment.

"Oh dear," said Joel at last, shaking his stocking, "I've got all there is. I wish there were forty Christmases coming!"

"I haven't!" screamed Davie. "There's something in the toe."

"It's an apple, I guess," said Joel. "Turn it up, Dave."

"'Tisn't an apple," exclaimed Davie; "'tisn't round - it's long and thin; here 'tis." And he pulled out a splendid long whistle on which he blew a blast long and terrible, and Joel immediately following, all quiet was broken up, and the wildest hilarity reigned.

"I don't know as you'll want any breakfast," at last said Mrs. Pepper, when she had got Phronsie a little sobered down.

"I do, I do!" cried Joel.

"Goodness!! After your candy?" said Polly.

"That's all gone," said Joel, tooting around the table on his whistle. "What are we going to have for breakfast?:

"Same as ever," said his mother, "it can't be Christmas all the time."

"I wish 'twas," said little Davie, "forever and ever!"

"Forever an' ever," echoed little Phronsie, flying up, her cheeks like two pinks, and Seraphina in her arms with her bonnet on upside down.

"Dear, dear!!" said Polly, pinching Ben to keep still as they tumbled down the little rickety steps to the Provision Room, after breakfast. The children, content in their treasures, were holding high carnival in the kitchen. "Suppose they should find it out now - I declare I should feel most awfully. Isn't it elegant?" she asked, in a subdued whisper, going all around and around the tree, magnificent in its dress of bright red and yellow balls, white festoons, and little candle ends all ready for lighting. "Oh, Ben, did you lock the door?"

"Yes," he said. "That's a mouse," he added, as a little rustling noise made Polly stop where she stood back of the tree and prick up her ears in great distress of mind. "'Tis elegant," he said, turning around in admiration, and taking in the tree which, as Polly said, was quite "gorgeous," and the evergreen branches twisted up on the beams and rafters and all the other festive arrangements. "I don't believe Jappy's is any better."

"I wish Jappy was here," said Polly, with a small sigh.

"Well, he isn't," said Ben. "Come, we must go back into the kitchen or all the children will be out here. Look your last, Polly; 'twon't do to come again till it's time to light up."

"Mammy says she'd rather do the lighting up," said Polly.

"Had she?" said Ben, in surprise. "Oh, I suppose she's afraid we'll set something afire. Well, then, we shan't come in till we have it."

"I can't bear to go," said Polly, turning reluctantly away, "it's most beautiful - Oh, Ben, is your Santa Claus dress all safe?"

"Yes," said Ben, "I'll warrant they won't find that in one hurry! Such a time as we've had to make it!"

"I know it." laughed Polly. "Doesn't that cotton wool look just like bits of fur, Ben?"

"Yes," said Ben, "and when the flour's shaken over me, it'll be Santa himself."

"We've got to put back the hair into mamsie's cushion the first thing tomorrow," whispered Polly, anxiously, "and we mustn't forget it, Bensie."

"I want to keep the wig awfully," said Ben. "You did make that just magnificent, Polly!"

"If you could see yourself," giggled Polly. "Did you put it in the straw bed, and are you sure you pulled the ticking over it smoothly?"

"Yes, sir," replied Ben, "sure's my name's Ben Pepper! If you'll only keep them from seeing me when I'm in it till we're ready - that's all I ask."

"Well," said Polly, a little relieved, "but I hope Joe won't look."

"Come, they're coming!" whispered Ben. "Quick!"

"Polly!" rang a voice dangerously near; so near that Polly, speeding over the stairs to intercept it, nearly fell on her nose.

"Where have you been?" asked one.

"Let's have a concert," put in Ben; Polly was so out of breath that she couldn't speak. "Come, now, each take a whistle, and we'll march round and round and see which can make the biggest noise."

In the rattle and laughter which this procession made all mystery was forgotten, and the two conspirators began to breathe freer.

Five o'clock! The small ones of the Pepper flock, being pretty well tired out with noise and excite-

ment, all gathered around Polly and Ben and clamored for a story.

"Do, Polly, do," begged Joel. "It's Christmas, and 'twon't come again for a year."

"I can't," said Polly, in such a twitter that she could hardly stand still, and for the first time in her life refusing, "I can't think of a thing."

"I will, then," said Ben. "We must do something," he whispered to Polly.

"Tell it good," said Joel, settling himself.

So for an hour the small tyrants kept their entertainers well employed.

"Ain't it growing awful dark?" said Davie, rousing himself at last, as Ben paused to take breath.

Polly pinched Ben.

"Mammy's going to let us know," he whispered in reply. "We must keep on a little longer."

"Don't stop," said Joel, lifting his head where he sat on the floor. "What are you whispering for, Polly?"

"I'm not," said Polly, glad to think she hadn't spoken.

"Well, do go on, Ben," said Joel, lying down again.

"Polly'll have to finish it," said Ben.

So Polly launched out into such and extravagant story that they all, perforce, had to listen.

All this time, Mrs. Pepper had been pretty busy in her way. And now she came into the kitchen and set down her candle on the table. "Children," she said. Everybody turned and looked at her - her tone was so strange; and when they saw her dark eyes shining with such a new light, little Davie skipped right out into the middle of the room. "What's the matter, mammy?"

"You may all come into the Provision Room," said she.

"What for?" shouted Joel in amazement, while the others jumped to their feet and stood staring.

Polly flew around like a general, arranging her forces. "Let's march there," said she. "Phronsie, you take hold of Davie's hand, and go first."

"I'm going first," announced Joel, squeezing up past Polly.

"No, you mustn't, Joe," said Polly decidedly. "Phronsie and David are the youngest."

"They're always the youngest," said Joel, falling back with Polly to the rear.

"Forward! MARCH!" sand Polly. "Follow mamsie!"

Down the stairs they went with military step, and into the Provision Room. And then, with one wild look, the little battalion broke ranks, and tumbling one over the other, in decidedly unmilitary style, presented a very queer appearance!

And Captain Polly was the queerest of all; for she just gave one gaze at the tree, and then sat right down on the floor, and said, "Oh, MY!"

Mrs. Pepper was flying around delightedly, and saying, "Please to come right in" and "How do you do?"

And before anybody knew it, there were the laughing faces of Mrs. Henderson and the parson himself, Dr. Fisher, and old Grandma Bascom, while the two Henderson boys, unwilling to be defrauded of any of the fun, were squeezing themselves in between everybody else, and coming up to Polly every third minute, and saying, "There - aren't you surprised?"

"It's Fairyland!" cried little Davie, out of his wits with joy. "Oh, aren't we in Fairyland, ma?"

The whole room was in one buzz of chatter and fun; and everybody beamed on everybody else; and nobody knew what they said till Mrs. Pepper called, "Hush! Santa Claus is coming."

A rattle at the little old window made everybody look there, just as a great snow-white head popped up over the sill.

"Oh," screamed Joel, "'tis Santy!"

"He's coming in!" cried Davie, in chorus, which sent Phronsie flying to Polly. In jumped a little old man, quite spry for his years; with a jolly, red face and a pack on his back, and flew into their midst, prepared to do his duty; but what should he do, instead of making his speech, "this jolly old saint" - but first fly up to Mrs. Pepper, and say, "Oh, mamsie, how did you do it?"

"It's Ben!" screamed Phronsie; but the little old saint didn't hear, for he and Polly took hold of hands, and pranced around that tree while everybody laughed till they cried to see them go!

And then it all came out!

"Order!" said Parson Henderson, in his deepest tones; and then he put into Santa Claus's hands a letter, which he requested him to read. And the jolly old saint, although he was very old,

didn't need any spectacles, but piped out in Ben's loudest tones;

"DEAR FRIENDS: - A Merry Christmas to you all! And that you'll have a good time, and enjoy it as much as I've enjoyed my good times at your house, is the wish of your friend, "Jasper Elyot King."

"Hurray for Jappy!" cried Santa Claus, pulling his beard; this ended in three good cheers - Phronsie coming in too late with her little crow - which was just as well, however!

"Do your duty, now, Santa Claus!" commanded Dr. Fisher, as master of ceremonies. And everything was as still as a mouse!

And the first thing she knew, a lovely brass cage, with a dear little bird with two astonished black eyes in it, was put into Polly's hands. The card on it said: "For Miss Polly Pepper, to give her music every day in the year."

"Mamsie," said Polly; and then she did the queerest thing of the whole performance - she just burst into tears!

"I never thought I should have a bird for my very own!"

"Hello!" said Santa Claus. "I've got something myself!"

"Santa Claus's clothes are too old," laughed Dr.
Fisher, holding up a stout, warm suit that a boy
about as big as Ben would delight in.

And then that wonderful tree just rained down
all manner of lovely fruit. Gifts came flying thick
and fast, till the air seemed full, and each one
was greeted with a shout of glee as it was put
into the hands of its owner. A shawl flew down
on Mrs. Pepper's shoulders; and a workbasket
tumbled on Polly's head; and tops and balls and
fishing poles sent Joel and David into a corner
with howls of delight!

But the climax was reached when a large wax
doll in a very gay pink silk dress was put into
Phronsie's hands, and Dr. Fisher, stooping
down, read in loud tones: ""For Phronsie, from
one who enjoyed her gingerbread boy."

After that, nobody had anything to say! Books
jumped down unnoticed, and gay boxes of
candy. Only Polly peeped into one of her books,
and saw in Jappy's plain hand, "I hope we'll
both read this next summer." And turning over
to the title page, she saw "A Complete Manual of
Cookery."

"The best is yet to come," said Mrs. Henderson,
in her gentle way. When there was a lull in the
gale, she took Polly's hand and led her to a little
stand of flowers in the corner concealed by a
sheet - pinks and geraniums, heliotropes, and

roses, blooming away, and nodding their pretty heads at the happy sight - Polly had her flowers.

"Why didn't we know?" cried the children at last, when everybody was tying on their hoods, and getting their hats to leave the festive scene, "how could you keep it secret, mammy?"

"They all went to Mrs. Henderson's," said Mrs. Pepper. "Jasper wrote me, and asked where to send them, and Mrs. Henderson was so kind as to say that they might come there. And we brought them over last evening, when you were all abed. I couldn't have done it," she said, bowing to the parson and his wife, "if it hadn't been for their kindness - never in the world!"

"And I'm sure," said the minister, looking around on the he bright group, "if we can help along a bit of happiness like this, it is a blessed thing!"

And here Joel had the last word. "You said 'twasn't going to be Christmas always, mammy. I say," looking around on the overflow of treasures and the happy faces, "it'll be just forever!"

CHRISTMAS AT BRACEBRIDGE HALL
WASHINGTON IRVING

A man might then behold
  At Christmas, in each hall
Good fires to curb the cold,
  And meat for great and small.
The neighbours were friendly bidden,
  And all had welcome true,
The poor from the gates were not chidden,
  When this old cap was new.

  -Old Song

There is nothing in England that exercises a more delightful spell over my imagination than the lingerings of the holiday customs and rural games of former times. They recall the pictures my fancy used to draw in the May morning of life, when as yet I only knew the world through books, and believed it to be all that poets had painted it; and they bring with them the flavour of those honest days of yore, in which, perhaps with equal fallacy, I am apt to think the world was more home-bred, social, and joyous than at present. I regret to say that they are daily growing more and more faint, being gradually worn away by time, but still more obliterated by modern fashion. They resemble those picturesque morsels of Gothic architecture which we see crumbling in various parts of the country, partly dilapidated by the waste of ages, and partly lost

in the additions and alterations of latter days. Poetry, however, clings with cherishing fondness about the rural game and holiday revel, from which it has derived so many of its themes,-as the ivy winds its rich foliage about the Gothic arch and mouldering tower, gratefully repaying their support by clasping together their tottering remains, and, as it were, embalming them in verdure.

Of all the old festivals, however, that of Christmas awakens the strongest and most heartfelt associations. There is a tone of solemn and sacred feeling that blends with our conviviality, and lifts the spirit to a state of hallowed and elevated enjoyment. The services of the church about this season are extremely tender and inspiring. They dwell on the beautiful story of the origin of our faith, and the pastoral scenes that accompanied its announcement. They gradually increase in fervour and pathos during the season of Advent, until they break forth in full jubilee on the morning that brought peace and good-will to men. I do not know a grander effect of music on the moral feelings than to hear the full choir and the pealing organ performing a Christmas anthem in a cathedral, and filling every part of the vast pile with triumphant harmony.

It is a beautiful arrangement, also derived from days of yore, that this festival, which commemorates the announcement of the religion of peace

and love, has been made the season for gathering together of family connections, and drawing
closer again those bands of kindred hearts
which the cares and pleasures and sorrows of
the world are continually operating to cast loose;
of calling back the children of a family who have
launched forth in life, and wandered widely
asunder, once more to assemble about the paternal hearth, that rallying-place of the affections, there to grow young and loving again
among the endearing mementoes of childhood.

There is something in the very season of the year
that gives a charm to the festivity of Christmas.
At other times we derive a great portion of our
pleasures from the mere beauties of nature. Our
feelings sally forth and dissipate themselves over
the sunny landscape, and we "live abroad and
everywhere." The song of the bird, the murmur
of the stream, the breathing fragrance of spring,
the soft voluptuousness of summer, the golden
pomp of autumn; earth with its mantle of refreshing green, and heaven with its deep delicious blue and its cloudy magnificence, all fill us
with mute but exquisite delight, and we revel in
the luxury of mere sensation. But in the depth
of winter, when nature lies despoiled of every
charm, and wrapped in her shroud of sheeted
snow, we turn for our gratifications to moral
sources. The dreariness and desolation of the
landscape, the short gloomy days and darksome
nights, while they circumscribe our wanderings,
shut in our feelings also from rambling abroad,

and make us more keenly disposed for the pleasures of the social circle. Our thoughts are more concentrated; our friendly sympathies more aroused. We feel more sensibly the charm of each other's society, and are brought more closely together by dependence on each other for enjoyment. Heart calleth unto heart; and we draw our pleasures from the deep wells of living kindness, which lie in the quiet recesses of our bosoms: and which when resorted to, furnish forth the pure element of domestic felicity.

The pitchy gloom without makes the heart dilate on entering the room filled with the glow and warmth of the evening fire. The ruddy blaze diffuses an artificial summer and sunshine through the room, and lights up each countenance into a kindlier welcome. Where does the honest face of hospitality expand into a broader and more cordial smile-where is the shy glance of love more sweetly eloquent-than by the winter fireside? and as the hollow blast of wintry wind rushes through the hall, claps the distant door, whistles about the casement, and rumbles down the chimney, what can be more grateful than that feeling of sober and sheltered security with which we look around upon the comfortable chamber and the scene of domestic hilarity?

The English, from the great prevalence of rural habits throughout every class of society, have always been fond of those festivals and holidays which agreeably interrupt the stillness of coun-

try life; and they were, in former days, particularly observant of the religious and social rites of
Christmas. It is inspiring to read even the dry
details which some antiquarians have given of
the quaint humours, the burlesque pageants,
the complete abandonment to mirth and good-
fellowship with which this festival was celebrated. It seemed to throw open every door, and
unlock every heart. It brought the peasant and
the peer together, and blended all ranks in one
warm generous flow of joy and kindness. The
old halls of castles and manor-houses resounded with the harp and the Christmas carol,
and their ample boards groaned under the
weight of hospitality. Even the poorest cottage
welcomed the festive season with green decorations of bay and holly-the cheerful fire glanced
its rays through the lattice, inviting the passenger to raise the latch, and join the gossip knot
huddled around the hearth, beguiling the long
evening with legendary jokes and oft-told Christmas tales.

One of the least pleasing effects of modern refinement is the havoc it has made among the
hearty old holiday customs. It has completely
taken off the sharp touchings and spirited reliefs
of these embellishments of life, and has worn
down society into a more smooth and polished,
but certainly a less characteristic surface. Many
of the games and ceremonials of Christmas have
entirely disappeared, and like the sherris sack of
old Falstaff, are become matters of speculation

and dispute among commentators. They flourished in times full of spirit and lustihood, when
men enjoyed life roughly, but heartily and vigorously; times wild and picturesque, which have
furnished poetry with its richest materials, and
the drama with its most attractive variety of
characters and manners. The world has become
more worldly. There is more of dissipation, and
less of enjoyment. Pleasure has expanded into a
broader, but a shallower stream, and has forsaken many of those deep and quiet channels
where it flowed sweetly through the calm bosom
of domestic life. Society has acquired a more
enlightened and elegant tone; but it has lost
many of its strong local peculiarities, its home-
bred feelings, its honest fireside delights. The
traditionary customs of golden-hearted antiquity, its feudal hospitalities, and lordly
wassailings, have passed away with the baronial
castles and stately manor-houses in which they
were celebrated. They comported with the shadowy hall, the great oaken gallery, and the
tapestried parlour, but are unfitted to the light
showy saloons and gay drawing-rooms of the
modern villa.

Shorn, however, as it is, of its ancient and festive honours, Christmas is still a period of delightful excitement in England. It is gratifying to
see that home feeling completely aroused which
seems to hold so powerful a place in every English bosom. The preparations making on every
side for the social board that is again to unite

friends and kindred; the presents of good cheer passing and repassing, those tokens of regard, and quickeners of kind feelings; the evergreens distributed about houses and churches, emblems of peace and gladness; all these have the most pleasing effect in producing fond associations, and kindling benevolent sympathies. Even the sound of the waits, rude as may be their minstrelsy, breaks upon the mid-watches of a winter night with the effect of perfect harmony. As I have been awakened by them in that still and solemn hour, "when deep sleep falleth upon man," I have listened with a hushed delight, and, connecting them with the sacred and joyous occasion, have almost fancied them into another celestial choir, announcing peace and good-will to mankind.

How delightfully the imagination, when wrought upon by these moral influences, turns everything to melody and beauty: The very crowing of the cock, who is sometimes heard in the profound repose of the country, "telling the nightwatches to his feathery dames," was thought by the common people to announce the approach of this sacred festival:

> *"Some say that ever 'gainst that season comes*
> *Wherein our Saviour's birth is celebrated,*
> *This bird of dawning singeth all night long:*
> *And then, they say, no spirit dares stir*
>   *abroad;*

*The nights are wholesome-then no planets
    strike,
No fairy takes, no witch hath power to charm,
So hallow'd and so gracious is the time."*

Amidst the general call to happiness, the bustle of the spirits, and stir of the affections, which prevail at this period, what bosom can remain insensible? It is, indeed, the season of regenerated feeling-the season for kindling, not merely the fire of hospitality in the hall, but the genial flame of charity in the heart.

The scene of early love again rises green to memory beyond the sterile waste of years; and the idea of home, fraught with the fragrance of home-dwelling joys, reanimates the drooping spirit,- as the Arabian breeze will sometimes waft the freshness of the distant fields to the weary pilgrim of the desert.

Stranger and sojourner as I am in the land,- though for me no social hearth may blaze, no hospitable roof throw open its doors, nor the warm grasp of friendship welcome me at the threshold,-yet I feel the influence of the season beaming into my soul from the happy looks of those around me. Surely happiness is reflective, like the light of heaven; and every countenance, bright with smiles, and glowing with innocent enjoyment, is a mirror transmitting to others the rays of a supreme and ever shining benevolence.

He who can turn churlishly away from contemplating the felicity of his fellow beings, and sit down darkling and repining in his loneliness when all around is joyful, may have his moments of strong excitement and selfish gratification, but he wants the genial and social sympathies which constitute the charm of a merry Christmas.

THE STAGE-COACH

Omne bene
Sine poena
Tempus est ludendi;
Venit hora,
Absque mora
Libros deponendi.

-Old Holiday School Song.

In the preceding paper I have made some general observations on the Christmas festivities of England, and am tempted to illustrate them by some anecdotes of a Christmas passed in the country; in perusing which, I would most courteously invite my reader to lay aside the austerity of wisdom, and to put on that genuine holiday spirit which is tolerant of folly, and anxious only for amusement.

In the course of a December tour in Yorkshire, I rode for a long distance in one of the public coaches, on the day preceding Christmas. The coach was crowded, both inside and out, with passengers, who, by their talk, seemed principally bound to the mansions of relations or friends to eat the Christmas dinner. It was loaded also with hampers of game, and baskets and boxes of delicacies; and hares hung dangling their long ears about the coachman's box,- presents from distant friends for the impending feast. I had three fine rosy-cheeked schoolboys for my fellow passengers inside, full of the buxom health and manly spirit which I have observed in the children of this country. They were returning home for the holidays in high glee, and promising themselves a world of enjoyment. It was delightful to hear the gigantic plans of pleasure of the little rogues, and the impracticable feats they were to perform during their six weeks' emancipation from the abhorred thraldom of book, birch, and pedagogue. They were full of anticipations of the meeting with the family and household, down to the very cat and dog; and of the joy they were to give their little sisters by the presents with which their pockets were crammed; but the meeting to which they seemed to look forward with the greatest impatience was with Bantam, which I found to be a pony, and, according to their talk, possessed of more virtues than any steed since the days of

Bucephalus. How he could trot! how he could run! and then such leaps as he would take-there was not a hedge in the whole country that he could not clear.

They were under the particular guardianship of the coachman, to whom, whenever an opportunity presented, they addressed a host of questions, and pronounced him one of the best fellows in the whole world. Indeed, I could not but notice the more than ordinary air of bustle and importance of the coachman, who wore his hat a little on one side, and had a large bunch of Christmas greens stuck in the button-hole of his coat. He is always a personage full of mighty care and business, but he is particularly so during this season, having so many commissions to execute in consequence of the great interchange of presents.

And here, perhaps, it may not be unacceptable to my untravelled readers to have a sketch that may serve as a general representation of this very numerous and important class of functionaries who have a dress, a manner, a language, an air, peculiar to themselves, and prevalent throughout the fraternity; so that, wherever an English stage-coachman may be seen, he cannot be mistaken for one of any other craft or mystery.

He has commonly a broad, full face, curiously
mottled with red, as if the blood had been forced
by hard feeding into every vessel of the skin; he
is swelled into jolly dimensions by frequent
potations of malt liquors, and his bulk is still
further increased by a multiplicity of coats, in
which he is buried like a cauliflower, the upper
one reaching to his heels. He wears a broad-
brimmed, low-crowned hat; a huge roll of
coloured handkerchief about his neck, know-
ingly knotted and tucked in at the bosom; and
has in summer-time a large bouquet of flowers
in his buttonhole; the present, most probably, of
some enamoured country lass. His waistcoat is
commonly of some bright colour, striped; and his
small-clothes extend far below the knees, to
meet a pair of jockey boots which reach about
half-way up his legs.

All this costume is maintained with much preci-
sion; he has a pride in having his clothes of
excellent materials; and, notwithstanding the
seeming grossness of his appearance, there is
still discernible that neatness and propriety of
person which is almost inherent in an Englishman. He enjoys great consequence and consideration along the road; has frequent conferences
with the village housewives, who look upon him
as a man of great trust and dependence; and he
seems to have a good understanding with every
bright-eyed country lass. The moment he arrives

where the horses are to be changed, he throws down the reins with something of an air, and abandons the cattle to the care of the hostler; his duty being merely to drive from one stage to another.

When off the box, his hands are thrust in the pockets of his greatcoat, and he rolls about the inn-yard with an air of the most absolute lordliness. Here he is generally surrounded by an admiring throng of hostlers, stable-boys, shoe-blacks, and those nameless hangers-on that infest inns and taverns, and run errands, and do all kinds of odd jobs, for the privilege of battening on the drippings of the kitchen and the leakage of the tap-room. These all look up to him as to an oracle; treasure up his cant phrases; echo his opinions about horses and other topics of jockey lore; and, above all, endeavour to imitate his air and carriage. Every ragamuffin that has a coat to his back thrusts his hands in the pockets, rolls in his gait, talks slang, and is an embryo Coachey.

Perhaps it might be owing to the pleasing seren-ity that reigned in my own mind, that I fancied I saw cheerfulness in every countenance through-out the journey. A stage-coach, however, carries animation always with it, and puts the world in motion as it whirls along. The horn, sounded at the entrance of a village, produces a general bustle. Some hasten forth to meet friends; some with bundles and bandboxes to secure places,

and in the hurry of the moment can hardly take leave of the group that accompanies them. In the meantime, the coachman has a world of small commissions to execute. Sometimes he delivers a hare or pheasant; sometimes jerks a small parcel or newspaper to the door of a public-house; and sometimes, with knowing leer and words of sly import, hands to some half- blushing, half-laughing housemaid an odd-shaped billet-doux from some rustic admirer. As the coach rattles through the village, every one runs to the window, and you have glances on every side of fresh country faces, and blooming, giggling girls. At the corners are assembled juntas of village idlers and wise men, who take their stations there for the important purpose of seeing company pass; but the sagest knot is generally at the blacksmith's, to whom the passing of the coach is an event fruitful of much speculation. The smith, with the horse's heel in his lap, pauses as the vehicle whirls by; the Cyclops round the anvil suspend their ringing hammers, and suffer the iron to grow cool; and the sooty spectre in brown paper cap, labouring at the bellows, leans on the handle for a moment, and permits the asthmatic engine to heave a long-drawn sigh, while he glares through the murky smoke and sulphureous gleams of the smithy.

Perhaps the impending holiday might have given a more than usual animation to the country, for it seemed to me as if everybody was in good looks and good spirits. Game, poultry, and

other luxuries of the table, were in brisk circulation in the villages; the grocers', butchers', and fruiterers' shops were thronged with customers. The housewives were stirring briskly about, putting their dwellings in order; and the glossy branches of holly, with their bright red berries, began to appear at the windows. The scene brought to mind an old writer's account of Christmas preparations:-"Now capons and hens, besides turkeys, geese, and ducks, with beef and mutton-must all die; for in twelve days a multitude of people will not be fed with a little. Now plums and spice, sugar and honey, square it among pies and broth. Now or never must music be in tune, for the youth must dance and sing to get them a heat, while the aged sit by the fire. The country maid leaves half her market, and must be sent again, if she forgets a pack of cards on Christmas eve. Great is the contention of Holly and Ivy, whether master or dame wears the breeches. Dice and cards benefit the butler; and if the cook do not lack wit, he will sweetly lick his fingers."

I was roused from this fit of luxurious meditation by a shout from my little travelling companions. They had been looking out of the coach-windows for the last few miles, recognising every tree and cottage as they approached home, and now there was a general burst of joy-"There's John! and there's old Carlo! and there's Bantam!" cried the happy little rogues, clapping their hands.

At the end of a lane there was an old sober-
looking servant in livery waiting for them: he
was accompanied by a superannuated pointer,
and by the redoubtable Bantam, a little old rat
of a pony, with a shaggy mane and long, rusty
tail, who stood dozing quietly by the roadside,
little dreaming of the bustling times that awaited
him.

I was pleased to see the fondness with which the
little fellows leaped about the steady old foot-
man, and hugged the pointer, who wriggled his
whole body for joy. But Bantam was the great
object of interest; all wanted to mount at once;
and it was with some difficulty that John arranged that they should ride by turns, and the
eldest should ride first.

Off they set at last; one on the pony, with the
dog bounding and barking before him, and the
others holding John's hands; both talking at
once, and overpowering him by questions about
home, and with school anecdotes. I looked after
them with a feeling in which I do not know
whether pleasure or melancholy predominated:
for I was reminded of those days when, like
them, I had neither known care nor sorrow, and
a holiday was the summit of earthly felicity. We
stopped a few moments afterward to water the
horses, and on resuming our route, a turn of the
road brought us in sight of a neat country seat.
I could just distinguish the forms of a lady and
two young girls in the portico, and I saw my little

comrades, with Bantam, Carlo, and old John,
trooping along the carriage road. I leaned out of
the coach-window, in hopes of witnessing the
happy meeting, but a grove of trees shut it from
my sight.

In the evening we reached a village where I had
determined to pass the night. As we drove into
the great gateway of the inn, I saw on one side
the light of a rousing kitchen fire beaming
through a window. I entered, and admired, for
the hundredth time, that picture of convenience,
neatness, and broad, honest enjoyment, the
kitchen of an English inn. It was of spacious
dimensions, hung round with copper and tin
vessels, highly polished, and decorated here and
there with a Christmas green. Hams, tongues,
and flitches of bacon were suspended from the
ceiling; a smoke-jack made its ceaseless clanking beside the fireplace, and a clock ticked in
one corner. A well scoured deal table extended
along one side of the kitchen, with a cold round
of beef and other hearty viands upon it, over
which two foaming tankards of ale seemed
mounting guard.

Travellers of inferior order were preparing to
attack this stout repast, while others sat smoking and gossiping over their ale on two high-
backed oaken seats beside the fire. Trim housemaids were hurrying backwards and forwards
under the directions of a fresh, bustling landlady; but still seizing an occasional moment to

exchange a flippant word, and have a rallying laugh, with the group round the fire. The scene completely realised Poor Robin's humble idea of the comforts of midwinter.

> *"Now trees their leafy hats do bare,*
> *To reverence Winter's silver hair;*
> *A handsome hostess, merry host,*
> *A pot of ale now and a toast,*
> *Tobacco and a good coal fire,*
> *Are things this season doth require."**

* Poor Robin's Almanack, 1684.

I had not been long at the inn when a postchaise drove up to the door. A young gentleman stepped out, and by the light of the lamps I caught a glimpse of a countenance which I thought I knew. I moved forward to get a nearer view, when his eye caught mine. I was not mistaken; it was Frank Bracebridge, a sprightly, good- humoured young fellow, with whom I had once travelled on the Continent. Our meeting was extremely cordial; for the countenance of an old fellow traveller always brings up the recollection of a thousand pleasant scenes, odd adventures, and excellent jokes. To discuss all these in a transient interview at an inn was impossible; and finding that I was not pressed for time, and was merely making a tour of observation, he insisted that I should give him a day or two at his father's country-seat, to which he was going to pass the holidays, and which lay at a

few miles' distance. "It is better than eating a
solitary Christmas dinner at an inn," said he;
"and I can assure you of a hearty welcome in
something of the old-fashion style." His reason-
ing was cogent; and I must confess the preparation I had seen for universal festivity and social
enjoyment had made me feel a little impatient of
my loneliness. I closed, therefore, at once with
his invitation: the chaise drove up to the door;
and in a few moments I was on my way to the
family mansion of the Bracebridges.

CHRISTMAS EVE

Saint Francis and Saint Benedight
Blesse this house from wicked wight,
From the night-mare and the goblin,
That is hight good-fellow Robin;
Keep it from all evil spirits.
Fairies, weezels, rats, and ferrets:
 From curfew time
 To the next prime.
   -CARTWRIGHT.

It was a brilliant moonlight night, but extremely
cold; our chaise whirled rapidly over the frozen
ground; the post-boy smacked his whip inces-
santly, and a part of the time his horses were on
a gallop. "He knows where he is going," said my
companion, laughing, "and is eager to arrive in
time for some of the merriment and good cheer
of the servants' hall. My father, you must know,
is a bigoted devotee of the old school, and prides

himself upon keeping up something of old English hospitality. He is a tolerable specimen of what you will rarely meet with nowadays in its purity, the old English country gentleman; for our men of fortune spend so much of their time in town, and fashion is carried so much into the country, that the strong, rich peculiarities of ancient rural life are almost polished away. My father, however, from early years, took honest Peacham* for his textbook, instead of Chesterfield: he determined, in his own mind, that there was no condition more truly honourable and enviable than that of a country gentleman on his paternal lands, and, therefore, passes the whole of his time on his estate. He is a strenuous advocate for the revival of the old rural games and holiday observances, and is deeply read in the writers, ancient and modern, who have treated on the subject. Indeed, his favourite range of reading is among the authors who flourished at least two centuries since; who, he insists, wrote and thought more like true Englishmen than any of their successors. He even regrets sometimes that he had not been born a few centuries earlier, when England was itself, and had its peculiar manners and customs. As he lives at some distance from the main road, in rather a lonely part of the country, without any rival gentry near him, he has that most enviable of all blessings to an Englishman, an opportunity of indulging the bent of his own humour without molestation. Being representative of the oldest family in the neighbourhood, and a great

part of the peasantry being his tenants, he is much looked up to, and, in general, is known simply by the appellation of 'The Squire;' a title which has been accorded to the head of the family since time immemorial. I think it best to give you these hints about my worthy old father, to prepare you for any little eccentricities that might otherwise appear absurd."

Peacham's "Complete Gentleman," 1622.

We had passed for some time along the wall of a park, and at length the chaise stopped at the gate. It was in a heavy, magnificent old style, of iron bars, fancifully wrought at top into flour-ishes and flowers. The huge square columns that supported the gate were surmounted by the family crest. Close adjoining was the porter's lodge, sheltered under dark fir-trees, and almost buried in shrubbery.

The post-boy rang a large porter's bell, which resounded through the still, frosty air, and was answered by the distant barking of dogs, with which the mansion-house seemed garrisoned. An old woman immediately appeared at the gate. As the moonlight fell strongly upon her, I had full view of a little primitive dame, dressed very much in the antique taste, with a neat kerchief and stomacher, and her silver hair peeping from under a cap of snowy whiteness. She came curtseying forth, with many expressions of simple joy at seeing her young master. Her

husband, it seems, was up at the house keeping Christmas eve in the servants' hall; they could not do without him, as he was the best hand at a song and story in the household.

My friend proposed that we should alight and walk through the park to the hall, which was at no great distance, while the chaise should follow on. Our road wound through a noble avenue of trees, among the naked branches of which the moon glittered as she rolled through the deep vault of a cloudless sky. The lawn beyond was sheeted with a slight covering of snow, which here and there sparkled as the moonbeams caught a frosty crystal; and at a distance might be seen a thin, transparent vapour, stealing up from the low grounds, and threatening gradually to shroud the landscape.

My companion looked round him with trans-port:-"How often," said he, "have I scampered up this avenue, on returning home on school vaca-tions! How often have I played under these trees when a boy! I feel a degree of filial reverence for them, as we look up to those who have cher-ished us in childhood. My father was always scrupulous in exacting our holidays, and having us around him on family festivals. He used to direct and superintend our games with the strictness that some parents do the studies of their children. He was very particular that we should play the old English games according to their original form and consulted old books for

precedent and authority for every 'merrie dis-
port;' yet I assure you there never was pedantry
so delightful. It was the policy of the good old
gentleman to make his children feel that home
was the happiest place in the world; and I value
this delicious home- feeling as one of the choicest gifts a parent can bestow."

We were interrupted by the clangour of a troop
of dogs of all sorts and sizes, "mongrel, puppy,
whelp, and hound, and curs of low degree," that,
disturbed by the ringing of the porter's bell, and
the rattling of the chaise, came bounding, open-
mouthed, across the lawn.

"— The little dogs and all,
Tray, Blanch, and Sweetheart— see, they bark at
me!"

cried Bracebridge, laughing. At the sound of his
voice the bark was changed into a yelp of delight, and in a moment he was surrounded and
almost overpowered by the caresses of the faithful animals.

We had now come in full view of the old family
mansion, partly thrown in deep shadow, and
partly lit up by the cold moonshine. It was an
irregular building of some magnitude, and
seemed to be of the architecture of different
periods. One wing was evidently very ancient,
with heavy stone-shafted bow windows jutting
out and overrun with ivy, from among the foliage

of which the small diamond-shaped panes of glass glittered with the moonbeams. The rest of the house was in the French taste of Charles the Second's time, having been repaired and altered, as my friend told me, by one of his ancestors, who returned with that monarch at the Restoration. The grounds about the house were laid out in the old formal manner of artificial flower-beds, clipped shrubberies, raised terraces, and heavy stone balustrades, ornamented with urns, a leaden statue or two, and a jet of water. The old gentleman, I was told, was extremely careful to preserve this obsolete finery in all its original state. He admired this fashion in gardening; it had an air of magnificence, was courtly and noble, and befitting good old family style. The boasted imitation of nature in modern gardening had sprung up with modern republican notions, but did not suit a monarchical government; it smacked of the levelling system. I could not help smiling at this introduction of politics into gardening, though I expressed some apprehension that I should find the old gentleman rather intolerant in his creed. Frank assured me, however, that it was almost the only instance in which he had ever heard his father meddle with politics; and he believed that he had got this notion from a member of Parliament who once passed a few weeks with him. The Squire was glad of any argument to defend his clipped yew-trees and formal terraces, which had been occasionally attacked by modern landscape gardeners. As we approached the house, we heard the sound of

music, and now and then a burst of laughter
from one end of the building. This, Bracebridge
said, must proceed from the servants' hall,
where a great deal of revelry was permitted, and
even encouraged, by the Squire throughout the
twelve days of Christmas, provided everything
was done comformably to ancient usage. Here
were kept up the old games of hoodman blind,
shoe the wild mare, hot cockles, steal the white
loaf, bob apple and snapdragon: the Yule log and
Christmas candle were regularly burnt, and the
mistletoe, with its white berries, hung up to the
imminent peril of all the pretty housemaids.*

* See Note A.

So intent were the servants upon their sports,
that we had to ring repeatedly before we could
make ourselves heard. On our arrival being
announced, the Squire came out to receive us,
accompanied by his two other sons; one a young
officer in the army, home on leave of absence;
the other an Oxonian, just from the University.
The Squire was a fine, healthy-looking old
gentleman, with silver hair curling lightly round
an open, florid countenance; in which a
physiognomist, with the advantage, like myself,
of a previous hint or two, might discover a singular mixture of whim and benevolence.

The family meeting was warm and affectionate;
as the evening was far advanced, the Squire
would not permit us to change our travelling

dresses, but ushered us at once to the company, which was assembled in a large old-fashioned hall. It was composed of different branches of a numerous family connection, where there were the usual proportion of old uncles and aunts, comfortably married dames, superannuated spinsters, blooming country cousins, half-fledged striplings, and bright-eyed boarding-school hoydens. They were variously occupied; some at a round game of cards; others conversing around the fireplace; at one end of the hall was a group of the young folks, some nearly grown up, others of a more tender and budding age, fully engrossed by a merry game; and a profusion of wooden horses, penny trumpets, and tattered dolls, about the floor, showed traces of a troop of little fairy beings, who, having frolicked through a happy day, had been carried off to slumber through a peaceful night.

While the mutual greetings were going on between Bracebridge and his relatives, I had time to scan the apartment. I have called it a hall, for so it had certainly been in old times, and the Squire had evidently endeavoured to restore it to something of its primitive state. Over the heavy projecting fireplace was suspended a picture of a warrior in armour standing by a white horse, and on the opposite wall hung helmet, buckler, and lance. At one end an enormous pair of antlers were inserted in the wall, the branches serving as hooks on which to suspend hats, whips, and spurs; and in the corners of the

apartment were fowling-pieces, fishing-rods, and other sporting implements. The furniture was of the cumbrous workmanship of former days, though some articles of modern convenience had been added, and the oaken floor had been carpeted; so that the whole presented an odd mixture of parlour and hall.

The grate had been removed from the wide overwhelming fireplace, to make way for a fire of wood, in the midst of which was an enormous log glowing and blazing, and sending forth a vast volume of light and heat; this I understood was the Yule-log, which the Squire was particular in having brought in and illumined on a Christmas eve, according to ancient custom.*

See Note B.

It was really delightful to see the old Squire seated in his hereditary elbow-chair by the hospitable fireside of his ancestors, and looking around him like the sun of a system, beaming warmth and gladness to every heart. Even the very dog that lay stretched at his feet, as he lazily shifted his position and yawned, would look fondly up in his master's face, wag his tail against the floor, and stretch himself again to sleep, confident of kindness and protection. There is an emanation from the heart in genuine hospitality which cannot be described, but is immediately felt, and puts the stranger at once at his ease. I had not been seated many min-

utes by the comfortable hearth of the worthy
cavalier before I found myself as much at home
as if I had been one of the family.

Supper was announced shortly after our arrival.
It was served up in a spacious oaken chamber,
the panels of which shone with wax, and around
which were several family portraits decorated
with holly and ivy. Beside the accustomed
lights, two great wax tapers, called Christmas
candles, wreathed with greens, were placed on a
highly-polished buffet among the family plate.
The table was abundantly spread with substantial fare; but the Squire made his supper of
frumenty, a dish made of wheat cakes boiled in
milk with rich spices, being a standing dish in
old times for Christmas eve. I was happy to find
my old friend, minced-pie, in the retinue of the
feast; and finding him to be perfectly orthodox,
and that I need not be ashamed of my predilec-
tion, I greeted him with all the warmth wherewith we usually greet an old and very genteel
acquaintance.

The mirth of the company was greatly promoted
by the humours of an eccentric personage whom
Mr. Bracebridge always addressed with the
quaint appellation of Master Simon. He was a
tight, brisk little man, with the air of an arrant
old bachelor. His nose was shaped like the bill
of a parrot; his face slightly pitted with the
smallpox, with a dry perpetual bloom on it, like
a frost-bitten leaf in autumn. He had an eye of

great quickness and vivacity, with a drollery and lurking waggery of expression that was irresistible. He was evidently the wit of the family, dealing very much in sly jokes and innuendoes with the ladies, and making infinite merriment by harpings upon old themes; which, unfortunately, my ignorance of the family chronicles did not permit me to enjoy. It seemed to be his great delight during supper to keep a young girl next him in a continual agony of stifled laughter, in spite of her awe of the reproving looks of her mother, who sat opposite. Indeed, he was the idol of the younger part of the company, who laughed at everything he said or did, and at every turn of his countenance. I could not wonder at it; for he must have been a miracle of accomplishments in their eyes. He could imitate Punch and Judy; make an old woman of his hand, with the assistance of a burnt cork and pocket-handkerchief: and cut an orange into such a ludicrous caricature, that the young folks were ready to die with laughing.

I was let briefly into his history by Frank Bracebridge. He was an old bachelor of a small independent income, which by careful management was sufficient for all his wants. He revolved through the family system like a vagrant comet in its orbit; sometimes visiting one branch, and sometimes another quite remote; as is often the case with gentlemen of extensive connections and small fortunes in England. He had a chirping, buoyant disposition, always

enjoying the present moment; and his frequent change of scene and company prevented his acquiring those rusty unaccommodating habits with which old bachelors are so uncharitably charged. He was a complete family chronicle, being versed in the genealogy, history, and inter-marriages of the whole house of Bracebridge, which made him a great favourite with the old folks; he was a beau of all the elder ladies and superannuated spinsters, among whom he was habitually considered rather a young fellow, and he was a master of the revels among the children; so that there was not a more popular being in the sphere in which he moved than Mr. Simon Bracebridge. Of late years he had resided almost entirely with the Squire, to whom he had become a factotum, and whom he particularly delighted by jumping with his humour in respect to old times, and by having a scrap of an old song to suit every occasion. We had presently a specimen of his last mentioned talent; for no sooner was supper removed, and spiced wines and other beverages peculiar to the season intro-duced, than Master Simon was called on for a good old Christmas song. He bethought himself for a moment, and then, with a sparkle of the eye, and a voice that was by no means bad, excepting that it ran occasionally into a falsetto, like the notes of a split reed, he quavered forth a quaint old ditty:

> *"Now Christmas is come,*
> *Let us beat up the drum,*

And call all our neighbours together;
And when they appear,
Let us make them such cheer
As will keep out the wind and the weather,"
etc.

The supper had disposed every one to gaiety, and an old harper was summoned from the servants' hall, where he had been strumming all the evening, and to all appearance comforting himself with some of the Squire's home-brewed. He was a kind of hanger-on, I was told, of the establishment, and though ostensibly a resident of the village, was oftener to be found in the Squire's kitchen than his own home, the old gentleman being fond of the sound of "harp in hall."

The dance, like most dances after supper, was a merry one; some of the older folks joined in it, and the Squire himself figured down several couples with a partner with whom he affirmed he had danced at every Christmas for nearly half a century. Master Simon, who seemed to be a kind of connecting link between the old times and the new, and to be withal a little antiquated in the taste of his accomplishments, evidently piqued himself on his dancing, and was endeavouring to gain credit by the heel and toe, rigadoon, and other graces of the ancient school; but he had unluckily assorted himself with a little romping girl from boarding-school, who, by her wild vivacity, kept him continually on the

stretch, and defeated all his sober attempts at elegance;-such are the ill- assorted matches to which antique gentlemen are unfortunately prone!

The young Oxonian, on the contrary, had led out one of his maiden aunts, on whom the rogue played a thousand little knaveries with impunity; he was full of practical jokes, and his delight was to tease his aunts and cousins; yet, like all madcap youngsters, he was a universal favourite among the women. The most interesting couple in the dance was the young officer and a ward of the Squire's, a beautiful blushing girl of seventeen. From several shy glances which I had noticed in the course of the evening, I suspected there was a little kindness growing up between them; and, indeed, the young soldier was just the hero to captivate a romantic girl. He was tall, slender, and handsome, and like most young British officers of late years, had picked up various small accomplishments on the Continent-he could talk French and Italian-draw landscapes,-sing very tolerably-dance divinely; but above all he had been wounded at Waterloo;-what girl of seventeen, well read in poetry and romance, could resist such a mirror of chivalry and perfection!

The moment the dance was over, he caught up a guitar, and lolling against the old marble fireplace, in an attitude which I am half inclined to suspect was studied, began the little French air

of the Troubadour. The Squire, however, exclaimed against having anything on Christmas
eve but good old English; upon which the young
minstrel, casting up his eye for a moment, as if
in an effort of memory, struck into another
strain, and, with a charming air of gallantry,
gave Herrick's "Night-Piece to Julia:"

> "Her eyes the glow-worm lend thee,
> The shooting stars attend thee,
>   And the elves also,
>   Whose little eyes glow
> Like the sparks of fire, befriend thee.
>
> "No Will-o'-the-Wisp mislight thee;
> Nor snake or glow-worm bite thee;
>   But on, on thy way,
>   Not making a stay,
> Since ghost there is none to affright thee.
>
> "Then let not the dark thee cumber;
> What though the moon does slumber,
>   The stars of the night
>   Will lend thee their light,
> Like tapers clear without number.
>
> "Then, Julia, let me woo thee,
> Thus, thus to come unto me;
>   And when I shall meet
>   Thy silvery feet,
> My soul I'll pour into thee."

The song might have been intended in compliment to the fair Julia, for so I found his partner was called, or it might not; she, however, was certainly unconscious of any such application, for she never looked at the singer, but kept her eyes cast upon the floor. Her face was suffused, it is true, with a beautiful blush, and there was a gentle heaving of the bosom, but all that was doubtless caused by the exercise of the dance; indeed, so great was her indifference, that she was amusing herself with plucking to pieces a choice bouquet of hothouse flowers, and by the time the song was concluded, the nosegay lay in ruins on the floor.

The party now broke up for the night with the kind-hearted old custom of shaking hands. As I passed through the hall, on the way to my chamber, the dying embers of the Yule-log still sent forth a dusky glow; and had it not been the season when "no spirit dares stir abroad," I should have been half tempted to steal from my room at midnight, and peep whether the fairies might not be at their revels about the hearth.

My chamber was in the old part of the mansion, the ponderous furniture of which might have been fabricated in the days of the giants. The room was panelled with cornices of heavy carved work, in which flowers and grotesque faces were strangely intermingled; and a row of black look-

ing portraits stared mournfully at me from the walls. The bed was of rich though faded damask, with a lofty tester, and stood in a niche opposite a bow window. I had scarcely got into bed when a strain of music seemed to break forth in the air just below the window. I listened, and found it proceeded from a band, which I concluded to be the waits from some neighbouring village. They went round the house, playing under the windows.

I drew aside the curtains, to hear them more distinctly. The moonbeams fell through the upper part of the casement, partially lighting up the antiquated apartment. The sounds, as they receded, became more soft and aerial, and seemed to accord with quiet and moonlight. I listened and listened-they became more and more tender and remote, and, as they gradually died away, my head sank upon the pillow and I fell asleep.

CHRISTMAS DAY

Dark and dull night, flie hence away,
And give the honour to this day
That sees December turn'd to May.

.   .   .   .

Why does the chilling winter's morne
Smile like a field beset with corn?
Or smell like to a meade new-shorne,
Thus on the sudden?-Come and see
The cause why things thus fragrant be.

-HERRICK.

When I awoke the next morning, it seemed as if all the events of the preceding evening had been a dream, and nothing but the identity of the ancient chamber convinced me of their reality. While I lay musing on my pillow, I heard the sound of little feet pattering outside of the door, and a whispering consultation. Presently a choir of small voices chanted forth an old Christmas carol, the burden of which was:

"Rejoice, our Saviour he was born
On Christmas Day in the morning."

I rose softly, slipped on my clothes, opened the door suddenly, and beheld one of the most beautiful little fairy groups that a painter could imagine.

It consisted of a boy and two girls, the eldest not more than six, and lovely as seraphs. They were going the rounds of the house, and singing at every chamber-door; but my sudden appearance frightened them into mute bashfulness. They remained for a moment playing on their lips with their fingers, and now and then stealing a shy glance, from under their eyebrows, until, as if by one impulse, they scampered away, and as they turned an angle of the gallery, I heard them laughing in triumph at their escape.

Everything conspired to produce kind and happy feelings in this stronghold of old-fashioned hospitality. The window of my chamber looked out upon what in summer would have been a beautiful landscape. There was a sloping lawn, a fine stream winding at the foot of it, and a tract of park beyond, with noble clumps of trees, and herds of deer. At a distance was a neat hamlet, with the smoke from the cottage chimneys hanging over it; and a church with its dark spire in strong relief against the clear, cold sky. The house was surrounded with evergreens, according to the English custom, which would have given almost an appearance of summer; but the morning was extremely frosty; the light vapour of the preceding evening had been precipitated by the cold, and covered all the trees and every blade of grass with its fine crystallisations. The rays of a bright morning sun had a dazzling effect among the glittering foliage. A robin, perched upon the top of a mountain-ash that

hung its clusters of red berries just before my window, was basking himself in the sunshine, and piping a few querulous notes; and a peacock was displaying all the glories of his train, and strutting with the pride and gravity of a Spanish grandee on the terrace-walk below.

I had scarcely dressed myself, when a servant appeared to invite me to family prayers. He showed me the way to a small chapel in the old wing of the house, where I found the principal part of the family already assembled in a kind of gallery, furnished with cushions, hassocks, and large prayer-books; the servants were seated on benches below. The old gentleman read prayers from a desk in front of the gallery, and Master Simon acted as clerk, and made the responses; and I must do him the justice to say that he acquitted himself with great gravity and decorum.

The service was followed by a Christmas carol, which Mr. Bracebridge himself had constructed from a poem of his favourite author, Herrick; and it had been adapted to an old church melody by Master Simon. As there were several good voices among the household, the effect was extremely pleasing; but I was particularly gratified by the exaltation of heart, and sudden sally of grateful feeling, with which the worthy Squire delivered one stanza: his eyes glistening, and his voice rambling out of all the bounds of time and tune:

"'Tis thou that crown'st my glittering hearth
With guiltlesse mirth,
And giv'st me wassaile bowles to drink,
Spiced to the brink:
Lord, 'tis Thy plenty-dropping hand,
That soiles my land;
And giv'st me for my bushell sowne,
Twice ten for one."

I afterwards understood that early morning service was read on every Sunday and saint's day throughout the year, either by Mr. Bracebridge or by some member of the family. It was once almost universally the case at the seats of the nobility and gentry of England, and it is much to be regretted that the custom is fallen into neglect; for the dullest observer must be sensible of the order and serenity prevalent in those households, where the occasional exercise of a beautiful form of worship in the morning gives, as it were, the key-note to every temper for the day, and attunes every spirit to harmony.

Our breakfast consisted of what the Squire denominated true old English fare. He indulged in some bitter lamentations over modern breakfasts of tea-and-toast, which he censured as among the causes of modern effeminacy and weak nerves, and the decline of old English heartiness; and though he admitted them to his table to suit the palates of his guests, yet there was a brave display of cold meats, wine, and ale, on the sideboard.

After breakfast I walked about the grounds with Frank Bracebridge and Master Simon, or Mr. Simon as he was called by everybody but the Squire. We were escorted by a number of gentleman-like dogs, that seemed loungers about the establishment; from the frisking spaniel to the steady old staghound; the last of which was of a race that had been in the family time out of mind: they were all obedient to a dog-whistle which hung to Master Simon's buttonhole, and in the midst of their gambols would glance an eye occasionally upon a small switch he carried in his hand.

The old mansion had a still more venerable look in the yellow sunshine than by pale moonlight; and I could not but feel the force of the Squire's idea, that the formal terraces, heavily moulded balustrades, and clipped yew-trees, carried with them an air of proud aristocracy. There appeared to be an unusual number of peacocks about the place, and I was making some remarks upon what I termed a flock of them, that were basking under a sunny wall, when I was gently corrected in my phraseology by Master Simon, who told me that, according to the most ancient and approved treatise on hunting, I must say a MUSTER of peacocks. "In the same way," added he, with a slight air of pedantry, "we say a flight of doves or swallows, a bevy of quails, a herd of deer, of wrens, or cranes, a skulk of foxes, or a building of rooks." He went on to inform me, that, according to Sir Anthony

Fitzherbert, we ought to ascribe to this bird "both understanding and glory; for, being praised, he will presently set up his tail chiefly against the sun, to the intent you may the better behold the beauty thereof. But at the fall of the leaf, when his tail falleth, he will mourn and hide himself in corners, till his tail come again as it was."

I could not help smiling at this display of small erudition on so whimsical a subject; but I found that the peacocks were birds of some consequence at the Hall, for Frank Bracebridge informed me that they were great favourites with his father, who was extremely careful to keep up the breed; partly because they belonged to chivalry, and were in great request at the stately banquets of the olden time; and partly because they had a pomp and magnificence about them, highly becoming an old family mansion. Nothing, he was accustomed to say, had an air of greater state and dignity than a peacock perched upon an antique stone balustrade.

Master Simon had now to hurry off, having an appointment at the parish church with the village choristers, who were to perform some music of his selection. There was something extremely agreeable in the cheerful flow of animal spirits of the little man; and I confess I had been somewhat surprised at his apt quotations from authors who certainly were not in the range of

every-day reading. I mentioned this last circumstance to Frank Bracebridge, who told me with a
smile that Master Simon's whole stock of erudition was confined to some half-a-dozen old authors, which the Squire had put into his hands,
and which he read over and over, whenever he
had a studious fit; as he sometimes had on a
rainy day, or a long winter evening. Sir Anthony
Fitzherbert's "Book of Husbandry;" Markham's
"Country Contentments;" the "Tretyse of Hunting," by Sir Thomas Cockayne, Knight; Izaak
Walton's "Angler," and two or three more such
ancient worthies of the pen, were his standard
authorities; and, like all men who know but a
few books, he looked up to them with a kind of
idolatry, and quoted them on all occasions. As
to his songs, they were chiefly picked out of old
books in the Squire's library, and adapted to
tunes that were popular among the choice spirits of the last century. His practical application
of scraps of literature, however, had caused him
to be looked upon as a prodigy of book-knowl-
edge by all the grooms, huntsmen, and small
sportsmen of the neighbourhood.

While we were talking we heard the distant toll
of the village bell, and I was told that the Squire
was a little particular in having his household at
church on a Christmas morning; considering it a
day of pouring out of thanks and rejoicing; for,
as old Tusser observed:

*"At Christmas be merry, and thankful withal,
And feast thy poor neighbours, the great and
the small."*

"If you are disposed to go to church," said Frank Bracebridge, "I can promise you a specimen of my cousin Simon's musical achievements. As the church is destitute of an organ, he has formed a band from the village amateurs, and established a musical club for their improvement; he has also sorted a choir, as he sorted my father's pack of hounds, according to the directions of Jervaise Markham, in his "Country Contentments;" for the bass he has sought out all the 'deep solemn mouths,' and for the tenor the 'loud ringing mouths,' among the country bumpkins; and for 'sweet mouths,' he has culled with curious taste among the prettiest lasses in the neighbourhood; though these last, he affirms, are the most difficult to keep in tune; your pretty female singer being exceedingly wayward and capricious, and very liable to accident."

As the morning, though frosty, was remarkably fine and clear, the most of the family walked to the church, which was a very old building of gray stone, and stood near a village, about half a mile from the park gate. Adjoining it was a low snug parsonage, which seemed coeval with the church. The front of it was perfectly matted with a yew-tree that had been trained against its walls, through the dense foliage of which apertures had been formed to admit light into the

small antique lattices. As we passed this sheltered nest, the parson issued forth and preceded
us.

I had expected to see a sleek, well-conditioned
pastor, such as is often found in a snug living in
the vicinity of a rich patron's table; but I was
disappointed. The parson was a little, meagre,
black-looking man, with a grizzled wig that was
too wide, and stood off from each ear; so that his
head seemed to have shrunk away within it, like
a dried filbert in its shell. He wore a rusty coat,
with great skirts, and pockets that would have
held the church Bible and prayer-book; and his
small legs seemed still smaller, from being
planted in large shoes decorated with enormous
buckles.

I was informed by Frank Bracebridge that the
parson had been a chum of his father's at Oxford, and had received this living shortly after
the latter had come to his estate. He was a
complete black- letter hunter, and would
scarcely read a work printed in the Roman character. The editions of Caxton and Wynkin de
Worde were his delight; and he was indefatigable
in his researches after such old English writers
as have fallen into oblivion from their worthless-
ness. In deference, perhaps, to the notions of
Mr. Bracebridge, he had made diligent investiga-
tions into the festive rites and holiday customs
of former times; and had been as zealous in the
inquiry as if he had been a boon companion; but

it was merely with that plodding spirit with which men of adust temperament follow up any track of study, merely because it is denominated learning; indifferent to its intrinsic nature, whether it be the illustration of the wisdom, or of the ribaldry and obscenity of antiquity. He had pored over these old volumes so intensely, that they seemed to have been reflected into his countenance indeed; which, if the face be an index of the mind, might be compared to a title-page of black-letter.

On reaching the church porch, we found the parson rebuking the gray-headed sexton for having used mistletoe among the greens with which the church was decorated. It was, he observed, an unholy plant, profaned by having been used by the Druids in their mystic ceremonies; and though it might be innocently employed in the festive ornamenting of halls and kitchens, yet it had been deemed by the Fathers of the Church as unhallowed, and totally unfit for sacred purposes. So tenacious was he on this point, that the poor sexton was obliged to strip down a great part of the humble trophies of his taste, before the parson would consent to enter upon the service of the day.

The interior of the church was venerable but simple; on the walls were several mural monuments of the Bracebridges, and just beside the altar was a tomb of ancient workmanship, on which lay the effigy of a warrior in armour, with

his legs crossed, a sign of his having been a crusader. I was told it was one of the family who had signalised himself in the Holy Land, and the same whose picture hung over the fireplace in the hall.

During service, Master Simon stood up in the pew, and repeated the responses very audibly; evincing that kind of ceremonious devotion punctually observed by a gentleman of the old school, and a man of old family connections. I observed, too, that he turned over the leaves of a folio prayer-book with something of a flourish; possibly to show off an enormous seal-ring which enriched one of his fingers, and which had the look of a family relic. But he was evidently most solicitous about the musical part of the service, keeping his eye fixed intently on the choir, and beating time with much gesticulation and emphasis.

The orchestra was in a small gallery, and presented a most whimsical grouping of heads, piled one above the other, among which I particularly noticed that of the village tailor, a pale fellow with a retreating forehead and chin, who played on the clarionet, and seemed to have blown his face to a point; and there was another, a short pursy man, stooping and labouring at a bass viol, so as to show nothing but the top of a round bald head, like the egg of an ostrich. There were two or three pretty faces among the female singers, to which the keen air of a frosty

morning had given a bright rosy tint; but the
gentlemen choristers had evidently been chosen,
like old Cremona fiddles, more for tone than
looks; and as several had to sing from the same
book, there were clusterings of odd physiognomies, not unlike those groups of cherubs we
sometimes see on country tombstones.

The usual services of the choir were managed
tolerably well, the vocal parts generally lagging a
little behind the instrumental, and some loitering fiddler now and then making up for lost time
by travelling over a passage with prodigious
celerity, and clearing more bars than the keenest
fox-hunter to be in at the death. But the great
trial was an anthem that had been prepared and
arranged by Master Simon, and on which he had
founded great expectation. Unluckily there was a
blunder at the very outset; the musicians became flurried; Master Simon was in a fever;
everything went on lamely and irregularly until
they came to a chorus beginning "Now let us
sing with one accord," which seemed to be a
signal for parting company: all became discord
and confusion; each shifted for himself, and got
to the end as well, or rather as soon, as he
could, excepting one old chorister in a pair of
horn spectacles bestriding and pinching a long
sonorous nose; who, happening to stand a little
apart, and being wrapped up in his own melody,
kept on a quavering course, wriggling his head,
ogling his book, and winding all up by a nasal
solo of at least three bars' duration.

The parson gave us a most erudite sermon on the rites and ceremonies of Christmas, and the propriety of observing it not merely as a day of thanksgiving, but of rejoicing; supporting the correctness of his opinions by the earliest usages of the Church, and enforcing them by the authorities of Theophilus of Cesarea, St. Cyprian, St. Chrysostom, St. Augustine, and a cloud more of Saints and Fathers, from whom he made copious quotations. I was a little at a loss to perceive the necessity of such a mighty array of forces to maintain a point which no one present seemed inclined to dispute; but I soon found that the good man had a legion of ideal adversaries to contend with; having, in the course of his researches on the subject of Christmas, got completely embroiled in the sectarian controversies of the Revolution, when the Puritans made such a fierce assault upon the ceremonies of the Church, and poor old Christmas was driven out of the land by proclamation of Parliament.* The worthy parson lived but with times past, and knew but a little of the present.

* *See Note C.*

Shut up among worm-eaten tomes in the retirement of his antiquated little study, the pages of old times were to him as the gazettes of the day; while the era of the Revolution was mere modern history. He forgot that nearly two centuries had elapsed since the fiery persecution of poor

mince-pie throughout the land; when plum-
porridge was denounced as "mere popery," and
roast beef as antichristian; and that Christmas
had been brought in again triumphantly with
the merry court of King Charles at the Restoration. He kindled into warmth with the ardour of
his contest, and the host of imaginary foes with
whom he had to combat; had a stubborn conflict
with old Prynne and two or three other forgotten
champions of the Round-heads, on the subject
of Christmas festivity; and concluded by urging
his hearers, in the most solemn and affecting
manner, to stand to the traditionary customs of
their fathers, and feast and make merry on this
joyful anniversary of the Church.

I have seldom known a sermon attended apparently with more immediate effects; for, on leaving
the church, the congregation seemed one and all
possessed with the gaiety of spirit so earnestly
enjoined by their pastor. The elder folks gathered in knots in the churchyard, greeting and
shaking hands; and the children ran about
crying, Ule! Ule! and repeating some uncouth
rhymes,* which the parson, who had joined us,
informed me had been handed down from days
of yore. The villagers doffed their hats to the
Squire as he passed, giving him the good wishes
of the season with every appearance of heartfelt
sincerity, and were invited by him to the Hall, to
take something to keep out the cold of the
weather; and I heard blessings uttered by several of the poor, which convinced me that, in the

midst of his enjoyments, the worthy old cavalier had not forgotten the true Christmas virtue of charity.

* *"Ule! Ule!*
  Three puddings in a pule;
  Crack nuts and cry ule!"

On our way homeward his heart seemed overflowing with generous and happy feelings. As we passed over a rising ground which commanded something of a prospect, the sounds of rustic merriment now and then reached our ears; the Squire paused for a few moments, and looked around with an air of inexpressible benignity. The beauty of the day was of itself sufficient to inspire philanthropy. Notwithstanding the frostiness of the morning, the sun in his cloudless journey had acquired sufficient power to melt away the thin covering of snow from every southern declivity, and to bring out the living green which adorns an English landscape even in midwinter. Large tracts of smiling verdure contrasted with the dazzling whiteness of the shaded slopes and hollows. Every sheltered bank on which the broad rays rested yielded its silver rill of cold and limpid water, glittering through the dripping grass; and sent up slight exhalations to contribute to the thin haze that hung just above the surface of the earth. There was something truly cheering in this triumph of warmth and verdure over the frosty thraldom of winter; it was, as the Squire observed, an em-

blem of Christmas hospitality, breaking through the chills of ceremony and selfishness, and thawing every heart into a flow. He pointed with pleasure to the indications of good cheer reeking from the chimneys of the comfortable farm-houses and low, thatched cottages. "I love," said he, "to see this day well kept by rich and poor; it is a great thing to have one day in the year, at least, when you are sure of being welcome wher-ever you go, and of having, as it were, the world all thrown open to you; and I am almost dis-posed to join with Poor Robin, in his malediction of every churlish enemy to this honest festival:

"Those who at Christmas do repine,
And would fain hence despatch him,
May they with old Duke Humphry dine,
Or else may Squire Ketch catch 'em.'"

The Squire went on to lament the deplorable decay of the games and amusements which were once prevalent at this season among the lower orders, and countenanced by the higher: when the old halls of castles and manor-houses were thrown open at daylight; when the tables were covered with brawn, and beef, and humming ale; when the harp and the carol resounded all day long, and when rich and poor were alike wel-come to enter and make merry.* "Our old games and local customs," said he, "had a great effect in making the peasant fond of his home, and the promotion of them, by the gentry made him fond of his lord. They made the times merrier, and

kinder, and better; and I can truly say, with one of our old poets:

> *"I like them well — the curious preciseness*
> *And all-pretended gravity of those*
> *That seek to banish hence these harmless*
>   *sports,*
> *Have thrust away much ancient honesty.'*

* See Note D.

"The nation," continued he, "is altered; we have almost lost our simple, true-hearted peasantry. They have broken asunder from the higher classes, and seem to think their interests are separate. They have become too knowing, and begin to read newspapers, listen to alehouse politicians, and talk of reform. I think one mode to keep them in good humour in these hard times would be for the nobility and gentry to pass more time on their estates, mingle more among the country people, and set the merry old English games going again."

Such was the good Squire's project for mitigating public discontent; and, indeed, he had once attempted to put his doctrine in practice, and a few years before had kept open house during the holidays in the old style. The country people, however, did not understand how to play their parts in the scene of hospitality; many uncouth circumstances occurred; the manor was overrun by all the vagrants of the country, and more

beggars drawn into the neighbourhood in one week than the parish officers could get rid of in a year. Since then, he had contented himself with inviting the decent part of the neighbouring peasantry to call at the Hall on Christmas Day, and distributing beef, and bread, and ale, among the poor, that they might make merry in their own dwellings.

We had not been long home when the sound of music was heard from a distance. A band of country lads, without coats, their shirt- sleeves fancifully tied with ribands, their hats decorated with greens, and clubs in their hands, were seen advancing up the avenue, followed by a large number of villagers and peasantry. They stopped before the hall door, where the music struck up a peculiar air, and the lads performed a curious and intricate dance, advancing, retreating, and striking their clubs together, keeping exact time to the music; while one, whimsically crowned with a fox's skin, the tail of which flaunted down his back, kept capering around the skirts of the dance, and rattling a Christmas-box with many antic gesticulations.

The Squire eyed this fanciful exhibition with great interest and delight, and gave me a full account of its origin, which he traced to the times when the Romans held possession of the island; plainly proving that this was a lineal descendant of the sword-dance of the ancients. It was now, he said, nearly extinct, but he had

accidentally met with traces of it in the neighbourhood, and had encouraged its revival; though, to tell the truth, it was too apt to be followed up by rough cudgel-play and broken heads in the evening.

After the dance was concluded, the whole party was entertained with brawn and beef, and stout home-brewed. The Squire himself mingled among the rustics, and was received with awkward demonstrations of deference and regard.

It is true, I perceived two or three of the younger peasants, as they were raising their tankards to their mouths when the Squire's back was turned, making something of a grimace, and giving each other the wink; but the moment they caught my eye they pulled grave faces, and were exceedingly demure. With Master Simon, however, they all seemed more at their ease. His varied occupations and amusements had made him well known throughout the neighbourhood. He was a visitor at every farm-house and cottage; gossiped with the farmers and their wives; romped with their daughters; and, like that type of a vagrant bachelor, the bumblebee, tolled the sweets from all the rosy lips of the country around.

The bashfulness of the guests soon gave way before good cheer and affability. There is something genuine and affectionate in the gaiety of the lower orders, when it is excited by the

bounty and familiarity of those above them; the warm glow of gratitude enters into their mirth, and a kind word or a small pleasantry, frankly uttered by a patron, gladdens the heart of the dependant more than oil and wine. When the Squire had retired, the merriment increased, and there was much joking and laughter, particularly between Master Simon and a hale, ruddy-faced, white-headed farmer, who appeared to be the wit of the village; for I observed all his companions to wait with open mouths for his retorts, and burst into a gratuitous laugh before they could well understand them.

The whole house, indeed, seemed abandoned to merriment. As I passed to my room to dress for dinner, I heard the sound of music in a small court, and, looking through a window that commanded it, I perceived a band of wandering musicians, with pandean pipes and tambourine; a pretty, coquettish housemaid was dancing a jig with a smart country lad, while several of the other servants were looking on. In the midst of her sport the girl caught a glimpse of my face at the window, and, colouring up, ran off with an air of roguish affected confusion.

THE CHRISTMAS DINNER

Lo, now is come the joyful'st feast!
  Let every man be jolly,
Eache roome with yvie leaves is drest,
  And every post with holly.
Now all our neighbours' chimneys smoke,
  And Christmas blocks are burning;
Their ovens they with bak't meats choke,
  And all their spits are turning.
    Without the door let sorrow lie,
      And if, for cold, it hap to die,
    We'll bury't in a Christmas pye,
      And evermore be merry.
            -WITHERS'S Juvenilia.

I had finished my toilet, and was loitering with
Frank Bracebridge in the library, when we heard
a distant thwacking sound, which he informed
me was a signal for the serving up of the dinner.
The Squire kept up old customs in kitchen as
well as hall; and the rolling-pin, struck upon the
dresser by the cook, summoned the servants to
carry in the meats.

  "Just in this nick the cook knock'd thrice,
  And all the waiters in a trice
    His summons did obey;
  Each serving man, with dish in hand,
  March'd boldly up, like our train-band,
    Presented and away." *

* *Sir John Suckling.*

The dinner was served up in the great hall, where the Squire always held his Christmas banquet. A blazing, crackling fire of logs had been heaped on to warm the spacious apartment, and the flame went sparkling and wreathing up the wide-mouthed chimney. The great picture of the crusader and his white horse had been profusely decorated with greens for the occasion; and holly and ivy had likewise been wreathed around the helmet and weapons on the opposite wall, which I understood were the arms of the same warrior. I must own, by the by, I had strong doubts about the authenticity of painting and armour as having belonged to the crusader, they certainly having the stamp of more recent days; but I was told that the painting had been so considered time out of mind; and that as to the armour, it had been found in a lumber room, and elevated to its present situation by the Squire, who at once determined it to be the armour of the family hero; and as he was absolute authority on all such subjects to his own household, the matter had passed into current acceptation. A sideboard was set out just under this chivalric trophy, on which was a display of plate that might have vied (at least in variety) with Belshazzar's parade of the vessels of the Temple: "flagons, cans, cups, beakers, goblets, basins, and ewers;" the gorgeous utensils of good companionship, that had gradually accumulated through many generations of jovial housekeepers. Before these stood the two Yule

candles, beaming like two stars of the first magnitude: other lights were distributed in
branches, and the whole array glittered like a
firmament of silver.

We were ushered into this banqueting scene
with the sound of minstrelsy, the old harper
being seated on a stool beside the fireplace, and
twanging his instrument with a vast deal more
power than melody. Never did Christmas board
display a more goodly and gracious assemblage
of countenances; those who were not handsome
were, at least, happy; and happiness is a rare
improver of your hard-favoured visage.

I always consider an old English family as well
worth studying as a collection of Holbein's portraits or Albert Durer's prints. There is much
antiquarian lore to be acquired; much knowledge of the physiognomies of former times. Perhaps it may be from having continually before
their eyes those rows of old family portraits, with
which the mansions of this country are stocked;
certain it is, that the quaint features of antiquity
are often most faithfully perpetuated in these
ancient lines; and I have traced an old family
nose through a whole picture-gallery, legiti-
mately handed down from generation to generation, almost from the time of the Conquest.
Something of the kind was to be observed in the
worthy company around me. Many of their faces
had evidently originated in a Gothic age, and

been merely copied by succeeding generations; and there was one little girl, in particular, of staid demeanour, with a high Roman nose, and an antique vinegar aspect, who was a great favourite of the Squire's, being, as he said, a Bracebridge all over, and the very counterpart of one of his ancestors who figured in the court of Henry VIII.

The parson said grace, which was not a short, familiar one, such as is commonly addressed to the Deity, in these unceremonious days; but a long, courtly, well-worded one of the ancient school.

There was now a pause, as if something was expected; when suddenly the butler entered the hall with some degree of bustle; he was attended by a servant on each side with a large wax-light, and bore a silver dish, on which was an enormous pig's head, decorated with rosemary, with a lemon in its mouth, which was placed with great formality at the head of the table. The moment this pageant made its appearance, the harper struck up a flourish; at the conclusion of which the young Oxonian, on receiving a hint from the Squire, gave, with an air of the most comic gravity, an old carol, the first verse of which was as follows:

> "*Caput apri defero*
> *Reddens laudes Domino.*
> *The boar's head in hand bring I,*

With garlands gay and rosemary.
I pray you all synge merily
Qui estis in convivio."

Though prepared to witness many of these little
eccentricities, from being apprised of the peculiar hobby of mine host; yet, I confess, the parade with which so odd a dish was introduced
somewhat perplexed me, until I gathered from
the conversation of the Squire and the parson
that it was meant to represent the bringing in of
the boar's head: a dish formerly served up with
much ceremony, and the sound of minstrelsy
and song, at great tables on Christmas Day. "I
like the old custom," said the Squire, "not
merely because it is stately and pleasing in
itself, but because it was observed at the College
of Oxford, at which I was educated. When I hear
the old song chanted, it brings to mind the time
when I was young and gamesome —and the
noble old college-hall — and my fellow students
loitering about in their black gowns; many of
whom, poor lads, are now in their graves!"

The parson, however, whose mind was not
haunted by such associations, and who was
always more taken up with the text than the
sentiment, objected to the Oxonian's version of
the carol: which he affirmed was different from
that sung at college. He went on, with the dry
perseverance of a commentator, to give the college reading, accompanied by sundry annota-
tions: addressing himself at first to the company

at large; but finding their attention gradually
diverted to other talk, and other objects, he
lowered his tone as his number of auditors di-
minished, until he concluded his remarks, in an
under voice, to a fat-headed old gentleman next
him, who was silently engaged in the discussion
of a huge plateful of turkey.*

See Note E.

The table was literally loaded with good cheer,
and presented an epitome of country abun-
dance, in this season of overflowing larders. A
distinguished post was allotted to "ancient sirloin," as mine host termed it; being, as he
added, "the standard of old English hospitality,
and a joint of goodly presence, and full of expectation."

There were several dishes quaintly decorated,
and which had evidently something traditionary
in their embellishments; but about which, as I
did not like to appear over curious, I asked no
questions. I could not, however, but notice a
pie, magnificently decorated with peacocks'
feathers, in imitation of the tail of that bird,
which overshadowed a considerable tract of the
table. This, the Squire confessed, with some
little hesitation, was a pheasant- pie, though a
peacock-pie was certainly the most authentical;
but there had been such a mortality among the
peacocks this season, that he could not prevail
upon himself to have one killed.*

* See Note F.

It would be tedious, perhaps, to my wiser readers, who may not have that foolish fondness for odd and obsolete things to which I am a little given, were I to mention the other makeshifts of this worthy old humourist, by which he was endeavouring to follow up, though at humble distance, the quaint customs of antiquity. I was pleased, however, to see the respect shown to his whims by his children and relatives; who, indeed, entered readily into the full spirit of them, and seemed all well versed in their parts; having doubtless been present at many a rehearsal. I was amused, too, at the air of profound gravity with which the butler and other servants executed the duties assigned them, however eccentric. They had an old- fashioned look; having, for the most part, been brought up in the household, and grown into keeping with the antiquated mansion, and the humours of its lord; and most probably looked upon all his whimsical regulations as the established laws of honourable housekeeping. When the cloth was removed, the butler brought in a huge silver vessel of rare and curious workmanship, which he placed before the Squire. Its appearance was hailed with acclamation; being the Wassail Bowl, so renowned in Christmas festivity. The contents had been prepared by the Squire himself; for it was a beverage in the skilful mixture of which he particularly prided himself, alleging that it was too abstruse and complex for the

comprehension of an ordinary servant. It was a
potation, indeed, that might well make the heart
of a toper leap within him; being composed of
the richest and raciest wines, highly spiced and
sweetened, with roasted apples bobbing about
the surface.*

See Note G.

The old gentleman's whole countenance beamed
with a serene look of indwelling delight, as he
stirred this mighty bowl. Having raised it to his
lips, with a hearty wish of a merry Christmas to
all present, he sent it brimming, around the
board, for every one to follow his example, according to the primitive style; pronouncing it
"the ancient fountain of good feeling, where all
hearts met together."*

See Note H.

There was much laughing and rallying, as the
honest emblem of Christmas joviality circulated,
and was kissed rather coyly by the ladies. When
it reached Master Simon he raised it in both
hands, and with the air of a boon companion
struck up an old Wassail chanson:

> *The browne bowle,*
> *The merry browne bowle,*
> *As it goes round about-a,*
> > *Fill*
> > *Still,*

Let the world say what it will,
And drink your fill all out-a.

The deep canne,
The merry deep canne,
As thou dost freely quaff-a,
   Sing,
   Fling,
Be as merry as a king,
And sound a lusty laugh-a.*

* *From "Poor Robin's Almanack."*

Much of the conversation during dinner turned upon family topics, to which I was a stranger. There was, however, a great deal of rallying of Master Simon about some gay widow, with whom he was accused of having a flirtation. This attack was commenced by the ladies; but it was continued throughout the dinner by the fat-headed old gentleman next the parson, with the persevering assiduity of a slow-hound; being one of those long-winded jokers, who, though rather dull at starting game, are unrivalled for their talents in hunting it down. At every pause in the general conversation, he renewed his bantering in pretty much the same terms; winking hard at me with both eyes whenever he gave Master Simon what he considered a home thrust. The latter, indeed, seemed fond of being teased on the subject, as old bachelors are apt to be; and he took occasion to inform me, in an

undertone, that the lady in question was a pro-
digiously fine woman, and drove her own
curricle.

The dinner-time passed away in this flow of
innocent hilarity; and, though the old hall may
have resounded in its time with many a scene of
broader rout and revel, yet I doubt whether it
ever witnessed more honest and genuine enjoyment. How easy it is for one benevolent being to
diffuse pleasure around him; and how truly is a
kind heart a fountain of gladness, making everything in its vicinity to freshen into smiles! The
joyous disposition of the worthy Squire was
perfectly contagious; he was happy himself, and
disposed to make all the world happy; and the
little eccentricities of his humour did but season, in a manner, the sweetness of his philanthropy.

When the ladies had retired, the conversation,
as usual, became still more animated; many
good things were broached which had been
thought of during dinner, but which would not
exactly do for a lady's ear; and though I cannot
positively affirm that there was much wit uttered, yet I have certainly heard many contests
of rare wit produce much less laughter. Wit,
after all, is a mighty tart, pungent ingredient,
and much too acid for some stomachs; but honest good humour is the oil and wine of a merry
meeting, and there is no jovial companionship
equal to that where the jokes are rather small,

and the laughter abundant. The Squire told
several long stories of early college pranks and
adventures, in some of which the parson had
been a sharer; though in looking at the latter, it
required some effort of imagination to figure
such a little dark anatomy of a man into the
perpetrator of a madcap gambol. Indeed, the
two college chums presented pictures of what
men may be made by their different lots in life.
The Squire had left the university to live lustily
on his paternal domains, in the vigorous enjoyment of prosperity and sunshine, and had flourished on to a hearty and florid old age; whilst
the poor parson, on the contrary, had dried and
withered away, among dusty tomes, in the silence and shadows of his study.

Still there seemed to be a spark of almost extinguished fire, feebly glimmering in the bottom of
his soul; and as the Squire hinted at a sly story
of the parson and a pretty milkmaid, whom they
once met on the banks of the Isis, the old gentleman made an "alphabet of faces," which, as far
as I could decipher his physiognomy, I verily
believe was indicative of laughter;-indeed, I have
rarely met with an old gentleman who took absolutely offence at the imputed gallantries of his
youth.

I found the tide of wine and wassail fast gaining
on the dry land of sober judgment. The company grew merrier and louder as their jokes
grew duller. Master Simon was in as chirping a

humour as a grasshopper filled with dew; his old songs grew of a warmer complexion, and he began to talk maudlin about the widow. He even gave a long song about the wooing of a widow, which he informed me he had gathered from an excellent black-letter work, entitled "Cupid's Solicitor for Love," containing store of good advice for bachelors, and which he promised to lend me. The first verse was to this effect:

"He that will woo a widow must not dally,
He must make hay while the sun doth shine;
He must not stand with her, Shall I, Shall I?
But boldly say, Widow, thou must be mine."

This song inspired the fat-headed old gentleman, who made several attempts to tell a rather broad story out of Joe Miller, that was pat to the purpose; but he always stuck in the middle, everybody recollecting the latter part excepting himself. The parson, too, began to show the effects of good cheer, having gradually settled down into a doze, and his wig sitting most suspiciously on one side. Just at this juncture we were summoned to the drawing-room, and, I suspect, at the private instigation of mine host, whose joviality seemed always tempered with a proper love of decorum.

After the dinner-table was removed, the hall was given up to the younger members of the family, who, prompted to all kind of noisy mirth by the Oxonian and Master Simon, made its old walls

ring with their merriment, as they played at romping games. I delight in witnessing the gambols of children, and particularly at this happy holiday-season, and could not help stealing out of the drawing-room on hearing one of their peals of laughter. I found them at the game of blind-man's buff. Master Simon, who was the leader of their revels, and seemed on all occasions to fulfil the office of that ancient potentate, the Lord of Misrule,* was blinded in the midst of the hall. The little beings were as busy about him as the mock fairies about Falstaff; pinching him, plucking at the skirts of his coat, and tickling him with straws. One fine blue-eyed girl of about thirteen, with her flaxen hair all in beautiful confusion, her frolic face in a glow, her frock half torn off her shoulders, a complete picture of a romp, was the chief tormentor; and from the slyness with which Master Simon avoided the smaller game, and hemmed this wild little nymph in corners, and obliged her to jump shrieking over chairs, I suspected the rogue of being not a whit more blinded than was convenient.

*See Note I.

When I returned to the drawing-room, I found the company seated around the fire, listening to the parson, who was deeply ensconced in a high-backed oaken chair, the work of some cunning artificer of yore, which had been brought from the library for his particular ac-

commodation. From this venerable piece of
furniture, with which his shadowy figure and
dark weazen face so admirably accorded, he was
dealing forth strange accounts of popular superstitions and legends of the surrounding country,
with which he had become acquainted in the
course of his antiquarian researches. I am half
inclined to think that the old gentleman was
himself somewhat tinctured with superstition,
as men are very apt to be who live a recluse and
studious life in a sequestered part of the country, and pore over black-letter tracts, so often
filled with the marvellous and supernatural. He
gave us several anecdotes of the fancies of the
neighbouring peasantry, concerning the effigy of
the crusader which lay on the tomb by the
church altar. As it was the only monument of
the kind in that part of the country, it had always been regarded with feelings of superstition
by the goodwives of the village. It was said to get
up from the tomb and walk the rounds of the
churchyard in stormy nights, particularly when
it thundered; and one old woman, whose cottage
bordered on the churchyard, had seen it,
through the windows of the church, when the
moon shone, slowly pacing up and down the
aisles. It was the belief that some wrong had
been left unredressed by the deceased, or some
treasure hidden, which kept the spirit in a state
of trouble and restlessness. Some talked of gold
and jewels buried in the tomb, over which the
spectre kept watch; and there was a story current of a sexton in old times who endeavoured to

break his way to the coffin at night; but just as he reached it, received a violent blow from the marble hand of the effigy, which stretched him senseless on the pavement. These tales were often laughed at by some of the sturdier among the rustics, yet when night came on, there were many of the stoutest unbelievers that were shy of venturing alone in the footpath that led across the churchyard. From these and other anecdotes that followed, the crusader appeared to be the favourite hero of ghost stories throughout the vicinity. His picture, which hung up in the hall, was thought by the servants to have something supernatural about it; for they remarked that, in whatever part of the hall you went, the eyes of the warrior were still fixed on you. The old porter's wife, too, at the lodge, who had been born and brought up in the family, and was a great gossip among the maid servants, affirmed that in her young days she had often heard say that on Midsummer eve, when it is well known all kinds of ghosts, goblins, and fairies become visible and walk abroad, the crusader used to mount his horse, come down from his picture, ride about the house, down the avenue, and so to the church to visit the tomb; on which occasion the church door most civilly swung open of itself: not that he needed it; for he rode through closed gates and even stone walls, and had been seen by one of the dairymaids to pass between two bars of the great park gate, making himself as thin as a sheet of paper.

All these superstitions, I found, had been very much countenanced by the Squire, who, though not superstitious himself, was very fond of seeing others so. He listened to every goblin tale of the neighbouring gossips with infinite gravity, and held the porter's wife in high favour on account of her talent for the marvellous. He was himself a great reader of old legends and romances, and often lamented that he could not believe in them; for a superstitious person, he thought, must live in a kind of fairyland.

Whilst we were all attention to the parson's stories, our ears were suddenly assailed by a burst of heterogeneous sounds from the hall, in which was mingled something like the clang of rude minstrelsy, with the uproar of many small voices and girlish laughter. The door suddenly flew open, and a train came trooping into the room, that might almost have been mistaken for the breaking up of the court of Fairy. That indefatigable spirit, Master Simon, in the faithful discharge of his duties as Lord of Misrule, had conceived the idea of a Christmas mummery, or masking; and having called in to his assistance the Oxonian and the young officer, who were equally ripe for anything that should occasion romping and merriment, they had carried it into instant effect. The old housekeeper had been consulted; the antique clothes-presses and wardrobes rummaged and made to yield up the relics of finery that had not seen the light for several generations; the younger part of the

company had been privately convened from the parlour and hall, and the whole had been bedizened out, into a burlesque imitation of an antique masque.*

* See Note J.

Master Simon led the van, as "Ancient Christmas," quaintly apparelled in a ruff, a short cloak, which had very much the aspect of one of the old housekeeper's petticoats, and a hat that might have served for a village steeple, and must indubitably have figured in the days of the Covenanters. From under this his nose curved boldly forth, flushed with a frost-bitten bloom, that seemed the very trophy of a December blast. He was accompanied by the blue-eyed romp, dished up as "Dame Mince-Pie," in the venerable magnificence of faded brocade, long stomacher, peaked hat, and high-heeled shoes. The young officer appeared as Robin Hood, in a sporting dress of Kendal green and a foraging cap with a gold tassel. The costume, to be sure, did not bear testimony to deep research, and there was an evident eye to the picturesque, natural to a young gallant in the presence of his mistress. The fair Julia hung on his arm in a pretty rustic dress, as "Maid Marian." The rest of the train had been metamorphosed in various ways; the girls trussed up in the finery of the ancient belles of the Bracebridge line, and the striplings bewhiskered with burnt cork, and gravely clad in broad skirts, hanging sleeves,

and full-bottomed wigs, to represent the characters of Roast Beef, Plum Pudding, and other
worthies celebrated in ancient maskings. The
whole was under the control of the Oxonian, in
the appropriate character of Misrule; and I observed that he exercised rather a mischievous
sway with his wand over the smaller personages
of the pageant.

The irruption of this motley crew, with beat of
drum, according to ancient custom, was the
consummation of uproar and merriment. Master
Simon covered himself with glory by the stateli-
ness with which, as Ancient Christmas, he
walked a minuet with the peerless, though giggling, Dame Mince-Pie. It was followed by a
dance of all the characters, which, from its med-
ley of costumes, seemed as though the old family
portraits had skipped down from their frames to
join in the sport. Different centuries were figur-
ing at cross hands and right and left; the dark
ages were cutting pirouettes and rigadoons; and
the days of Queen Bess jigging merrily down the
middle, through a line of succeeding generations.

The worthy Squire contemplated these fantastic
sports, and this resurrection of his old ward-
robe, with the simple relish of childish delight.
He stood chuckling and rubbing his hands, and
scarcely hearing a word the parson said, not-

withstanding that the latter was discoursing most authentically on the ancient and stately dance at the Paon, or Peacock, from which he conceived the minuet to be derived.* For my part, I was in a continual excitement, from the varied scenes of whim and innocent gaiety passing before me. It was inspiring to see wild-eyed frolic and warm-hearted hospitality breaking out from among the chills and glooms of winter, and old age throwing off his apathy, and catching once more the freshness of youthful enjoyment. I felt also an interest in the scene, from the consideration that these fleeting customs were posting fast into oblivion, and that this was, perhaps, the only family in England in which the whole of them were still punctiliously observed. There was a quaintness, too, mingled with all this revelry that gave it a peculiar zest; it was suited to the time and place; and as the old Manor House almost reeled with mirth and wassail, it seemed echoing back the joviality of long-departed years.

*See Note K.

But enough of Christmas and its gambols; it is time for me to pause in this garrulity. Methinks I hear the questions asked by my graver readers, "To what purpose is all this?-how is the world to be made wiser by this talk?" Alas! is there not wisdom enough extant for the instruction of the world? And if not, are there not thousands of

abler pens labouring for its improvement? —
It is so much pleasanter to please than to
instruct — to play the companion rather than
the preceptor.

What, after all, is the mite of wisdom that I could
throw into the mass of knowledge? or how am I
sure that my sagest deductions may be safe
guides for the opinions of others? But in writing
to amuse, if I fail, the only evil is my own disappointment. If, however, I can by any lucky
chance, in these days of evil, rub out one
wrinkle from the brow of care, or beguile the
heavy heart of one moment of sorrow; if I can
now and then penetrate through the gathering
film of misanthropy, prompt a benevolent view of
human nature, and make my reader more in
good humour with his fellow beings and himself,
surely, surely, I shall not then have written
entirely in vain.

THE END.

NOTE A.
 The misletoe is still hung up in farmhouses and kitchens at Christmas; and the young men have the privilege of kissing the girls under it, plucking each time a berry from the bush. When the berries are all plucked, the privilege ceases.

NOTE B.
The Yule-clog is a great log of wood, sometimes the root of a tree, brought into the house with great ceremony, on Christmas eve, laid in the fireplace, and lighted with the brand of last year's clog. While it lasted there was great drinking, singing, and telling of tales. Sometimes it was accompanied by Christmas candles, but in the cottages the only light was from the ruddy blaze of the great wood fire. The Yule-clog was to burn all night; if it went out, it was considered a sign of ill luck.

Herrick mentions it in one of his songs:

> "Come, bring with a noise
> My merrie, merrie boyes,
> The Christmas log to the firing:
> While my good dame, she
> Bids ye all be free,
> And drink to your hearts' desiring."

The Yule-clog is still burnt in many farmhouses and kitchens in England, particularly in the

north, and there are several superstitions connected with it among the peasantry. If a squint-
ing person come to the house while it is burning,
or a person barefooted, it is considered an ill
omen. The brand remaining from the Yule-clog
is carefully put away to light the next year's
Christmas fire.

NOTE C.
From the Flying Eagle, a small gazette, pub-
lished December 24, 1652: "The House spent
much time this day about the business of the
Navy, for settling the affairs at sea; and before
they rose, were presented with a terrible remon-
strance against Christmas day, grounded upon
divine Scriptures, 2 Cor. v. 16; 1 Cor. xv. 14, 17;
and in honour of the Lord's Day, grounded upon
these Scriptures, John xx. I; Rev. i. 10; Psalm
cxviii. 24; Lev. xxiii. 7, 11; Mark xvi. 8; Psalm
lxxxiv. 10, in which Christmas is called Anti-
Christ's masse, and those Mass-mongers and
Papists who observe it, etc. In consequence of
which Parliament spent some time in consultation about the abolition of Christmas day,
passed orders to that effect, and resolved to sit
on the following day, which was commonly
called Christmas day."

NOTE D.
An English gentleman at the opening of the
great day, i. e. on Christmas day in the morning,
had all his tenants and neighbours enter his hall
by daybreak. The strong beer was broached,

and the black jacks went plentifully about with toast, sugar, nutmeg, and good Cheshire cheese. The hackin (the great sausage) must be boiled by daybreak, or else two young men must take the maiden (i.e. the cook) by the arms and run her round the market-place till she is shamed of her laziness.-Round about our Sea-coal Fire.

NOTE E.

The old ceremony of serving up the boar's head on Christmas day is still observed in the hall of Queen's College, Oxford. I was favoured by the parson with a copy of the carol as now sung, and as it may be acceptable to such of my readers as are curious in these grave and learned matters, I give it entire.

> "The boar's head in hand bear I,
> Bedeck'd with bays and rosemary;
> And I pray you, my masters, be merry,
>   Quot estia in convivio.
>   Caput apri defero
>   Reddens laudes Domino.
>
> "The boar's head, as I understand,
> Is the rarest dish in all this land,
> Which thus bedeck'd with a gay garland
>   Let us servire cantico.
>   Caput apri defero, etc.

"Our Steward hath provided this
In honour of the King of Bliss,
Which on this day to be served is
In Reginensi Atrio.
Caput apri defero,"
        Etc., etc., etc.

NOTE F.

The peacock was anciently in great demand for stately entertainments. Sometimes it was made into a pie, at one end of which the head appeared above the crust in all its plumage, with the beak richly gilt; at the other end the tail was displayed. Such pies were served up at the solemn banquets of chivalry, when knights-errant pledged themselves to undertake any perilous enterprise; whence came the ancient oath, used by Justice Shallow, "by cock and pie."

The peacock was also an important dish for the Christmas feast; and Massinger, in his "City Madam," gives some idea of the extravagance with which this, as well as other dishes, was prepared for the gorgeous revels of the olden times:

"Men may talk of country Christmasses,
Their thirty pound butter'd eggs, their pies of carps' tongues:
Their pheasants drench'd with ambergris; the carcases of three fat wethers bruised for gravy, to make sauce for a single peacock!"

NOTE G.

The Wassail Bowl was sometimes composed of ale instead of wine; with nutmeg, sugar, toast, ginger, and roasted crabs; in this way the nut-brown beverage is still prepared in some old families, and round the hearths of substantial farmers at Christmas. It is also called Lambs' Wool, and is celebrated by Herrick in his "Twelfth Night:"

> *"Next crowne the bowle full*
> *With gentle Lambs' Wool,*
> *Add sugar, nutmeg, and ginger,*
> *With store of ale too;*
> *And thus ye must doe*
> *To make the Wassaile a swinger."*

NOTE H.

The custom of drinking out of the same cup gave place to each having his cup. When the steward came to the doore with the Wassel, he was to cry three times, Wassel, Wassel, Wassel, and then the chappel (chaplain) was to answer with a song.-Archaeologia.

NOTE I.
At Christmasse there was in the Kings's house, wheresoever hee was lodged, a lorde of misrule, or mayster of merry disportes; and the like had ye in the house of every nobleman of honour, or good worshippe, were he spirituall or temporall.- Stow.

NOTE J.
Maskings or mummeries were favourite sports at Christmas in old times; and the wardrobes at halls and manor-houses were often laid under contribution to furnish dresses and fantastic disguisings. I strongly suspect Master Simon to have taken the idea of his from Ben Jonson's "Masque of Christmas."

NOTE K.
Sir John Hawkins, speaking of the dance called the Pavon, from pavo, a peacock, says: "It is a grave and majestic dance; the method of dancing it anciently was by gentlemen dressed with caps and swords, by those of the long robe in their gowns, by the peers in their mantles, and by the ladies in gowns with long trains, the motion whereof, in dancing, resembled that of a pea-cock."-History of Music.

THE SELFISH GIANT
OSCAR WILDE

Every afternoon, as they were coming from school, the children used to go and play in the Giant's garden.

It was a large lovely garden, with soft green grass. Here and there over the grass stood beautiful flowers like stars, and there were twelve peach-trees that in the springtime broke out into delicate blossoms of pink and pearl, and in the autumn bore rich fruit. The birds sat on the trees and sang so sweetly that the children used to stop their games in order to listen to them. "How happy we are here!" they cried to each other.

One day the Giant came back. He had been to visit his friend the Cornish ogre, and had stayed with him for seven years. After the seven years were over he had said all that he had to say, for his conversation was limited, and he determined to return to his own castle. When he arrived he saw the children playing in the garden.

"What are you doing there?" he cried in a very gruff voice, and the children ran away.

"My own garden is my own garden," said the Giant; "any one can understand that, and I will

allow nobody to play in it but myself." So he built a high wall all round it, and put up a notice-board.

TRESPASSERS WILL BE PROSECUTED

He was a very selfish Giant.

The poor children had now nowhere to play. They tried to play on the road, but the road was very dusty and full of hard stones, and they did not like it. They used to wander round the high wall when their lessons were over, and talk about the beautiful garden inside. "How happy we were there," they said to each other.

Then the Spring came, and all over the country there were little blossoms and little birds. Only in the garden of the Selfish Giant it was still winter. The birds did not care to sing in it as there were no children, and the trees forgot to blossom. Once a beautiful flower put its head out from the grass, but when it saw the notice-board it was so sorry for the children that it slipped back into the ground again, and went off to sleep. The only people who were pleased were the Snow and the Frost. "Spring has forgotten this garden," they cried, "so we will live here all the year round." The Snow covered up the grass with her great white cloak, and the Frost painted all the trees silver. Then they invited the North

Wind to stay with them, and he came. He was
wrapped in furs, and he roared all day about the
garden, and blew the chimney-pots down. "This
is a delightful spot," he said, "we must ask the
Hail on a visit." So the Hail came. Every day for
three hours he rattled on the roof of the castle
till he broke most of the slates, and then he ran
round and round the garden as fast as he could
go. He was dressed in grey, and his breath was
like ice.

"I cannot understand why the Spring is so late
in coming," said the Selfish Giant, as he sat at
the window and looked out at his cold white
garden; "I hope there will be a change in the
weather."

But the Spring never came, nor the Summer.
The Autumn gave golden fruit to every garden,
but to the Giant's garden she gave none. "He is
too selfish," she said. So it was always Winter
there, and the North Wind and the Hail, and the
Frost, and the Snow danced about through the
trees.

One morning the Giant was lying awake in bed
when he heard some lovely music. It sounded so
sweet to his ears that he thought it must be the
King's musicians passing by. It was really only a
little linnet singing outside his window, but it
was so long since he had heard a bird sing in his

garden that it seemed to him to be the most beautiful music in the world. Then the Hail stopped dancing over his head, and the North Wind ceased roaring, and a delicious perfume came to him through the open easement. "I believe the Spring has come at last," said the Giant; and he jumped out of bed and looked out.

What did he see?

He saw a most wonderful sight. Through a little hole in the wall the children had crept in, and they were sitting in the branches of the trees. In every tree that he could see there was a little child. And the trees were so glad to have the children back again that they had covered themselves with blossoms, and were waving their arms gently above the children's heads. The birds were flying about and twittering with delight, and the flowers were looking up through the green grass and laughing. It was a lovely scene, only in one corner it was still winter. It was the farthest corner of the garden, and in it was standing a little boy.

He was so small that he could not reach up to the branches of the tree, and he was wandering all round it, crying bitterly. The poor tree was still quite covered with frost and snow, and the North Wind was blowing and roaring above it. "Climb up! little boy," said the Tree, and it bent its branches down as low as it could; but the boy was too tiny.

And the Giant's heart melted as he looked out. "How selfish I have been!" he said; "now I know why the Spring would not come here. I will put that poor little boy on the top of the tree, and then I will knock down the wall, and my garden shall be the children's playground for ever and ever." He was really very sorry for what he had done.

So he crept downstairs and opened the front door quite softly, and went out into the garden. But when the children saw him they were so frightened that they all ran away, and the garden became winter again. Only the little boy did not run, for his eyes were so full of tears that he did not see the Giant coming. And the Giant stole up behind him and took him gently in his hand, and put him up into the tree. And the tree broke at once into blossom, and the birds came and sang on it, and the little boy stretched out his two arms and flung them round the Giant's neck, and kissed him. And the other children, when they saw that the Giant was not wicked any longer, came running back, and with them came the Spring. "It is your garden now, little children," said the Giant, and he took a great axe and knocked down the wall. And when the people were going to market at twelve o'clock they found the Giant playing with the children in the most beautiful garden they had ever seen.

All day long they played, and in the evening they came to the Giant to bid him good-bye.

"But where is your little companion?" he said: "the boy I put into the tree." The Giant loved him the best because he had kissed him.

"We don't know," answered the children; "he has gone away."

"You must tell him to be sure and come here to-morrow," said the Giant. But the children said that they did not know where he lived, and had never seen him before; and the Giant felt very sad.

Every afternoon, when school was over, the children came and played with the Giant. But the little boy whom the Giant loved was never seen again. The Giant was very kind to all the children, yet he longed for his first little friend, and often spoke of him. "How I would like to see him!" he used to say.

Years went over, and the Giant grew very old and feeble. He could not play about any more, so he sat in a huge armchair, and watched the children at their games, and admired his garden. "I have many beautiful flowers," he said; "but the children are the most beautiful flowers of all."

One winter morning he looked out of his window
as he was dressing. He did not hate the Winter
now, for he knew that it was merely the Spring
asleep, and that the flowers were resting.

Suddenly he rubbed his eyes in wonder, and
looked and looked. It certainly was a marvellous
sight. In the farthest corner of the garden was a
tree quite covered with lovely white blossoms. Its
branches were all golden, and silver fruit hung
down from them, and underneath it stood the
little boy he had loved.

Downstairs ran the Giant in great joy, and out
into the garden. He hastened across the grass,
and came near to the child. And when he came
quite close his face grew red with anger, and he
said, "Who hath dared to wound thee?" For on
the palms of the child's hands were the prints of
two nails, and the prints of two nails were on the
little feet.

"Who hath dared to wound thee?" cried the
Giant; "tell me, that I may take my big sword
and slay him."

"Nay!" answered the child; "but these are the
wounds of Love."

"Who art thou?" said the Giant, and a strange
awe fell on him, and he knelt before the little
child.

And the child smiled on the Giant, and said to him, "You let me play once in your garden, to-day you shall come with me to my garden, which is Paradise."

And when the children ran in that afternoon, they found the Giant lying dead under the tree, all covered with white blossoms.

INDEX